MEDIA OWNERSHIP AND CONTROL

Competition and diversity in media and communications are fundamental to a healthy economy and democracy. In India and internationally there is no consensus on the exact manner and scope of interventions that are appropriate to protect competition and pluralism in media markets.

Many emerging economies including India are seeking to adopt their own regulation in this area taking their lead from the UK. The issues have been brought into sharp focus in India in recent years. First, the enactment and implementation of modern—but sector neutral—competition law under the Competition Act 2002 has caused a step change in regulation towards an economics and effects-based approach. Second, in 2013 the India telecoms regulator launched controversial reform proposals to apply a media-specific approach to ownership regulation.

As academics, lawyers, businesses, regulators and policy-makers in India cast a glance at the international experience, this book examines the legal, economic and policy issues relating to regulation of ownership and control of media markets. The focus of comparative assessment is on examples from the European Union, EU Member States and the US.

Volume 8 in the series Hart Studies in Competition Law

Hart Studies in Competition Law

Volume 1: *Intellectual Property, Antitrust and Cumulative Innovation in the EU and the US*
Thorsten Käseberg

Volume 2: *State Aid and the European Economic Constitution*
Francesco de Cecco

Volume 3: *The Private Enforcement of Competition Law in Ireland*
David McFadden

Volume 4: *Cross-Border EU Competition Law Actions*
Edited by Mihail Danov, Florian Becker and Paul Beaumont

Volume 5: *European Merger Remedies: Law and Policy*
Dorte Hoeg

Volume 6: *Sanctions in EU Competition Law: Principles and Practice*
Michael Frese

Volume 7: *Fairness in Antitrust: Protecting the Strong from the Weak*
Adi Ayal

Media Ownership and Control

Law, Economics and Policy in an Indian and International Context

Suzanne Rab and Alison Sprague

·HART·
PUBLISHING
OXFORD AND PORTLAND, OREGON
2017

Hart Publishing
An imprint of Bloomsbury Publishing Plc

Hart Publishing Ltd
Kemp House
Chawley Park
Cumnor Hill
Oxford OX2 9PH
UK

Bloomsbury Publishing Plc
50 Bedford Square
London
WC1B 3DP
UK

www.hartpub.co.uk
www.bloomsbury.com

Published in North America (US and Canada) by
Hart Publishing
c/o International Specialized Book Services
920 NE 58th Avenue, Suite 300
Portland, OR 97213-3786
USA

www.isbs.com

First published in hardback, 2014
Paperback edition, 2017

British Library Cataloguing-in-Publication Data
A catalogue record for this book is available from the British Library.

ISBN: HB: 978-1-84946-635-6
PB: 978-1-50991-389-3

Typeset by Compuscript Ltd, Shannon

Prologue

PICTURE THE SCENE

India's 1.2 billion people are on the threshold of gargantuan economic and social change and a clash between modernity and traditionalism. A decade ago it was scarcely credible to think that affordable real-time engagement would be possible with the widely-spread and diverse population, but that is changing before our eyes. A backstreet market in Mumbai is a place where the arts of the ancients attract goggle-eyed audiences. Dancers and glass-eating warriors practice their breathtaking routines, while shoppers move from stall to stall sampling the produce that is on offer. Meanwhile, onlookers are firmly connected to the twenty-first century through their 'always-on' smartphone and other mobile devices. Whether it is a download of a Bollywood movie on the internet, or an e-version of the *Times of India*, *The Hindustan* or some vernacular language daily, the media and communications mélange is a juxtaposition of the old and the new. It is a vibrant 'mediaplace' where the media and entertainment industry has grown from INR 728 billion in 2011 to INR 821 billion in 2012 with an overall growth of 12.6 per cent[1]—the fastest growing digital community in the Brazil, Russia, India and China (BRIC) region.

Now, let's picture a scene where what is on offer or broadcast from the various vendors or channels is available at the same bundled price, and which consumers grudgingly pay because there is no alternative. Some smaller operators entered the market, but they were quickly forced out by the incumbent who owns the prime content and already has a big subscriber base. The remaining few platforms are struggling to make a profit, despite running a lean cost structure and having some innovative content. Over time, the biggest operator blocks the channels of the newer entrants and starts to push its own content, which is badly made and probably infringes someone else's copyright. There used to be a balanced mix of quality programmes and news stories, but now there are five advertising breaks per hour promoting political propaganda. What's worse, this operator has made deals with the local housing agencies so that tenants cannot avail themselves of services from rival operators. And when they do take up the service, the rate is exorbitant and customers face being cut-off selectively with no grievance mechanism.

[1] KPMG, 'FICCI—KPMG Media & Entertainment Report 2013', 12 March 2013.

The two images described above present two very different pictures of India's media and communications landscape. It can be challenging to distinguish between anticompetitive and abusive practices and the functioning of a competitive market. The first scenario presents a somewhat idealised picture of competition. Traditional consumption patterns are being challenged and new players enter the market with innovative products and services. What could be happening in the second scenario is inconclusive. It could be that the few operators in the market have called a truce on competition and decided not to undercut each other on price and service. As a result of this understanding they can reap the rewards of a quiet life where they do not have to offer better and more innovative services at lower prices in order to keep and grow their customer base and make a profit. But it is not clear why the channel operator is now able to offer sub-standard service and exclude competing content. It could be that it has bought out competitors or signed long-term exclusive distribution deals with the housing agencies. The use of the media to distort the news agenda has a more sinister side to it but it does not tell the full story. It is not apparent what other sources of news and current affairs are available to the audience, other than on the small screen. All in all, further inquiry is needed to understand what is happening, why it is happening and what might be done to promote choice and diversity and without stultifying investment and growth.

The related issues of competition and pluralism—or viewpoint diversity—illustrated above also have an important dimension beyond the Indian market. Experience in Australia, the European Union, the United Kingdom, the United States and beyond suggests that India is not unique in facing these challenges. The stylised scenarios recounted above reflect pervasive themes worldwide. They set the scene for the popular debate and the legal, economic and policy inquiry that is the subject of this book. We explore what international comparative insights and experience can contribute to this debate. We compare media and communications companies operating in an unregulated environment with those which are subject to regulation (of varying forms) to see if there are expected benefits depending on whether tighter or lesser controls are introduced. We consider the delicate relationship between pluralism and competition. We venture policy recommendations on media and communications regulation as India stands poised to decide its future ownership regulation and structures.

We have watched, and participated in, the ongoing debate about how to tackle the issue of plurality in the UK, in Europe, and internationally. Some of this has been through first-hand experience and representing industry interests. There is, perhaps, no other subject that engages, affects and is shaped more by the media. We hope that through this international review we have taken the debate further. First, we have shown that there are always at least two sides to a story. Second, however emotive the subject matter and the personalities involved, there are some issues that can be debated rationally and objectively. Third, many of the international regimes have been developed and are developing over time in different contexts. They have their recognised imperfections which are only now becoming apparent.

A FEW FACTS

In order to frame the discussion that follows, it is useful to try to map out the contours of the Indian media landscape with a few pertinent facts about who owns what and why there is so much interest in media ownership and control in India. In fact, an initial observation may be that there appears to be a lack of information or transparency on media ownership. The result is a story of contrasts. At one level, the multiplicity of players in terms of absolute numbers is suggestive of competition and choice where players of all sizes have entered the fray to jostle for a share of audience. At another level, the web of political and corporate affiliations presents a more complex picture which has fuelled a popular cause to examine what this means for preserving a healthy market and viewpoint heterogeneity.

A few facts will illustrate these themes. First, the media and communications market has seen tremendous change, especially in the past decade. With India opening its markets and embracing globalisation, the market has seen an influx of new companies.

With respect to television, India graduated from the traditional cable network connection to the new and more modern method of direct-to-home (DTH) satellite broadcasting. The early years of modernisation were characterised by players such as DishTV and TataSky (a tie-up between the Indian company, Tata and its UK counterpart, Sky), but the market today provides a wider range of service providers. In terms of the genre of entertainment, today India stands shoulder to shoulder with other countries by showcasing programmes in a manner suited to the Indian palate. Quite apart from domestic entertainment genres, in common with many other countries India has adapted global formats to the local market and culture. Programmes such as *Indian Idol* have been adapted from their British and US counterparts (*Pop Idol* and *American Idol*) and *Jhalak Dikhla Ja* is based on the show *Dancing with the Stars*.

Radio risked becoming largely redundant in the cities, but then dusted itself off and picked itself up in the early 2000s and two or three new radio channels emerged. The new channels brought a fresh lease of life to the medium of mass communication. The number of channels continued to increase for two to three years and today multiple channels compete for the largest audience.

The print media has witnessed growth. There has been an increase in the number of newspapers that provide news in a 'daily capsule' form. The *Hindustan Times* perhaps took the first step towards the introduction of such formats. India also has national editions of a number of foreign magazines such as *Good Housekeeping*, *GoodHomes* and the like. The dependence on advertising revenues means that the growth of the print industry is dampened by the macro-economic situation. However, 2012 saw an improvement in circulation revenues.[2] The concept of free

[2] Ibid.

newspapers, as published in the UK, is not yet significant but consumers may hope that such a concept will be introduced soon to further facilitate the greater dissemination of opinions and information. In the coming years, it will be interesting to see whether the industry adopts a differentiated pricing strategy as an attempt to penetrate new markets.

The telecoms sector has grown. With more and diverse companies providing services and plans at competitive rates, the end-user has a range of choices. The leading companies include Airtel, Vodafone, Idea, Reliance, Aircel, MTNL and Tata. With number portability being introduced as a feature, companies have even greater incentives to outplay others. In the face of a more crowded market and more legacy providers, a newer-comer may find it tough to make and sustain its place. When Aircel (a telecoms service provider) entered the market, it could hardly find any takers. Even today, the brand attempts to provide one of the best deals, but due to less than complete network coverage, the company may not be the most popular.

India has seen access to the internet grow at an unprecedented rate. A number of telecommunications companies have come and gone. The government-owned MTNL/BSNL which was the sole telecoms provider also ventured into this field. However, due to poor performance and poor customer satisfaction, it does not have a significant presence today. Companies such as Satyam, which was one of the first private companies to provide internet services, have shut down after a few years. Many more companies, including Airtel, Tata, MTS and Reliance, then entered the market. These companies are strong competitors today. It is, however, interesting to note that in a few areas one or a limited number of companies enjoy close to monopoly positions over service provision in a particular region.

The internet further changed the way in which content could be delivered, for example with online versions of newspapers. A number of newspapers including *The Times of India* provide such a facility. More and more people in the metropolitan cities such as Mumbai and Delhi and other growing cities have taken up the habit of online shopping. Internet banking and similar services have provided greater convenience for Indian consumers. While a number of metrics could be cited to illustrate the growth of online activity and digitisation in India, perhaps the most striking is the growth in internet use which showed a year-on-year growth of 51 per cent from 2011 to 2012.[3]

Second, in terms of media outlets, the numbers suggest a crowded and even abundant market. A recent article from *The Hindu*[4] has cited over 840 registered TV channels (of which 300 cover news and current affairs) and 82,000 registered publications. Yet behind the absolute numbers of outlets and entities, questions have been raised as to the concentration of control. That is to say, despite the quantity of players in the market, there have been calls to examine further the

[3] comScore, *The State of Digital*, Q4 2012.

[4] *The Hindu*, 'Media cross-holding in cross hairs' 24 March 2013.

ultimate controllers and whether their disparate holdings across and within media segments may confer dominance in particular markets.

Third, the resulting fragmentation–concentration dichotomy has emerged relatively unchecked by government regulation or restriction on ownership across and within the media. It was not until quite recently that mergers and acquisitions (M&A) have been subject to mandatory merger control review on competition grounds with the coming into force of merger control on 1 June 2011 pursuant to the Competition Act 2002.

Fourth, the closeness of the media with political parties and individuals controlling or being affiliated with sections of the media has raised concerns that policy-making may be being subverted by partial presentation of views in the media. The concerns are reminiscent of experiences in other countries where political figures have used the media to further their interests. This has led to concerns that India may be having its own 'Berlusconi moment'.[5]

Fifth, the corporate structure of India's corporate conglomerates has a media dimension through the diversification of corporate holdings across and within a range of businesses, including media. This is evident through cross-ownership across different sectors of the media as well as vertical integration across the media supply chain from content production and ownership through to distribution. Numerous examples could be cited. At the risk of being too selective and of the examples not fully reflecting the evolving market: Essel and Sun are active in print, TV and FM radio as well as DTH; Bhaskar group, Times Group, ABP and Malayala count at least three media segments in their corporate stable; and the Ambani group has interests across a range of media. However, in a sector where such features may be explained by the pursuit of efficiencies or a logical outcome of converging media offerings, the cross-web of ownership across and within the media industry can be consistent with a competitive outcome.

Finally, recent acquisitions add to the increasingly complex media-holding structure. At the beginning of 2012, Reliance Industries Limited (RIL) became India's largest media conglomerate through various multi-layered funding operations including with Network 18, an Indian mass media company with interests in television, print, online, film, mobile content and allied businesses. A few months later, Indian multinational conglomerate Birla Group acquired almost a third of Living Media India, an Indian media conglomerate with interests in magazines, newspapers, books, radio, television, printing and the internet. Oswal Green, a Delhi-based chemicals and fertilisers company, also acquired New Delhi Television in two transactions at the end of 2012. While none of these transactions has raised any competition concerns, the trend of consolidation underlines the importance of identifying who is really in control of India's media.

[5] Silvio Berlusconi was Italy's longest-serving prime minister since the Second World War. He is also known to be a prominent owner of the media.

TELECOM REGULATORY AUTHORITY OF INDIA CONSULTATIONS

These issues come into sharp focus with the launch of a consultation in February 2013 by the Telecom Regulatory Authority of India (TRAI).[6] This was spurred by the Ministry of Information and Broadcasting, urging the regulator to look again at the state of horizontal and vertical integration in India's media, with the mandate of protecting viewpoint diversity and choice. Four years earlier, the TRAI had put forward a plan for regulating the sector, recommending a market study and threatening restrictions on media cross-ownership. Despite the commissioning by the TRAI of a study of India's media landscape three years later, nothing had been done prompting questions about what action, if any, would be taken and when.

Enter now the TRAI's media ownership consultation in 2013. The consultation was presented on the basis of 2009 market study findings which formed the backdrop to a series of questions relating to how to regulate India's media markets. Comparisons from jurisdictions as far away as the UK, US, Germany and France provided purported inspiration for a vast overhaul of India's up to now relatively unrestricted media market.

The issues are wide ranging and cover topics such as: media consumption measures; the definition of control; the threshold for allowing M&A; and the nature of information disclosures. There are three standout themes which give a particular insight into where the TRAI's consultation intimated it could be heading in terms of the overall policy.

First, there is the question of who should be prohibited from entering the media. The potential candidates to be embargoed from entering the media include: political bodies, religious groups, government departments and bodies funded by the state. The apparent aim is to dismantle what has been an uncomfortable use of the public service news media to promote partisan interests.

Second, should an enterprise be permitted to own media interests in a variety of media sectors: potentially print, TV, radio and any other of the emerging new media? Companies would, of course, like to preserve their ability to expand into other media segments. In fact, such growth may be almost inevitable in the face of convergence—a catchphrase used to describe technical changes which have allowed for newer forms of delivery and functionality and which are blurring the traditional demarcations between media. The consultation postulates elaborate metrics as a possible methodology to decide when 'enough is enough'. Although the TRAI observes that similar measures have been used internationally, some have been abandoned in recent years in favour of more flexible approaches. The UK, for example, has seen a steady rolling back of absolute controls on media ownership and the US abandoned its complex media diversity index which purported to determine the influence of specific companies over the media.

[6] See, further, Telecom Regulatory Authority of India, *Consultation Paper on Issues relating to Media Ownership*, 15 February 2013.

Third, should vertical integration be permitted at all? Or putting it another way, should a company be allowed to hold interests across the media supply chain, say from content ownership through to broadcasting and distribution giving it end-to-end connectivity with the customer? In a sector where vertical integration is not only a fact of life but often a business imperative, the suggestion by the TRAI that vertical integration beyond a 20 per cent interest could be unlawful without further inquiry has troubled economists, lawyers and business managers alike. Economic theory and empirical evidence provides, at best, a nuanced view of the competition effects of vertical integration and restraints.

To add further impetus to the reform agenda, only a few months after the ink had dried on the media ownership consultation, there emerged a further inquiry by the TRAI into the cable sector echoing similar themes to the general media ownership consultation.[7]

Media Pluralism and Plurality

The concern that viewpoint diversity may be under threat has been put forward as an argument in favour of tougher measures to safeguard plurality of the media. The regulation of media ownership is often justified on two main grounds. The first is to maintain competition or to ensure that economic power does not become concentrated in the hands of a particular entity so that it may raise prices above competitive levels or reduce quality or innovation. The second argument, in some cases related to the former but distinct, is to protect plurality of the media. The doctrine of pluralism simply means 'many' (in this case viewpoints, opinions or views). The aim is to create and preserve an environment which is conducive to freedom of expression where no viewpoint should be allowed to control the news 'agenda'. Putting it differently, no person (individual, corporate group or political party) should be able to escape criticism or scrutiny in a plural media market environment.

In India, media pluralism also has a constitutional foundation. The Constitution of India under Article 19(1)(a) accords the freedom of speech and expression to all its citizens. Steadily, over time, the courts have held and reiterated that freedom of the press comes within the ambit of Article 19(1)(a). The freedom is not absolute in nature and is subject to the corresponding reasonable restrictions imposed under Article 19 itself. The TRAI has previously called this provision in aid of its reform proposals.

The media can be a very powerful mechanism to deliver a message and it is vital that no viewpoint is favoured or marginalised. In fact, some of the most pressing social concerns facing India, ranging from female foeticide to honour killings and domestic violence are being aired in the media. In many respects this media visibility can contribute to breaking down centuries of silence and concomitant oppression.

[7] Telecom Regulatory Authority of India, *Consultation Paper on Monopoly/Market dominance in Cable TV services*, 3 June 2013.

The world of television has witnessed a huge growth in the 'crime drama or crime documentary' genre. We conjecture whether this is an apt expression to use but we are assured by Indian viewers that that is how they see it as well. TV shows such as *Crime Patrol* and *Savdhaan India* (translated as 'Caution India') aim to recreate the events of many solved cases (primarily criminal in nature) and broadcast them. These shows are broadcast most nights after 11 pm to avoid exposing young children to them. They have helped expose numerous incidents and cases that occur disturbingly frequently, such as domestic violence, robberies, murders, rapes, other forms of sexual abuse, frauds and so on. These have not only made people more aware of such incidents but also have a strong moral underpinning in raising the public consciousness about issues that previously were not discussed in public. These are issues facing real Indians today; they are not some 'other worldly' polemic but topics and life stories that are only now being aired and subject to open debate. That is why a free media matters in India.

While there is general support for media pluralism as a 'good thing' there is also a degree of equivocation internationally in terms of how to measure media plurality and, indeed, what is meant by a sufficiently plural media market. Certainly, plurality has a quantitative and qualitative dimension. This was recognised by the UK Court of Appeal when it examined the UK media public interest test under the Enterprise Act 2002 in relation to British Sky Broadcasting's proposed acquisition of a 17.9 per cent interest in ITV, a commercial public service TV broadcaster.[8] Under the UK legal framework certain media mergers will be judged against whether, post-transaction, there remains sufficient plurality of control of the media. Plurality, then, means that more than one viewpoint remains. How many more than one is sufficient, however, has not yet been decided by India, or indeed by any other democracy that seeks to regulate this area. As a starting point, it may be postulated that at the time of enactment of the UK Communications Act 2003 media plurality was sufficient since the legislation itself represented a rolling back of controls on media ownership. However, the question of sufficiency of plurality is once against before the UK authorities which are reviewing the entire regulatory framework further inviting consideration of whether the concept of sufficiency (of plurality) needs to be made more explicit. The TRAI has entered this area on the basis of regulating ownership issues. However, the thrust of its proposals has implications for freedom of expression.

International Insights

India has entered the international debate on how best to ensure that the increasing concentration of the media does not compromise competition and viewpoint

[8] *British Sky Broadcasting Group Plc v The Competition Commission* [2010] EWCA Civ 2.

pluralism. While India may have come to this debate later than some other countries, it will not find that it can leverage neatly off policies that have been shown to be effective elsewhere.

Perhaps the only recurrent theme is that there is no 'one size fits all' international standard in terms of how media pluralism is to be protected. As countries around the world have reassessed their own regulation in this area, it is clear how their policies have been shaped by the very specific cultural, economic and political context which makes plurality almost a product of national identity.

The international models of regulation can range from no specific controls at all (eg in Sweden and Finland) to more elaborate plurality tests which determine whether a media merger will pass muster (eg in the UK and Germany). Some countries may be somewhere in between, deploying caps on ownership in certain segments of the media but allowing mainstream competition law tests to assess whether a merger will be approved by a specialist competition regulator (eg in France and Italy).

Another prevailing theme is ongoing debate and scrutiny about whether existing media ownership rules need to be relaxed or made more flexible (as in the Netherlands and United States) or even strengthened (as in Australia and the UK). A related trend is an inquiry into whether the mechanism for regulating the press should be put on a more formal footing, as seen in the UK recently with a proposal for a Royal Charter with 'statutory underpinning' in response to a judicial inquiry.

Against this background, India certainly has plenty of inspiration and examples which it could borrow—or reject. However, the real challenge is how to cut through the morass of rules and create something that works for India and which addresses its specific challenges. If one of the biggest concerns is political capture of the press, then a remedy that targets that may well be warranted. However, it is questionable whether a wholesale importation of plurality regulation which has not necessarily been workable elsewhere is a proportionate solution, at least in the absence of an assessment of the alternatives.

LOOKING AHEAD

Important questions remain: how to ensure that politics does not distort the free expression of views and opinion; how to create and sustain an environment where diverse business models can thrive; and how to adapt to the realities of changing economic times where consolidation is inevitable. How India develops the regulatory framework for the media sector will determine the extent to which such issues are addressed.

The analysis here has the modest aim of informing that debate; a debate that has become polarised in terms of the solutions that have been put forward. The debate about the ownership of the media has historical antecedents. Even the nation's first minister, Nehru, criticised the 'jute press' which was singled out as a mouthpiece of the central jute mills. Today, similar concerns have arisen where what is postulated is a control of the media by some of the country's biggest industrial groups. Faced with the increasing politisation and in some segments consolidation of India's media, and following at least two regulatory consultations, there is a clamour to 'do something'. Understandably, the targets of increased regulatory restrictions would like to preserve the status quo and be allowed to expand their businesses free of regulation.

As we watch other versions of this story play out globally, the overriding theme of this book is consistent with the sledgehammer principle. A blunt instrument can, of course, be used to crack a nut but carries a danger that, in so doing, anything else that is in the line of attack may be damaged. This is a comment about sledgehammers and nuts and is certainly not a counsel of regulatory forbearance or do nothing. Rather, it calls for consideration of a more precise instrument in dealing with one of the most difficult and perplexing regulatory dilemmas facing most modern democracies; how to balance media pluralism and competition.

Our analysis also supports a competition-based approach. This suggests that the most effective enabler of new entry, and better products and services, at lower prices, is competition. This is in opposition to a hypothesis of introducing additional *ex ante* regulatory schemes that may restrict services and products. It also builds on India's recent history of enacting and implementing competition law. The early experience shows that the Competition Commission of India (CCI) is not afraid of assertive action, although it is still too early in its history to make a definitive prognosis.

When it comes to protecting media plurality, competition law can go a long way to ensure that one voice does not become so overwhelming due to its economic and political power that it crowds out other viewpoints. However, a consensus is emerging that media pluralism and competition are distinct and that there is, in principle, a regulatory 'gap' where competition law alone cannot address some of the challenges presented by individuals or groups using their influence to distort the media. The question, then, is how to plug that gap? This may call for tighter restrictions on the types of entities that can control the media such as political parties or government agencies. However, it will be important in devising any change from the status quo that any additional controls do not result in replacing one form of objectionable 'control' with another, under the guise of state supervision of the media.

In these circumstances, it is difficult to be too enthusiastic about a total rewrite of India's media regulation to ban any form of market expansion across the media supply chain or a blanket threshold on the level of permitted interest in a related sector—at least without more detailed inquiry as to what economic considerations dictate that approach or the set threshold level.

It is quite possible that as the competition–plurality debate continues, different regimes will continue to emerge internationally and in terms of their underlying philosophy and specific content. While a first blush analysis might suggest that there should be convergence in the regulatory systems on this aspect, a closer inspection casts doubt on this sweeping conclusion. Owing to the very specific way in which the media markets and attendant regulation have grown up in the various jurisdictions, it is perhaps understandable that they will continue to reflect their own cultural, economic and political identities.

This book should therefore be viewed as part of a discovery process for those seeking a better understanding of the role of policy, regulation, law and economics in shaping and sustaining healthy media markets. And it should always be read with the particular market, legal and economic context firmly in sight.

Suzanne Rab

London, December 2013

Acknowledgements

It is barely two years on from the 'go live' of Indian merger control in June 2011 and the publication of my first international comparative book on Indian competition law. I did not believe that I would be penning a further and third book on India's competition law so soon. Still less did I think that a whole book could and should be devoted to the impact on one particular sector so soon in the history of India's modern competition law. This book on regulation of ownership and competition in the media and communications sector comes at an early stage in the development of India's competition law and at a time when many issues remain unresolved. Despite the book being probably ahead of its time, there are many people who have supported its early appearance and without whom publication would not have been possible.

It was in early 2013 when I first thought that the media and communications sector merited special treatment from an India–international comparative perspective. My first book—*Indian Competition Law, an International Perspective*—had already been well received. Yet India's competition law and regulatory landscape had not stood still and the media and communications sector was particularly active. There have been numerous agreements and abuse of dominance investigations and the Competition Commission of India (CCI) already has a fair number of merger reviews under its belt. The role of the sector regulators and competition regulator has been tabled as a topic for future legislative reforms in a Bill put before the Lok Sabha (the lower house of the Indian Parliament) in late 2012. These developments must be seen against the changes that Indian competition law has already undergone since the adoption of the Competition Act 2002 and the establishment of the CCI in the mid-2000s under the helm of Vinod Dhall, the first acting Chair of the CCI and 'founding father' of Indian competition law. My interactions with him and the first Chairman, Dhanendra Kumar, over the years have always been a source of inspiration and renewal. As with my previous books on this subject, their comments and insights have continued to stimulate the ongoing process of examination.

It was two consultations in 2013 which really put the sector's challenges into sharp focus. They put into perspective the need for a detailed examination of how similar regulatory and sector-specific issues were being treated internationally. Specifically, the Telecom Regulatory Authority of India was consulting on wide reforms to the regulation of the media and communications sector through controversial proposals to impose ownership caps and bans on vertical integration. It claimed to take its inspiration from regulation overseas. It was then that my co-author Alison Sprague and I were asked to prepare commentary on the proposals from an international comparative perspective. We had already gained practical experience navigating similar rules and regulation in our own home jurisdictions—the UK and the EU. It is fair to say that the appropriate scope of media and communications regulation in the UK and in many countries internationally remains one of the most pressing and controversial regulatory issues of the day. So, first and foremost, we would like to thank the Cable and Satellite Broadcasting Association of Asia (CASBAA), an industry association that represents a range of players in the media and communications sector in Asia, for being the catalyst for this work. They were the inspiration for the initial comparative review and the idea to build a study which took as its starting point the current market realities in India. Much of the early comparative thinking for this work was stimulated by the CASBAA. Special mention must go to John Madeiros who has enhanced the industry perspective immeasurably.

Further industry rigour and insight and from the Indian perspective has come from Mukul Shastry of the Reserve Bank of India, and Abhishek Saxena of Phoenix Legal, among others. Over the years, I have been educated by their 'on the ground' perspective of what it is like to advise businesses in India seeking to navigate new legal regimes.

We would also like to acknowledge the contributions of international subject experts, content originators and reviewers. Without such commitments and input it would not have been possible to write and coordinate a multi-disciplinary and multi-jurisdictional work of this nature. Particular thanks go to our economist contributors. We are grateful to Philip Kalmus who provided the critical economics assessment on vertical issues. On the economics of cable, we are grateful for the contribution and insights of Paul Reynolds. Both are full-time economics expert practitioners. Above all, we sought an economics contribution which would be practical and accessible while maintaining academic and theoretical robustness.

Special mention must go to the originators of the country comparative case studies for the cable sector. In no particular order other than alphabetically by county, we would like to thank country contributors Len Hawkes (Belgium); Denis Alves Guimarães and Leopoldo Pagotto (Brazil); Jet Zhisong Deng (China); Pedro Marques Bom (Portugal); Alla Naglis, Alexander Kudelin and Xenia Melkova (Russia); Kee-Hong Chun (South Korea); SAI Law & Economics (Mexico); and Karen Alderman Lucas (United States). Their contributions have considerably enhanced the currency and authenticity of the international comparisons at the sector level.

We must also thank the reviewers who subjected the book to critical comment from the original roadmap and conception through to the final content. Many of them would prefer to remain anonymous and understate their contribution, but in their distinct way they helped the manuscript evolve and improve. Thanks are due to them and should be recorded for posterity here. On Indian competition law and regulation we are grateful to Professor Versha Vahini of the National Law School of India University Bangalore, one of India's pioneer law and academic institutions. We would also like to thank Professor Tony Appleyard (Professor of Finance at Newcastle University), an expert in regulatory accounting and finance, for his perspective.

I cannot omit a final note of thanks to my friends Rakesh, Diksha and Yashita Munjal. They have supported and inspired me throughout my visits to India and projects relating to Indian competition law. All have contributed to practical and academic discourse in the field of law through their work as advocate, university research associate and student. Beyond the law, their insights have helped to shape the local relevance of a book whose subject matter is a reflection of the cultural life of a country.

In a book which is intended to be relevant to regulators and policy-makers, we are grateful to the guidance of Professor George Yarrow, the current Chair of the Regulatory Policy Institute in Oxford (amongst many other accolades). George is without comparator as a 'doyen' of regulatory policy in the UK and internationally. His comments and steering along the way have provided inspiration and discipline.

All errors and omissions, of course, remain those of the authors and we would be grateful to hear from readers who have comments on how this work may be corrected, improved or developed.

Suzanne Rab

London, December 2013

Table of Contents

Biographies

AUTHORS

Suzanne Rab

Suzanne Rab is a barrister practising at Serle Court, a leading chambers based in Lincoln's Inn in London. She has over 15 years' experience advising businesses, regulators and competition authorities on EU, UK and international competition law across the range of competition law, merger control and regulatory matters.

Suzanne has particular experience advising on transactions and commercial agreements and practices, including in proceedings before the UK competition and regulatory authorities and the European Commission. She has worked on some of the most high profile merger, market and cartel investigations in Europe and the UK. She has advised on a range of competition law issues in the media sector including in matters relating to telecommunications, newspapers, online distribution, pay TV, sports rights and licensing of copyright.

In the telecoms sector, Suzanne has advised a UK mobile operator on the licensing, competition and regulatory aspects of the UK Competition Commission's calls to mobiles investigation including price control imposed on operators with Significant Market Power, through the reference, price control, market investigation and judicial review. At EU level, she has advised on the European Commission's competition investigation into differential pricing of iTunes in the EU Member States. She has also advised on the EU and UK competition law, regulatory and merger control issues relating to Video-on-Demand, which was subject to a second stage review by the UK Competition Commission.

In the print media, Suzanne's representative engagements include advising a UK investor on the competition law and public interest aspects of its proposed investment in a major UK newspaper and a regional newspaper on the competition law implications of its distribution arrangements. She has also conducted legal and economics analysis of competition and consolidation in the UK regional newspaper sector with PwC Economics.

Suzanne has advised at the cutting edge of media plurality issues including advising News Corporation on the UK and EU competition law and public interest aspects of its proposed acquisition of the shares in British Sky Broadcasting Group that it does not already own. Together with co-author Alison Sprague, she has given evidence to the House of Lords in relation to the 2013 Select Committee Inquiry into UK media regulation.

In the audio-visual sector, she has advised a range of players from start-ups to major content owners and broadcasters. She has advised a leading venue operator and promoter on its participation in the UK merger control aspects of the merger between Live Nation and Ticketmaster, before the UK Office of Fair Trading and the Competition Commission. Suzanne's representative engagements in the film sector include advising the American Society of Composers, Authors and Publishers on implementation of the European Commission's controversial *CISAC* decision which was upheld in part by the EU General Court in 2013. She has advised a French channel on the EU competition law issues relating to exclusive licensing of its movie rights. She has also advised start-up film companies on the competition law implications of the UK Competition Commission's investigation into pay TV movie rights.

In the sports sector, she has advised British Telecommunications on competition law issues relating to access to and distribution of sports media rights; the English Cricket Board on the competition aspects of commercial practices; and various beverage suppliers on the competition law issues related to their sponsorship and distribution of products at sporting events.

Suzanne has advised extensively on the intersection between intellectual property and competition law including advising Dow Jones on the European Commission's Reuters Instruments Codes investigation under the EU abuse of dominance prohibition in Article 102 Treaty on the Functioning of the EU. She also represented a major US pharmaceutical company on the European Commission's inquiry into the pharmaceutical sector, including attendance at the dawn raid which initiated the inquiry.

Suzanne has wide experience of advising businesses, governments and regulators on developing and implementing new laws and regulatory regimes in line with international best practices, including in network industries. This includes advising an industry association on its submissions to the Telecom Regulatory Authority of India in relation to proposed reforms to regulation of ownership of communications and media enterprises. Her advice to regulators includes advising the European Commission and conducting market analysis to inform the identification of criteria to evaluate projects of common regional European interest in the electricity sector. She has also advised the Commission for Electricity Regulation in Ireland on the EU law and regulatory aspects of a scheme to allocate scarce capacity in the Irish natural gas network. In 2013 Suzanne led a project with the Oxford-based Regulatory Policy Institute Working for the Legal Services Board to examine barriers to entry, exit and mobility in the legal services profession in England and Wales and to inform policy-making in this area.

Suzanne has wide expertise and reputation advising businesses, legal practitioners and regulators in emerging competition law regimes (both outbound in relation to EU law comparative expert opinions and inbound in relation to the application of EU and UK law to international businesses). Examples include advising Reliance Industries (India-EU); PETRONAS (Malaysia-EU) and Monsanto (Mexico-EU). She has also advised international businesses on new competition laws introduced in 2013 in the United Arab Emirates and Mozambique and modelled on EU law.

Suzanne regularly speaks at conferences, presenting on a variety of competition-related topics including merger control, sector regulation, and the role of economics in competition cases. Suzanne has made media appearances on competition law and regulatory matters, including for BBC Radio, BBC Worldwide and Bloomberg.

Suzanne publishes in a range of legal and trade journals including Competition Law Insight, European Competition Law Review, Journal of European Competition Law and Practice and Utilities Journal. She is regularly quoted in the quality press and media on competition law topics, including in *Bloomberg*, *The Deal*, *Dow Jones*, *European Voice*, *Financial Times*, *The Guardian*, *Reuters*, and *Wall Street Journal*.

Suzanne is the author of *Indian Competition Law, an International Perspective* (first published by Wolters Kluwer, May 2012; with a supplement on cartel regulation published in January 2013). The book is the first of its kind international comparative analysis of the Competition Act 2002 published contemporaneously with the coming into force of Indian merger control in 2011. Suzanne was involved in the international engagement on the modern Indian competition law, including through her participation in an International Competition Network Working Group. She maintains a keen interest in the development of Indian competition law and has given seminars on Indian competition law from an international comparative perspective, including as a guest speaker at the Indian Law Institute. She has also been involved in industry initiatives to promote international engagement on Indian competition law including through advocacy with the US-India Business Council and Indo-German Chamber of Commerce.

Suzanne holds an MA in jurisprudence and a post-graduate Bachelor of Civil Law degree specialising in competition law, intellectual property, evidence and conflict of laws, both from the University of Oxford. She is a Visiting Fellow of Imperial College London specialising in competition cases with an antitrust/IP dimension. She has also taught at the University of Oxford. She is a senior research associate and member of the Advisory Board of the Regulatory Policy Institute.

In private practice and prior to joining the bar, Suzanne has held positions and most recently partnership at leading international antitrust law practices including Slaughter and May, Freshfields Bruckhaus Deringer, Hogan Lovells and King & Spalding. She has also held the role of director at PricewaterhouseCoopers working within its strategy, economics and forensics team.

Alison Sprague

Dr Alison Sprague is a partner in the London office of Competition Economists Group (CEG). Alison has more than 15 years' economics consulting experience and specialises in the media, entertainment and telecommunications sectors, advising private and public sector clients in the UK and overseas. Her sector experience includes television, radio, film, internet, music, sport, gambling, music, publishing and fixed/mobile telecoms. She has led numerous strategy and economics projects, providing commercial, competition, policy and regulatory advice. She has additionally conducted research into brands and advertising effectiveness and led a number of expert witness reports. Several projects have employed econometric techniques.

Clients encompass companies, regulators, governments, and their legal advisers, in the UK and overseas.

Alison developed a significant number of advertising revenue forecasting models including for numerous successful franchise applications and renewals—Channel 3, Channel 5, Teletext, DTT, Classic FM, INR2, Talk Radio, and DAB. She has also developed projections for overseas markets including Eire, Macedonia, Hong Kong, several Eastern European countries, the Netherlands and Scandinavia. Contexts include competition, deregulation, litigation, due diligence and privatisation. She has also examined funding models, public value and economic impact in relation to public service broadcasters and conducted two major studies of pay TV markets in the EU as inputs to a client's submission to Ofcom's pay TV investigation. She has also assessed possible uses, values and bidders for the UK's 'digital dividend' (UHF) spectrum. She additionally examined the likely impact of changing the amount of permitted advertising minutage on TV and appraised the reach projections for BBC i-Player. She has written several reports, submissions and presentations on media plurality matters. She advised Ofcom on the viability of local TV and its costs by platform.

Alison's media competition experience includes a merger in the Netherlands TV market, EU roaming charges, UK transport pricing, the collective selling of UK sports rights, UK newspaper and magazine distribution, EU and UK fixed-to-mobile termination rates, the UK outdoor advertising sector, EU local loop and leased lines, GSM spectrum in the Netherlands and EU pay TV sectors. She recently appraised international media plurality and competition regimes as part of a regulatory response on behalf of a major satellite industry association.

Alison has examined sports rights on a number of occasions—she estimated the implicit value of the rights to the Champions League in terms of advertising and sponsorship revenue, examined the revenue distribution model of the Premier League as part of the assessment of another sport, examined the regulatory and competition issues in respect of the Premier League's sale of its broadcast rights and reviewed an expert report in respect of the collective selling of football rights following an investigation by the UK Office of Fair Trading.

Many of the studies Alison has led have been published, including a report on the BBC's educational activities for the BBC Trust, two reports on the European pay TV sector in support of client submissions to an Ofcom market investigation, two empirical studies on advertising effectiveness, a report on the economic impact of the BBC, two studies on how Ofcom takes into account the consumer interest in its formation and implementation of regulation for the Ofcom Consumer Panel and a review of the assumptions underpinning the reach projections for BBC iPlayer as input to the public value test. She has also written numerous thought leadership papers on local newspapers, government policy, copyright, gambling, consumer policy and the competition regime in the UK.

Alison has three degrees in economics and has written several publications. Following her first degree she began her career as a Research Assistant to Professor Patrick Minford and for her MPhil and DPhil theses, she was supervised by Professor Stephen Nickell. She was also a college lecturer at Oxford University. Prior to joining CEG, she held positions at FTI, PwC, KPMG and NERA.

CONTRIBUTORS

ECONOMISTS

Dr Philip Kalmus is Vice President in the Antitrust & Competition Economics Practice at Charles River Associates. Previously a Vice President at FTI and a Director at LECG, Dr Kalmus specialises in applying economic theory to analyse relevant economic facts in competition cases. Philip has a Theoretical Economics PhD, and in his professional career has worked on a large number of antitrust cases with a particular focus on complex vertical and horizontal competition issues. Vertical issues include margin squeeze cases, retroactive and share-of-demand rebates, the incentive and effect of giving access to upstream infrastructure and vertical pricing restraints in online markets.

Contributor to vertical integration.

Paul Reynolds is a partner with the economic consultancy, CEG Europe. Paul advises on economic issues in competition law, regulation and damages cases particularly related to the communications and media sector. He has advised on competition and regulatory issues in relation to the cable industry in a number of European markets as well as in Australasia and North America. Paul previously led a team of economists in the telecommunications group of the Australian Competition and Consumer Commission.

Contributor to cable TV.

COUNTRY PROFILES—CABLE

EUROPE

Belgium

Leonard Hawkes' particular interest is in the application of EU and UK competition law and regulation to network industries. He focuses on the communications (including post), audiovisual, media and energy sectors. Len has practised from Brussels since 1984. He is a Solicitor and Juriste Conseil (member of the European

List of the French speaking Order of the Brussels Bar). He has advised on national regional investment and PPP financing for regional broadband, establishment of the second fixed network operator in South Africa; as well as on investments in satellite broadcasting in Western Africa and on fixed/mobile interconnection agreements in Malaysia, Botswana and Rwanda. He has notified EU and UK mergers to the respective competition authorities and conducted litigation before the European Courts in Luxembourg, including on exchanges of information between competitors. He was European Counsel in Brussels and London to a leading international law firm (1995–2003) and is currently Counsel to DBB Law in Brussels.

Portugal

Pedro Marques Bom has practised as a lawyer since 2001. He is the Director of the Legal Service at the Portuguese Competition Authority (since October 2013). He was a Senior Associate of the EU and Competition Law department at PLMJ law firm (2009–2013). Prior to joining PLMJ, he was Adviser to the Board of the Portuguese Competition Authority (2007–2008), the Director of the Competition and Regulation Department at the Portuguese Health Authority (2006–2007) and Legal Officer at the Portuguese Competition Authority (2003–2006). He holds postgraduate diplomas in competition and industrial property law, from the University of Santiago de Compostela (Spain) and in banking and capital markets, from the University of Coimbra (Portugal).

Russia

Alla Naglis is a partner in King & Spalding's Moscow office focusing on corporate law, mergers and acquisitions and telecommunications, media and entertainment law, and advising major US, European, and Russian parties. She has significant experience advising Russian and international media and entertainment companies on virtually all issues in the film and TV industry, including film and TV production and financing projects, distribution, TV broadcasting and intellectual property issues in Russia, and has been consistently ranked as one of the leading Russian TMT lawyers.

Alexander Kudelin is counsel in King & Spalding's Moscow office. Alexander has more than 17 years' experience with domestic and cross-border mergers and acquisitions, joint ventures, private equity investments, securities, secured and project finance transactions, debt restructurings and general transactional matters. He advises clients in various industries including telecommunications, oil and gas, metals and mining, automotive, food and banking.

Xenia Melkova is an associate in King & Spalding's Moscow office and specialises in advising on Russian mass media and telecom regulation. Xenia's experience includes establishing a Russian presence for a number of worldwide TV channels. She also advises on intellectual property matters with a focus on film co-production and distribution in Russia, and software development and licensing.

AMERICAS

Brazil

Leopoldo Pagotto holds a law degree from the University of São Paulo (USP) Law School (1999), an MSc in Economic Law from the University of São Paulo Law School (Thesis: Competition in the Brazilian Banking System) (2004), an MSc in Regulation from the London School of Economics and Political Science (Thesis: Institutional analysis of the Brazilian Antitrust Authorities) (2005) and a PhD in Economic Law (Dissertation: Anticorruption in Brazil). He regularly writes in several specialised reviews in both Brazil and abroad, besides being the Communication and Website Officer of the IBA Anticorruption Committee. He is also a judge of the Ethics Tribunal of the São Paulo Bar Association. Admitted to the São Paulo Bar Association, Leopoldo has been working as an antitrust practitioner and has been involved in several antitrust cases (merger reviews and conduct cases). He also has knowledge in regulatory and litigation areas of practice. Before his professional experience as an antitrust attorney, he was a trainee at the Administrative Council for Economic Defense (CADE), Brasília, and at Secretariat of Economic Law (SDE), Brasília. After graduating, Leopoldo practised litigation before the courts and in the administrative sphere in the Audit Tribunal, Electoral Courts, Parliamentary Investigation Commissions.

Denis Alves Guimarães is Partner with Alves Guimarães Política Regulatória AGPR, a legal, business and economics consultancy in public policies and government affairs, notably antitrust, regulation and anti-corruption.

He practised law in leading Brazilian law firms (2006–13), advising global law firms and companies on all areas of antitrust in many sectors of the economy, as well as on regulatory matters and international trade.

In the public sector (2003–05), Denis was an attorney at the Secretariat of Economic Law of the Ministry of Justice of Brazil, where he worked on antitrust and pharmaceutical regulation investigations, as well as on antitrust and regulatory advocacy before international organisations and the Brazilian Legislative Branch and government bodies.

In academia, he is a Michigan Grotius Research Scholar (University of Michigan), and has a PhD in Economic and Public Finance Law from the University of Sao Paulo (USP) Law School.

Denis is Advisory Board Member of the Brazilian Institute of Studies on Competition, Consumer Affairs and International Trade—IBRAC (2014–15), and Member of the Committee of Studies on Competition and Economic Regulation of the Brazilian Bar Association, Sao Paulo Section—CECORE OAB SP (2013–15), and of the Committee of Competition of the Sao Paulo Institute of Attorneys—IASP (2013–15). He has co-edited the book *Concorrência e Regulação no Setor de Saúde Suplementar* (Competition and Regulation in the Healthcare Sector, co-edited by L. Farina and published by Singular in Sao Paulo, Brazil, 2010), co-authored the books *Comentários à Nova Lei de Defesa da Concorrência* (Comments to the New Brazilian Competition Law, co-edited by L. Pagotto, co-authored by D. Andreoli et al. and published by Forense/Método in Rio de Janeiro/

Sao Paulo, Brazil, 2012) and *Competition Law in the BRICS Countries* (co-edited by A. Emch/J. Regazzini/V. Rudomino, co-authored by M. Calliari, T. Janssens, G. Oliveira et al. and published by Kluwer Law International/International Bar Association—IBA in Alphen aan den Rijn, The Netherlands, 2012) and the article Brazilian Cartel Enforcement: From Revolution to the Challenges of Consolidation (co-authored by M. Calliari and published in the Antitrust magazine, Section of Antitrust Law, American Bar Association—ABA, Summer 2011, Vol. 25, NO. 3). He has authored dozens of publications and works on antitrust, regulation, legislative reform, state reform and public policy.

Mexico

SAI Law & Economics provides consulting services with a law and economics interdisciplinary approach, integrating renowned lawyers and economists. The Competition Practice Group participated in the preparation of the Mexico contribution to the cable sector review in this book.

Lucia Ojeda is partner with SAI and has been head of the Competition Practice Group since 2002. In her professional practice she has, for more than 10 years, assisted clients from diverse sectors in obtaining authorisations from the Mexican competition agency in respect of global, regional and national transactions. She represents clients bringing cases for anticompetitive conduct and defends companies subject to antitrust investigations. Due to her extensive practice in competition/antitrust issues, Lucia has participated in the consulting group of specialised private lawyers that was formed at the request of the competition agency to consider the initiative to amend the Mexican Federal Law on Economic Competition, its Regulations and other related administrative provisions. She obtained her law degree with honours at the Instituto Tecnológico Autónomo de México.

Luis Alberto Aziz is a founding partner and head of the Competition Practice Group and the Corporate Law Practice Group of SAI. His areas of expertise are cross-border counselling, mergers and acquisitions, arbitration and competition. In relation to competition issues he has advised companies on the notification of global and national mergers, on complaints against commercial practices. He has defended companies on antitrust investigations in several sectors such as soft drinks, beer, cement, hotels etc. He led the SAI legal team in the preparation of antitrust reports to the competition agency on the practices of the two leading airlines in Mexico. He has been selected by *Chambers* and *Who's Who Legal* as one of the top lawyers in the antitrust field in Mexico and as the recommended lawyer for Mexico by Global Law Experts. He obtained his law degree *magna cum laude* at the Universidad Nacional de México.

Itziar Esparza has been the senior associate head of the Competition Practice Group and the Trade Remedies Practice Group at SAI since 2011. Her practice has focused on competition law, international trade remedies and investment and commercial arbitration. She has represented clients in pre-merger filings with the competition agency in complex trans-border transactions relating to the food, natural gas, and aviation industries, and in cartel investigations in the aviation and autoparts markets.

Felipe García has been a senior associate in the SAI Competition Practice Group since 2013. Before joining SAI he served as a consultant with the Mexican Federal Competition Commission and other governmental agencies, including the National Commission of the Retirement System. In his antitrust practice he has assisted clients regarding possible relative monopolistic practices and mergers in a range of markets including aviation, agriculture, telecommunications, food and energy.

Gabriela Schafler has been a junior associate in the SAI Competition Practice Group and the Trade Remedies Practice Group since 2011. Her practice in competition matters includes the assessment and defence before Mexico's competition agency of various companies in investigations and mergers in global and regional transactions.

United States

Karen Alderman Lucas has significant international antitrust experience in Europe, the United States and Asia. Her practice covers multi-national mergers and acquisitions and investigations into alleged monopolisation and anticompetitive conduct.

Karen has authored and edited a number of publications, including 'BRIC in the International Merger Review Edifice', (2010) 43 *Cornell International Law Journal*. 73 (co-authored with Terry Calvani). More recently, she co-edited a guest symposium edition of the Antitrust Bulletin, to which she also contributed the 'Survey of International Jurisdictions Providing for Judicial Merger Prohibition Decisions', Antitrust Bulletin, *The Journal of American and Foreign Antitrust and Trade Regulation* (co-authored with Robert Schlossberg).

From February 2005 to November 2009 Karen was an associate at Freshfields Bruckhaus Deringer in Germany, the United Kingdom and the United States, and from January 2010 to December 2011 was a foreign legal consultant at Kim & Chang in South Korea. She graduated with an LLB from the University of Cambridge in 2002. Karen is admitted in England and Wales as a solicitor and is a member of the New York bar.

ASIA-PACIFIC

China

Jet Zhisong Deng is a partner at Dacheng Law Offices in Beijing. He practises in the areas of antitrust and international trade law in China. Since 2005 he has focused on Chinese antitrust law—three years before China's Anti-Monopoly

Law took effect. He holds a PhD in international law and is a research fellow at the University of International Business and Economics.

South Korea

Kee-Hong Chun is an attorney at Kim & Chang, specialising in competition law and M&A. He has extensive experience in representing multinational and domestic companies in connection with various antitrust issues, including cartels, joint venture formation, distribution arrangements, intellectual property and competitor collaborations. Kee-Hong has also defended companies subject to merger investigation and other civil and criminal investigations in a wide variety of industries, including cable TV, pharmaceuticals, online markets, superstores, chemicals, IT, aviation and heavy industries.

Kee-Hong was a visiting attorney at Shearman & Sterling's New York office in 2012 and 2013, and at Hankun Law Offices in Beijing in 2007 and 2008. He received his LLB from the Seoul National University College of Law in 1999 and his LLM from UC Berkeley, School of Law in 2012. He graduated from the Judicial Research and Training Institute of the Supreme Court of Korea in 2003. He is admitted to the Korean and New York bars.

List of Tables and Figures

List of Tables

List of Figures

Table of Cases

India

Agreements and commercial practices

Mergers

European Union

European Commission

Belgium

Brazil

France

Germany

Mexico

Portugual

Russian Federation

South Korea

United Kingdom

United States

Table of Legislation

India

European Union

Belgium

Brazil

Mexico

Portugal

Russian Federation

South Korea

United Kingdom

Primary legislation

Secondary legislation

United States

International

'The Indian media industry is a dynamo, poised to achieve great success—and to propel India onto the global scene as a generator of cultural content that can be consumed in many parts of the world. Indian TV channels are already achieving great success in places as diverse as Southeast Asia, the Middle East, the USA and Europe—building on the strength of content creation skills developed at home, to suit Indian audiences. It's hard to imagine that only 20 years ago, India had a broadcasting monopoly. The ensuing two decades of rapid investment and development by private entrepreneurs have created an environment where consumers have a plethora of choice. The current market is characterized by a very large number of competing voices—with the number set to multiply further, as broadband penetration increases and Indians begin to watch more and more television content on the Internet.

So whither, now? India clearly does not want to return to the days of 'only one voice' in broadcasting—whether the government's or anyone else's! So concerns have emerged about how pluralism can be encouraged. And politics rears its ugly head, with very real concerns that partisan political control lies occulted behind some of the voices heard in the media. Even accepting that regulators are confronted with some real problems in need of attention, however, it needs to be recognized as well that India also has an unfortunate history of regulatory overreach—cable price controls and 'must provide' mandates from the last decade are two excellent examples of measures that were not adequately analyzed before enactment, were too sweeping and inflexible, and have had lasting negative effects on the cable industry.

In consideration of India's future policies on media ownership, lessons can be drawn from other countries' experiences—India doesn't have to re-invent the 'competition policy' wheel. And one important lesson from overseas is that clear-headed analysis of likely 'regulatory impacts' is essential <u>before</u> measures are implemented. India is only just starting down that road; the necessary analytical and procedural tools need to be put in place sooner, rather than later'.

John Madeiros, Chief Policy Officer, CASBAA

1

Introduction

1.1 THE CONTEXT: MARKET, LEGAL AND REGULATORY TRENDS SHAPING THE MEDIA AND COMMUNICATIONS SECTOR IN INDIA AND INTERNATIONALLY

Competition and diversity in media and communications are fundamental to a competitive economy and healthy democracy. In India, and internationally, there is no consensus in terms of the manner and scope of interventions that are appropriate to protect competition and pluralism in media markets. In recent years the relationship between competition and pluralism has been brought into sharp focus in India by two main developments. First, the enactment and implementation of modern—but sector neutral—competition law under the Competition Act 2002 (Competition Act) represents a step change in competition regulation towards an economics- and effects-based approach. Second, in 2013 the Telecom Regulatory Authority of India (TRAI) launched controversial reform proposals to introduce a media-specific approach to regulation that diverges in some important respects from international best practices.[1]

The academic, legal and policy significance of competition in media and communications is exemplified by the fact that there is no one-size-fits-all solution across jurisdictions and there are polar extremes in terms of the content and intrusiveness of regulation. The regimes range from no specific rules to address media plurality beyond competition law, to elaborate schemes to capture the nuances of content and viewpoint diversity.

Many emerging economies, including India, are seeking to adopt their own regulation in this area taking their lead from the UK. Yet there are doubts whether India has the institutional infrastructure to address the issues even where there is an empirical basis for intervention and consensus on the appropriate form of regulation that is required.

Established regimes have revisited their lighter touch regulation in this area, sometimes in response to popular pressure. Reform of media regulation has

[1] See, further, Telecom Regulatory Authority of India, *Consultation Paper on Issues relating to Media Ownership*, 15 February 2013; and Telecom Regulatory Authority of India, *Consultation Paper on Monopoly/Market dominance in Cable TV services*, 3 June 2013.

been a high profile issue in the UK—with the Leveson Inquiry[2], Royal Charter and its aftermath—and internationally. A European Commission proposal for an EU-wide measure on media plurality emphasises that this issue is to be seen in a wider international context.[3] March 2013 also saw the proposal and withdrawal of controversial reforms to Australian media ownership, and the regulation of media professionals.[4] The 'Media Package' as it became known sparked criticism from the media industry's most prominent leaders. Concerns ranged from the content of the proposals to the swift manner of their introduction without adequate consultation.

In the media and communications sector, there has been a notable trend towards vertical integration and this is a feature of commercial transactions that has been examined closely by the competition authorities.

A related development is 'convergence' which has become a familiar word used to describe the technological and market changes that have occurred in the media and communications industries. There are a number of implications of convergence for a review of media and communications market developments in India and elsewhere. They include: (i) a transition from scarcity in distribution to abundance; (ii) an increased use of distribution networks; and (iii) the possibility of new and potentially complex industry structures emerging. Individually or collectively, these phenomena are likely to render the issues addressed in this book relevant to a range of industries, beyond the traditional media as presently understood.

As academics, lawyers, business managers, regulators and policy-makers in India cast a glance at the international experience there is a compelling need to review in a consolidated and dispassionate manner the relevance of the comparative analysis to India. The modest aim of this book is to contribute to that debate.

This book does not seek to provide an exhaustive review of the issues or jurisdictions covered. In a number of areas the state of regulatory development is very much in flux. This is illustrated by the many outstanding consultations on media regulation and plurality which have not resulted in reform measures at the time of writing.

Rather, by providing examples of recurrent themes in an international context and by locating these trends firmly within the context of proposed and ongoing reforms in India, we seek to illustrate that India is not alone in the challenges it faces. It can benefit from and contribute to insights from other countries, some of which have encountered serious problems in their own regulation of the media and are seeking to correct these. While the challenges faced by India and other

[2] Lord Justice Leveson, 'An inquiry into the culture, practices and ethics of the press' Report No 0780 2012–13, 29 November 2012.

[3] See, further, chapter 9, section 9.3 below.

[4] See, further, chapter 9, section 9.5 below.

economies globally will differ to some extent, a competitive and diverse media and communications markets is a common goal and one worth the time and investment to pursue.

1.2 WHY FOCUS ON OWNERSHIP AND CONTROL?

Why focus on ownership and control since this is only one facet of regulation and competition law control of the media? Such issues are at the forefront of the regulatory 'agenda' in India and internationally. Among the critical questions that have arisen in debates about media ownership and control have been whether the 'gatekeepers' of the networks or content will show a preference for their own operations and discriminate against rivals? Should those who control the medium or means of transmission also control the message? And what would be the effect on competition, consumers and the public interest? Moreover, can competition law on its own protect viewpoint diversity or what is commonly referred to as 'plurality'?

The impact of cross-media ownership also raises interesting questions and views can differ. Should a media owner be allowed to control interests across the media supply chain from content acquisition to delivery to the end consumer, and across the different types of media? Those in the 'yes' camp claim that cross-ownership and vertical integration allow for economies of scale and scope to be realised. More money can be invested in content, there is a better assumption and alignment of risk and, ultimately, more choice for consumers.[5] However, arguments have been raised that such interests should not go unchecked given that the vertically-integrated operator or conglomeration of interests may have the ability and incentive to favour its own operations to the detriment of rivals and competition.

The authors have made a choice to focus on the issue of ownership and control as the central case for this book, recognising a very obvious trade-off between coverage and depth.

To the extent that ownership raises particular issues in the media and communications sector, such issues tend to relate chiefly to news but also relate to current affairs and material contained in documentaries, investigative journalism and so on. At the same time, there are also issues in the broadcasting of sports and sporting events and movies. For example, in the case of sports events we find that market forces or even policies may designate a limited number of entrants—these are essentially the 'rules of the game' and may not raise competition issues at all. Policy-makers may consider that it is important to ensure that such events are carried over multiple media as well as on pay TV so as to be widely available.

[5] See, further, chapter 6 on vertical integration in the media sector.

We believe that since our immediate focus is on the situation in India viewed in an international context, ownership and control issues are sufficiently significant to support this work—particularly given the linguistic and cultural diversity of India which implies that the issues will arise in different contexts. At the same time, we note the global prominence of India in the production of movies (Bollywood) and in sports (eg cricket). The application of competition law to such areas can thus be expected to be of wide and growing interest to consumers, business managers, policy makers and academics in India as it is internationally.

We recognise the intersection between regulation and mainstream competition law insofar as the two impact on ownership and control. This is due not least to the on-going debate about whether competition law alone is sufficient to guard against harm to the consumer interest or whether *ex ante* restrictions on ownership are warranted.[6]

1.3 SCOPE

The following areas are covered in this book:

— Achieving policy objectives—a consideration of the rationale for regulation (why, what, how and who) and the need to ensure that policy objectives are identified early and targeted with appropriate instruments, using methods that minimise secondary effects; the effect of convergence on policy objectives and regulatory approaches; trends in regulatory approaches (eg technology neutrality, *ex ante* vs *ex post* interventions) (chapter 2);

— Market definition and delineation—an exploration of the role of market definition and demarcation in competition cases and its particular significance in media and communications cases. This identifies the role of market definition as a tool in a core competition law analysis, whether in relation to agreements, commercial practices or mergers. It examines the particular challenges that have arisen in applying traditional technical approaches to market delineation in media and communications cases before proceeding to sketch out a more coherent framework that takes account of the specific features of the sector and the role of the consumer (chapter 3);

— Competition law—a discussion of competition law issues in the media and communications sector; an examination of how the Competition Commission of India (CCI) has used the Competition Act prohibitions on agreements and abuse of dominance in the media and communications sector (chapter 4);

[6] We note that there is a separate and related issue about the regulation of media owners and particularly the press (whether by industry or other bodies). Such regulation pertains to regulation of the conduct of media professionals. This topic is not addressed specifically in this book, outside of our more general discussion on plurality and reform of media regulation. See, further, chapters 5 and 9 below.

- Media ownership and control—a discussion of possible high-level models to regulate control of the media, citing international examples and the pros and cons of the various approaches (chapter 5);
- Vertical integration—an outline of the economics of vertical integration (costs and benefits), citing examples to demonstrate the approaches of regulatory and competition authorities (including *ex-ante* vs *ex post* approaches) (chapter 6);
- Cable sector—an international comparative assessment of how regulation and competition law have been applied in the cable sector. As this sector has received particular attention as a candidate for regulatory reform in India, we explore how a range of international regulatory regimes have addressed the economic and competition challenges facing the sector. Examples are provided from Europe, the Americas and Asia and from countries which are similar to and differ from India in terms of their economic, cultural and geopolitical dimensions (chapter 7);
- The effect of the internet—an assessment of the effects of the internet on media consumption and distribution. The internet widens the distribution, service delivery and availability of media for consumers across all genres. We also provide a case study on news consumption and provision: the internet lowers barriers to entry, widens the market for 'news' and increases plurality (chapter 8);
- Shaping the future regulatory agenda in India and internationally—an examination of ongoing regulatory reform in India, the UK, the EU, the US and Australia as the basis for identifying the lessons learned for design of policy in India and internationally (chapter 9); and
- Conclusions and implications for policy—a reflection on the key trends emerging in terms of where the media and communications regulatory 'agenda' is heading internationally and the implications for design and implementation of effective policy and regimes in India (chapter 10).

The focus of our comparative assessment has been on examples from the EU and individual Member States and the US.

We observe the dynamic nature of media regulation. While we have endeavoured to capture the most up-to-date regulatory and policy positions, we recognise the evolving nature of this area. In particular, at the time of writing an overhaul of the UK framework for competition law and regulation is underway with the merger of the UK's first and second stage competition authorities (the Office of Fair Trading (OFT) and the Competition Commission respectively) to form the Competition and Markets Authority (CMA) with effect from 1 April 2014. While references in this book to the application of competition law in the sector relate to the historic experience of the UK competition authorities (the OFT and the Competition Commission) and the UK media and communications sector regulator (Ofcom) they are informative when considering the roles of Ofcom and the CMA in the reformed UK competition law regime.

Our comments on jurisdictions beyond the UK and EU are based on our in-house knowledge of the local regimes at the time of writing.

1.4 SOURCES OF FURTHER INFORMATION

In compiling this work we drew on information from a wide range of sources including competition authority, regulatory authority and government policy papers, academic publications and competition law cases.

Supplementary information is provided in the following appendices:

— Appendix 1 contains additional material relevant to our discussion of achieving policy objectives;
— Appendix 2 contains additional material relevant to our discussion of media ownership and merger control and summarises the media ownership and merger control rules (if any) applying in the media and communications sector in the selected international regimes within our study;
— Appendix 3 provides additional material on the competition review of newspaper mergers in the UK and economic features of the sector;
— Appendix 4 provides more detailed reviews of the regulatory and competition law frameworks and experience in relation to the cable sectors in selected jurisdictions in Europe, the Americas and Asia;
— Appendix 5 provides a number of metrics relevant to access to the internet and online user behaviour in India; and
— Appendix 6 contains additional material on the status of and contributions to ongoing regulatory review of media and communications regulation internationally.

2

Achieving Policy Objectives

2.1 INTRODUCTION

This chapter considers the rationale for regulation (why, what, how and who) and the need to ensure that policy objectives are clearly identified and targeted with appropriate instruments. We outline: the principles that policy goals should be achieved using methods that minimise secondary effects; the effect of convergence on policy objectives and regulatory approaches; and trends in regulatory approaches (eg technology neutrality, *ex ante* vs *ex post* interventions).

Convergence has significant implications for both future regulation and the transition period, that is the present time, as technology, companies and services undergo digital transformation. Old style regulation suited to old style markets is no longer appropriate. Indeed, the application of such regulation may stifle investment and innovation.

The European Commission, for example, published its Green Paper on the implications of convergence in the late 1990s.[1] Internationally, regulators continue to address convergence challenges, and common themes include technological neutrality and balancing flexibility and legal certainty, necessity and proportionality. Globally, policy-makers have paid extensive attention to convergence implications over a considerable period of time.

As we go on to explain, as a bare minimum, regulators should acknowledge that convergence implies that they should show caution when intervening.

Moreover, the internet operates within a convergent environment where distinctions between various media and telecommunications services and networks become blurred. Online is also truly cross-media. This poses specific challenges to regulators in respect of a number of key areas—what and how to regulate, how to define and measure markets, and how to define and measure plurality.

Regulation is in any case an imperfect tool to mimic competitive forces or to achieve market outcomes that policy-makers believe would not occur without intervention. But regulation has its costs as well as benefits. There is a danger that high costs might be incurred if inappropriate tools are applied to solve specific problems and/or if 'old style' regulation is applied to markets subject to dynamic

[1] European Commission, 'Green Paper on the Convergence of the Telecommunications, Media and Information Technology Sectors, and the Implications for Regulation' COM (97) 623, 3 December 1997.

change, for example, as a result of technological advances. Companies may relocate or have unsustainable business models. Investment may be chilled. Consumers may be adversely affected: prices, quality, service range, or service availability may be negatively shaped by regulation, thereby reducing consumer benefits.

2.2 GUIDING PRINCIPLES

In developing a new regulatory regime and reassessing the effectiveness of existing regulation, policy-makers need to be cognisant of a few general principles. Questions to consider include:

— Why regulate? What are the objectives of the intervention?
— What to regulate? Which services or areas of activity should be regulated?
— How to regulate? What instruments should be used? and
— Who should regulate and who should be regulated? What are the institutional aspects?

When designing new regulatory regimes, the following precepts, while obvious once stated, should be observed:

— Define public policy objectives clearly—distinguishing economic efficiency areas from public interest areas, even if one is at the cost of the other;
— Identify the policy instruments available and the potential economic effects (including enforcement costs) of each;
— Identify why the market left to itself and/ or current regulatory tools are unlikely to lead to the achievement of the objective. Sufficient analysis and relevant evidence are required to justify intervention; and
— Choose the most appropriate form of regulatory intervention—the best instrument targeted to the problems identified, assessing the potential economic effects—and identify whether there could be unintended consequences.

Generally, well-targeted policies will:

— address the specific problem or concern;
— lead to small secondary economic effects; and
— have minimum enforcement/compliance effects.

In contrast, poorly directed policies tend to create substantial economic distortions (ie 'unintended consequences' that are not related directly to their primary purpose) and/or tend to be costly to enforce.

In reaching definitive policy proposals, therefore, the why, what, how and who questions should be asked at each stage of the media and communications value chain, supported by analysis of the segments in respect of both economic efficiency and public interest objectives. We provide a summary in Figure 1.

The distinction between economic efficiency objectives and public interest objectives is fundamental and pursuing both may require different approaches. The

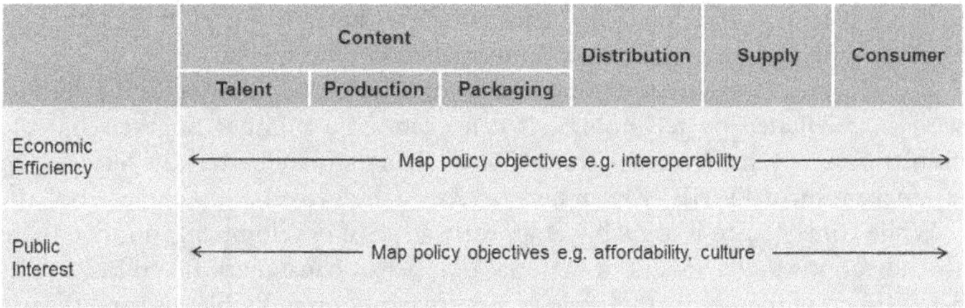

Figure 1: Policy objectives and the media value chain

Source: Authors' analysis and FTI Consulting, Strictly Media Policy, FTI Briefing

regulatory approach to the former should be based purely on economic analysis, whereas the latter tends to involve more subjective assessments, even though economic considerations should play an important role, especially the need to make them explicit and to minimise secondary effects.

As the UK's government department responsible for media (the Department for Culture Media & Sport (DCMS)) stated in its submission to the Leveson Inquiry: 'any [media ownership] rules inevitably act as a potential constraint on that market so it is essential that they be proportionate and do not unnecessarily restrict growth and innovation'.[2]

It is important to reference the extensive research programme that the UK communications regulator (the Office of Communications (Ofcom)) undertook in respect of media plurality as it demonstrates that there are significant challenges and no easy answers. Ofcom spent some seven months on a public consultation on how to measure plurality. The consultation involved stakeholder engagement (including written submissions), academic seminars, international benchmarking, extensive consumer research, an in-depth study of the provision of news, and a review of the academic literature.

Ofcom concluded that assessments of media plurality should not be boiled down to simple market share metrics and that:

> The literature suggests that qualitative factors, including the type of ownership, should also be considered when thinking about plurality. Some writers in this area, including Barnett, have suggested that regulation to promote quality journalism (a form of positive content regulation), rather than a focus on media ownership rules, may be a way to secure outcomes in the public interest.[3]

[2] Department for Culture, Media & Sport, *Media Ownership: Summary*, available at: www.levesoninquiry.org.uk/wp-content/uploads/2012/07/DCMS-submission_Narrative-on-media-ownership.pdf.

[3] Ofcom, *Media plurality and news: a summary of contextual academic literature*, Annex 7, 29 June 2012.

It is important to develop a regulatory regime that is sufficiently flexible and forward-looking to harness future 'convergence' developments.

Convergence is essentially the coming together of audiovisual and telecoms services, facilitated by technology. It can occur at a number of levels—at the industrial level (eg a telecoms company acquiring a broadcaster), in services (eg internet protocol TV (IPTV)), in networks, and in devices.

While convergence is arguably at an early stage of development in India, there are indications that a small but material number of consumers are embracing its benefits—as witnessed by the explosion in smartphone and tablet use and the use of online and social media.

Any regulations imposed on the sector need to take into account possible future technological developments. India will not want to lag behind its BRIC (Brazil, Russia, India and China) counterparts by applying 'old style' regulation to 'new style' companies/markets. Traditional companies will require a regime that gives them the room to invest and to leverage the opportunities of digital transformation. India will want the proportion of digital 'have nots' to decline, not increase.

We consider next the instruments of competition and regulatory policy that may be deployed to promote competitive media and communications markets and otherwise promote the public interest.

2.3 INSTRUMENTS OF COMPETITION AND REGULATORY POLICY—MAPPING OUT THE LANDSCAPE

Over 100 countries have some form of competition law which applies to all sectors of the economy. The position in the media sector is more complex, where competition law and sector regulation may often apply on the same facts.

Our comparative study seeks to identify international best practices that emerge in the regulatory regimes of countries which already exhibit some market, legal and institutional similarities with India (although not necessarily all of these or to the same degree). We focus on comparisons with countries that have already acquired experience in developing regulatory regimes in the media and communications sector.

India's own competition law provides an important backdrop against which our findings should be assessed. India's modern competition law is contained in the Indian Competition Act 2002 (Competition Act) and is enforced by the Competition Commission of India (CCI). The Competition Act contains many features which resemble EU competition law (and, to a lesser extent, US antitrust law). We therefore profile the EU model as starting point benchmark comparator.

Within the EU, we also examine the position in selected Member States with a focus on the UK. The comparison with the UK is apposite, not least since it is a country with which India shares a common history and many aspects of Indian law and procedure are based on English law. We supplement this analysis with comparative vignettes from other key antitrust jurisdictions, including the

United States. In so doing, we emphasise that despite the historical and economic similarities in the relevant markets, India should be slow to emulate particular approaches for their own sake, unless those approaches are appropriate for India now and are considered against a coherent policy on what it is desired to achieve.

To set the scene for what follows, we identify the key instruments of competition and regulatory policy that we consider in this work.

2.4 COMPETITION LAW

Competition laws contain two basic types of rules that affect commercial agreements and practices (outside of control of mergers and acquisitions):

— prohibitions on restrictive agreements;[4] and
— prohibitions on the abuse of a dominant position.[5]

2.5 SECTOR REGULATION

It is a feature of the media and communications sector that companies operating in the sector may be subject to additional sector-specific regulation by a specialist regulator. Even where sector-specific rules do not apply or sector approvals are not strictly required, the sector regulator may liaise closely with the competition regulator in considering which rules or a combination of them are best suited to address a particular issue.

The EU electronic communications sector is subject to supra-national regulation under an umbrella structure known as the 'EU regulatory framework' which is implemented in the national laws of the EU Member States. The EU regulatory framework dates back to 2002 and the latest set of significant amendments, adopted in 2009, took effect on 26 May 2011.[6]

[4] The EU prohibition on restrictive agreements is contained in Article 101 of the Treaty on the Functioning of the EU (TFEU) and national law equivalents (including Chapter I of the Competition Act 1998 in the UK). The counterpart prohibition in Indian law is contained in section 3 of the Competition Act. The most serious form of anticompetitive agreement is a cartel formed to fix prices or share markets or customers.

[5] The EU prohibition on abuse of dominance is contained in Article 102 TFEU and national law equivalents (including Chapter II of the Competition Act 1998 in the UK). The counterpart prohibition in Indian law is contained in section 4 of the Competition Act. Typical types of behaviour that have been sanctioned as an abuse of dominance include pricing abuses (excessive pricing, predatory pricing, margin squeeze and discriminatory pricing), and non-pricing abuses (eg refusal to supply, refusal to license, and abusive litigation).

[6] The EU regulatory framework comprises Directive 2009/140 amending the Framework Directive (2002/21/EC), the Access Directive (2002/19/EC) and the Authorisation Directive (2002/20/EC) [2009] OJ L337/37; Directive 2009/136 amending the Universal Services Directive (2002/22/EC), the E-Privacy Directive (2002/58/EC) and Regulation 2006/2004 on consumer protection co-operation [2009] OJ L337/11; and Regulation 1211/2009 establishing a new Body of European Regulators (BEREC) [2009] OJ L337/1.

The EU regulatory framework is predicated on the following principles of 'good governance'. These include:

— basing regulation on clearly defined policy objectives;
— proportionate and 'light-handed' regulation, so that *ex ante* regulation is limited to the minimum necessary (eg *ex ante* obligations are reserved to those operators who are found to enjoy Significant Market Power (SMP) in a relevant market);
— technological neutrality;
— balancing flexibility and legal certainty;
— harmonisation of national regulatory regimes; and
— periodic review of the EU Regulatory Framework.

2.6 MERGER CONTROL

Merger control refers to the procedure of reviewing mergers and acquisitions (or 'concentrations') under competition law. Typically, parties involved in a concentration that meets the relevant thresholds (which may be turnover, asset or market-share based) are required to notify their transaction to a specialist authority for approval.

India's mandatory merger control system became effective on 1 June 2011. The CCI has already built up experience in this area. We consider the role of merger control when discussing media ownership rules, protection of plurality, and vertical integration in chapters 5 and 6.

2.7 CONVERGENCE

Convergence has become a familiar phrase, or even a 'buzzword', to describe the changes that have occurred in the media and communications industries, particularly in the last decade. In order to frame the discussion that follows, it is helpful to describe two parameters of convergence that are instructive when considering the competition and policy implications of convergence—technical convergence and economic convergence.

Technical convergence blurs the lines between traditional audiovisual and telecommunications services, networks and devices. In respect of its economic effects, while the characteristics of the 'end-point' of convergence (if it exists) are unknown, there are a number of practical implications of convergence. These include:

— a transition from scarcity in distribution to abundance;
— increased use of distribution networks; and
— the emergence of new and potentially complex industry structures.

From scarcity to abundance	Use of networks	Market structure
Additional expenditure on new services	Economies of scale	Vertical integration
Expansion in range of services	Economies of scope	Horizontal integration
New types of transactions	Lower prices	First mover advantages
From public good towards private good	Competing technologies	
New bundling/unbundling possibilities		
New revenue and pricing models		
Cross-border service provision		

Figure 2: Economic implications of convergence

Source: KPMG, Public Policy Issues Arising From Telecommunications and Audiovisual Convergence, a report prepared for DG XIII, London, 1996

Moreover, it is unclear whether the 'end point' will be economically efficient or socially desirable.[7] However, as set out in a report that underpinned the European Commission's Convergence Green Paper, there are a number of potential economic implications of convergence.[8] These are summarised in Figure 2.

Thus in today's dynamic market the traditional lines between formerly discrete sectors of the media or communications markets are no longer sustainable as rigid demarcations. Telecoms providers are entering the broadcasting arena; device manufacturers are entering the media sector; application providers (eg Microsoft) are entering related markets; social networks (eg Facebook) have revolutionised the way in which content is distributed and consumed; and search engines (eg Google) are transforming their businesses to become multi-platform media companies.

In a paper discussed at the OECD's 2013 Global Forum on Competition, Mr Allan Fels commented on the market uncertainties presented by convergence and their implications for the design of regulatory policy. The first uncertainty is demand uncertainty which has become apparent in markets in which online services are supplied. A second source of uncertainty concerns new technologies, where technology risks have increased. Third, despite notable success stories, uncertainty remains as to whether and, if so what, a profitable business model for a particular service might be. Finally, uncertainty arises as to the potential sources of competitive products.

[7] This does not necessarily imply that unduly restrictive regulation should be applied today.

[8] KPMG, 'Public Policy Issues Arising From Telecommunications and Audiovisual Convergence, a report prepared for DG XIII', London, 1996.

When commenting on the policy implications of convergence, Mr Fels is cognisant of the need to be vigilant to the potential for competitive harm, while recognising the dangers of inappropriate (over- or under- zealous) regulation:

> 48. In combination, these four types of uncertainty flowing from convergence generate significant market uncertainty. Furthermore, the above discussion underlines the deep uncertainty that exists about where profit opportunities lie in the emerging, but as yet poorly understood, markets. A heavy investor in the wrong parts of the industry may find its asset is used, but the real profits accrue to a supplier somewhere else in the production chain.
>
> ...
>
> 56 ... However, technological change is also reducing the entry barriers into the production of content and expanding the range of transmission options—both of which should serve to reduce competition concerns. At the same time, *the speed and unpredictability of technological change makes it vital competition authorities recognise the risks of 'getting it wrong'*: in the sense of mistaking transient commercial success for market power; or, conversely, in over-estimating the corrective efficacy of entry and of new competition. *Striking the balance between these errors will undoubtedly be challenging for competition regulators, and at times frustrating for market participants, in developed and developing countries alike.* (emphasis added)[9]

From a regulatory perspective, the technological and economic phenomena of convergence point to a more integrated approach to media policy. This does not necessarily require a uniform approach to regulation of all sectors as there should be scope for variations, where appropriate. However, it does require a coordination of regulatory functions and rules.

2.8 'TECHNOLOGY NEUTRAL'

In the EU, economic policy in the telecoms and media sectors is based upon liberalisation of national markets. The telecoms and media sectors are subject to different regulation.

However, convergence of the sectors has also led to a degree of convergence in regulation, with EU policy being technologically neutral for the 'electronic communications' sector. Accordingly, the EU regulatory framework does not use specific, different legal definitions for 'telecoms', 'media' or 'IT' and covers the conveyance of signals (of all types, including voice and data) by electronic communications networks (of all types, including fixed and wireless networks, the public switched telephone network (PSTN), internet protocol (IP) data networks, cable networks and radio and television broadcast networks).

[9] Organisation for Economic Co-operation and Development, 'Competition issues in television and broadcasting', Contribution from Mr Allan Fels (DAF/COMP/GF (2013)6).

This concept is reflected in the legal definitions in the Framework Directive as follows:

> 'electronic communications network' means transmission systems and, where applicable, switching or routing equipment and other resources, including network elements which are not active, which permit the conveyance of signals by wire, radio, optical or other electromagnetic means, including satellite networks, fixed (circuit- and packet-switched, including Internet) and mobile terrestrial networks, electricity cable systems, to the extent that they are used for the purpose of transmitting signals, networks used for radio and television broadcasting, and cable television networks, irrespective of the type of information conveyed.[10]

The concept of technological neutrality has at least two implications for the design of regulatory regimes. First, the concept of the media should not depend on any specific form of platform or means of transmission. Second, the rights and obligations that apply to media enterprises should apply regardless of the underlying technology that they use, provided that they conform to the technology-neutral definition.

2.9 REGULATION: SECTOR-SPECIFIC VS COMPETITION LAW

In general, a number of key distinctions have been identified as demarcating the line between sector regulation and competition law which tend to correspond, broadly, to the '*ex ante*' and '*ex post*' labels.

To frame the discussion which follows (and to reveal the over-simplification) it is useful to start with a few key distinctions to define the boundaries between sector regulation and competition law.

- Sector regulation is generally applied *ex ante* enabling 'regulators' to control the activities of natural or unnatural monopolies. Once markets have been opened up to competition, market forces come into play. It is maintained that competition law can then be applied to intervene if—and only if—there have been observable restrictions on competition or evidence of likely violations of law (*ex post*).
- Sector regulators tend to have an ongoing relationship with regulated companies and benefit from a stream of information on the sector derived from carrying out their supervisory functions. On this view, competition authorities generally rely on complaints and obtain information in the context of specific enforcement actions.

[10] Directive 2002/21/EC of the European Parliament and of the Council of 7 March 2002 on a common regulatory framework for electronic communications networks and services [2002] OJ L108, Article 2 as amended.

— Sector regulators impose and monitor detailed behavioural remedies. Competition authorities, if the distinction is maintained, typically elect for structural-based remedies addressing specific activities.
— Sector regulators have a broad range of policy objectives. These may include industrial policy objectives as well as consumer welfare objectives. Competition authorities have a narrower remit, typically to promote consumer welfare or total welfare.

As will be apparent from the analysis which follows, the above distinctions should not be taken as polar extremes in demarcating how sector regulation and competition operate or interact. Rather, the '*ex ante*' and '*ex post*' distinctions are relevant to our study of how sector regulation and competition can combine in India to achieve the optimum balance between preventing the creation or entrenchment of market power and providing companies with incentives to invest and innovate.

First, some kind of temporary market power may be needed to achieve efficiencies connected with investment and innovation. Second, it is apparent that markets may not always be left on their own to address the challenges presented by technological development if consumers find it costly to switch to new products and services.

This situation may give rise to complex balancing that does not always have a clear-cut policy solution. The implication is that it is vital that regulators limit themselves to intervention *ex ante* only where this is demonstrated to be necessary to prevent the likely foreclosure of entry, competition and innovation.

2.10 EU EXPERIENCE

Competition law plays a complementary role to sector-specific regulation, particularly in the telecoms sector. The relationship between regulation and competition law was described by Competition Commissioner Joaquín Almunia in 2010:

> The telecommunications sector is a great example of regulation and competition working hand in hand. It is typically the sort of industry where ex ante regulation has been a necessary complement to competition enforcement, because there are enduring economic bottlenecks, namely non-replicable legacy facilities. So regulation of access to networks has been necessary to allow market entry.
>
> But *regulation is being progressively phased out, as competition in the market develops*, ultimately, electronic communications will be governed by competition law only. Under the current EU Regulatory Framework for electronic communications, regulation is the exception rather than the rule. The Commission, alongside national regulatory authorities, has a role to play in ensuring that regulation is imposed *only where it is necessary*. (emphasis added)[11]

[11] Joaquín Almunia, 'Competition v Regulation: where do the roles of sector specific and competition regulators begin and end' Brussels, 23 March 2010.

2.11 ALLOCATION OF COMPETENCES BETWEEN SECTOR REGULATOR AND COMPETITION AUTHORITY

2.11.1 Regulatory 'Models'

An important issue raised by regulatory policy-makers relates to the allocation of functions between regulators. The following are conceptual models of regulation:

- Separate: Separate competition authority and sector regulator applying competition law and sector regulation respectively (eg as seen in India).[12]
- Combined: Consolidated regulatory authority applying competition law and sector regulation (eg proposal to create the Comisión Nacional de la Competencia y los Mercados in Spain).
- Concurrency: Separate competition and regulatory authority applying competition law and sector regulation respectively; sector regulator has power to apply competition law in its own sector (eg as seen in the UK).

2.11.2 Indian Experience

The jurisdiction of the CCI under the Competition Act must be distinguished from that of the sector regulators. The Competition Act is designed to promote competition in all sectors of the Indian economy through its system of effectively prescribing what companies should not do, that is, engage in certain pricing behaviour, cartels, collusion and so on. The sector regulators provide a framework which companies in the sector are obliged to follow regarding tariffs, industry standards, entry conditions and service obligations.

The Competition Act as originally enacted contemplates a synergised relationship between the CCI and the sector regulators in that:

- the CCI can make a reference to a statutory authority if, in the course of a proceeding before the CCI, an issue is raised by any party (if any decision which such statutory authority has taken, or proposes to take, is or would be, contrary to any of the provisions of the Competition Act), and if the implementation is entrusted to a statutory authority;
- where, in the course of a proceeding before any statutory authority, an issue is raised by any party that any decision which such statutory authority has taken or proposes to take, is or would be, contrary to any of the provisions of the Competition Act, then such statutory authority can make a reference in respect of such issue to the CCI; and

[12] As at December 2013, the CCI has exclusive competence to determine whether there has been a violation of Indian competition law.

— the CCI can make an own-initiative reference to, or receive a reference from, a statutory authority.

However, there is as yet no specific guidance concerning the relationship between the CCI and the sector regulators, which has raised the question of potentially overlapping or duplicative regulation.

The end of 2012 saw developments towards amendments to Indian competition law. On 7 December 2012 the Lok Sabha (the lower house of the Indian Parliament) passed the Competition (Amendment) Bill, 2012 (Competition Amendment Bill). Before this becomes law, it needs to be passed by the Rajya Sabha (the upper house of the Indian Parliament). It must then be notified by the government. The exact timing and scope of implementation of the Competition Amendment Bill are unclear. However, there is momentum to push ahead the sweeping changes to the existing Competition Act, whose provisions on anticompetitive agreements and commercial practices have been in operation since May 2009 and whose merger control provisions have been active since June 2011.

There are two legislative proposals which are significant when considering the balance of powers between the CCI and Indian sector regulators. First, a new provision is proposed to give central government the power to specify different values of assets and turnover for any class of enterprises for merger control purposes. This would give the government the power to introduce specific merger thresholds by market sector such as the media sector.

Second, there will be a provision for mandatory references of issues by statutory authorities (including sector regulators) to the CCI and from the CCI to the statutory authorities. Currently, such references between the CCI and statutory authorities occur on a discretionary basis as described above. This should allow for a more streamlined approach to dealing with competition issues in regulated sectors such as the media.

2.11.3 UK Experience

Companies operating in the regulated industries in the UK will be familiar with the 'concurrent' application of competition by the competition authority and the various sector regulators. The sector regulators for these purposes include Ofcom, the sector regulator for the media and communications industries.

The sector regulators share, broadly, the same powers as the Competition and Markets Authority to enforce UK and EU competition law in their respective sectors.

When concurrency was introduced, arguments were put forward both for and against the system. In favour of concurrency it was argued that: (i) sector regulators had developed specialist expertise and knowledge of their sectors that could be applied effectively in competition cases; (ii) there was overlap between the sector licensing regimes and competition law; and (iii) concurrency would encourage sector regulators to move away from reliance on *ex ante* regulation to using *ex post* competition law.

Against concurrency it was argued that: (i) concurrency is rare in other jurisdictions including the EU; (ii) the sector regulators lacked expertise in EU competition law analysis and investigations experience; (iii) there would be a less efficient use of regulatory resources given the number of bodies that could potentially apply competition powers; (iv) there was a risk of inconsistency in decision making; and (v) there was a risk of 'double jeopardy' where companies operating in more than one sector might face multiple investigations.

Over the years, various bodies have put forward suggestions as to how the perceived difficulties with the current concurrency regime might be addressed.[13]

2.12 RESTRICTIONS ON COMPETITION

Competition authorities have applied competition law prohibitions on restrictive agreements in a range of media and communications contexts. The CCI has already applied Indian competition law in this area as will be discussed in chapter 4.

In the absence of evidence of market power ('dominance') the authorities have used the prohibition on restrictive agreements to sanction arrangements between independent undertakings that are likely to foreclose new entry. Such interventions have generally been pursued with the aim of bringing about lower prices, better quality, increased innovation and, ultimately, greater consumer choice.

In the EU, for example, the European Commission has applied the EU equivalent to section 3 of the Indian Competition Act (Article 101 TFEU) to a range of media and communications contexts. This includes pricing of music downloads,[14] simulcast broadcasting,[15] and collective purchasing by broadcasters and collective licensing by sports associations of sports rights.[16]

[13] The relationship between the competition and sector regulators remains controversial. The UK Enterprise and Regulatory Reform Act 2013 makes provision which would allow the Secretary of State by order to remove from a sector regulator all or any of their concurrent competition powers discussed above.

[14] European Commission press release, 'Antitrust: European Commission welcomes Apple's announcement to equalise prices for music downloads from iTunes in Europe' (IP/08/22) 9 January 2008.

[15] European Commission press release, 'Commission clears one-stop agreements for the licensing of TV and radio music via the Internet' (IP/02/1436) 8 October 2002.

[16] See, further, European Commission press releases: 'Commission clears UEFA's new policy regarding the sale of the media rights to the Champions League' (IP/03/1105) 24 July 2003; 'Details of broadcasting rights commitments made by the German Football League' (MEMO/05/16) 19 January 2005.

A recent example of the application of competition law rules on restrictive agreements in the telecoms sector is the European Commission's January 2013 fine on Telefónica (exceeding EUR 66 million) and Portugal Telecom (exceeding EUR 12 million). The case concerned a non-compete arrangement in the context of Telefónica's acquisition of sole control over Vivo, a Brazilian mobile operator that had previously been jointly owned by the parties under a joint venture.[17]

The potential application and limits of applying the competition law prohibition on restrictive agreements is illustrated by an EU case involving collecting societies. On 12 April 2013 the EU General Court gave its judgments in proceedings brought by the International Confederation of Societies of Authors and Composers (CISAC) and 21 of its collecting society members.[18] This related to the European Commission's 2008 decision finding that the collecting societies had violated Article 101(1) TFEU through the provisions in their reciprocal representation agreements.[19] While the General Court upheld the findings of the European Commission in part,[20] the main interest in the appeal was the challenge to the finding of the existence of a concerted practice relating to national territorial limitations. The General Court held that the European Commission had not proven to a sufficient legal standard that there was concertation among the societies in respect of the provisions relating to territorial limitations. The outcome on this element has been welcomed by the collecting societies. However, almost a decade of legal wrangling in this case raises issues about the proper balance between protecting competition and ensuring that creators and rights holders are able to develop licensing models that meet market needs.

[17] European Commission press release, 'Antitrust: Commission fines Telefónica and Portugal Telecom €79 million for illegal non-compete contract clause' (IP/13/39) 23 January 2013.

[18] *CISAC* judgments in Case T-392/08 *AEPI v Commission*; Case T-398/08 *Stowarzyszenie Autorów 'ZAiKS' v Commission*; Case T-401/08 *Säveltäjäin Tekijänoikeustoimisto Teosto v Commission*; Case T-410/08 *GEMA v Commission*; Case T-411/08 *Artisjus Magyar Szerzõi Jogvédõ Iroda Egyesület v Commission*; Case T-413/08 *SOZA v Commission*; Case T-414/08 *AKKA/LAA v Commission*; Case T-415/08 *IMRO v Commission*; Case T-416/08 *EAU v Commission*; Case T-417/08 *SPA v Commission*; Case T-418/08 *OSA v Commission*; Case T-419/08 *LATGA-A v Commission*; Case T-420/08 *SAZAS v Commission*; Case T-421/08 *Performing Right Society v Commission*; Case T-422/08 *Sacem v Commission*; Case T-425/08 *KODA v Commission*; Case T-428/08 *STEF v Commission*; Case T-432 *AKM v Commission*; Case T-433/08 *SIAE v Commission*; Case T-434/08 *TONO v Commission*; Case T-442/08 *CISAC v Commission*; Case T-451/08 *Stim v Commission*, judgments of 12 April 2013 finding anticompetitive conduct on the part of collecting societies.

[19] European Commission press release, 'Antitrust: Commission prohibits practices which prevent European collecting societies offering choice to music authors and users' (IP/08/1165) 16 July 2008. *CISAC* (Case COMP/C2/38.698—*CISAC*, Commission decision of 16 July 2008).

[20] The General Court upheld the finding of the European Commission that there was a violation of Article 101 in respect of the clauses which prevented CISAC members from accepting as a member an author who was already a member of another society. Similarly, the General Court upheld the finding of a restriction of EU competition law in respect of clauses which provided for one society to confer on the other, reciprocally, the exclusive right in the territories in which the other operates to grant the requisite authorisations for public performances.

2.13 MARKET POWER

Control of market power in the media and communications sector has been a focus of the CCI as we will discuss in chapter 4. Here, we provide a brief reference to the approach of regulators internationally. A variety of regulatory tools have been deployed, ranging from enforcement of the competition law rules on abuse of dominance to sector-specific regulation and market-wide investigations.

To illustrate some prevailing themes, we contrast in Appendix 1 the approach of the EU and UK authorities in the telecoms and broadcasting sectors respectively.

The EU experience of competition law enforcement in the telecoms sector must be considered in its market and historical context. In the early years, competition law enforcement of the EU prohibition on abuse of dominance was directed towards curbing the market power of former state monopolies which, by virtue of their incumbent positions and control of infrastructure, actually or potentially had the ability and incentive to restrict new entry. The pattern of enforcement today is still influenced by this background and is aimed at addressing observable abuses of market power. It will be recalled that Indian competition law has the very same powers of intervention through section 4 of the Competition Act should there be concerns that any communications (or media) operator is abusing market power.

The UK experience of sector and market regulation in the broadcasting sector illustrates how the UK has sought to address concerns that markets may not be working as well as they might but there has been no evidence of a violation of competition law. In such a situation the need to encourage innovation and keep markets contestable remains considerable. Two case studies in Appendix 1 illustrate the potential for 'getting it wrong'. First, the UK's attempts to impose intrusive sector-specific regulation in the form of a wholesale must-offer obligation on British Sky Broadcasting Limited (BSkyB) in respect of its sports channels did not survive a judicial challenge. Second, after a two-year-long market investigation before the UK Competition Commission (CC), it was decided that there was no adverse effect on competition (AEC) in relation to the supply and distribution of pay TV movie content.[21]

Thus, the implication for India as it contemplates charting a new path in media and communications regulation should be one of caution. Like the UK and the EU, India has a modern competition law and a specialist regulator that is charged with competition law enforcement. This does not necessarily mean that enforcement policy should be more lenient. Rather, it should preserve the flexibility to

[21] During a period of 10 months, the CC reversed its preliminary decision that BSkyB's position gave rise to an AEC to conclude that BSkyB did not have such an advantage over its rivals when competing for pay TV subscribers as to harm competition. The CC noted the increasing trend of audiovisual content being delivered over the internet which had increased competition and consumer choice. The ultimate conclusion reached by the CC demonstrates the reluctance of a competition authority to impose remedies in a rapidly changing and uncertain market place.

adapt to the particular challenges of media and communications markets where the blunt instrument of rigid *ex ante* controls in the absence of observable harm risks being counterproductive.

2.14 CONCLUSIONS AND IMPLICATIONS FOR POLICY

A number of implications for design of policy and regulatory interventions emerge:

— Costs and benefits: Regulation is an imperfect tool to mimic competitive forces or to achieve market outcomes that policy-makers believe would not occur absent intervention. But regulation has costs as well as benefits. There is a danger that high costs are incurred if there is the application of inappropriate tools to solve specific problems and/or if 'old style' regulation is applied to markets subject to dynamic change, for example, owing to technology. Companies may relocate or suffer unsustainable business models. Investment may be chilled. Consumers may be adversely affected: prices, quality, service range or service availability may be negatively shaped by the regulations, thereby reducing consumer benefits. A rigorous Regulatory Impact Assessment is needed to inform reform proposals, demonstrating that departure from the status quo would produce benefits that outweigh the potential harm that is likely to result from ill-targeted regulation.

— Regulatory best practices: Despite differences in policy towards the regulation of the media and communications sectors internationally, there are some prevailing themes. These include: technological neutrality and balancing flexibility and legal certainty, necessity and proportionality.

— Allocation of regulatory functions: A question arises as to the proper balance in regulatory functions between the sector regulator and competition regulator. In any event, concurrent application of competition law by competition and sector regulators is rare internationally. Overall, there is evidence of a move away from concurrent application of competition law and a consolidation of competition functions in the relevant competition authority (eg in the UK). India adopts the 'separate' but synergistic model where the CCI is exclusively responsible for competition law enforcement. At the very least, this focuses attention on the application of competition law by specialist authorities. At the same time, it does not mean that sector regulatory experience of the media and communications sector cannot be deployed to good effect in working with the CCI to apply competition law in a measured way to secure a healthy and vibrant market in India.

— Risk of errors: The intervention by sector regulators or competition regulators in cases where there is no violation of competition law but concerns arise due to the organic growth of the company, is highly controversial. These cases are inherently fact-intensive and the scope for error or 'getting it wrong' must not be underestimated. Too precipitous an intervention and there is a risk of implementing over-corrective measures. Conversely, the countervailing threat of new entry must be credible. A competition authority such as the CCI is best equipped to address such issues, benefiting, where appropriate, from the information and insights which may be more readily available to the sector authority but where the CCI takes the final decision on whether or how to use its competition law powers.

When designing new regulatory regimes, underlying principles, while obvious once stated, should include:

— Achieving public policy objectives: Objectives should be clearly defined, distinguishing economic efficiency areas from public interest areas, even if one is at the cost of the other. The policy instruments available should be identified along with the potential economic effects (including enforcement costs) of each. Sufficient analysis is required to justify intervention; and the most appropriate form of regulatory intervention selected, to minimise unintended consequences.
— Convergence: Despite convergence, there remains fragmentation in the approaches adopted by regulators towards intervention in telecoms and other sectors. However, issues of access, network neutrality, non-discrimination and protection of intellectual property rights are recurrent themes. These are issues that are familiar to competition authorities. Moreover, technological changes may break down these demarcations further. However, the real challenge that convergence poses is increased uncertainty in respect of the speed of technical change and its effects in the short and longer term. Regulators or competition authorities run the risk of 'getting it wrong' by applying old style, stringent regulations and/or by mistaking transitory profitability for abuse. A cautious and flexible approach is required. The application of old style regulations to such evolving markets is not recommended; it may stifle investment and innovation. Regulation should be flexible enough to take account of the evolving market dynamic and be informed by the best assessment of how markets are likely to evolve.
— Evolving markets: There may be gaps in competition law in that it is unable to address market failings which may not be attributable to an infringement of competition law or breach of sector regulatory law by any company. The UK has sought to address this through the market investigations regime but this is a lengthy and resource-intensive process. The outcome may be a clean bill of health but only after a detailed inquiry and years after the initial concerns were raised. For example, the recent UK *BSkyB* case[22] involving movies

[22] Competition Commission, 'Movies on pay TV market investigation: A report on the supply and acquisition of subscription pay TV movie rights and services', 2 August 2012.

on pay TV has highlighted that the way in which retail pay TV services are provided is evolving and this can alter the incentive and ability of a firm to exercise market power.[23] India does not have such a market investigations regime but even where it operates in the UK we detect a level of regulatory forbearance in the media sector.

[23] See, further, Appendix 1.

3

Market Delineation and Definition in Media

3.1 INTRODUCTION

This book is about the regulation of ownership and control of media and communications, a sector that is undergoing major market, regulatory and technological development.

A threshold issue arises as to an appropriate delineation of the subject matter: what exactly do we mean by media and communications, and why the focus on ownership and control?

The phenomenon of convergence presents an important starting point from which to map out the parameters of the subject matter. This recognises that technical and regulatory developments are leading to a blurring of distinctions and alignments between what were previously considered to be separate segments of the media. To take one example, audiovisual content might be available via a TV broadcast or over the internet. Different technical means of transmission may be used but, gradually, the differences are being eroded. This raises a question about whether the broadcaster and internet service provider are in the same market at all now, or whether they will be in the future, and whether it really matters when considering competition between them.

Market definition plays an important role in competition law analysis. Commercial practices and pricing strategies that would be acceptable for a company with a modest market position may be prohibited when practised by a company with market power. In the context of mergers and acquisitions, the key question from a merger control standpoint is whether the transaction will give rise to a significant or substantial reduction in competition or lead to the creation or strengthening of a dominant position in the relevant market. This is particularly relevant to India where many of the core issues covered by the Competition Act 2002 (Competition Act) are predicated on the notion of an 'appreciable adverse effect' (AAE) on the *relevant market* in India. Thus, market definition is often a first-line indicator of the likely legal treatment of many of the commercial decisions that a company may decide to take. It is, therefore, a useful starting point when framing any discussion of competition and regulation.

Given that this book retains a relatively narrow focus (ownership and control of the (converging) media) we must start by putting those issues in a coherent frame of reference by defining the relevant economic activities. We therefore begin with an excursion into the economic and legal principles underlying market definition. Thus, one of the big issues in the sector has been the extent to which different channels of communication, such as free-to air-TV, pay TV, newspapers and the internet, compete with each other. Is there a broad market for news and current affairs content or are individual channels sufficiently distinct that issues of competition and plurality arise for each of them, as well as at a broader cross-media level? What is the significance of the fact that consumers may have access to news and current affairs via multiple media including online? Viewed in this way, the topic of market definition—or delineation—would seem to be a useful starting point to frame the debate that follows.

We are not concerned exclusively with goods or services that are easily measured in terms of economic value or price. Value is influenced by the link between the media and cultural aspects or freedom of expression. While it is beyond the scope of this book to revisit the theoretical discussion on the fundamental freedom of expression,[1] it is an important factor when considering pluralism and diversity. Indeed, safeguarding the democratic goal of freedom of expression is one of the reasons why many legal systems have rules which protect plurality in the first place. Given the intersection between the media and culture, which can itself be a mechanism of promoting national or narrower interests, it is ever more important to delineate the 'boundaries of the field'. This is one way ensuring that laws and regulations that impact the media and seek to pursue goals which are not wholly related to competition are applied in a balanced and justifiable way, taking account of traditional and newer forms of transmission.

Finally, there is an important temporal aspect which is brought into sharp perspective by the converging nature of media markets. The phenomenon of convergence is again relevant. We do not know where this will lead or what the end point will be and over what timeframe, but this does not mean that we should abandon the challenge of framing a reasonable time period for mapping out the subject matter. This inquiry into the temporal dimension of relevant markets and competition is familiar to competition authorities, for example, when considering the likelihood of entry (whether through new technologies or new companies entering a market).

The remainder of this chapter is structured as follows. First, we provide an assessment of the role of market definition in competition analysis. Second, we consider the role of the consumer in media regulation. Third, we identify the key challenges in identifying relevant markets in the media and communications sector. Fourth, we explore how, in light of those challenges, relevant markets are

[1] In most countries, including in the EU, freedom of expression is fundamental to the democratic order. It is defined in Article 10 European Convention on Human Rights as embracing the freedom to seek, impart and receive information. The Constitution of India under Article 19(1)(a) provides for the freedom of speech and expression to all its citizens.

identified in the media and communications sector in practice. We conclude with a preliminary sketch of a conceptual framework for identification of relevant markets in the media communications sector to frame the analysis that follows.

3.2 THE ROLE OF MARKET DEFINITION IN COMPETITION ANALYSIS

Most modern competition laws are based on three core concepts: (i) anticompetitive agreements (including cartels); (ii) prevention of abuse of dominance or market power; and (iii) merger control.

In each of these cases, a key aspect to the assessment is the relevant market. In relation to anticompetitive agreements, while it may not be necessary to define the relevant market in all cases which involve a violation of the prohibition on restrictive agreements,[2] the focus is on the prevention, restriction or distortion of competition in the market. In the case of abuse of dominance or monopoly, it is clear that such assessment cannot take place independently of an inquiry into market definition since the logically prior question of whether an enterprise is abusing a dominant position is whether it in fact holds a dominant position in a relevant market.

In relation to mergers, the substantive test is frequently articulated around such concepts as a substantial lessening of,[3] or significant impediment to effective competition,[4] or the creation or strengthening of a dominant position,[5] by definition in a relevant market.

[2] For example, the EU has distinguished cartel cases where it is necessary to define the relevant market. The EU Court discussed this case law in *Greek Ferries* (Case T-61/99 *Adriatica di Navigazione SpA v Commission of the European Communities* [2003] ECR II-5349):

> For the purposes of applying Article 85, the reason for defining the relevant market is to determine whether the agreement, the decision by an association of undertakings or the concerted practice at issue is liable to affect trade between Member States and has as its object or effect the prevention, restriction or distortion of competition within the common market. That is why, for the purposes of Article 85, the objections to the definition of the market adopted by the Commission cannot be seen in isolation from those concerning the impact on trade between Member States and the impairing of competition (SPO and Others v Commission, cited above, paragraph 75, and Case T-348/94 Enso Española v Commission [1998] ECR II-1875, paragraph 232). It has also been held that an objection to the definition of the relevant market is of no consequence provided that the Commission has rightly concluded, on the basis of the documents referred to in the contested decision, that the agreement in question distorted competition and was liable to have an appreciable effect on trade between Member States (Joined Cases T-25/95, T-26/95, T-30/95 to T-32/95, T-34/95 to T-39/95, T-42/95 to T-46/95, T-48/95, T-50/95 to T-65/95, T-68/95 to T-71/95, T-87/95, T-88/95, T-103/95 and T-104/95 Cimenteries CBR and Others v Commission [2000] ECR II-491, paragraph 1094)' (Greek Ferries, paragraph 27). Thus, the correct definition of the relevant market is not necessary where the European Commission has already concluded (correctly) that the agreement in question distorted competition and was liable to have an appreciable effect on trade. By contrast, the EU Court has also provided a detailed explanation of the categories of cases where the relevant market should be defined, including where a complex infringement is involved and the failure to correctly define the relevant market could result in the imposition of liability for an infringement on a market where it does not participate (Greek Ferries, paragraphs 31 to 33).

[3] For example, under UK or Australian merger control.

[4] For example, under EU merger control.

[5] For example, under Saudi Arabian merger control.

It is clear that competition law analysis under the Competition Act cannot be carried out without an inquiry into the relevant market definition. One of the key concepts underpinning Indian competition law is the notion of an AAE on competition in India.

Section 3(1) of the Competition Act prohibits agreements which cause, or are likely to cause, an AAE on competition within India. Section 4(1) of the Competition Act prohibits abuse of a dominant market position. Determination of the relevant market by reference to which an AAE on competition within India and a dominant position is to be assessed is of critical importance to the application of the prohibitions of anticompetitive agreements and abuse of a dominant position. However, there is no statutory requirement to prove an AAE on competition under section 4.

The substantive test for the review of mergers and combinations under section 6(1) of the Competition Act is whether the combination causes, or is likely to cause, an AAE on competition within the relevant market in India. Identification of the relevant market is also important when determining what remedies may be needed to address competition concerns on the relevant markets. This assessment is to be made using what is, essentially, an economic assessment and should be conducted in relation to both the relevant 'product' and 'geographic' market. It can be expected that the Competition Commission of India (CCI) will want to focus on the impact of the relevant practices at the Indian (national, regional and local) level, even if the relevant geographic market may be wider or even worldwide. However, this should not preclude a broader economic analysis where the markets are open to competition from outside India. It is noteworthy that section 19(6) of the Competition Act indicates that factors such as language, consumer preferences, trade barriers and transportation costs are relevant when determining the relevant geographic market, which could suggest that the relevant markets are wider than India in appropriate cases.

Despite the differences in content and policy between jurisdictions it is possible to discern an element of commonality as regards the core elements of market definition and its dimensions. Market definition is typically approached from the perspective of the relevant product and geographic divisions.

In the EU, the European Commission's 1997 notice on the relevant market[6] states that:

> A relevant product market comprises all those products and/or services which are regarded as *interchangeable* or substitutable by the consumer, by reason of the products' characteristics, their prices and their intended use (emphasis added).[7]

[6] Commission notice on the definition of relevant market for the purposes of Community competition law, OJ C372 (Commission notice on the relevant market).

[7] Ibid, paragraph 7.

Relevant geographic markets are defined as follows:

> The relevant geographic market comprises the area in which the undertakings concerned are involved in the supply and demand of products or services, in which the conditions of competition are sufficiently homogeneous and which can be distinguished from neighbouring areas because the conditions of competition are appreciably different in those area.[8]

Underlying these approaches is the concept of substitutability, whether from the demand or the supply side.

In relation to demand-side factors the European Commission states that 'the assessment of demand substitution entails a determination of the range of products which are viewed as substitutes by the consumer'.[9] Supply-side factors may also be relevant 'in those situations in which its effects are equivalent to those of demand substitution in terms of effectiveness and immediacy'. Effectively 'this means that suppliers are able to switch production to the relevant products and market them in the short term without incurring significant additional costs or risks in response to small and permanent changes in relative prices'.[10]

There is also a temporal dimension in that market definition is not a 'once and for all' assessment but must be considered over a relevant time frame. This may differ depending on whether the inquiry relates to commercial practices (anticompetitive agreements or abuse of dominance) or merger control. In this context the European Commission notes that:

> The different time horizon considered in each case might lead to the result that different geographic markets are defined for the same products depending on whether the Commission is examining a change in the structure of supply, such as a concentration or a cooperative joint venture, or examining issues relating to certain past behaviour.[11]

The importance of integrating a timing factor cannot be underestimated, particularly if competition authorities are concerned with a forward-looking analysis in merger cases (ie what would be the effect of the merger on the relevant market) and if they want to promote new entry and the evolution of markets in the future. The temporal dimension is clearly highly relevant to appreciating the sensitivities of converging media markets that form the core of this work where it may be more difficult to predict market developments.

The approach described above is typical of approaches adopted in other competition laws including the US and national competition laws in the EU and worldwide. The approach is also congruent with the so-called 'hypothetical

[8] Ibid, paragraph 8.
[9] Ibid, paragraph 15.
[10] Ibid, paragraph 20.
[11] Ibid, paragraph 12.

monopolist test', conveniently labelled as the 'SSNIP' test.[12] In essence, this test seeks to assess the reactions of consumers in response to a company increasing its prices by, say, 5 to 10 per cent over a period of about a year. The European Commission describes this exercise and its role in defining the relevant product and geographic market as follows:

> The question to be answered is whether the parties' customers would switch to readily available substitutes or to suppliers located elsewhere in response to a hypothetical small (in the range 5% to 10%) but permanent relative price increase in the products and areas being considered. If substitution were enough to make the price increase unprofitable because of the resulting loss of sales, additional substitutes and areas are included in the relevant market. This would be done until the set of products and geographical areas is such that small, permanent increases in relative prices would be profitable. The equivalent analysis is applicable in cases concerning the concentration of buying power, where the starting point would then be the supplier and the price test serves to identify the alternative distribution channels or outlets for the supplier's products.[13]

We return to the practical application of the SSNIP test when considering some of the specific challenges of market definition in the media sector in section 3.4 below.

Market definition therefore performs an important role in framing the assessment of commercial practices and mergers by competition authorities. It also has a role in providing an element of legal certainty and predictability for businesses subject to regulation as a bright line indicator for intervention and compliance. This is clear in the case of abuse of dominance where practices that may be acceptable for a non-dominant company may be prohibited when engaged in by a company with market power.

In relation to agreements, market definition and market shares can also provide the basis for determining when restrictions in agreements may give rise to competition law scrutiny. For example, where the relevant conditions of an EU block exemption are satisfied, including market share thresholds and the non-inclusion of certain prohibited restrictions, the agreement automatically falls outside the prohibition in Article 101 of the Treaty on the Functioning of the European Union (TFEU) and does not require further assessment. Such block exemptions have proved particularly useful in the EU for companies seeking to 'self-assess' compliance of their arrangements with competition law and where, since 1 May 2004, there has no longer been a general procedure for an advance ruling by the European Commission on specific practices. For example, EU law currently provides for block exemptions for vertical agreements,[14] research and development

[12] 'SSNIP' denotes a small but significant non-transitory increase in price.

[13] Commission notice on the relevant market, paragraph 17.

[14] Regulation No 330/2010 of 20 April 2010 on the application of Article 101(3) of the Treaty on the Functioning of the EU to categories of vertical agreements and concerted practices [2010] OJ L102.

agreements,[15] specialisation agreements[16] and technology transfer.[17] While there are currently no blanket exemptions for defined categories of agreements under India competition law that could be compared to the block exemptions which exist in the EU competition regime, market share is expected to be a relevant factor when determining an AAE under India competition law.

Previous approaches of the competition authorities are not necessarily predictors of how similar cases will be dealt with in the future. However, when this notion underpins the question of which types of behaviour would be allowed and which would be sanctioned as unacceptable, it can be a valuable clue to enable businesses to know which commercial decisions to adopt.

3.3 THE ROLE OF THE CONSUMER IN MEDIA REGULATION DEBATES

3.3.1 The Consumer and Different Types of Regulation

The consumer interest lies at the heart of debates on whether and how to regulate, especially in media, even if this is not always made explicit. Both *ex ante* economic regulation and *ex post* competition interventions aim to correct market failures, with the objective of improving market efficiency and delivering superior outcomes for consumers than would otherwise be the case. The European Commission, for example, on launching its new package of telecommunications regulations in September 2013—its 'most ambitious plan in 26 years of telecoms market reform'—couched its elements solely in terms of 10 benefits for consumers.[18]

Additionally, there is the question of what may be termed 'paternalistic regulation' related to consumer policy. This focuses on firms and their interactions with consumers dealing with areas such as unfair trading practices and contract terms. This is concerned less with market structures and more with consumer protection and fairness from the consumer perspective. Indeed, consumer policy is often applied in competitive markets.

The rationale for market intervention by governments may broadly be segmented into two main types: economic efficiency reasons and public interest reasons. The former aim to correct market failures on economic grounds, whereas

[15] Regulation No 1217/2010 of 14 December 2010 on the application of Article 101(3) of the Treaty on the Functioning of the EU to categories of research and development agreements [2010] OJ L335.

[16] Regulation No 1218/2010 of 14 December 2010 on the application of Article 101(3) of the Treaty to categories of specialisation agreements [2010] OJ L335.

[17] Regulation (EC) No 316/2014 of 21 March 2014 on the application of Article 101(3) of the Treaty on the Functioning of the EU to categories of technology transfer agreements [2014] OJ L93/17.

[18] Commission press release, 'Commission proposes major step forward for telecoms single market' (IP/13/828) 11 September 2013.

the latter tend to be concerned more generally with matters such as access, affordability and consumer protection.

3.3.2 The Consumer vs the Citizen

In considering the role of the consumer in media regulation debates, a further distinction may be made between the consumer and the citizen. While these two concepts are closely related, the UK communications regulator, Ofcom, explains the nuances between the consumer and the citizen in relation to its policies as follows:

> The purpose of consumer policy is to facilitate the operation of markets, to remove barriers and correct market failures which might otherwise prevent them delivering what consumers want. Citizen-related policy is concerned with changing market outcomes in order to meet broader social, cultural or economic objectives.[19]

Thus, the concepts of both the consumer and the citizen play an important role in media regulation debates and design.

3.3.3 Rationale for Regulation

Figure 3 provides a summary of the economic efficiency and public interest rationales for regulatory intervention, mapped along the audiovisual value chain.[20] The stages of the chain, at a high level, are as follows: talent—the raw inputs to audiovisual content; production—the mechanics of combining the talent inputs into audiovisual content (eg a TV programme); and packaging—the compilation of content into products for delivery (eg a TV channel). This includes both marketing and advertising sales; distribution—the broadcasting and subsequent transmission (terrestrial, cable, satellite or IP-based) of the TV channel(s) to the home; and supply—the final stage to the consumer interface, usually, but necessarily, involving a set top box. In the case of free-to-air television this stage does not entail a direct relationship with the consumer whereas for pay services, there is a billing relationship between the pay TV retailer and the consumer.

[19] Ofcom, Ofcom's consumer policy available at stakeholders.ofcom.org.uk/consultations/ocp/statement.

[20] We cast the description in terms of television services for illustrative purposes.

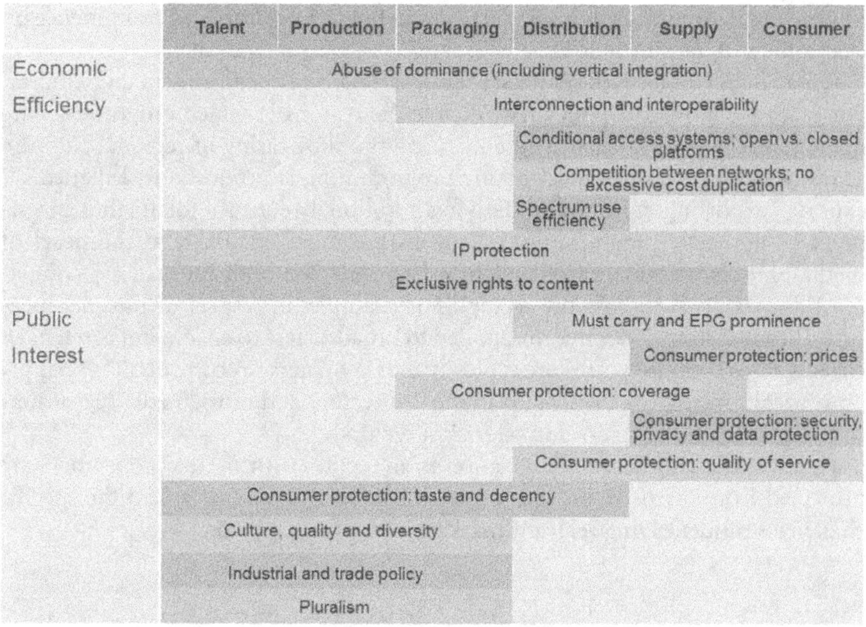

Figure 3: Rationale for regulation mapped across the audiovisual chain

Source: Authors' analysis and KPMG, Public Policy Issues Arising From Telecommunications and Audiovisual Convergence, a report prepared for DG XIII, London, 1996

As can be seen from Figure 3, all of the economic efficiency rationales are aimed at making markets work more effectively by increasing competition which, all other things being equal, leads to reduced prices and increased choice for consumers. Arguably, such rationales are generic competition issues that apply across all markets that may not mimic competitive markets. In the above case, such tools tend to be applied with greater readiness in the media sector than in other sectors. This contrasts with many of the categories in the public interest segment of the figure where the fact that the market is the media sector, drives the objectives of the intervention.

There is a complex array of public interest objectives in the public interest section that cover a wide range of areas. As shown, such areas range from media-specific matters, such as ensuring service coverage (to ensure all citizens have the ability to receive broadcast services), through to more generic consumer privacy issues, such as security and data protection. Others are concerned with the quality of service and prices.

Then there is regulation that is much more media-specific; citizens are at the heart of this. For example, there is regulation aimed at ensuring that there is a wide range of high-quality programming produced, programming that reflects domestic talent and local, regional and national viewpoints. Policies directed at ensuring universal access to and discoverability of public service programming impose regulations such as 'must carry' on network operators and prominence on electronic programme guides.

Other policy objectives may have spillover effects on consumers and citizens. For example, industrial policy may dictate the regions in which programmes are made (creating employment and enhancing the showcasing of regional culture). Trade policy may ensure that specific programming is produced to enhance TV exports (exporting culture and deriving additional revenues for further investment in domestic programming). Citizens are most obviously at the heart of media pluralism regulation. Regulations here may be both internal (to companies) and external (across the sector). For example, in respect of internal measures, broadcasting codes may be applied to broadcasters to ensure impartial news coverage. External measures are typically media ownership controls. These apply both within media (eg ownership in the TV sector) and cross-media (eg ownership across the newspapers and television sectors).

Finally, taste and decency regulation is aimed at ensuring that consumers are protected from offensive on-screen media content. We consider next the specific challenges of identifying relevant markets in the media sector.

3.4 CHALLENGES IN IDENTIFYING RELEVANT MARKETS IN THE MEDIA SECTOR

The definition of the relevant market, while intuitively simple and anchored in economic theory and legal precedents, can present particular issues in the media sector.

3.4.1 Market Definition and the New Media

The term 'new media' may be used loosely to describe the forms of media that have evolved in recent years and which use newer technologies and digitisation. Digitisation allows computers to store, manipulate and transmit information in the form of speech, text, data and video more efficiently, cheaply and quicker than previously.

This development has been taking place since the 1970s, although it has progressed significantly since the 1990s. In many respects, the advent of the internet and the changes and possibilities it brings for communication and information dissemination may be likened to the challenges of the telegraph in the 1840s. The internet promotes the desire to be competitive in an increasingly global marketplace. It provides businesses, consumers and countries with access to a larger area for trade, education and cultural exchange. In describing such developments, 'frontier' metaphors may be used, evoking a radical shift that to where it is no longer 'business as usual'. Whatever the end point, there is a growing belief that the new media is essential for economic transformation and empowerment, away from an industrial economy to service economies in pursuit of the so-called 'innovation agenda'.

From a legal perspective, this invites the question of how such developments can be accommodated within the existing legal framework. Is this a case of existing tools being capable of application to the new phenomena or do we need a fundamental re-think or new legal rules and principles?

From a consumer perspective, the new media raises interesting opportunities and not always welcome perspectives. From a sceptical perspective, there may be a readiness to question everything that is heard, seen or read in the new media, to conclude that somewhere someone is trying to make money, and to assume that everywhere there is a threat to personal privacy.

At the outset, it would seem sensible to outline the basic characteristics of the 'new media'. We return to these characteristics at the end of this chapter when considering whether there is an underlying logic to media markets that can serve as a guide to authorities and businesses when evaluating the implications for competition and public policy.

— Interpersonal: Traditional telephony or two-way communication involves discretionary contact between two willing participants. The telecommunications companies are not responsible for the content of the message that is communicated. In the new media and distribution over the worldwide web, such distinctions no longer hold and the boundaries between the public and the private spheres become blurred. The ability to access, monitor or 'hack' material which users or owners believe to be private is another area where the distinctions between the public and the personal break down.

— Multiple: By definition, the internet brings about mass communication with a potentially global audience. However, it is possible to conceive of narrower audiences where the coverage is self-selected by users, such as broadcasts to friends on Facebook.

— Convergence. This refers to the merging of what were previously separate industries: telecommunications, computing and broadcasting. We return to the concept of convergence throughout this work when considering its implications for market definition and the evaluation of competition in converging media markets.

3.4.2 Market Definition in Fast-moving Markets

A common theme in the discussion of markets that are subject to innovation and technical change is the difficulty of formulating an accurate market definition that takes account of new and prospective entry and even displacement of market power by new products and services. This issue has particular prominence in media markets which are characteristically subject to evolution.

Competition and regulatory authorities are faced with the challenge of anticipating the likely reactions of consumers, suppliers and competitors over time. The time horizon issue also has special significance in a remedies context: will commitments be sufficient to address concerns over time or might they be disproportionate and actually constrain the ability of markets to develop in their own way?

Authorities may find that they are placed between a rock and a regulatory hard place when faced with arguments of the parties that suggest there is no need to worry, and complaints from competitors. The experience of hindsight and the real risk of regulatory myopia is illustrated by the *Vivendi/Canal+/Seagram* case.[21] The Vizzavi joint venture (JV) was approved by the European Commission subject to remedies due to concerns of market dominance on account of Vivendi and Canal+ in a number of EU pay TV and content markets. This is not the place to question that decision or the principles that were articulated in it. However, the subsequent failure of Vizzavi does illustrate the necessarily *ex ante* approach of merger assessment and the challenges for regulators in anticipating future developments.

3.4.3 Limitations of the SSNIP Test

The practical application of the SSNIP test gives rise to some thorny issues and particularly in media markets. It will be recalled that the market identification process in which we are engaged is not an end itself but a process intended to inform a legal assessment. The SSNIP test incorporates elements from economics and intrinsic uncertainties.

At a general level, it is a familiar criticism of the SSNIP test that it is predicated on the assumption that the initial price is competitive. Determining the competitive level may itself require substantial information collation and analysis (if available). Furthermore, the test prescribes that any increase by 5 to 10 per cent above the already 'competitive' price will lead consumers to switch to an alternative and so on. However, as any student of economics will know, a switch to another product or service may simply reflect the fact that the existing price is far above the competitive level and not merely by the 'small but significant' 5 to 10 per cent level which underpins the SSNIP test. This phenomenon may actually lead to perverse outcomes which do not reflect genuine substitution. This is the so-called 'cellophane fallacy'.[22]

The difficulties are compounded when assessing the effect of a price increase in media markets which may relate to infrastructure access, intangible goods or intellectual property rights (IPR). The determination of the competitive price or the impact of a price increase may be even more delicate and uncertain in situations

[21] Case No COMP/M.2050—*Vivendi/Canal+/Seagram*, Commission decision of 13 October 2000.

[22] The expression is derived from the reasoning in a US Supreme Court case and the subsequent response in economic literature (see, further, *US v E I du Pont* 351 US 377, 76 S Ct 994, 100 L Ed 1264 (1956)).

which do not involve the consumption of a physical product. For instance, some markets may be characterised by significant upfront costs such as network build costs (eg cable or satellite platform) or the underlying goods may be more subjective to value (eg copyright over films). The determination of a competitive price may be rendered more complex in relation to network upgrades, the cost of which will need to be recouped over time and reflected in the assessment of price. So-called 'premium services', such as live sports broadcasts or movie channels, may raise more complex pricing issues should there be no obvious substitute content.

The time factor complicates the assessment. Identifying customer reactions (or likely reactions) over one year or more may not necessarily provide an answer to the question of whether an entity is subject to competitive constraints in a converging media market. The question of what consumers might (hypothetically) do in response to a (hypothetical) increase in price in relation to a market which, by definition, may be very different even a year from now, is an exercise that becomes increasingly divorced from realities.

Furthermore, the SSNIP test uses prices as its sole determinant of substitution. This does not take account of other benchmarks of competition on which media players differentiate themselves: innovation, quality, diversity, service levels and so on. Thus, the hypothetical reaction of consumers to a hypothetical price increase may reveal little about genuine competitive constraints. For this purpose, a more detailed examination is needed of the relevant economic agents and their horizontal and vertical relationships across the supply chain.

3.4.4 Products and Services

Many of the tools that are used in market definition such as prices for raw materials, 'sales' to end users, distribution, marketing and transportation costs, tend to be more suited to traditional physical-type products markets. The media sector, by contrast, tends to comprise markets which correspond more to services (eg internet services, TV subscription, etc). Even if the product is tangible—for example, a newspaper—an analysis focused solely on prices of products may not properly reflect the constraints to which a supplier is subject. For example, a newspaper may be provided 'free' to readers with the publisher earning its revenues through other sources, such as advertising.

Although the distinction between products and services is a fact of modern life, market definition in competition cases has not yet caught up with the subtleties of the distinction.

3.4.5 Identifying the Limits of Convergence

Convergence has acquired a particular impetus when considering competition and regulation in the media sector. There is wide recognition of the need to take account of market evolution in the media sector and a variety of decisions purport to address convergence when approaching relevant markets and analysis.

Microsoft's acquisition of Skype illustrates how telecommunications companies expanding globally are often driven by a search for complementarity and opportunities to enter new markets. Microsoft develops a vast range of software products including network and desktop operating systems, personal communications services, computer and mobile entertainment services, search portals, and business and office applications. In 2011, Microsoft made the largest acquisition in its history through the purchase of the Skype internet phone service provider. Skype provides free software voice communications over internet protocol and chargeable internet calls to fixed lines and mobiles. The main driver of this transaction for Microsoft was the cost reduction in building internet protocol telephony and innovation.[23]

On 7 October 2011 the European Commission gave an unconditional clearance to the transaction in a Phase I EU merger control procedure.[24] The European Commission's appreciation of the phenomenon of convergence is evident its observation that:

> As a consequence of this ongoing convergence, the traditional distinctions between data and voice, between hardware and software, and between the various distinct products and services that are offered by enterprise communications companies are blurring.[25]

The European Commission identified minimal overlaps at the horizontal level and did not identify any adverse competition effects. However, this was as a result of an extensive inquiry spanning multiple product markets and indicating a readiness to grapple with the realities of converging telecommunications and related markets. The European Commission thus stated:

> For the purpose of the assessment of the present transaction, it can be left open whether the market for enterprise communications services needs to be segmented according to functionalities (advanced telephony, unified messaging—email, fax, voice messaging combined, web, voice and videoconferencing, IM/presence, collaborating tools etc.).[26]

In the course of this assessment, while lip service is given to convergence there is no attempt to identify the limits of convergence. While this was not necessary for the decision at hand, it gives little guidance to those seeking clarification about what convergence means in practice for media market analysis.

Further, the analysis focuses heavily on supply-side factors when assessing the different technologies that may be used to deliver products and services

[23] It does not appear that there were other serious bidders for Skype at the time. Wall Street Journal, 'Microsoft Dials Up Change, CEO Ballmer Defends Hefty $8.5 Billion Price Tag for Internet-Phone Firm Skype', 11 May 2011, available at: online.wsj.com/article/SB10001424052748703730804576314854222820260.html.

[24] Case COMP/M.6291—*Microsoft/Skype*, Commission decision of 7 October 2011 *(Microsoft/Skype)*.

[25] *Microsoft/Skype*, paragraph 50.

[26] *Microsoft/Skype*, paragraph 46.

to the consumer. This observation does not mean that the approach is wrong or misguided. It simply reflects the apparent opposite focus in conventional approaches to market definition which tend to focus more on demand-side factors. This may slow down the tendency to rush to the conclusion that technological convergence in and of itself indicates that products and services are substitutable from the perspective of consumers and, hence, provide a ready-made answer to the quandaries of market definition. For example, the same technology may be used to deliver pay and free-to-air TV to the consumer but competition authorities may not regard the two as being in the same economic market.

3.4.6 Relationship with Public Interest and Plurality

Market delineation in the media sector becomes a more sophisticated exercise when considered in relation to policies and goals which are not founded exclusively on the promotion of competition, although they may be informed by the latter.

Here we are concerned with the fact that some media products and services have cultural, social and political dimensions and therefore contribute to viewpoint diversity or pluralism. Given the different aims pursued by competition law and laws protecting plurality it would seem vital to be careful to ensure a balanced and justifiable frame of reference when considering the issues at stake. While it might be tempting to transplant economic concepts of market definition into the area of plurality assessment, this misses the point that market concentration and plurality are different issues. For example, it is quite possible to find an economic market which is not concentrated but where plurality concerns nevertheless arise. This might be where one controller with a relatively modest market share has a disproportionate influence over the news agenda which is not in any way related to its market share.

News Corporation's recent proposed acquisition of the shares in British Sky Broadcasting (BSkyB) that it does not already own illustrates the interaction between competition law and public interest assessment. It highlights that the latter assessment is not purely an issue of concentration in a relevant market. The transaction involved the proposed acquisition of control over a pay TV broadcaster (BSkyB) by a newspaper owner (News Corporation). The transaction was approved unconditionally by the European Commission at Phase I under the EU Merger Regulation (EUMR)[27] due to the absence of a significant impediment to effective competition in the relevant markets.[28] However, the European Commission observed that its decision was without prejudice to the assessment of the UK authorities on media plurality grounds. The transaction was subject

[27] Regulation (EC) No 139/2004 of 20 January 2004 on the control of concentrations between undertakings [2004] OJ L24.

[28] Case No COMP/M.5932—*News Corporation/BSkyB*, Commission decision of 21 December 2010.

to a detailed review by the UK authorities on media plurality grounds. The UK communications sector regulator, Ofcom, provided input and advice to the UK Secretary of State as to the impact on media plurality at the national level. Ultimately, the transaction was referred to the UK Competition Commission for an in-depth review but the reference was withdrawn because News Corporation withdrew its bid.[29] While the Competition Commission was denied an opportunity to decide the relevant audience for plurality purposes, the basic point remains sound: a relevant audience for plurality purposes may differ from the relevant market for competition purposes.

3.4.7 The Social Dimension and Information Gap

Beyond the public interest questions of freedom of speech and plurality lies an important social aspect arising from the role of the media in furthering dissemination of information, ideas and education. This issue gains added importance from the perspective of emerging economies such as India who are behind some other economies on the path to cyberspace. The impact of the internet on media market analysis is addressed in chapter 8.

For market delineation purposes, it is useful to note that it happens that richer consumers and the more educated elite will be the first to embrace the internet and technology. The poorer, less educated consumer will tend to adopt the technology later which forces the public policy debate about what can and should be done to redress the balance. Capturing such issues in any market definition or economic frame of reference which stands above the social policy agenda is no easy task. However, this is an important issue for India and other economies where internet penetration is increasing while there are still high levels of illiteracy.[30]

3.4.8 A Lot at Stake

A further complexity when seeking to arrive at a workable market definition in the media sector is that there is a lot at stake for businesses, consumers and governments. This is especially the case where IPR or new technology are involved. Inventors of new technology or content may generate new patents or copyright. When the market becomes established, the rights may be transferred or litigated.

[29] Competition Commission press release 41/11, 'CC Formally Cancels News Corp/BSkyB Inquiry', 25 July 2011.

[30] The Indian literacy rate grew to 74.04% in 2011 from 12% at the end of British rule in 1947 (Government of India Ministry of Home Affairs, 'Census of India, 2011', available at: censusindia.gov.in).

Incumbents may even block the development of rival technologies or platforms or buy out emerging ones. If a new technology threatens an incumbent business then it may seek to undercut that new entry. If investing in new technology becomes too risky, then new services may not be developed at all or may be developed to a lesser extent than would otherwise have been the case. This is the delicate trade-off between new and old technologies which has special prominence in the media sector where debates about market power have typically focused on access to content and infrastructure.

Whether a company is found dominant in a relevant market will determine whether it is subject to more onerous competition law and regulatory obligations. In extreme cases, this can entail a 'must offer' or access obligation or the supply of IPR on fair terms. When compounded with some of the delicate economics and theoretical issues, it can mean that there is a great deal to argue about which can swing a case either way. Thus, interested parties have a real incentive to deploy whatever financial and intellectual resources they have at their disposal to put their case. This can result in protracted investigations which may not result in a definitive view on the relevant market even if they reach a conclusion.

Moreover, such cases often raise strong emotions and consumer reaction. Almost anything that we care passionately about—whether it be mobile phone communications, a movie, a sports channel or a TV programme—can arouse deep consumer appeal and sentiment. Thus media competition and regulatory cases rarely go unnoticed by the public. The high profile nature of such cases and their impact on everyday life provides yet another strategic constraint on decision-makers. They must resist the temptation to pander to popular interests or the pleas of interested parties.

3.5 BETWEEN THEORY AND PRAGMATISM: IDENTIFYING RELEVANT MARKETS IN PRACTICE

While theoretical approaches to market definition have limits as outlined above, the decisional practice appears to depart from the theory. This creates its own set of problems in terms of how to respond operationally—whether from the perspective of business, regulators or policy-makers.

3.5.1 Information Limits

Those involved in applying the SSNIP test to actual cases will be aware that the data needed to substantiate the substitutability test will rarely be available in the form that the textbook requires.

In practice, the type of information which is available or useful in any particular case will vary. The following are the types of evidence that the European

Commission considers relevant in assessing whether two products are demand substitutes:

— Evidence of substitution in the recent past: In certain cases, it is possible to analyse evidence relating to recent past events or shocks in the market that offer actual examples of substitution between two products.
— Quantitative tests: There are a number of quantitative tests that have been specifically designed for the purpose of delineating markets. These tests consist of various econometric and statistical approaches to derive estimates of elasticities and cross-price elasticities for the demand of a product, including those based on price movements over time.
— Views of customers and competitors: Reasoned answers of customers and competitors may be used as a proxy for the reactions to the 5 to 10 per cent price increase postulated by the SSNIP test.
— Consumer preferences: Marketing studies and consumer surveys on usage patterns and attitudes, data from consumers' purchasing patterns, the views expressed by retailers, and more generally, market research studies can be used to inform whether products are subsumable from a demand perspective.
— Barriers and costs associated with switching demand to potential substitutes: These may include regulatory or legal barriers, IPR and so on.
— Different categories of customers and price discrimination: The extent of the product market might be narrowed in the presence of distinct groups of customers that could be subject to price discrimination.[31]

The list of potential 'proxy' measures of substitution is not exhaustive but demonstrates that the identification of substitutes is rarely an exact science; rather it calls for an element of pragmatism.

3.5.2 Demand-side Considerations

We observe that the concept of demand is not an immutable concept. Typically, this notion is examined from the (end-)consumer perspective. This approach is not the only one. For example, the media sector displays the characteristics of so-called 'two-sided markets' so that it may be necessary to look at a number of different relationships. For example, a newspaper publisher may have two sets of customers or income streams—the readers of newspapers and advertisers. In order to understand the competitive constraints faced by the proprietor, an inquiry into the effect on (marginal) customers (ie readers) in the event of a 5 to 10 per cent price increase will tell only part of the story on competitive constraints.

[31] Commission notice on the relevant market, (above n 6) paragraphs 35–43.

3.5.3 Geographic Boundaries

A notable feature when examining the approach of competition and regulatory authorities to market definition is the rather limited focus accorded to questions of geographic market definition in the cases decided by the competition authorities.

This issue can be particularly significant when considering, for example, the extent to which an owner of a network covering a distinct geographic area, such as a cable operator, is subject to competition or whether owners or licensees of media rights on a territorial basis should be considered dominant.

Another factor that tends to be overlooked is the importance of local, regional or national languages which may have a bearing on the geographic scope of the relevant market or audience where media cultural products are concerned.

It is likely that the question of the correct geographic scope of reference is going to be increasingly important when evaluating media and competition cases in India. This is due to the sheer size of the country and the richness and diversity of the language and culture within it. While case precedents from other jurisdictions may generally be a useful starting point, in this instance EU case law might not be relevant. First, in the EU an element of national pride may prompt a national competition authority or regulator to view a market as national. Second, owing to the allocation of functions between the European Commission and the national competition authorities under the EU merger control framework[32] and following modernisation under Regulation 1/2003[33] there can be some confusion between

[32] The EU merger control regime, set out in the EUMR, applies to the enlarged European Economic Area (EEA). The EUMR is based on the 'one stop shop' principle which confers on the European Commission exclusive jurisdiction to review transactions which constitute a concentration (within the meaning of Article 3 EUMR) and which meet the turnover thresholds set out in Article 1(2) or (3) EUMR (and therefore have a Union dimension). In consequence, Member States are precluded by virtue of Article 21(3) EUMR from applying their national competition laws to such concentrations with a Union dimension.

[33] Regulation (EC) No 1/2003 of 16 December 2002 on the implementation of the rules on competition laid down in Articles 81 and 82 of the Treaty [2002] OJ L1. The enforcement of EU competition law also displays interesting features from the perspective of the interaction between the European Commission and the Member State authorities. Pursuant to the Modernisation Regulation, the European Commission, the national competition authorities (NCAs) and the national courts have the competence to apply EU competition law to anticompetitive agreements and practices. Undertakings are required to self-assess whether their agreements fall within Article 101(1) TFEU and, if so, whether they meet the exemption conditions of Article 101(3) TFEU. Furthermore, the Modernisation Regulation also confirms the allocation of responsibilities when NCAs and the national courts apply Articles 101 and 102 TFEU. In respect of an agreement or practices that affect trade between Member States, NCAs and national courts are bound to apply Articles 101 and 102 TFEU and cannot prohibit pursuant to national law an agreement that is compatible with Article 101 TFEU. Such authorities are permitted to apply the stricter provisions of national law to prohibit unilateral conduct even if such conduct would not be in violation of Article 101 TFEU. In order to ensure the uniform application of Union law, where national courts rule on agreements, decisions or practices under Article 101 or Article 102 TFEU which are already the subject of a European Commission decision, they cannot take decisions running counter to the decision adopted by the European Commission. Furthermore, they must avoid giving decisions which would 'conflict' with a decision contemplated by the European

the jurisdiction of the national authority and the definition of the relevant geographic market. This can lead authorities to conclude that the relevant market is national in cases where their national law applies. Third, since in the EU competition law goals and single market integration goals tend to elide there can be a readiness to view markets as wider than national in the absence of any obvious barriers to intra-EU trade.

The implication for countries such as India, which have competition laws that currently operate on a national basis, is that they should appreciate the relevance of infra-national aspects and focus on this question when considering the relevant market. The Telecom Regulatory Authority of India (TRAI) in its recent cable consultation appears to have appreciated this significance when considering the extent to which certain states may have more concentrated cable markets than others.[34] India should be able to determine this question on the merits without the distraction of other factors such as the allocation of case load between various competition authorities. That is not to say that other more local or political turf wars are not relevant, but it is a reminder of the need for a coherent and honest approach on the geographic market.

3.5.4 Divergent Approaches

Differences in the approaches taken by authorities in defining the relevant market can present challenges when trying to reach a globally accepted standard methodology, outcomes aside. Divergence in approach and conclusion can be particularly pronounced in relation to newer markets or when considering the relationships with other (non-media) markets such as financing of media operations. Sometimes the differences may relate not to the end conclusion but to the factors that the authority considered relevant in reaching its decision.

Using the example of pay TV, when considering broadcasting there is broad consensus in terms of the basic distinctions between upstream access to the raw content (whether media or sports rights) and, from the perspective of the consumer/viewer, between pay and free TV. However, within those broad generalisations there can be nuances and different approaches in terms of the competitive constraints at the periphery or when formulating the rationale for the decision.

In the UK, the Competition Commission in its market investigation into the supply of movies on pay TV considered that pay TV providers impose a sufficiently strong constraint on each other for pay TV retailing to be a separate

Commission in proceedings it has initiated. Finally, national competition law in the Member States (which tends to be very similar to EU competition law) may be applied by the national competition authorities.

[34] Telecom Regulatory Authority of India, 'Consultation Paper on Monopoly/Market dominance in Cable TV services', 3 June 2013.

market.[35] This market includes subscription video on-demand services, whether offered alongside linear services or on a stand-alone basis.

France has considered whether there might be a wider market for digital terrestrial and pay TV, either over satellite or cable.[36] However, it is not clear whether this relates only to pay TV.

Germany has distinguished a market for free TV on the one hand and pay TV in all its forms, relying on the nature of the contractual relationship with the customer in the case of the latter.[37]

On a cursory examination, the fact that different authorities may approach what appears to be a very similar question differently is not a concern in itself. Differences in approach may arise from the fact that the authorities were asked different substantive questions or were presented with different evidence on which to base their decisions. Therefore, it is quite understandable that an authority asked to decide whether service 1 is a substitute for service 2 may answer the question differently to one who is asked whether there is substitutability between service 1 and service 3. What this means in practice is that precedents should be viewed in context rather than *in abstracto* since it is important to inquire what the authority was being asked to determine and what it was not asked to consider.

3.5.5 Limits of Precedent

As case law develops internationally, it can be tempting for authorities and market participants to seek to rely on or draw inspiration from past decisions whether from their own jurisdiction or from another relevant jurisdiction. This is so even in situations where there is no formal doctrine of precedent and cases from other jurisdictions or tribunals are relied on as an aid to reasoning for their 'persuasive' value.

This approach is useful and necessary since it allows for a principled development of the law. It also facilitates some cohesion at least at the jurisdictional level where today's decisions need to be reconciled with previous decisions. However, there are serious issues which need to be confronted. First, it may be that existing case law did not deal directly with the issue at hand or that it avoided the issue entirely on the basis that the issue of market definition was not critical to the authority's findings so could be left open. This might be after postulating a number of (hypothetical and narrow) market definitions that further complicate the analysis. Second, the existing case law can be self-fulfilling resulting in a reluctance to depart from precedent,

[35] Competition Commission, 'Movies on pay TV market investigation, A report on the supply and acquisition of subscription pay TV movie rights and services', 2 August 2012.

[36] See, opinion no 98-A-14 of the Competition Council of 31 August 1998, *Havas and Cie Générale des Eau.*

[37] BKartA 1 October 1998 WuW/E DE-V 53, 58, Premiere: Report of the Federal Cartel Office 1997/1998 BT Drs 14/1139, p 163.

at least in a first phase procedure, while recognising that a more developed perspective could be argued out through a longer procedure.[38] Third, and perhaps obviously, existing precedents may be of limited relevance if the market has moved on in light of new technology or the appearance of new entrants.

3.5.6 Effect on Market Participants and the Quest for Predictability

The tension between theory and practice outlined above raises important issues for the coherence of a legal or regulatory system where market definition can be an important determinant of liability. This is a worry where: (i) the imposition of *ex ante* obligations can be predicated on the identification of market power in a relevant market; (ii) companies found dominant are subject to responsibilities which would not apply to non-dominant players; (iii) the assessment of a merger may depend on effects in a given market; (iv) restrictions on competition may be viewed differently depending on the level of market share of the parties.

In a dominance context, the issue is particularly pronounced due to the difficulty in defining both dominance and abuse. In the EU there has long been a debate about the relationship between dominance and abuse. Does the fact that a company is able to refuse to supply competitors with content or access to infrastructure provide prima facie evidence of dominance? The issues are separate but the risk of market definition becoming a self-fulfilling determinant of dominance and therefore abuse should be recognised. For example, the Court of Justice of the EU (CJEU) in *United Brands v Commission*[39] agreed with the principle that the conduct of an allegedly dominant firm could be taken into account when deciding whether it is dominant.

A further factor for enterprises seeking to anticipate the reaction of the authorities to their agreements, commercial practices or concentrations is the tendency of competition authorities to define markets narrowly or on a cautious basis. Even if the narrow market approach is not determinative in a particular case the fact that it was considered—or left open—may be of significance for evaluation of future cases. It can also lead to companies deciding not to engage in otherwise pro-competitive or benign activity on the basis of the more strict approach to market definition that

[38] The UK Office of Fair Trading (OFT) cleared Northcliffe Media Limited's acquisition of Topper Newspapers Limited. It considered that the relevant product scope in this case consisted of the supply of print newspapers (and advertising space in them) in Nottingham taking due account of separate advertising categories where appropriate. The parties had not provided sufficient evidence to demonstrate that the product scope should be wider than print newspaper titles. Ultimately, this issue was not decisive for the first phase clearance decision although conceivably such issues would be open for re-examination in the event of a second phase procedure (Office of Fair Trading, 'Anticipated acquisition by Northcliffe Media Limited of Topper Newspapers Limited, The OFT's decision on reference' 1 June 2012).

[39] Case 27/76 *United Brands Company and United Brands Continental BV v Commission* [1978] ECR 207, paragraphs 448–59.

was suggested and hence conclude (wrongly) that they have market power. Thus the strategy of conforming behaviour to the lowest common denominator where a company assumes that it is dominant on the basis of a narrow market definition, can result in constraining its margin of commercial manoeuvre.

There is a further paradox in that the very existence of precedent can also contribute to a lack of certainty and predictability. If the inquiry into past case law produces a series of inconclusive speculations on ever narrower segmentations by technology, platform, customer group and geography, where questions are increasingly and persistently left open, this can actually make it more difficult for parties to evaluate their behaviour and anticipate how it would be viewed by a relevant authority. Where the commercial practices at issue straddle multiple jurisdictions taking the same inconclusive approach, the complexity increases. The need for a transparent and coherent framework that reflects, in practical terms, the actual analytical approach to market delineation and what really matters to decision-making is thus fundamental.

3.6 CASE STUDY: MARKET DEFINITION UNDER THE EU COMMUNICATIONS REGULATORY FRAMEWORK

3.6.1 The EU Regulatory Framework: Introduction

Regulation of the communications sector in the EU provides an interesting case study with which to examine the role of market definition as a key analytical tool when considering the imposition of *ex ante* regulatory obligations.[40] Overall, the process reflects a reeling back of *ex ante* regulation over time in preference for a reliance on (*ex post*) competition law enforcement except in relation to operators which are found to enjoy a position of Significant Market Power (SMP).

We begin with a brief explanation of the evolution of the regulatory regime and the analysis of relevant markets. We then consider how the framework has developed through market definition, market analysis, and the assessment of and the adoption of regulatory measures. We also consider some remaining challenges and unresolved questions.

The framework must be understood against the institutional context where regulatory activities in the EU communications sector are conducted by a range of institutions. The super-structure is based on two-level regulation and a division of competencies between the European Commission and the Member States. The framework is underpinned by two principles. The first is harmonisation in the form of legislative and other legal measures that are enacted at

[40] See, further, Tintor, V et al, 'The Legal and Economic Framework of EU Telecom Market Regulation' (2010) *Economic Annals* Volume LV, No 185, April–June 2010, 107–28.

EU level by the European Commission, and which are then implemented at national level in the Member States. The second is the principle of delegation whereby national sector competencies are the responsibility of the Member States, subject to close monitoring by the European Commission. While this model is not readily transferable across legal systems worldwide, some of the issues that the European Commission and Member States have confronted when trying to adapt their legal rules to the changes in the communications sector over the last two decades will be familiar.

3.6.2 Evolving Approach

The process of deregulation in the EU telecommunications sector has been gradual. By the 1990s most EU Member States had completely or partially privatised their public telecommunications operators paving the way for market liberalisation. It is useful to set the scene with a brief historical explanation of the evolution of the measures aimed at regulating competition in the sector.

The 1998 EU regulatory framework aimed to eliminate exclusive rights that were previously granted to the state incumbents. National regulatory authorities were established in the Member States whose responsibility was to ensure objective and non-discriminatory conditions for all operators. A two-stage analysis was conducted. The first stage involved the identification of operators within the relevant service market with a market share of 25 per cent in the area in which it had been granted a licence. Where market share fell below the 25 per cent threshold the national regulatory authority (NRA) had to identify additional criteria, such as lack of countervailing buyer power or ready access to capital, in order to establish market power. According to this approach markets that were susceptible to *ex ante* regulation were identified, although it should be emphasised that the relevant markets were not defined according to standard competition law principles. Regulatory remedies were then imposed on operators according to the identification of SMP.

The 2002 regulatory framework[41] reflected the need for a more precise identification of relevant markets. It also reflected the principle of technological neutrality, the primacy of competition law as the basis for protecting and promoting competition and innovation, and an increased role for the European Commission in relation to the decision. The new framework was also driven by the phenomenon of

[41] The current regulatory framework consists of the following: Directive 2002/21/EC on a common regulatory framework for electronic communications networks and services (Framework Directive); Directive 2002/20/EC on the authorisation of electronic communications networks and services (Authorisation Directive); Directive 2002/19/EC on access to, and interconnection of, electronic communications networks and associated facilities (Access Directive); Directive 2002/22/EC on universal service and users' rights relating to electronic communications networks and services (Universal Service Directive); and Directive 2002/58/EC concerning the processing of personal data and the protection of privacy in the electronic communications sector (E-privacy Directive).

convergence in the area of electronic communications. In contrast to the approach under the 1998 regulatory framework, the European Commission and each NRA, when identifying markets susceptible to *ex ante* obligations and when assessing which operators have SMP, should apply the principles and methodologies under competition law. The European Commission published a Recommendation on relevant markets[42] and guidelines for market analysis and the assessment of SMP in accordance with the principles of competition law.[43]

The 2007 regulatory framework[44] represented yet another development in the EU approach to identifying relevant markets susceptible to *ex ante* regulation. This crystallised in the European Commission's 2007 Recommendation which eliminated 11 relevant markets from the list and unified two others resulting in only seven markets for regulation. Out of those seven only one market is retail (access to the public telephone network at a fixed location for residential and non-residential customers) and the rest are wholesale. Some retail markets were fully deregulated.

The telecommunications 'relevant markets' that should be subject to *ex ante* regulation remain subject to evaluation. The European Commission has received advice from external experts advising that fewer markets should be included on the European Commission's list and that no new markets should be added.[45] The advice will inform the European Commission's review of the 2007 Recommendation.

Table 1 illustrates the transformation in the number and designation (ie whether or not subject to *ex ante* regulation) of framewords from 2002 to 2007 based on the 2003 and 2007 Recommendations. Each NRA remains free within this framework to analyse other markets in its national context or a relevant event with cross-border dimensions.

[42] Commission recommendation of 11 February 2003 on relevant product and service markets within the electronic communications sector susceptible to ex ante regulation in accordance with Directive 2002/21/EC of the European Parliament and of the Council on a common regulatory framework for electronic communication networks and services (notified under document number C 497) [2003] OJ L114 (2003 Recommendation).

[43] Commission guidelines on market analysis and the assessment of significant market power under the Community regulatory framework for electronic communications networks and services, OJ C165.

[44] In 2007, the European Commission published proposals for two Directives and a Regulation to amend the regulatory framework, and adopted Commission recommendation of 17 December 2007 on relevant product and service markets within the electronic communications sector susceptible to ex ante regulation in accordance with Directive 2002/21/EC of the European Parliament and of the Council on a common regulatory framework for electronic communication networks and services (OJ L344 (2007 Recommendation)). In November 2009, the Council and European Parliament adopted the following proposals: Directive 2009/140/EC amending Directives 2002/21/EC, 2002/19/EC and 2002/20/EC (Better Regulation Directive); Directive 2009/136/EC amending Directive 2002/22/EC, Directive 2002/58/EC and Regulation (EC) 2006/2004 (Citizens' Rights Directive); and Regulation (EC) 1211/2009 establishing the Body of European Regulators for Electronic Communications (BEREC).

[45] European Commission MEMO/13/875, 'Telecoms relevant markets expert advice received by Commission—suggests fewer markets should be regulated', 10 October 2013.

Table 1: Transition from 2003 to 2007 Recommendations

Number		Relevant Market	Regulation	Number		Relevant Market	Regulation
2003	2007			2003	2007		
1	1	Access to the public telephone network at a fixed location—residential customers	***Ex ante***	10		Transit services in the fixed public telephone network	None
2		Access to the public telephone network at a fixed location—non-residential customers		11	4	Wholesale unbundled access (including shared access) to metallic loops and sub-loop for the purpose of providing broadband and voice services	***Ex ante***
3		Publicly available local and/or national telephone services provided at a fixed location—residential customers	None	12	5	Wholesale broadband access	
4		Publicly available international telephone services provided at a fixed location—residential customers		13	6	Wholesale terminating segments of leased lines	
5		Publicly available local and/or national telephone services—non-residential customers		14		Wholesale trunk segments of leased lines	None
6		Publicly available international telephone services—non-residential customers		15		Access and call origination on public mobile telephone networks	
7		Minimum set of leased lines	***Ex post***	16	7	Voice call termination on individual mobile networks	***Ex ante***
8	2	Call origination on the public fixed network at a fixed location	***Ex ante***	17		Wholesale national market for international roaming on public mobile networks	EU roaming
9		Call termination on individual public telephone networks provided at a fixed location		18		Broadcasting transmission services to deliver broadcast content to end-users	***Ex post***

3.6.3 Some Remaining Difficulties

The EU approach to the regulation of the telecommunications sector has morphed over the years and reflects a transition from monopoly to the introduction of alternative operators. However, this process has been criticised. A number of issues remain, as discussed below, which are dealt with in detail in the academic literature (Baudrier, 2006;[46] de Streel, 2005;[47] and Dobbs, 2004[48]).

The final list of relevant markets has not been determined and Member States remain free to analyse other markets, albeit subject to obligations to publish the results of its analysis. Some commentators (Knieps, 2009[49]) suggest that only markets 1 and 4 should be regulated. It may also be surprising that a wider than national market has not been defined within the EU. This may develop in future years.

The regulatory approach is not without its costs. The process of identifying relevant markets and conducting market analysis involves the gathering of data from operators and regulatory resources, all of which comes at a cost. The first stage of implementation resulted in at least 450 analyses of relevant national markets in the EU for the then 25 Member States. In each case the European Commission was required to accept or reject the approaches of the NRAs. The 2007 regulatory framework has reduced the number of relevant markets and regulatory burdens but this is an ongoing process.

The EU approach accords a degree of flexibility to NRAs, although recent developments have seen the balance shift more towards the European Commission performing a coordinating role. The question of multi-layering of regulation, modification of decisions and the resulting uncertainty it can yield is not unique to the EU. India will need to confront the question of possible overlap or inconsistency in decision-making between the CCI and the TRAI if the allocation of competencies is not clearly defined.

This raises a question about the relevance of the analysis to markets that were 'born competitive' in that they do not bear the legacy of a monopoly provider. The internet is an obvious example. The EU approach derived from the legacy of state control of EU telecommunications markets and has now been extended beyond its traditional base to the wider electronic communications sector. With convergence this evolution seems almost inevitable, but it raises the question of

[46] Baudrier, A, 'The EU Regulatory Framework for Electronic Communications: Relevance and Efficiency Three Years Later' (2006) *Communications & Strategies*, No 61, 1st quarter.

[47] de Streel, A, 'A First Assessment of the New European Regulatory Framework for Electronic Communications' (2005) *Communications & Strategies*, No 58, 2nd quarter.

[48] Dobbs, I and Richards, P, 'Innovation and the New Regulatory Framework for Electronic Communications in the EU' (2004) *European Competition Law Review* No 25.

[49] Knieps, G and Zenhausern, P, 'The reform of the European regulatory framework for electronic communications: The unexploited phasing-out potentials' (2009) paper presented at the 2nd Annual Conference on Competition and Regulation in Network Industries, Centre for European Policy Studies (CEPS) Brussels, 20 November 2009.

the relevance of the approach to newer markets which do not generally conform to natural monopolies or bottlenecks.

The EU regulatory framework applies to telecommunications or electronic communications. It does not apply to broadcasting where the EU has generally stepped back. Convergence has forced the question of the justification for this approach and whether market distortion may result from the asymmetry in regulation between communications and broadcasting (the latter having developed more on national lines). In the UK, the Department for Culture, Media & Sport (DCMS) has published 'Connectivity, content and consumers: Britain's digital platform for growth'.[50] A key question posed by the DCMS is: 'is there a risk of unfairness or market distortion if firms are more—or less—regulated because they are subject to one form of regulation rather than another?'

3.7 TOWARDS A COHERENT FRAMEWORK FOR MARKET ANALYSIS IN THE MEDIA AND COMMUNICATIONS SECTOR?

The challenges of market definition more generally, and the particular issues arising in relation to the media sector, raise the issue of the usefulness of traditional approaches such as the SSNIP test in the media sector.

In order to provide a guide to whether the factual evidence may raise competition or other concerns, it would seem that market definition needs to meet at least three basic requirements. First, it should reflect the market as it operates in practice over a reasonable time period; it should not be subject to the whims of fleeting trends, unproven technology or untested approaches. Second, it should be straightforward to understand and implement. Third, it should be consistent with accepted economic and legal principles. This reflects the fact that in the context of a competition law or regulatory procedure market definition is ultimately a legal tool informed by economics.

The realisation of such goals in a sector that is fast-moving may seem somewhat elusive. The approach put forward here is to start with a presentation of a stylised media value chain that incorporates, as far as possible, the elements which tend to define the relationships between the various actors in the media value chain. At the risk of simplification, it emerges from the above assessment that many forms of media conform to the same underlying logic as far as the supply and demand relationships are concerned. The value chain may be divided broadly into various links and relationships from the upstream development and acquisition of content (whether for traditional print, broadcasting, TV or online). Depending on the different media concerned, the downstream distribution may vary in terms of the type of economic agents that interface with one another in order to reach the end consumer. The value chain may be divided broadly into links and relationships from

[50] Department for Culture, Media & Sport, 'Connectivity, Content and Consumers Britain's digital platform for growth', July 2013.

the upstream development and acquisition of content (whether for traditional print, broadcasting, TV or online). Depending on the different media concerned the downstream distribution may vary according to the type of economic agents that interface with one another in order to reach the end consumer. This is displayed graphically with special relevance for the TV sector in Figure 4 below.

From Figure 4 it can be seen that the chain involves:

- Access to content whether in the form of (i) talent (eg production companies, production departments, actors/writers, sports bodies and channel owners); (ii) production (through content producers); or (iii) packaging (ie different agents such as TV broadcasters, channel owners or pay TV retailers acquire and package content in a different form to meet the preferences of their customers).
- Distribution whether via terrestrial, cable, satellite, copper or fibre.
- Supply to the consumer reader, viewer or listener and whether via TV, Set-top-box, PC, laptop, smartphone or home hub.

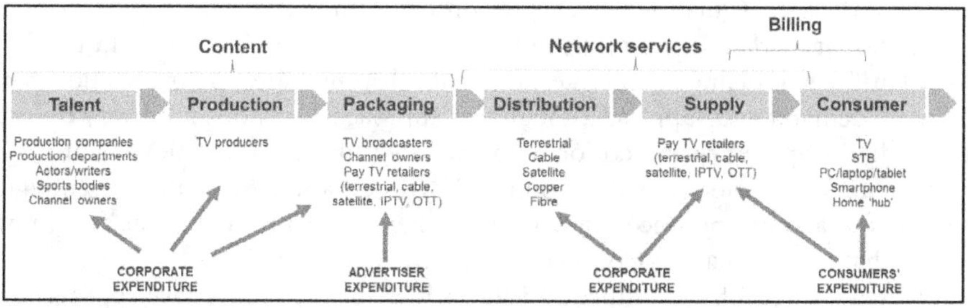

Figure 4: A stylised media value chain in the broadcasting sector

Source: Authors' analysis

To minimise complexity, Figure 4 shows the 'cash injections' at each stage of the chain but not the revenue flows. For the present, the above interactions may correspond to different and separate industry segments and economic markets, even though they relate to the same value chain. However, owing to convergence such discrete elements are now being produced within the same entity or firm and may elide over time. This development is further promoted by the liberalisation of regulation, as exemplified in the EU.[51]

It should be noted that the use of the value chain as an analytical tool in a competition, regulatory or merger analysis is not new.[52] However, it may be a useful

[51] See, further, chapter 2, section 2.10 on the EU regulatory framework.

[52] The concept was described by Michael Porter in *Competitive Advantage: Creating and Sustaining Superior Performance* (Simon and Schuster, 1985): The idea of the value chain is based on the process view of organisations, the idea of seeing a manufacturing (or service) organisation as a system, made up of subsystems each with inputs, transformation processes and outputs. Inputs, transformation processes, and outputs involve the acquisition and consumption of resources—money, labour, materials, equipment, buildings, land, administration and management. How value chain activities are carried out determines costs and affects profits.

starting point to identify the relationships between the various actors. It may also help to identify the value that should be placed on a particular product or service when considering the optimum level of regulation and how regulatory interventions may undermine or enhance the value chain and consumer welfare.

Furthermore, the identification of a value chain may also provide a better reflection of the positions of businesses that are affected by a regulatory intervention. The views of such actors are prominent in competition law and regulatory investigations as can be seen by the number of complaints-led investigations in the media sector. However, such arguments need to be thoroughly tested by any policy-maker or authority given that the perspectives advanced may not be entirely disinterested. The value chain approach may therefore provide an appropriate means to collate the positions of the various parties and to understand the connections between them.

Using the value chain it may be possible to develop a more relevant analytical framework within which to appraise a particular issue (whether in relation to competition law, regulation or merger control). While the value chain is not a substitute for market definition in an economics-sense it provides a starting point for identifying or delineating the key issues of substitutability and the relationship between demand and supply. Although this approach may not sound very different to that adopted by competition authorities worldwide in traditional competition inquiries, it is not dependent on the SSNIP test and may be flexible enough to take into account non-economic goals, such as the public interest and cultural issues, that are characteristic of media markets.

Before we discuss how competition authorities and regulators have approached ownership and control in media markets in practice, we remind the reader of Figure 3 in this chapter (the overview of how the multi-faceted competition, regulatory and public interest issues appear and often elide across the value chain. As convergence continues, such an approach may be increasingly relevant in other contexts).

This work seeks to incorporate both factual and discursive material, covering the relevant economic theory, policy and actual practice in a range of international regimes. The intrinsic tensions between the need to be theoretically and academically robust, factually accurate and up-to-date in an area where the law is evolving at a slower pace than the markets themselves, highlight the limitations of the approach set out here. We do not purport to draw definitive operational conclusions that are readily translatable into each and every regulatory context in the media sector. Rather, we seek to provide an analytical framework that is informed by the relevant literature and experience and which may serve as a practical guide to operational decision-making in India and elsewhere.

4

Competition Law

4.1 INTRODUCTION

Countries around the world have seen significant interventions in media and communications markets resulting from competition law concerns.

During the first four years of the active implementation of India's Competition Act 2002 (Competition Act) investigations carried out by the Competition Commission of India (CCI) focused on potential restrictions of competition through horizontal and vertical agreements and arrangements, as well as abuse of a dominant market position.

Media convergence, built upon technological changes, is based on linking the value of different products and services. Convergence involving media platforms and producers creates challenges for competition, through development of media product portfolios across the value chain, creating network effects that may limit competition and access to the value chain. While this issue may invite examination, of itself it does not necessarily require intervention.

This chapter reviews the early experience of the CCI in applying the Competition Act provisions on anticompetitive agreements (section 3) and abuse of dominance (section 4) to the media and communications sector. This assessment provides the background for determining whether competition law alone can be effective in ensuring a competitive and healthy media and communications sector. We return to this question in chapter 10 when considering the implications of the interaction between competition law and other interventions for the design and implementation of effective and sustainable legal and regulatory structures.

4.2 AGREEMENTS

4.2.1 Indian Competition applied to Cartel-like Behaviour in the Media Sector

The CCI has been applying mainstream Indian competition law under section 3 of the Competition Act to traditional anticompetitive agreements which restrict the ability of independent players to participate in a market. In this way, the application of competition law indirectly protects pluralism by supporting the conditions for market entry and expansion for a range of players. Rules against cartels, such as those outlined in section 3 of the Competition Act, may also guard against foreclosure in markets which facilitate collusion due to increased concentration. In this way, *ex post* application of competition law operates as a corrective mechanism in cases where there is no legal basis to intervene against the change in market structure but where market players participate in restrictive agreements or arrangements.

There are several examples of the CCI applying the prohibition on anticompetitive agreements to the media sector. For example, the CCI has found a violation of section 3 of the Competition Act in a case involving associations of film producers, distributors and exhibitors acting as regulators for the distribution and exhibition of films in their respective territories.[1] It was alleged by the complainant, a producer of a major Hindi film due for theatrical release, that the associations made it compulsory for every film distributor to become a member of the associations and register films with them before the exhibition of a film. Any distributor that refused to become a member or to register its film was not permitted to distribute the film in the territories regulated by the respective associations. It was alleged that third-party cinema exhibitors were not willing to take the risk of exhibiting the film of a distributor that was not a member of the relevant associations, or whose film had not been registered with them. The CCI ordered the associations to end the practice of penalising distributors and to modify their rules. In respect of one regional association which also restricted its members from dealing with non-members, the CCI imposed a penalty of INR12,89,735 (representing 10 per cent of its average turnover for the previous three financial years).

4.2.2 The Concept of an 'Appreciable Adverse Effect' on Competition has been Construed Widely to Capture Local and Regional Effects

Section 3 of the Competition Act prohibits any agreement in respect of the production, supply, distribution, storage, acquisition or control of goods or provision of services which causes, or is likely to cause, an appreciable adverse effect (AAE) on competition within India. Section 3 has been held to apply in circumstances where the anticompetitive agreement produces local or regional effects.

The CCI decided a case involving regional markets against the Eastern India Motion Picture Association and Coordination of Artist and Technicians of West Bengal Film and Television Industry (collectively EMPA).[2] The case was brought by a complainant engaged in the distribution of serial films in Eastern India.

[1] Case 56/2011 *M/s Cinergy Independent Film Services Pvt Ltd v Telangana Telugu Film Distribution Association & Ors*, 1 January 2013.

[2] Case 16/2011 *Mr Sajjan Khaitan v Eastern India Motion Picture Association & Ors*, 9 August 2012.

The complainant had been granted a licence to dub the serial *Mahabharata* into Bengali. It entered into an agreement with television channels to telecast the dubbed serial.

The CCI found that the EMPA had sought to impose restrictions on the telecast of the dubbed serials and had adopted methods to prevent telecasts of the serial on one of the two channels on which the serial was due to be telecast. The CCI found that the conduct was in violation of section 3 of the Competition Act because it limited the control and distribution of dubbed serials in the relevant areas of operation. The CCI directed the EMPA to stop the anticompetitive practices and to modify its articles of association and rules accordingly.

4.3 ABUSE OF DOMINANCE

4.3.1 Challenges of applying Competition Law in the Media and Communications Sector

A number of features of media and communications markets highlight some of the challenges in applying competition law and particularly prohibitions on the abuse of a dominant position in such markets.

The markets are consumer facing. The sector embraces products consumers care about passionately—movies, music, phones, internet, gadgets and so on. There are, therefore, opportunities for significant consumer and public relations benefits from intervention—but also dangers of chilling investment by getting it wrong.

The definition of the relevant market may not be straightforward in a new technology or media which has not previously existed but which may replace existing technology (eg SMS as a substitute for a phone call, and Twitter providing a new social network and news platform). These considerations affect the threshold question of whether a company is dominant at all in a relevant market since only in such circumstances can it be abusing a dominant (market) position.

Today's market share may understate tomorrow's market power in a fast-moving market, particularly where the internet is shaping new forms of distribution and consumer choice. It is difficult to draw the line between dominance acquired legitimately through superior business acumen and abuse which needs to be curtailed.

There is a tension between static and dynamic competition. It may be necessary to allow some short-term restriction of competition to stimulate investment in the long term.

The question of the appropriate remedy is controversial. Where intellectual property rights (IPR) are concerned, as is often the case in the media and communications industry, compulsory licensing and access remedies tend to challenge property rights and freedom of contract.

It is difficult to determine what constitutes a competitive price where there is value in brand and IP which it may not be straightforward to quantify.

The distinct market dynamic in India in particular raises its own challenges. Traditionally, there has been relatively limited IPR protection. India is globally acclaimed as a centre of innovation and excellence but needs to attract and retain investment if it is to stay ahead. India has a massive consumer market which is expected to match the US in gross domestic product by 2050.[3]

In these circumstances, the CCI as a specialist competition regulator has an important role to play in keeping markets open and maintaining India's position as a centre for investment. However, there is a real potential for unintended and damaging consequences where regulatory interventions are misplaced.

4.3.2 No General Exception for Protection of IPR

The limited exception to the prohibition of anticompetitive agreements under Indian competition law which allows reasonable conditions to protect any rights conferred under specific intellectual property legislation[4] does not apply to cases of abuse of dominance. In any event, this exception would seem to be of narrow scope under the Competition Act, in particular, since it does not strictly extend to IPR arising under the laws of jurisdictions outside India.

It should be noted that intellectual property cases form a considerable proportion of the cases considered by competition authorities, particularly in the EU, in the area of abuse of dominance. Notable examples include: Microsoft's tying of its Windows Media Player with its operating system and refusal to supply interoperability information;[5] the European Commission inquiry into the pharmaceutical sector and follow-on cases;[6] and a challenge involving allegations that Rambus had charged excessive royalties resulting in commitments by it to license its patents on fair, reasonable and non-discriminatory (FRAND) terms.[7]

India is therefore poised to use its competition law to sanction abuse of dominance in appropriate cases involving IPR. There are ample precedents on which to draw internationally but such interventions have been controversial.

[3] PricewaterhouseCoopers Economics, 'World in 2050: The BRICs and beyond: prospects, challenges and opportunities', January 2013.

[4] Competition Act, section 3(5).

[5] Case T-201/04 *Microsoft Corporation v Commission* [2007] ECR II-3601.

[6] European Commission, 'Pharmaceutical Sector Inquiry, Final Report', 8 July 2009.

[7] Case COMP/38.636 *Rambus*, Commission decision of 9 December 2009.

4.3.3 Indian Competition Law has already been applied to Abuse of Dominance in the Media and Communications Sector

The CCI has enforced section 4 of the Competition Act on abuse of a dominant position in the media and communications sector.

In a relatively early Competition Act case the CCI imposed a penalty of Rs 8 crore on three entities of cable TV operator, Fastway Group.[8] The penalty represented 6 per cent of its average turnover for the three previous financial years.

The CCI's order was passed after an investigation prompted by information provided by Kansan News that broadcasts the news and current affairs TV channel *Day and Night News*. It was alleged by the complainant channel that the Fastway Group had abused its dominant position, controlling transmission and broadcasting of TV channels, resulting in denial of market access to the channel and violating section 4 of the Competition Act. The CCI found that Fastway Group had over 85 per cent of the total subscribers in Punjab and Chandigarh. As a result, the CCI found that broadcasters were dependent on Fastway Group's network and that consumers in the regions did not have any effective alternative. The CCI found that Fastway Group had denied the opportunity for transmission of the complainant channel by termination of the agreement between them without any sound justification.

4.3.4 Complaints-led Cases

A notable feature of cases before the CCI is that they are complaints-led. Complainants have included individuals, opposite parties in contractual disputes, and consumer associations. For example, the Consumer Unity and Trust Society (CUTS) filed a complaint against Google alleging that Google had been abusing its market power in search engines.[9]

The complaints-led nature of competition cases in the media and communications sector is not surprising. The industry is worth billions of euro, dollars and crores of business. In short, this is a high-stakes business. The corollary is that it may be worth fighting cases to the end, regardless of their intellectual merits, owing to the point of legal principle at issue. Strategic or tactical issues also come into play where an ongoing regulatory investigation can mean months if not years of commercial uncertainty. There are no easy solutions—complainants and investigated parties as well as their lawyers and economists have plenty to debate.

[8] Case 36/211 *M/s Kansan News Pvt Ltd v M/s Fastway Transmission Pvt Ltd & Ors*, 3 July 2012.

[9] The Hindu Business Line, 'Consumer rights body CUTS takes Google to competition panel', 13 June 2012, available at: www.thehindubusinessline.com/industry-and-economy/consumer-rights-body-cuts-takes-google-to-competition-panel/article3524715.ece.

In these circumstances, the challenge for the competition authority is to ensure that complaints are thoroughly tested while recognising that all sides to an argument may have their axes to grind. The potential for nuisance complaints is multiplied when parties can bring cases in multiple venues. This should not foreclose different or even parallel avenues of redress but it does raise a question about which authorities are best placed to handle such issues effectively.

A case illustrating the potential for unmeritorious complaints in the media sector considered tie-in arrangements in the context of distributors and single-screen cinemas.[10] It was alleged that prior to the release of one of its films, *Ek Tha Tiger*, Yash Raj Films Private Limited (YRF) had imposed a condition on single-screen cinemas that if they wanted to exhibit the film they would have to agree to exhibit another of YRF's films which was scheduled for release during Diwali 2012. The CCI rejected the complaint. The complainant had not provided data to prove that YRF and its associated companies were dominant. Furthermore, the CCI found no AAE on competition for the purposes of section 3 of the Competition Act. The complainant applied to the Competition Appellate Tribunal (Compat) for a temporary injunction on the Diwali release of YRF's film. Compat refused to grant any relief on the basis that there was neither a prima facie case nor irreparable injury to the complainant.

4.3.5 International Dimension

Many global media and communications companies are already active in India (eg Apple, BT, Disney, Google, Intel and News Corporation). The CCI has investigated, or is investigating, competition cases in relation to companies or issues that have been, or are, the subject of investigation by international competition law counterparts, including in the EU and US.

For example, in May 2012 press reports indicated that the CCI has launched an investigation into Google's suspected abusive and discriminatory practices relating to its AdWords programme, in contravention of section 4 of the Competition Act.[11] The European Commission has also investigated Google for alleged abuse of dominance and considered commitments offered by Google to resolve the case.[12]

A case that has raised questions in this area concerns Apple's iPhones and iPads. The CCI received a complaint under section 4 of the Competition Act that Apple was allegedly curbing customer choice by limiting the availability of iPhones

[10] Case 66/2012 *Ajay Devgn Films v Yash Raj Films Pvt Ltd & Ors*, 5 November 2012.

[11] Economic Times, 'CCI orders probe in Google's AdWords programme', 6 March 2012, available at: articles.economictimes.indiatimes.com/2012-05-06/news/31597590_1_google-s-adwords-google-spokesperson-bharatmatrimony.

[12] European Commission press release, 'Antitrust: Commission seeks feedback on commitments offered by Google to address competition concerns' (IP/13/371) 25 April 2013.

and iPads in India to a limited number of service providers, outside its signature stores. It was alleged that the latest version of iPhones was available in India through Aircel and Bharti AirTel, while iPads were sold only through the Apple store. The complainant also alleged that a user can only download software from the iStore and that other versions are not recognised by the device and that Apple phones could only be serviced in Apple service centres, which charge high rates for servicing. However, there has been no final decision in this case.

A number of learnings emerge from these cases. First, it is clear that the CCI is being confronted with competition cases in the media and communications sector raising similar issues to those that have been before international regulators. Second, as a newer authority, the CCI is taking a cautious approach in this area rather than rushing to a decision in cases which raise complex issues of fact and law. Third, given the nascent stage of competition law enforcement in India, there are good arguments for concentrating enforcement within a specialist body such as the CCI rather than creating further risks of inconsistent decisions in India and between India and international regulators who are examining similar issues.

Collective Dominance

The CCI has addressed the question of whether Indian competition law applies to abuse of a collectively dominant position. In the EU abuse of a dominant position 'by one or more undertakings' is prohibited under Article 102 of the Treaty of the Functioning of the EU. This covers abuse of a collective dominant position. Collective dominance tends to occur where there are a smaller number of businesses in a market who take strategic decisions by taking into account the prospective conduct of their rivals. The practical difficulty is that businesses are entitled to adapt their own market strategy to the existing or anticipated conduct of their competitors without there being an infringement.[13]

So far, the CCI has stated that the concept of collective dominance is inapplicable under Indian competition law.

In a case in the cable industry, while finding a group dominant the CCI stated that an independent enterprise cannot be part of an independent group's dominance:

> Since there cannot be a case of any anticompetitive agreement of the nature mentioned in section 3(3) of the Act among the entities of same group, it cannot be said that the Opposite Parties have formed a cartel. … The Commission also observes that the OP-4 is a Public limited company promoted by Essel group. As per the findings of DG, OP-1 or any other Opposite Parties do not have either 26% share in OP-4 or power to appoint more than fifty percent members of Board of Directors of OP-4. There is no structural relationship between the OP-4 and remaining Opposite Parties which establishes that OP4 is part of the common group.[14]

[13] Case C-7/95P *John Deere v Commission* [1993] ECR I-1375.

[14] Case 36/211 *M/s Kansan News Pvt Ltd v M/s Fastway Transmission Pvt Ltd & Ors*, 3 July 2012.

However, this position would change following proposed amendments to Indian competition law discussed in chapter 2, section 2.11.2. One proposed amendment would extend the prohibition on abuse of a dominant position to cover 'collective dominance'. If enacted, this would mean that the CCI may in the future find a dominant position where no company is individually dominant but where, together, two or more companies hold a dominant position. This should allow the CCI to find more scope for infringement action where it does not have evidence of an anticompetitive agreement or single dominance.

4.4 INITIAL CONCLUSIONS

The following tentative conclusions may be drawn from the early competition law enforcement experience of the CCI in the media and communications sector.

In relation to agreements, Indian competition law has been applied to anticompetitive behaviour in the media sector even where dominance is not established. The concept of an AAE on competition has been construed widely and does not depend on an anticompetitive effect at national level.

In relation to abuse of a dominant position, cases tend to have high stakes, with a concomitant potential for error. This raises a question about the balance between competition and sector regulatory enforcement and expertise. The importance of sector-specific expertise in understanding the potential for harm in such cases suggests an important role for the sector regulator in contributing to the quality of decision-making. Whether the actual investigation and enforcement should be concentrated exclusively in the hands of the competition authority is one of the most topical regulatory issues, in India and abroad.

There is no general and comprehensive exception under Indian competition law for protection of IPR resulting in a patchwork of legal protections. It is not obvious why IPR conferred under laws outside of India should warrant less protection. Abuse of IPR in the media and communications sector can be sanctioned in appropriate cases.

Cases tend to be complaints-led, emphasising the need to balance the costs and the benefits of creating additional layers of enforcement at a time when complaints show no sign of relenting. The CCI has investigated or is investigating competition cases in relation to companies or issues that have been or are the subject of investigation by their international competition law counterparts including in the EU and US. There is a need for consistency and avoidance of duplication in regulatory decision-making in India and internationally.

The CCI may in the future find a dominant position where no company is individually dominant but where, together, two or more companies hold a dominant position. However, such cases have been difficult to establish in the EU, not least due to the ambivalence surrounding fulfilment of the conditions for collective dominance.

5

Media Ownership and Control

5.1 INTRODUCTION

This chapter examines the structural regulation of the media and communications sector and the regulatory policy instruments that can be used to address the twin challenges of (i) concentration in the media, and (ii) the need to safeguard plurality.

This chapter provides:

— an appraisal of the relationship between competition and pluralism and how these different but related goals interact;
— a survey of the main regulatory mechanisms that have been deployed internationally to regulate market structure in the media sector through any or all of a combination of direct controls on media ownership (including ownership caps), competition review in merger control, or sector-specific tests designed to address plurality; and
— observations on the emerging features of regulatory architecture with a view to identifying their implications for design of optimal regulatory instruments.

Appendix 2 summarises the media ownership and merger control rules (if any) which apply in the media and communications sector in selected countries within our study. The focus is on media ownership rules based on shareholding and interest and not on nationality (ie foreign ownership). The latter presupposes that a policy decision has been taken to limit foreign ownership, an issue which is beyond the scope of this book.

5.2 PROTECTING COMPETITIVENESS AND PLURALISM

5.2.1 What is Pluralism or Plurality?

A February 2013 consultation paper on media cross-ownership by the Telecom Regulatory Authority of India (TRAI) places pluralism as an important goal, noting in the first paragraph that 'media pluralism is a cornerstone of democracy and this fact should be reflected in the plurality of independent and autonomous media and in diversity of media content'.[1]

The consultation paper sets as a goal the design of rules to balance pluralism and competitiveness:

> In order to ensure media pluralism and counter the ills of monopolies, it is felt that reasonable restrictions need be put in place on ownership in the media sector. The Media Ownership Rules should be so designed so as to strike a balance between ensuring a degree of plurality of media sources and content, and a level playing field for companies operating in the media sector on the one hand and providing freedom to companies to expand, innovate and invest on the other.[2]

These goals are congruent with the aims of most modern democracies, although there are differences in the approaches that have been adopted to seek to achieve these ends.

When the UK sought to develop its own laws in this area the relevant government minister said in 2003 that

> [media] plurality is important for a healthy and informed democratic society. The underlying principle is that it would be dangerous for any person to control too much of the media because of his or her ability to influence opinions and set the political agenda.[3]

In relation to broadcasting and cross-media mergers, the relevant media plurality considerations are set out in section 58(2C) of the UK Enterprise Act 2002 and include

> the need, in relation to every different audience in the United Kingdom or in a particular area or locality of the United Kingdom, for there to be a sufficient plurality of persons with control of the media enterprises serving that audience.

UK communications regulator Ofcom conducted a significant research study and extensive stakeholder consultation on plurality matters between November 2011 and June 2012. Following a request by the Secretary of State (SoS) in October 2011, Ofcom stated that:

> We have defined plurality as a) ensuring there is a diversity of viewpoints available and consumed across and within media enterprises and b) preventing any one media owner or voice having too much influence over public opinion and the political agenda.[4]

To set the context for what follows, we define pluralism as a situation where no single voice/ viewpoint can control the news agenda, restrict ideas or debate, or allow government, or indeed other players, to escape scrutiny.

[1] Telecom Regulatory Authority of India, 'Consultation Paper on Issues relating to Media Ownership', 15 February 2013, Introduction, paragraph (i).

[2] Ibid, Introduction, paragraph (v).

[3] Hansard, Lord McIntosh of Haringey (Parliamentary Under Secretary, DCMS), 2 July 2003.

[4] Ofcom, 'Measuring media plurality, Ofcom's advice to the Secretary of State for Culture, Olympics, Media and Sport', 6 June 2012.

Another relevant distinction is between external plurality (achieving plurality through a number of media outlets) and internal plurality (ensuring content diversity through a single supplier). Both these mechanisms for contributing to plurality are accepted, for example, in the UK. In the context of British Sky Broadcasting's (BSkyB) proposed acquisition of a 17.9 per cent interest in ITV, the UK Competition Commission thought 'that it was appropriate to distinguish between the range of information and views that are provided across separate independent media groups (external plurality) and the range that are provided within individual media groups (internal plurality)'.[5]

Finally, we distinguish between 'plurality' (the fact of there being many) and 'pluralism' (the policy goal or doctrine).

5.2.2 Relationship between Pluralism and Competition Law

Pluralism is designed to capture issues other than those that are covered by competition inquiries into market concentration. The analysis also has to encompass the capacity of an entity to unacceptably influence public debate quite separately from any competition issues.

UK guidance on this issue explains how pluralism and competition are distinct but can inform one another:

> *[The plurality test] is not intended to replicate or import aspects of the substantial lessening of competition test that applies in relation to mergers raising competition concerns.* This test will be applied separately by the competition authorities, where appropriate. An example of concerns regarding the impact of consolidation on the need for a plurality of views in newspapers in the UK can be seen in the (then Monopoly and Mergers Commission's) MMC's report on the proposed acquisition by Daily Mail & General Trust of Nottingham Evening Post. In that case, the MMC concluded that the increase in regional concentration of ownership could be expected to pose a risk to the maintenance of diversity of opinion in the region and would in turn jeopardize accurate presentation of news and free expression of opinion. (emphasis added)[6]

Contrasting the different analytical inquiries that are involved in a plurality and competition assessment it is noted that:

> These *media public interest considerations invoked by the Secretary of State are distinct from the competition-based test* applied by the competition authorities. The aim of this competition analysis is to prevent a level of concentration of ownership which could

[5] Competition Commission, *Acquisition by British Sky Broadcasting Group Plc of 17.9 per cent of the shares in ITV Plc, Report sent to Secretary of State (BERR) 14 December 2007* (BSkyB/ ITV), Executive Summary, paragraph 30.

[6] Department of Trade and Industry, 'Guidance on the operation of the public interest merger provisions relating to newspapers and other media mergers', Guidance Document, May 2004, paragraph 5.15.

> give rise to a substantial lessening of competition. However, there is *a recognisable overlap between this competition assessment and at least the first of the broadcasting and cross-media public interest considerations, which posits the need for there to be a sufficient plurality of persons controlling media enterprises.* (emphasis added)[7]

However, it may be that interventions that are aimed at safeguarding competition can also promote pluralism:

> Although she will remain conscious of the distinctions between the competition and the public interest regimes, the Secretary of State anticipates that *in some cases she may take the view that action to safeguard competition in a market will by itself be likely to provide a sufficient plurality of control.* (emphasis added)[8]

The government department responsible for media in the UK, the Department for Culture, Media & Sport (DCMS), provided the following in its submission to the Leveson Inquiry:

> Policy and legislation has been designed overall to achieve a range of different media 'voices' which enable consumers to have access to a range of views which help them actively participate in the democratic process in the widest sense. … While imperfect, ownership restrictions act as an effective 'proxy' for media plurality.[9]

We note here an important conceptual issue: ownership is used as a proxy for viewpoints because owners of media outlets are assumed to be in a position to influence what is said and how it is said. However, one Canadian commentator, Kenneth Goldstein, pointed out that the proxy is just that and is therefore imperfect:

> Given the imperfect nature of the proxy, we conclude that public policy should proceed with great caution in this area. As a corollary, we suggest that we should avoid the construction of rigid rules or strict guidelines in this area, because those rules or guidelines would be, by definition, based on that imperfect proxy.[10]

The case studies in Appendix 2 illustrate the proposition that plurality and competition are different goals but regulatory interventions which are designed to protect competition can contribute to pluralism. However, since pluralism is not predicated on the presence of market power in an economic sense, there can be plurality issues even where competition law issues do not arise.

5.2.3 Initial Conclusions on Competition and Plurality Tests

The following are the key implications of the above assessment when considering the relationship between competition and plurality tests.

[7] Ibid, paragraph 7.3.

[8] Ibid, paragraph 7.4.

[9] Department for Culture, Media & Sport, 'Media Ownership: Summary', available at: www.levesoninquiry.org.uk/wp-content/uploads/2012/07/DCMS-submission_Narrative-on-media-ownership.pdf.

[10] Communications Management Inc, Letter of 17 November 2011, available at: stakeholders.ofcom.org.uk/binaries/consultations/measuring-plurality/responses/kenneth-goldstein.pdf.

First, competition tests and plurality tests seek to capture very similar and frequently overlapping issues. This is not surprising since both place an importance on ensuring that markets are not controlled by a limited number of controllers.

Second, there may be cases where a pure competition test does not address the more complex—and inherently more difficult to define—concept of plurality. Such cases tend to be easily identifiable, for example, where a controversial media owner seeks control of the press for political purposes, or where religious viewpoints are marginalised.

Third, the vast majority of cases can be dealt with by robust application of competition law by a specialist regulator. If—and only if—further issues are identified, targeted rules can be developed on a case-by-case basis such as restrictions on political parties controlling a television station.

Finally, the experience in the UK which has an elaborate media plurality regime bears out the above. In the decade since the current regime was put into operation, only three cases have raised plurality 'issues' such as to warrant a further inquiry. Critically, there has been no final determination in a case involving only plurality issues. None of these cases provide support for export of the same or a similar plurality regime into another jurisdiction and certainly not without a Regulatory Impact Assessment being conducted.

In *BSkyB/ITV*, BSkyB had acquired material influence over ITV, an important UK broadcast news provider. Even in those circumstances, the Competition Commission concluded that sufficient plurality remained for each major audience in the UK, both for a TV audience and a cross-media audience (taking into account the readership of News International's newspapers). BSkyB was required to divest its shareholding in ITV to below 7.5 per cent, for reasons connected with competition and not media plurality.

The second case involved News Corporation's proposed acquisition of the shares in BSkyB that it did not already own.[11] This was a highly unusual case which is unlikely to have international counterparts. The case did not reach a final decision by the SoS so provides no definitive support for the efficacy or otherwise of plurality controls. Quite the contrary; the case contributed to a full review of whether the existing media plurality test in the UK is workable in practice.

The third case is *Global Radio/GMG Radio*. On 24 June 2012, Global Radio acquired the entire issued share capital of GMG Radio Holdings Limited (GMG), the third-largest UK commercial radio operator and the operator of several radio stations across the UK. On 3 August 2012, the SoS issued a public interest intervention notice.[12] The intervention notice was issued on the basis that the media

[11] The competition aspects of the transaction were cleared by the European Commission. See, further, European Commission press release, 'Mergers: Commission clears News Corp's proposed acquisition of BSkyB under EU merger rules' (IP/10/1767) 21 December 2010.

[12] Ofcom, 'Guidance note for public interest test on the completed acquisition of GMG Radio Holdings Limited by Global Radio Limited', 3 August 2012.

plurality public interest test[13] might be relevant to consideration of the merger. Of most importance for present purposes, despite the issue of the intervention notice on 11 October 2012, the SoS announced that, on the advice of Ofcom, she would not refer the acquisition to the Competition Commission on media plurality public interest grounds.[14] The case was nevertheless referred to the Competition Commission but only on competition grounds.[15] The Competition Commission published its final report on 21 May 2013.[16] Global was required to partially divest some of the stations it had acquired or its own stations in each of the overlap areas to address the substantial lessening of competition found by the Competition Commission.

The result is that for the rare cases that raise only genuine plurality issues, experienced regulators internationally have not yet found effective and workable tools to address this discrete issue. There is no 'tried and trusted' approach that commands universal support and developed regimes have been subject to criticism as being prone to political interference.

5.3 INDIAN MERGER CONTROL IN THE MEDIA AND COMMUNICATIONS SECTOR

5.3.1 Introduction

In order to set in context the debate that follows, we outline a number of key trends in the application of Indian merger control in the media and communications sector.

- Enforcement: Mergers in media and communications have been subject to Indian merger control since mandatory merger control became effective under the Competition Act 2002 (Competition Act) on 1 June 2011.
- Minority interests: Indian merger control captures the acquisition of a minority interest in excess of 25 per cent. If anything, there is a movement towards lighter control of minority acquisitions.
- Wide reach: Cases involving corporate restructurings have highlighted the wide reach of Indian merger control.

[13] Here, the need, in relation to every different audience in the UK, or in a particular area or locality of the UK, for there to be a sufficient plurality of persons with control of the media enterprises serving that audience.

[14] Department for Culture, Media & Sport, 'Global Radio and Guardian Media Group Radio merger not to be considered on media plurality grounds', 11 October 2012.

[15] Office of Fair Trading press release, 'OFT refers Global Radio's acquisition of GMG Radio to the Competition Commission', 11 October 2012.

[16] Competition Commission, 'Global Radio Holdings Limited and GMG Radio Holdings Limited, A report on the completed acquisition by Global Radio Holdings Limited of GMG Radio Holdings Limited', 21 May 2013.

— Reform: Ongoing development of the Indian competition law and merger control framework is already underway and will address the balance of enforcement between the Competition Commission of India (CCI) and sector regulators.

5.3.2 Indian Merger Reviews in Media and Communications

Since mandatory merger control became effective in India on 1 June 2011, the CCI has reviewed mergers in a variety of sectors, including the media and communications sector.

Most of the merger cases that have come before the CCI have not raised significant substantive issues. For example, the CCI cleared News Corporation's acquisition of ESPN's[17] 50 per cent equity interest in sports broadcaster, ESS.[18] The CCI concluded that the combination would not result in an appreciable adverse effect (AAE) on competition in India. The CCI stated, amongst other things, that although the proposed combination resulted in the transfer of joint control to sole control it would not result in the elimination of any competitor. The joint venture partners, News Corporation and ESPN, were not competitors for broadcasting of sports channels in India.

The CCI has shown that it is ready to probe complex competition issues in appropriate cases. For example, the CCI has approved an acquisition by IMT, a trust established by Reliance Industries Ltd, of an interest in the media entity Network 18.[19] Approving the merger, the CCI observed that 'new television channels can be started with ease in India with sufficient scope for innovation and competition'. The CCI concluded that the proposed combination will not have any adverse effect on competition in the supply of TV channels in India. This was one of the more complex merger cases before the CCI which involved both horizontal and vertical issues.

Similarly, the CCI has approved a joint venture between Disney UTV Group, UGBL and IndiaCast, a TV18 and Viacom 18 alliance for the aggregation of TV channels.[20] As a result of the combination, IndiaCast will hold 74 per cent of the new distribution joint venture, while the remaining 26 per cent will be held by Disney UTV. Approving the transaction, the CCI observed that the market for aggregation of TV channels was competitive stating that 'even after the combination there will be 24 aggregators in the market which would provide enough competition in the market'.

[17] ESPN is a provider of sports coverage.
[18] Case C-2012/07/64 *Notice for acquisition by STARTV ATC Holding Limited*, 28 September 2012.
[19] Case C-2012/03/47 *Notice for acquisition filed by Independent Media Trust*, 28 May 2012.
[20] Case C-2013/01/107 *Notice for acquisition given by UTV Global Broadcasting Limited*, 19 February 2013.

5.3.3 Merger Control and Minority Interests

Schedule I of the Competition Commission of India (Procedure in regard to the transaction of business relating to combinations) Regulations 2011 (No 3 of 2011)[21] lists the categories of transactions not likely to have AAE on competition in India and which would typically qualify for exemption from filing. In other words, there is normally no need to file a notice when the combination falls under one of these categories.

One particular category relates to the acquisition of a minority interest. There is no requirement to file a notification where the transaction involves an acquisition of shares or voting rights that does not exceed 25 per cent of the total shares or voting rights held by the acquirer in the company, solely as an investment or in the ordinary course of business, not leading to an acquisition of control. The 25 per cent threshold was put in place to align Indian merger control with the position under the takeover regulations. In these circumstances, any attempt to lower the threshold would run counter to the developments under merger control. In light of yet further proposals to reform Indian merger control referred to in chapter 5, section 5.3.5, there is every reason to seek consistency in the regulation of mergers and combinations under the different rules.

5.3.4 Cases Involving Corporate Restructurings

The combinations that have come under CCI scrutiny have ranged from transactions between undertakings that prior to the combination were entirely independent, to internal restructurings. This is due in large part to two features of Indian merger control. First, as noted, Indian merger control captures the acquisition of a minority interest exceeding 25 per cent. Second, the exemption for intra-group transactions currently applies only to transactions where the relevant parties are wholly owned by a common parent.

To illustrate the potentially wide reach of Indian merger control to corporate restructurings which do not affect the competitive landscape, on 28 August 2012 the CCI approved the proposed combination of WBBS Delhi, WBBS Kerala, and WBBS Haryana into Wireless Business Services Private Limited pursuant to a scheme of amalgamation.[22] The CCI approved the combination unconditionally observing that the shareholding pattern of the parties was essentially the same before and after the transaction. The case is one of many similar restructurings that have been examined by the CCI and considered by it as raising no substantive issues. The case further highlights the 'belt and braces' nature of Indian merger control that applies to a variety of transactions and structures.

[21] As amended by the Competition Commission of India (Procedure in regard to the transaction of business relating to combinations) Amendment Regulations 2012 (No 1 of 2012).

[22] Case C-2012/07/66 *Notice for merger of WBBS Delhi, WBBS Kerala and WBBS Haryana into Wireless Business Services Private Limited*, 28 August 2012.

5.3.5 Ongoing Development of the Indian Competition Law and Merger Control Framework

The Competition (Amendment) Bill, 2012 seeks to confer increased autonomy on the CCI in enforcing the Competition Act, as well as some fine-tuning in the investigatory functions of the CCI.

A number of proposed changes are significant from the perspective of the CCI's ability to review transactions generally and in the media and communications in particular:

— Group: The threshold in order to constitute a 'group' when determining the relevant turnover or assets for merger control is increased to 50 per cent. The current provision defines a group as two or more enterprises that exercise 26 per cent voting rights in each other. This development indicates a trend towards reeling back of enforcement.

— Sector-specific merger control thresholds: A new provision will give the Central Government the power to specify different values of assets and turnover for any class of enterprises for merger control purposes. This could lead to different thresholds for the media and communications sector.

— References from and to statutory authorities: Mandatory references of issues by statutory authorities (including sector regulators) to the CCI and from the CCI to the statutory authorities. Currently, such references between the CCI and statutory authorities occur on a discretionary basis. This should allow for more streamlined enforcement within the CCI as the specialist competition regulator in consultation with relevant sector authorities including the TRAI.

5.4 COMPARATIVE SURVEY OF REGULATORY MODELS

5.4.1 Methodology

We examine the regulatory models that countries have adopted to seek to address concentration in the media and to promote pluralism.

Our survey is primarily descriptive and deliberately selective, focusing on a sample of regulatory regimes which exhibit a range of features, political and cultural contexts and different stages of evolution.

5.4.2 Countries Surveyed

The country regimes addressed in this chapter include: Belgium, Denmark, the EU, Finland, France, Germany, Greece, Italy, the Netherlands, Spain, Sweden, the UK and the US. Our review is based on the law, regulation and policy in the countries profiled at the time of writing.[23] Our examination is not intended to be an exhaustive commentary on the particular regimes; rather we illustrate key themes supplemented by the use of case study examples or 'vignettes'.

We note for comparative purposes that the European regulatory regime reflects a multi-layered system and division of competencies between the EU and the 28 Member States. Sector-neutral merger control applies at EU level where 'concentrations with a Union dimension' (ie large cross-border transactions meeting certain thresholds) are generally reviewed exclusively by the European Commission under the EU Merger Regulation (EUMR).[24] The substantive test for clearance is a competition test. The EUMR also contains mechanisms for the reallocation of jurisdiction between the European Commission and the national authorities to review mergers on competition grounds[25] and also on grounds of 'legitimate interest'.[26] The concept of legitimate interest covers plurality of the media.

The EU-wide regulatory system is complemented by the national merger control systems in the EU, which apply where the EUMR thresholds are not satisfied, which all have different tests for intervention.

The structure is also complicated by a patchwork of different national regulatory regimes including sector-specific controls and regulators (whether at national, regional or local level as the case may be). The result is a multi-faceted allocation of competencies within the EU.

A similar plethora of controls is present, though to a lesser extent, in the US. There are multiple federal (national), state and local government agencies potentially involved. The basic sector-specific Act is the Communications Act of 1934. The national regulator, the Federal Communications Commission (FCC), regulates interstate and international telecommunications, non-military uses of the radio frequency spectrum, over-the-air broadcast television and radio, and certain aspects of cable television content, but generally not internet backbone networks or peering arrangements. State and territorial public utilities commissions regulate intrastate telecommunications services. The Federal Trade Commission (FTC) regulates trade practices, marketing, privacy, and data protection in the communications sector, except for common-carrier services.

5.4.3 Regime Type

The regulatory regimes differ in the extent to which they employ one or a combination of: (i) regulation of ownership including cross-ownership through cross-ownership restrictions; (ii) mainstream merger control using a competition-based

[23] December 2013.

[24] Regulation (EC) No 139/2004 of 20 January 2004 on the control of concentrations between undertakings, [2004] OJ L24.

[25] EUMR, Articles 4(4), 4(5), 9 and 22.

[26] EUMR, Article 21.

substantive assessment; and (iii) modification of merger control or cross-ownership rules to address plurality.

Although the regimes differ and are influenced by cultural and political perspectives, some common features emerge in terms of the regulatory models that can be identified. These vary in their complexity and media-specificity (Model A = least media-specific and simplest; Model C = highly media-specific and complex).[27] We summarise these regime models in Figure 5 below. We adopt our categorisation based on the features that the country regulation displays as a whole and not on its application within a particular segment of the media (eg newspapers).

It should be noted that within the broad 'models' particular regimes may differ, sometimes markedly, in terms of the approaches adopted. For example, within Model B we discern a variety of approaches towards ownership cap restrictions (whether in the form of hard caps based on market share, audience share or some other metric). Within Model C, the manner in which countries apply a modified substantive approach to capture plurality issues can range from a competition law proxy in terms of market share (Greece) to a more targeted qualitative approach (UK).

Model	Description
Model A	No media ownership rules and sole application of competition rules in merger control
Model B	Media ownership rules and sole application of competition rules in merger control
Model C	Media ownership rules and modified application of competition rules in merger control

Figure 5: Regime models

Source: Authors' analysis

In presenting these models a number of overriding themes emerge.

First, the media regulatory environment as it affects ownership and plurality is diverse and complex. Second, the technical descriptions of these regimes and their market, political and cultural context emphasises that they cannot be separated from that context. They should not be taken as a blueprint for export into a wholly different market environment where the local context is very different. Third, even those regimes, such as that of the UK, which are more complex, have developed over a number of years and are not without costs. The regimes have been implemented by specialist regulators that have had a track record of dealing with similar issues.

Further, recent attempts to incorporate plurality tests without a Regulatory Impact Assessment and proper consultation with industry have floundered. The month of March 2013 saw the release—and eleventh hour withdrawal—of hotly contested reforms to Australian media regulation.[28] The proposed reforms comprise four Bills affecting media ownership and regulation of media

[27] A similar high-level conceptual categorisation is identified in Mediadem, 'The regulatory quest for independent media', July 2012.

[28] See, further, chapter 9, section 9.5.

professionals, and incorporated a controversial plurality test. They attracted vociferous condemnation from the media industry's most prominent leaders including public statements from News Limited and Ten Networks. Serious reservations were expressed about the content of the Bills, and the fact that they were presented without proper consultation with industry and the Opposition. The political repercussions of the aborted proposals are only just being felt. This recent experience, should, at the very least, urge newer regulators to apply caution in implementing radical reforms without an assessment of underlying regulatory failure and the appropriateness of the proposed regime for the specific market.

5.5 CASE STUDIES

To illustrate the operation of the above models in their market context it is useful to examine examples of regimes which correspond to the various models. The level of ownership concentration differs across the countries surveyed with some regimes having stricter or more flexible regimes than others.

We note that the rules operating in a particular country cannot be separated from the legal, economic and, most importantly, political context in which they take place. This is inherent in the nature of plurality which is designed to safeguard values that are commonly recognised as underpinning modern democracies. It is possible—indeed expected—that the rules discussed in our report will change. For example, in Italy, changes in government are expected to influence the future direction of Italian media ownership.

5.5.1 Model A: No Media Ownership Rules and Sole Application of Competition Rules in Merger Control

Sweden

Sweden's media industry is the largest in Scandinavia. Over the years, the Swedish and other Scandinavian governments have cooperated to seek to ensure effective competition and to address fears that more financially powerful Swedish companies will be able to gain market power across the Scandinavian media sector. This has contributed to an environment where there are few restrictions on media ownership. There are no sector-specific controls on ownership of the media in Sweden and mainstream competition-based merger control applies to mergers and acquisitions (M&A) and joint ventures in the sector.

The Netherlands

The Netherlands was comparatively late in liberalising its media and terrestrial broadcasting sector with the first commercial and private broadcasting licences issued in 1990. Since then it has made significant advances and has now removed restrictions on companies merging or acquiring assets in individual media segments and across the media beyond mainstream competition law.

As of 1 January 2011, the Netherlands withdrew temporary legislation on media concentrations which prohibited cross-ownership of daily newspapers, radio and television activities in one group if the individual market share on any of these three markets was higher than 35 per cent, and the sum of the individual market shares (on either two or three markets) after the transaction exceeded 90 per cent.[29] Therefore, there are no specific rules dealing with cross-ownership. Hence cross-ownership of media companies is only assessed under competition-based merger control and competition laws.

It should be noted that the outcomes in Model A regimes may be achieved in countries which adopt more complex controls and where reviews by the sector regulator and the competition authority achieve the same result.

A case in point is the US where both the FCC and the antitrust agency may scrutinise a transaction in the media and communications sector. On 10 October 2002, the US communications authority, the FCC, announced that it had declined to approve the transfer of licences from EchoStar Communications Corporation, and Hughes Electronics Corporation, a subsidiary of General Motors Corporation, to a new entity. The FCC effectively rejected any idea that the transaction could be modified to allay its concerns, notwithstanding that it had approved transactions after accepting commitments from the merged entity.

The FCC reached its decision before the Antitrust Division of the Department of Justice reached its own decision welcoming the decision by the parties to abandon the transaction.[30] This is not the place to discuss the merits or otherwise of this outcome. Rather, the case points to the fact that mainstream competition-based merger control and sector-specific controls can lead to the same result by different routes.

5.5.2 Model B: Media Ownership Rules and Sole Application of Competition Rules in Merger Control

France

France has stringent and complex media ownership rules. For example, in the broadcasting sector, French law provides for a maximum holding of 49 per cent of a company that has an authorisation to provide a national terrestrial television

[29] See, further, Commissariaat voor de Media, 'Media Monitor, The Dutch Media in 2010', February 2011.

[30] Department of Justice press release, 'Statement by R. Hewitt Pate on the abandonment of the Hughes/Echostar Transaction', 10 December 2002, available at: www.justice.gov/atr/public/press_releases/2002/200539.htm.

service, where the average audience for this service (whether digital or analogue) exceeds 8 per cent. Any person who already holds a national terrestrial television service, where the average audience for this service exceeds 8 per cent, may not directly or indirectly hold more than 33 per cent of a company that has an authorisation to provide a local terrestrial television service.

Cross-media ownership in France is not prohibited outright but is subject to controls. The granularity of the regulation is cited here not as an example of an approach that should necessarily be emulated, but to illustrate that it is at the extreme of media-specific regulation. The holder of more than 15 per cent of a company operating a national terrestrial television channel may not hold more than 15 per cent of another company active in the same sector. The holder of more than 5 per cent of two companies with authorisation to provide a national terrestrial television channel service may not hold more than 5 per cent of a third company.

There is also a 'two-in-three' rule whereby operators may not, beyond certain thresholds, operate or control more than two out of three of certain types of media. This applies at French national, regional and local level.

Although the regulations in France may be regarded as a textbook example of the application of rigid media ownership caps, the regime has to be understood in its political and cultural context. France has a long history of government censorship going back to the sixteenth and eighteenth centuries. Today, the freedom of the press is guaranteed by the French Constitution.

It is not surprising that in the context of this distinctly Gallic culture there has also been an impetus to resist any form of 'economic' censorship as a result of any voice becoming overwhelmingly powerful owing to a concentration of media ownership. This has manifested itself, on the one hand, in strict formulaic ownership controls. That said, this has stopped short of any special media rules in the merger control context where a pure competition analysis is deemed sufficient. Thus, even a country that may be considered to be an outlier in terms of media ownership regulation has elements of moderation in its pure competition based approach to merger control in the media sector.

5.5.3 Model C: Media Ownership Rules and Modified Application of Competition Rules in Merger Control

United Kingdom

Regulation of the UK media industry has a long history. Over the years the government has stripped away restrictions on media ownership which has created a more attractive environment for investment.

The Communications Act 2003 substantially removed former restrictions on cross-media ownership in the UK by removing certain prohibitions and raising the relevant market share thresholds. The Media Ownership (Radio and Cross-media) Order 2011[31] was enacted in June 2011 and removed all local cross-media ownership restrictions.

However, the UK currently displays one of the more complex systems for control of media concentration and plurality. A detailed summary of the media plurality merger control regime in the UK is set out in Appendix 2.

The first case under the current legislation where the SoS has intervened in a (media) merger on public interest grounds was the aborted acquisition of BSkyB by News International/News Corporation.[32] Another newspaper case where the SoS considered the case for intervention was Northern & Shell's acquisition of Channel 5 from RTL.[33] This transaction completed on 23 July 2010, without prior notification to the Office of Fair Trading (OFT). The SoS did not, however, intervene in this case, largely on the basis that Channel 5 was not a major source of news in the UK. In addition, Northern & Shell newspaper titles (the *Daily Star*, *Daily Express* and the *Sunday Express*) had a significantly lower market share—in the region of 10 to 14 per cent—compared to 37 per cent for News International titles at the time.

The public interest procedure continues to evolve and there is limited government guidance apart from the (old) guidance of the Department of Trade and Industry (now Business, Innovation & Skills) on the operation of the public interest provisions relating to newspaper and other media mergers.[34] This is despite a decade of experience by specialist regulators in implementing the rules. Ofcom has, however, provided new guidance to government on specific aspects of plurality, which we discuss below.

5.6 THE ONGOING DEBATE ON MEDIA PLURALITY

Our brief survey has been primarily descriptive of the status quo in the relevant regimes. However, the debate among regulators and policy-makers in this area is on-going and remains polemic. A few examples will serve to illustrate the issues that have been faced even by countries who have had experience applying controls on plurality. In short, there is no 'one size fits all' and while pockets of consensus emerge, this is not universal.

[31] The Media Ownership (Radio and Cross-media) Order 2011, SI 2011/1503.

[32] Department for Business, Innovation & Skills press release, 'Secretary of State for Business, Vince Cable, has today issued an intervention notice on News Corp's proposal to acquire the BSkyB shares that it does not already own', 4 November 2010, available at: news.bis.gov.uk/content/Detail.aspx?ReleaseID=416355&NewsAreaID=2.

[33] RTL press release, 'RTL Group sells UK broadcaster Five', 23 July 2010, available at: www.rtlgroup.com/www/htm/home_news.aspx?ID=C57D4206AF294A979A24C3EE4270E175.

[34] Department of Trade and Industry, 'Guidance on the operation of the public interest merger provisions relating to newspapers and other media mergers', Guidance Document, May 2004.

Clearly, media plurality is important; a crucial feature of a democratic society and a valid policy objective. However, it is difficult to define (more so in practice than in theory) and challenging to measure. In particular, identifying a definitive way to measure cross-media plurality remains tricky; there is no acceptable cross-media exchange rate. This boils down to the fact that 'impact' or 'influence' is almost impossible to assess. Thus, trying to calculate the consumption of TV, radio, newspaper and online news is fraught with difficulties.

5.6.1 Academic Perspectives

The European Commission has engaged a consortium of consultants and academics to conduct a major study on media plurality across EU Member States. Its objectives were to consider appropriate metrics to measure media plurality, and to monitor and indicate risks to media plurality. It developed a diagnostic tool, the 'Media Pluralism Monitor' which comprises more than 160 indicators.[35] And while a report was published in 2009, there appear to be no subsequent developments. This is not surprising—it seems unlikely that 28 Member States would compile and monitor 166 metrics.

Another study critically reviews how a number of plurality regimes have worked in practice, covering the Diversity Index in the US (2003), the public interest or plurality test in the UK (2003), the integrated communications system (SIC) in Italy (2004), and the German Commission on Concentration in the Media (KEK) approach to weighting the influence of various media in the context of its merger decision on ProSiebenSAT.1 Media AG and Axel Springer Media AG (2006).[36] The observations made in the paper are worth reproducing.

The study recognises the challenges of measuring media concentration where:

> The convergence of media, telecommunications and information technologies adds a new dimension to this problem as it results in changing market structures, exacerbating among other things the handling of cross-ownership and market definitions, and in claims for a greater emphasis on empirical evidence.[37]

However, it questions the KEK's approach commenting that:

> The instruments are novel but imperfect responses to the issues surrounding today's communications policy making. They have been appraised cautiously due to their methodological shortcomings and have been criticized outright: the [UK] plurality test applies only to mergers that would have been covered by the rules prior to their removal

[35] See, further, European Commission, 'Independent Study on Indicators for Media Pluralism, A monitoring tool for assessing risks for media pluralism in the EU Member States'. Details can be found at: ec.europa.eu/digital-agenda/en/independent-study-indicators-media-pluralism#the-final-output.

[36] Just, N, 'Measuring media concentration and diversity instruments in Europe and the US', DOI: 10.1177/0163443708098248, (2009) 31 *Media Culture & Society* 97.

[37] Ibid.

> by the 2003 Communications Act, the [US] DI neglects variations in size of media companies, the KEK's weighting approach arbitrarily assigns the equivalence of audience share in television to other media, and the SIC's market definition is too broad, thus rendering it unlikely that a company will have a dominant position under it.[38]

The study is highly critical of the various plurality regimes assessed, stating that none of the approaches are reliable or objective, and, importantly that there is a 'lack of sound empirical proof of whether they achieve what they are supposed to'.[39]

5.6.2 Regulatory Policy Perspectives

We also detect on the part of regulators themselves a trend of questioning of once 'tried-and-tested' mechanisms to see whether they are effective or need to be changed.

In the UK, the Leveson Report[40] and ongoing review of media ownership regulation has again reviewed the role that tighter or more sophisticated rules could play in promoting plurality. Ofcom has made some sensible recommendations in identifying the market characteristics that when present are indicative of sufficient plurality. Its suggestion that it is appropriate to examine a range of metrics 'in the round' and make a subjective judgement is sensible and echoes the approach adopted by the Competition Commission in *ITV/BSkyB*.[41] However, this conclusion comes after many years of soul searching by an experienced regulator and many distractions along the way. It by no means follows that an approach 'in the round' is appropriate in all regulatory regimes given the inherent subjectivity of such a benchmark.

In the US there is still vigorous debate on the scope and content of media ownership rules. On 22 December 2011 the FCC proposed changes to its media ownership rules.[42] The FCC is required by statute to review its media ownership rules every four years to determine whether they are 'necessary in the public interest as the result of competition'. The final vote on the new rules was expected to take place in early 2013. However, on 26 February 2013 the FCC announced a delay while the FCC conducts an impact study on how cross-ownership affects minority ownership.

Chapter 9 provides further details on the ongoing media ownership regulatory debate internationally. In the UK concerns have arisen that the plurality test is subjective and vague and could be subject to political interference. In the US

[38] Ibid.

[39] Ibid.

[40] Lord Justice Leveson, 'An inquiry into the culture, practices and ethics of the press' Report No 0780 2012–13, 29 November 2012.

[41] Competition Commission, *Acquisition by British Sky Broadcasting Group Plc of 17.9 per cent of the shares in ITV Plc, Report sent to Secretary of State (BERR) 14 December 2007.*

[42] For a more detailed discussion, see chapter 9, section 9.6.

concerns have arisen that hard limits on media ownership should themselves be subject to discretionary application but with as yet no clear consensus on how that should be applied. Reforms have been proposed at EU level and in Australia. The protracted and, at the time of writing, ultimately inconclusive positions in these countries have led observers to question whether these tests provide a benchmark to be emulated overseas and in countries which have no prior experience of applying media ownership controls.

5.7 NEWSPAPERS—A SPECIAL CASE?

5.7.1 Background

Newspapers, news and current affairs are at the heart of democracy, holding governments, businesses and individuals to account. A healthy and vibrant press is vital to free speech. The relationship between competition and pluralism is well illustrated by the case study of the print media.

In India, the story of the print media presents some interesting contrasts. According to KPMG, the Indian print industry grew by 7.3 per cent from INR 209 billion in 2011 to INR 224 billion in 2012.[43] While this was lower than the analyst expected, it still represents a year-on-year growth whereas in many other countries, including the UK, the press is in long-term decline. Of the more than 70,000 newspapers printed in India, around 90 per cent are published in Hindi and other vernaculars. The market ranges from national dailies such as *Times of India*, *Hindu*, *Hindustan*, *Indian Express*, *Statesman* and *Telegraph*, to smaller dailies published in Hindi.

The growth of the sector and the sheer number of offerings, however, should not obscure the need for a closer inquiry into how the print media is functioning and the issues it presents from a competition and public interest perspective.

5.7.2 Drivers of Consolidation

A high dependence on advertising revenues means that the growth of the Indian print industry will inevitably be dampened by stagnated economic performance. Following global trends, the Indian economy achieved a slower growth of only 5 per cent in 2012 to 2013 compared with 6.2 per cent in 2011 to 2012.[44] These economic pressures are not helped by the fall in the value of the rupee, which has a concomitant effect on the cost of imported newsprint.

[43] KPMG, 'FICCI—KPMG Media & Entertainment report 2013', 12 March 2013.
[44] Ibid.

In these circumstances, it can be expected that print houses will look to consolidation rather than aggressive organic expansion. While the CCI has not yet developed its analytical approach in relation to newspaper mergers, it will be interesting to see how it grapples with the attempts of merging parties to achieve cost efficiencies through consolidation.

A different story seems to be emerging at the national and regional levels, with the regional press exhibiting signs of more promising growth. However, only time will tell whether, and to what extent, this is sustainable. As KPMG's Head of Media and Entertainment in India has observed:

> The print industry's dependence on advertising resulted in lower than expected growth in 2012. National advertisers revised plans although regional markets still proved to be an area of growth. We see this trend continuing in 2013 and beyond as regional continues to be the engine of growth.[45]

Appendix 3 provides a case study examination of how the UK and US have grappled with economic and competition issues in the print sector. It will be evident from the experience to date that there have been some policy blunders along the way, in the UK at least. For many print houses in the UK, consolidation was the only way forward since remaining small scale did not make economic sense. The lessons for India, which is experiencing some growth in the print sector, are not yet clear and we cannot discern the conclusion of such trends. However, it is hoped that as the print story plays out in India the regulators will examine what has happened overseas and will resist creating obstacles that might imperil the sector's future viability.

5.7.3 Paid News, Politics and Pluralism

The relationship between India's political and business leaders and the press has become a topic of intense scrutiny in the ensuing debate on controls over media ownership. A selection of examples will serve to illustrate the somewhat uneasy association between public figures and news groups. For example, there is no shortage of high-profile political figures who also enjoy prominent ties to media groups: Bhartia of the *Hindustan* group, the Marans of the *Sun* group and Chandan Mitra of *The Pioneer* to name only some.

In itself, the fact that specific individuals who enjoy a public or political persona also have affiliations with a news outlet should not lead to the conclusion that any such link should be banned. To do so would amount to a form of censorship reminiscent of an earlier era.

However, the proximity between the media and India's political figures raises tensions and risks confusion over policy priorities. A focus of the TRAI's media

[45] Ibid.

ownership consultation was on whether there should be an absolute ban on any category of person owning a segment of the media.[46] Behind this question lurks a thinly disguised concern over the relationship between politicians and the media and between the political process and the news business.

It is one thing to place restraints on political parties owning, controlling or otherwise being affiliated with the media. However, to extend that principle to a limit on corporate control simply because an individual promoter espouses views which may be considered extreme or objectionable, raises more complex issues. In such a debate it is vital to distinguish the two issues of plurality and fitness to own a media enterprise.

For example, it may be that a particular transaction would result in a loss of plurality owing to the simple reduction in controllers. However, if the criteria by which acceptable plurality is measured relates to post-transaction sufficiency (of plurality), a merger which reduces the number of independent voices may still not raise plurality issues assuming that there remains sufficient plurality in the overall media landscape.

The plurality inquiry described above is separate from the question of whether the particular media owner should be allowed to control the relevant enterprise or if his conduct otherwise makes him unfit. Such a dichotomy has been debated at length in the *News of the World* hacking incident in the UK and will not be repeated here. Suffice to say that policy-makers devising rules to combat exploitation of the media for political ends need to be clear on the issue of concern and then develop rules which properly address the concern (whether it is plurality, competition, or fitness to own a media enterprise).

5.7.4 Emerging Insights from the UK

Our examination of how economic forces driving consolidation are playing out in the UK regional press yields some important insights for those reviewing and dealing in the sector. At present, the Indian regional press seems to be in a healthier state than its UK counterpart. There is, therefore, even more of an imperative for regulators to take a long hard look at what has happened overseas and to consider how they might (with the benefit of ongoing regulatory experience internationally) do things differently in their own jurisdiction faced with actual or prospective challenges. Although the CCI has yet to develop a detailed analytical framework for appraising mergers in the print sector, a review of the UK case experience may suggest some departure points.

[46] Telecom Regulatory Authority of India, 'Consultation Paper on Issues relating to Media Ownership', 15 February 2013.

There can be merger control jurisdiction over what appears to be a 'small' part of the nation or market. In one UK case, *Topper*,[47] the number of households potentially affected amounted to just over 1 per cent of total UK households, yet this was deemed enough to constitute a 'substantial part of the UK'. The share of supply test for determining jurisdiction under UK merger control is not an economic market test. Although the jurisdictional test under Indian merger control is a turnover and asset test, the question of the effect on the market—and whether this is an AAE—will be relevant at the stage of substantive assessment.

There is a relatively low threshold for referrals to a second-stage review in cases where there are material (narrowly defined) geographic overlaps. The UK adopts a cautious approach. However, the prospect of a lengthy review (between six and eight months) can sometimes lead to the transaction being abandoned by the parties irrespective of its commercial merits. A similar delay can occur under Indian merger control which has up to a review period.

The market analysis and evidence to support the competition case needs to be detailed and compelling. The UK considers advertising markets very narrowly and does not appear to have embraced the major changes taking place in the consumption and provision of news and, specifically, the effects of online and social media. However, it remains open to the parties to argue such constraints at the second stage. Such issues should be factors that the CCI (which decides both the first and second stage under Indian merger control) should examine.

Ex post market share per se is not the issue; rather the issue is whether *ex post* there is a substantial lessening of competition (a very similar test to that under Indian merger control which is an inquiry as to whether the merger produces an AAE on competition in the relevant market in India). In determining this issue, the UK takes into account both the closeness of competition between the parties, and competitive constraints. Consequently, it is significant whether the merger is between rivals or non-rivals in any particular market.

The UK provides a precedent for involvement of the sector regulator Ofcom in the local market appraisal. Although the final decision on whether to clear or refer a transaction remains that of the competition authority, Ofcom can provide analysis informed by its specialist expertise. Not all cases will require the same intensity of analysis but there may be a role for the TRAI to supplement the CCI's assessment in appropriate cases. Merging parties should do their homework by assessing the most narrow markets conceivable before merging and be prepared to offer remedies (usually divestment), if appropriate.

[47] Office of Fair Trading, *Anticipated acquisition by Northcliffe Media Limited of Topper Newspapers Limited, The OFT's decision on reference*, 1 June 2012.

5.8 CONCLUSIONS AND IMPLICATIONS FOR POLICY

Our survey of media ownership rules has been primarily descriptive and narrative. This is deliberate and serves to illustrate the history and market context underpinning the relevant regimes and how they have developed. Only after having considered that context can India decide whether, given elements of congruence (if any) between the overseas regimes and India, it is appropriate to draw inspiration from that experience when designing India's approach.

We identify below the key trends which are emerging. The omnipresent trend is that there is no 'one size fits all' and the regime design choice cannot be divorced from the political and cultural environment in which it takes place. However, some features tend to be recurrent.

— General application of competition law: In all the countries in our survey, competition law and mainstream sector-neutral merger control is applicable regardless of the sector. India has a solid platform with a modern competition authority—the CCI—already actively enforcing competition law and competition-based merger control in the media and communications sector.
— Sole application of competition law: Some countries adopt only sector-neutral regulation where the media sector is subject to the same regulation as other sectors and there are no additional requirements or controls (eg Denmark, the Netherlands and Sweden). In India, the CCI is building up experience in this area. It has issued significant decisions in the media and communications sector and beyond in relation to mergers, agreements and commercial practices. No arguments or evidence have been put forward by the TRAI or others to demonstrate that the CCI is not able to address threats to competition effectively. No assessment has been put forward to demonstrate that there are significant 'gap' cases where competition law cannot address concerns as to media diversity. This would imply that reliance on competition law alone is the most appropriate option for India unless and until a robust Regulatory Impact Assessment of the alternatives is conducted.
— Cooperation between competition and sector regulator: In the absence of sector-specific regulation—and even where there are sector specific rules—there is cooperation between the competition authority and the sector regulator (eg Finland, the UK). Refraining from implementing media-specific controls in India does not mean that sector insights cannot complement and enhance the operation of the competition regime. There are already initiatives underway in India through the pending reform to competition law that are designed to bring about a more efficient and predictable division of functions between the CCI and sector regulators.
— Targeted ownership restrictions: Where ownership restrictions or caps apply, there tend to be differences depending on the type of media or concentration. There is no universally accepted approach among regulators. Rather, there is an appreciation of the need to take account of the

specifics of individual media market segments. The trend is away from a 'sledgehammer' use of a blunt instrument to tackle complex issues. There tend to be few restrictions on ownership of the press or concentration between newspaper companies. Where cross-media regulation is present, this tends to be applicable mainly to the broadcasting sector (eg Germany). The position in India is fundamentally different, where there is no licensing of private terrestrial broadcasters. Any risk of a private broadcaster using or leveraging its broadcasting presence into other segments of the media is not present.

— Cross-media ownership regulation places no impediment on ownership across traditional and new media (ie a print newspaper provider distributing online). The evolution of new media affects media regulators in two main ways. First, at the definitional level there is no compelling need to differentiate between traditional and new media in terms of the regulation imposed provided there is functional equivalence. Second, the explosion of new media in the last decade has radically transformed the media landscape. This in itself creates additional diversity which tends to obviate the need for intrusive controls that were developed for a very different regulatory era.

— Licensing: The licensing system is also used to supplement competition law or sector-specific controls, particularly in the broadcasting sector (eg in Belgium, France and the UK). This impacts both the number of licensed providers, and the content that is disseminated. In this way, the licensing system may serve as a screen which seeks to promote pluralism by ensuring that licensed providers observe certain minimum requirements such as impartiality and accuracy. Such controls may resemble the controls on political parties owning segments of the media. A targeted approach that is the minimum necessary to address a demonstrable market failing would be consistent with international norms and could supplement the role of the CCI. Indeed, this would be consistent with regimes which have some sector-specific modifications for the media sector. In this way, the two laws inform each other and the strictest rule applies—whether that is a sector-specific rule or general competition law. This is not a matter of treating media as a 'special case' but of finding a problem and seeking to correct it with a targeted solution.

— Sector-specific rules on plurality: Some countries have supplemented their media ownership rules and mainstream merger control with sector-specific substantive rules or presumptions. These tend to be the exception and vary in sophistication. Two approaches emerge (i) adoption of proxies for measuring plurality such as market share thresholds (eg in Greece); and (ii) employing a specific substantive quantitative and qualitative assessment which seeks to define plurality more accurately (eg in the UK). A 'bright line' market share threshold may have advantages in terms of ease of application but it suffers in being a blunt instrument that gives no scope for qualitative assessment. The latter approach has been criticised as expensive, complex and unclear in its application.

— Evolution: The regulatory regime is subject to evolution. Overall, there can be seen to be a reeling back of ownership regulations whether in the form of ownership caps or restrictions by category of owner (eg in the Netherlands and the UK).
— Risk of political capture: It is also important to keep in sight that many of these laws take place against a background of lobbying by interest groups. It is observed that ownership caps are often influenced by the need for the preservation of incumbent interests (or, conversely, may be targeted to address certain combinations which were deemed inimical to the public interest). At a time when India is keen to maintain its position as a destination for investment and a 'halo' jurisdiction among the BRIC countries,[48] it should be wary of embarking on additional layers of regulation that are politically expedient in the short term and damaging to economic growth in the longer term.
— Risk of unintended consequences: In the absence of a Regulatory Impact Assessment there is a significant risk that India could embark on regulation that is not fit for purpose and is based on outdated market research. Far from correcting a market failure that has not been demonstrated, the result could be significant damage to markets. Such a course is also likely to undermine the credibility of the Indian regulatory regime. This is particularly worrying at a time when India's regulatory system is gaining credibility internationally and in particular through the work of the CCI. An example of the political repercussions of regulation proposed in the absence of a Regulatory Impact Assessment and amid vehement opposition is the recent collapse of the Australian media reforms as discussed further in chapter 9, section 9.5.
— Inherent challenges of measuring plurality: Policy-makers around the world are facing similar challenges: how best to measure plurality, whether or not online media should be included, and how best to achieve a balance between fulfilling policy objectives and not restricting markets. Where they exist, ownership restrictions tend to be simple and crude (albeit arbitrary) for both mono- and cross-media cases; complex measurement systems are not an observed trend. This is not surprising as weighting the relative influence of the various news media is problematic; it is subjective, subject to challenge and difficult to justify on empirical or *a priori* grounds. This situation raises serious doubts about whether India should embark on specific plurality controls at a nascent phase in the evolution of its competition regime. At the very least, there is much to be said for allowing the CCI to consider a number of cases—and cases that have withstood judicial scrutiny where appropriate—before embarking on a more elaborate regime.

[48] Brazil, Russia, India and China.

6

Vertical Integration

6.1 INTRODUCTION

Consolidation of previously distinct enterprises (whether through merger, acquisition, joint venture or strategic alliance) can be viewed through a number of different lenses, depending on where the companies operate and interact in the supply chain.

A convenient economic distinction is between: (i) horizontal issues (ie arising in mergers between companies operating at the same level in the supply chain, such as between two mobile telephony networks); (ii) vertical issues (ie arising in mergers between companies operating at different but related levels in the supply chain, such as between a film producer and distributor; (iii) conglomerate (ie arising in mergers between companies who operate in different markets which may be upstream, downstream or neighbouring such as between a newspaper, internet service provider and TV channel).

In the media and communications sector, there has been a notable trend towards vertical integration and this is a feature of concentrations that has been examined closely by the competition authorities. The extension of the presence of a company across the value chain brings economic efficiencies. At the same time, it can present competition issues where the company possesses market power at one or more levels in the supply chain.

In this chapter we outline:

— the economic drivers of mergers in the media and communications sector and the economic issues raised by vertical integration;
— recurrent themes in the competition assessment of vertical integration; and
— the ways competition authorities internationally have approached the issue of vertical integration and how they have sought to balance the goals of economic efficiency and competition, permitting consolidation in the sector with or without conditions.

6.2 A SCHEMATIC OF THE MEDIA VALUE CHAIN

While relatively high-level, Figure 6 provides a schematic of the media value chain (drawn to encompass various media such as newspapers, pay TV, radio, free-to-air broadcasting etc). Clearly there are various technical interfaces between each of the stages (such as middleware, content distribution systems, conditional access systems etc) but the diagram indicates the important elements from 'ideas' through to a specific service delivered to the consumer. The diagram is important as it sets out a framework within which the competitive nature of each stage may be assessed should competition concerns arise. It is also useful in that it depicts at a high level structures that are observed in 'real world' companies.

Talent	Production	Packaging	Distribution	Supply	Consumer
Production companies	TV producers	TV producers	Fixed:(satellite/cable/terrestrial/copper/fibre)	FTA	TV
Sports bodies	Radio producers	Radio producers	Mobile/3G/4G	Content retailer	Radio
Actors/writers	Games producers	Games producers	Road/rail/post	Fixed telco	PC/laptop
Musicians/singers	Record producers	Record producers		Mobile telco	Tablet
Games developers	News producers	News producers		ISP	Smartphone
App developers	Web producers	Web producers		Publisher	Set-top box
Editors		ISPs/portals		Store	Home 'hub'
		Newspaper publishers			Printed copy

Figure 6: Indicative media value chain

Source: Authors' analysis and FTI Consulting

6.3 VERTICAL INTEGRATION IN AN ECONOMIC CONTEXT

The economic understanding of vertical integration and its practical implementation in competition policy and merger control has undergone substantial 'swings'. The changes in scholarly opinion and antitrust and merger practice reflect the fact that there are both positive effects from vertical integration in the form of efficiencies (such as consumer benefits arising from, say, lower prices), and potentially negative effects in the form of foreclosure of non-integrated rivals.

The swings also reflect a shift from competition policy as a tool for protecting competition to a tool for protecting consumers. Vertical integration may make it more difficult for non-integrated companies to compete and therefore competition policy would interfere frequently if the protection of competition/competitors was the objective.

However, due to the inherent efficiencies of vertical integration the greater difficulty for non-integrated competitors does not necessarily translate into harm for consumers. Instead, the difficulty could arise because non-integrated firms face a more efficient rival. Therefore, when competition policy's objective is to protect consumers, on this theory there should be less intervention.

6.3.1 Three Phases of Economic and Competition Policy Thought

Three phases can be distinguished in the development of economic and competition policy. Until around 1970, vertical integration and vertical mergers were judged very critically. This was due to the focus on protecting competition and competitors, combined with a failure to recognise the efficiencies of vertical integration.

The Chicago Law School then argued strongly and successfully for the efficiency rationale of vertical integration. It was argued that vertical integration arises due to these efficiencies rather than with the aim to foreclose competitors. It was also argued that there is only one profit to be made in the market and a single integrated firm might be better placed to exploit that profit.

More recently, a more nuanced approach has been developed. The context of individual situations now plays a more important role. However, the pendulum of research and opinion has by no means swung back to a damning view of vertical integration. On the contrary, there is a presumption that vertical integration and vertical mergers are less harmful than horizontal mergers. This view is stated most clearly in the non-horizontal merger guidelines by the European Commission:

> Non-horizontal mergers are generally less likely to significantly impede effective competition than horizontal mergers.
>
> First, unlike horizontal mergers, vertical or conglomerate mergers do not entail the loss of direct competition between the merging firms in the same relevant market. As a result, the main source of anti-competitive effect in horizontal mergers is absent from vertical and conglomerate mergers.
>
> Second, vertical and conglomerate mergers provide substantial scope for efficiencies.[1]

The 2013 consultation by the Telecom Regulatory Authority of India (TRAI) on media ownership raises a concern over vertical integration between programming (broadcasting/content services) and access to consumers (distribution services).[2] The consultation paper states that

> [m]ore and more broadcasting companies owning television channels are venturing into various distribution platforms ... Similarly, many companies owning distribution platforms are also entering into television broadcasting.
>
> Though the vertical integration of various entities within a particular sector results in reduction in cost to the company as well as offers economies of scale, it often manifests in the form of ills of monopolies viz. higher cost to the consumers, blocking of competition, higher entry barrier for the new players to venture into the sector, deter innovations, deterioration of the quality of service to the consumers in the long run etc.[3]

This thinking appears quite similar to US and European antitrust thought before the Chicago Law School's arguments, that is, prior to the 1970s. It is hostile to vertical integration. We believe that the approach would benefit from the advances

[1] Commission guidelines on the assessment of non-horizontal mergers under the Council Regulation on the control of concentrations between undertakings, [2008] OJ C265/07, paragraphs 11–13.

[2] Telecom Regulatory Authority of India, 'Consultation Paper on Issues relating to Media Ownership', 15 February 2013, paragraph 6.1.

[3] Telecom Regulatory Authority of India, 'Consultation Paper on Issues relating to Media Ownership', 15 February 2013, paragraphs 6.1–6.2.

in economic thinking that have led to a more positive but still nuanced view of vertical integration.

6.3.2 A Last Preliminary: Vertical Integration and Vertical Restraints

A further initial insight into vertical integration is that such integration is not the only way for an upstream firm (a broadcaster) to enforce a certain type of behaviour on a downstream firm (the distributor). For this reason, economic theory has introduced the more general term 'vertical restraint'. An upstream firm can vertically restrain a downstream firm through a particular type of contract or conduct rather than owning the firm outright. The simplest such contract, which is viewed with hostility in many countries, is resale price maintenance. Under resale price maintenance, an upstream firm sets the retail price of the downstream firm. There are other contractual forms available to vertically restrain the behaviour of downstream firms: franchising, exclusive contracts and rebates are all ways in which an upstream firm attempts to influence the behaviour downstream.

Given that contractual restraints emulate vertical integration, it is correct for the TRAI to discuss these together. There are provisions in place by the TRAI that limit the use of vertical restraints. These include the requirement that every broadcaster must provide on request signals of its TV channels on a non-discriminatory basis to all distributors of TV channels including cable networks, Direct-to-home, Headend in the Sky. Further, no exclusive contracts are permitted between broadcasters and distributors of TV channels. In addition, broadcasters may not insist on guaranteed, minimum subscription amounts from distributors of TV channels.[4]

Given these basic provisions, which are already quite strict limitations on vertical restraints, it is advisable not to impose strict additional rules, such as market-share thresholds, above which vertical integration is no longer allowed. In such cases, firms might circumvent the regulation of vertical integration and instead use contracts to enforce vertical restraint by downstream (or upstream) companies that would still be allowed under the TRAI provisions. Such vertical restraint contracts, while having similar effects, may in some cases not yield the same efficiencies that would be obtained under vertical integration, such that the prohibition of vertical integration may lead to the undesired outcome of vertical restraint without compensating efficiency gains.

In our view, the vertical restraint limits in place combined with a review of vertical mergers on a case-by-case basis, and a review of other vertical clauses on the basis of existing Indian competition law, are significant regulatory tools which can be used to curb adverse market outcomes as a result of vertical integration. In this way, the risk of an efficiency loss through vertical separation would be minimised.

[4] Ibid, paragraph 6.7.

6.3.3 The Treatment of Vertical Restraints under Indian Competition Law

Indian competition law already has tools to address vertical restraints as discussed in chapter 4.

The treatment of agreements under the Competition Act 2002 (Competition Act) differs depending on whether horizontal arrangements (ie between enterprises or persons operating at the same level in the supply chain) or vertical arrangements (ie between enterprises or persons operating at different levels in the supply chain) are concerned. The treatment of vertical agreements is more nuanced than that relating to horizontal agreements, reflecting the need for an effects-based approach.

Horizontal arrangements, relating to price fixing, limitations on production or supply, market-sharing and bid-rigging, are presumed to have an appreciable adverse effect (AAE) on competition under section 3(3) of the Competition Act.

Vertical agreements, such as those between a supplier and a distributor, will be subject to a rule of reason-type analysis. Section 3(4) provides that vertical agreements (specifically, including resale price maintenance, exclusive supply or distribution agreements, tie-in arrangements or refusal to deal) will be considered agreements contained within the prohibition of anticompetitive agreements under section 3(1) if that agreement causes, or is likely to cause, an AAE on competition within the relevant markets in India.

Figure 7 contrasts the treatment of horizontal and vertical agreements under Indian competition law.

Horizontal agreements Between enterprises or persons operating at the same level in the supply chain	*Vertical agreements* Between enterprises or persons operating at different levels in the supply chain
Cartels (fixing directly, or indirectly, purchase or sale prices) *Limiting or controlling production, supply, markets or technical development, investment or provision* *Sharing markets or source of production or provision of services by allocation of geographic area of market, type of goods or services, number of customers in the market etc.* *Refusal to deal* *Bid rigging or collusive tendering*	*Tie in arrangements* *Exclusive supply* *Exclusive distribution* *Refusal to deal* *Resale price maintenance*
Presumed to have an appreciable adverse effect on competition	Subject to rule of reason-type approach (i.e. need to be assessed for effect on competition)

Figure 7: Horizontal and vertical agreements under Indian competition law

Source: Authors' analysis

6.3.4 Economic Reasoning of Vertical Integration: The Initial Sceptical View

The initial antitrust and merger control view which was held until around 1970, was that exclusive contracts and other types of vertical restraints were bad and that vertical mergers should be viewed with suspicion since they could foreclose competitors.

The foreclosure concern can apply both upstream and downstream. When an upstream firm and a downstream firm merge, the upstream firm may decide to no longer supply independent downstream competitors in order to avoid creating competition for its own downstream business. The downstream firm can, however, also decide to no longer buy from a rival of its new upstream parent and in this way foreclose the upstream firm's access to consumers. The thinking was that when a content firm and a distribution firm merge, the content firm may no longer provide content to other distributors; and the distributor may no longer buy content from other firms.

While the ability to foreclose rivals is present in these instances, the question of whether the vertically integrated firm has incentives to foreclose upstream or downstream is a further issue that needs to be understood. The reaction against the pre-Chicago Law School orthodoxy was that, usually, there is no such incentive to foreclose, and that, moreover, the reason why firms vertically integrate is for reasons of efficiency. Such efficiencies can be operational in their nature, but, more importantly, they can arise from overcoming the inefficiency of vertically separate contracting. The TRAI 2013 media ownership consultation does not appear to recognise that efficiencies are not only of an operational, but also of a contractual, nature.

6.3.5 Efficiency Gain of Vertical Integration: Avoiding Double Marginalisation

In addition to operational efficiencies, the competitive rationale for both vertical integration and the use of contracts to impose vertical restraints is the existence of the efficiency loss caused by 'double marginalisation' under separate ownership.

The reasoning is that when one compares vertically integrated firms with firms that are vertically separated, retail prices in the separated scenario can be higher since downstream firms' input prices already face a margin, to which they add a second margin. By adding a second margin, downstream firms do not take into account that the second margin leads to lower sales for the upstream firm. If, instead, the upstream and downstream firm agree on just one margin that is applied to the downstream price, prices would be lower and industry profits higher. An intuitive way to see this problem is that by fighting over the margin, upstream and downstream firms lose sight of the customer.

For the downstream firm, it is better to have a higher share of the total margin, even if the overall profit pool declines due to prices being too high for profit maximisation.

In the academic literature, the existence of double marginalisation has been shown to exist, for example, in the US cable industry.[5] It is shown that vertically integrated cable operators that both produce content and distribute TV have a larger subscriber base suggesting that they have better pricing. Further detail on the economic and competition law issues arising in the cable industry and from an international comparative perspective is provided in chapter 7.

The TRAI consultation appears unconvinced of economic efficiency in relation to vertical integration. This, however, is due to a narrow interpretation of economic efficiency as 'economies of scale' and therefore of an operational nature.[6] In contrast, the economic efficiency that is considered under the topic of 'double marginalisation' does not refer to greater operational efficiency and a lower cost of output, but to efficiency in contracting.

Once the efficiency of double marginalisation is considered, the question of foreclosure takes on a different meaning. A vertically merged firm will have incentives to use its downstream operation for efficiency reasons. This might mean that other downstream firms will not get the same favourable contractual conditions as the integrated retail arm.

The vertical merger, from a competition point of view, should, however, still go ahead since the other firms could still access the services. It is only the fact that they are more expensive to use for the upstream firm (and therefore less efficient) that they will get worse trading terms. In the worst case, the upstream firm will offer the monopoly price, but this still leaves the downstream firm able to operate. The upstream firm will not set a price higher than the monopoly price since that would hurt its own profits. Since there is only one profit to be made in the market, offering the monopoly price to downstream rivals does not undermine the integrated firm's vertically integrated business model. It has little reason to truly foreclose a rival.

6.3.6 More Nuanced Post-Chicago View

During the last decade or so, a 'post-Chicago' literature has developed which has introduced some nuances in this thinking. These include the potential foreclosure of upstream (content) firms through exclusive contracts if those firms are too

[5] Waterman, D and Weiss, A, 'The Effects of Vertical Integration between Cable Television Systems and Pay Cable Networks' (1996) 72 *Journal of Econometrics* 357–95.

[6] Telecom Regulatory Authority of India, 'Consultation Paper on Issues relating to Media Ownership', 15 February 2013, paragraphs 6.1–6.3.

small to satisfy the demand for the downstream firms.[7] A further nuance is the possibility that tacit collusion (coordinated behaviour) is enhanced by vertical mergers since the vertically integrated firm would be harmed less by a punishing price war, than it would benefit from lower wholesale prices.[8] There are further such examples. They all rely on special conditions that apply in certain circumstances, but not in others. The insight from this development for regulation of vertical integration should be that each vertical situation should be considered on its own merit.

Even with these new contributions to the literature that provide more nuance to the Chicago Law School view that vertical integration does not matter, it is not the case that the previous school of thought, that vertical integration was bad since foreclosure would occur, has been resurrected. This is due to the existence of double marginalisation. (ie, the problem of what happens to social welfare, prices and profits when one monopoly sells to another monopoly)

From the perspective of economic theory, therefore, there is little support for the TRAI's view of vertical integration as espoused in its 2013 consultation.

6.3.7 Efficiency Gain of Vertical Integration: Flexibility to Technological Change

In the media and communications industry, there is a further important element to vertical integration in addition to double marginalisation: technological change in communications results in supply and cost shocks that can very rapidly change the competitive position of market participants in the value chain.

Three examples suffice to illustrate this force. First, the digitalisation of distribution channels—whether via fibre, digital subscriber line (xDSL) terrestrial, cable or satellite—increases the supply of distribution very significantly over the previous analogue transmission. As a result, there is less of a technical bottleneck for the provision of media content.

Moreover, this increase in distribution supply is extended to practically unlimited supply of content via the internet through cable, fixed network or broadband wireless lines. Since the internet represents effectively a one-to-one connection between a content provider and a user of content for the time of transmission of the content, there is no longer a technical limitation to how much content a user can access. In fact, a user can switch seamlessly between different content providers. This change represents a very substantial supply shock for distribution networks. Without the technical limitations of distribution, they also have much lower economic incentives to foreclose content providers. As soon as there is a

[7] Fumagalli, C and Motta, M, 'Buyer Miscoordination, Entry and Downstream Competition' (2008) 118 *Economic Journal* 1196–222.

[8] Nocke, V and White, L, 'Do Vertical Mergers Facilitate Upstream Collusion?' (2005) PIER Working Paper No 05-013.

degree of competition in internet distribution, for example, via different mobile networks, foreclosure of content providers seems highly unlikely.

A similar technological supply shock has occurred in the creation and provision of content, which has been made much cheaper through technological innovation in recording and sound equipment.

In this environment of hundreds of TV channels, unlimited content access through internet services and cheap content production, it would be very difficult to economically foreclose entrants, particularly news services. This new supply situation probably also played a role in the 'Arab spring' in that even authoritarian states were no longer able to suppress plurality.

In such an environment, many existing business models are no longer viable. For example, while the Indian press is still stable, there is a worldwide secular decline in traditional print newspapers, which occurred with the widespread adoption of the internet. This has accelerated with the fast adoption of smartphones.

Newspaper publishers need to be able to react to such a shock to their industry segment if they are to survive. A parallel argument can be made for cable operators, content providers and all other companies in the value chain.

Companies react to these changes by entering different parts of the value chain. As has been shown in print, it is often not sufficient to simply produce print content as internet content in order to stabilise revenues and profits. This is particularly the case since, in most countries, a significant part of internet advertising revenues is captured by Google. Print companies, therefore, need to respond to the erosion of print advertising and new competition in internet advertising revenues with different business models.

Several print companies have started to use their distribution network to sell other products, such as mobile phone contracts, or they provide transactions-based services such as travel booking services or financial advisory services. Most of these services are not only horizontally distinct from print, but are also different in the vertical sense. Rules that would not allow the development of such differentiated business models as a response to technological change would burden the entire industry.

In this context, one should note that the most successful global companies in the media and communications industry have been expanding upstream and downstream from their original business models.

Apple, which used to be a hardware and software manufacturer, is now a significant content distributor for the music and film industry, and with its communications applications is an 'over-the-top' (OTT) telecommunications provider.

Google, originally a search engine, is a content provider with YouTube, an application service provider with its various mapping, information and communications services, has recently started operating a fibre network in Kansas, and has entered the mobile phone devices business with the acquisition of Motorola. It also participated in a Federal Communications Commission (FCC) auction for wireless frequencies.

Qualcomm, the world's largest mobile chip manufacturer, has been active as a mobile operator, a mobile content platform provider, a handset manufacturer, an internet protocol technology provider, a network equipment provider and so on.

Where regulators restrict such movement between different parts of the value chain, this hinders enterprise. There may well be individual cases of an exercise of market power. However, one would probably think that these are rare instances that would not warrant general ownership restrictions but could instead be dealt with on a case-by-case basis. Moreover, such concerns are more likely to arise over premium content rather than news or investigative journalism.

6.4 VERTICAL COMPETITION ISSUES IN MERGERS IN THE MEDIA AND COMMUNICATIONS SECTOR

Competition authorities have had to balance the efficiency benefits of vertical integration with potential threats to the competitive process. The multiplicity of markets involved and the often dynamic nature of media markets and communications concomitantly increase the challenges in formulating appropriate and measured responses.

One consequence of vertical integration may be that this alters the incentives of the merged entity to continue to deal with third parties in granting access to content or infrastructure on competitive terms. Such a change in the competitive dynamic may take the form of an outright refusal to supply, or pricing strategies where the third party is offered terms which are less favourable than those offered to the merged entity's own operations. However, the competition authorities accept that such practices may have pro-competitive effects and are already present to a large extent in the competitive dynamic of the sector. For example, a platform owner may offer its own pay TV services, internet and telephony over its own infrastructure as well as granting access to third parties to distribute their third-party content over the platform.

Below we outline some recurrent issues that have arisen in merger control proceedings involving vertical integration in the media and communications sector. We return to these theories of harm when we consider solutions that have been accepted by the authorities in concrete cases.

6.4.1 Access to Content

A company may control a key input that is of value to other companies operating in the sector. In the media sector, this will typically be the company holding the content/and or copyright of an audiovisual product (whether films, music or TV programmes). This control will be relevant to the competition analysis depending on whether the nature and scope of products and the relevant rights enjoyed allow the holder to gain a competitive advantage over rivals such that it may engage in exclusionary or discriminatory practices and thereby restrict competition.

6.4.2 Access to Infrastructure

A company may possess infrastructure or technology know-how that allows it to exercise control in the form of access to a certain market or customer base. The degree of control over the infrastructure will be relevant from a competition perspective only to the extent that the holder enjoys a significant degree of market power where the infrastructure is critical for a new entrant to gain market access and expand its presence. The role occupied by the holder of the infrastructure has often been described as that of a 'gate-keeper'.

6.4.3 Leverage

A related theme concerning vertical integration is a concern of potential 'leverage' or the ability to transfer market power into adjacent or neighbouring markets. This concern may arise where media companies seek to distribute their products across multiple platforms.

However, it is important to note that concerns about market leverage can arise without a merger. A notable example is Microsoft's bundling of its operating system and media player. This was the subject of competition law challenges before the EU and US authorities using competition law powers.[9]

6.4.4 Network Effects

Convergence in the media communications industry may reflect the phenomenon of network effects. In simple terms, a 'network effect' occurs when the benefit of an individual who is connected to the network increases with the addition of other individuals to the network.

This circumstance tends to invite scrutiny by the competition authorities when evaluating mergers in the media and communications sector. The concern is that the combination of network effects and market power may raise barriers to entry and result in market foreclosure of rival operators.

[9] See, further, the judgment of the General Court in Case T-201/04 *Microsoft Corporation v Commission* [2007] ECR II-3601.

6.4.5 Removal of a Maverick

In the telecoms sector the competition authorities' interest has not been limited to traditional access issues but in recent years has shown a readiness to examine whether the merger might jeopardise the survival of disruptive players or 'mavericks' in concentrated markets.

At the EU national level in *Belgacom/Scarlet*[10] the Belgian competition authority found that Belgacom's acquisition of DSL provider Scarlet would deprive the Belgian market of an innovative competitor with a developed optical glass fibre network, quite apart from its small market share. This case may be contrasted with *Iliad/Liberty Surf*[11] where the merger between two telephone and internet providers was investigated. The French Competition Authority found that rather than eliminating a maverick player the merger would likely strengthen a vibrant competitor (Iliad). The merger was cleared unconditionally.

6.5 VERTICAL INTEGRATION AND MERGER REMEDIES

6.5.1 Remedies Typology

In this section we illustrate the types of remedies that competition authorities have deployed to address vertical concerns arising out of mergers in the media and communications sector.

A broad distinction can be drawn between structural remedies (essentially divestments) and behavioural remedies (commitments on conduct). Within these broad categorisations, there are variations on the precise formulation of the remedy. For ease of classification we have considered remedies within the type groupings set out in Figure 8.[12]

[10] E-Competitions, 'The Belgian Competition Council approves upon remedies the takeover of alternative DSL-provider by the incumbent', 7 November 2008, no 23527.

[11] E-Competitions, 'The French Minister of economics clears telecom merger without remedies after investigating possible coordinated effects and elimination of a maverick', 22 August 2008, no 23603.

[12] This classification is based on the categorisation of merger remedies by type in the examination of national merger control remedies in the information and communications sector contained in the analysis by Hoehn, T, Rab, S and Saggers, G, 'Breaking up is hard to do—National Merger Remedies' (2009) 9 *European Competition Law Review*. The project which formed the basis for this analysis involved a review of over 500 merger remedies decisions across 30 European countries, including all the EU Member States, in order to examine trends in the number and types of remedies.

Structural remedies	Behavioural remedies
Divestiture of a controlling stake in a viable standalone business	Granting of access to content
Divestiture of a business carved out from a company structure	Granting of access to technology
Divestiture of assets	Granting of access to infrastructure
Divestiture or grant of long-term licence	Termination of exclusive vertical agreements
Commitment to exit from a jv	Other behavioural
Other structural	

Figure 8: Merger remedies by type

Source: Based on categorisation in National Merger Remedies cited at footnote 12

6.5.2 EU Experience

(a) Structural Remedies

A case involving a combination of structural and behavioural remedies is *Vivendi/ Seagram/ Canal Plus.*[13]

Vivendi was a large company in the media and communications sector with interests spanning mobile telephony, film production and distribution, and pay TV. Seagram was a Canadian company whose interests included the Universal music and film business.

The merged entity would hold the world's second-largest film library and the second-largest TV programme library in the European Economic Area. It would occupy the leading position in recorded music and enjoy a significant presence in publishing rights. The European Commission was concerned that the merged entity's considerable access to premium content presented a risk that if the merged entity had exclusive access this would raise barriers to entry to other pay TV operators.

The European Commission obtained a commitment that the merged entity would not supply its downstream pay TV platform with more than 50 per cent of the premium films available, thereby making the remainder available to competitors.

Vivendi also divested its interest in British Sky Broadcasting (BSkyB), thereby severing the link with Fox and reducing the amount of premium content that was owned by the merged entity.

[13] Case COMP/M.2050 *Vivendi/ Seagram/Canal Plus*, Commission decision of 24 July 2000.

(b) *Behavioural Remedies*

(i) Granting access to content

Access remedies have been typical in media and communications mergers raising vertical concerns. An all-embracing example of this is the 2006 merger between TPS and Canal Sat, two satellite broadcasting and TV service providers in France. The merger was approved subject to an extensive package of commitments.[14] Fifty-nine remedies were involved, most of which were aimed at granting access to broadcasts rights, programmes and channels by non-satellite operators. There was close coordination between the French Competition Authority and the sector regulators in this case.

(ii) Granting access to infrastructure

Newscorp/Telepiu[15] is an example of a case where the European Commission approved a merger raising vertical issues subject to an extensive package of commitments including granting access to infrastructure.

Newscorp controlled the Italian satellite pay TV platform Stream jointly with Telecom Italia. Telepiu, controlled by Vivendi Universal, was the dominant pay TV operator in Italy and started operating its platform in 1991 (analogue-terrestrial) before launching satellite in 1996.

The main affected markets were (i) the markets for pay TV services; and (ii) the markets for content acquisition (ie premium films, football events, other sports and TV channels).

The European Commission raised concerns that the merger would give rise to significant horizontal overlaps and would increase entry barriers through the creation of a near monopoly in the Italian market for pay TV and close to monopsony positions in the related markets for the acquisition of rights.

The commitments accepted by the European Commission comprised three main groups: (i) access to infrastructure; (ii) access to content; and (iii) withdrawal from terrestrial broadcasting activities.

With respect to access to infrastructure, the parties committed to grant to third parties access to the merged entity's satellite platform and access to the application programme interface (API) and conditional access system (CAS), according to a fair and non-discriminatory pricing formula. The merged entity was also subject to the obligation of entering into simulcrypt agreements in Italy as soon as reasonably possible and in any event within nine months from the written request from an interested third party.

[14] E-competitions, 'The French Minister of Economics clears the merger between the two pay-TV operators with 59 commitments after consultation of both the audiovisual regulator and the NCA (TPS/Canal Sat)', 30 August 2006, no 12542.

[15] Case COMP/M.2876 *Newscorp/Telepiu*, Commission decision of 2 April 2003.

(iii) Guaranteeing terms of supply

The UK Competition Commission accepted extensive behavioural remedies in a merger-to-monopoly situation in the merger of Arqiva (a subsidiary of Macquarie Broadcast Ventures Ltd) and National Grid Wireless Group.[16] The parties were the only two broadcast wireless transmission network operators in the UK.

Despite the preference of competition authorities for structural remedies, the Competition Commission listened to the views of customers who stated that they would prefer discounts and guarantees of service over a divestment of parts of the network.

The remedies package was underpinned by supporting provisions including a commitment that the new company would allow access at fair prices; the establishment of an Adjudication Scheme to decide disputes between the new company and third parties; and the appointment of a compliance officer who was responsible for monitoring compliance and liaising with the Office of Fair Trading, the adjudicator and Ofcom.

The solution was innovative and complex and was facilitated by the involvement of the parties' customers and the sector regulator Ofcom in the design of an appropriate remedy package.

(iv) Facilitating new entry

In *T-Mobile Austria/tele.ring*[17] the European Commission found that the merger would result in the elimination of a firm which, prior to the merger, had exerted a significant competitive constraint on the pricing of T-Mobile Austria and its principal competitor, Mobilkom.

The commitments provided that T-Mobile would sell 5 MHz 3G/UMTS frequency blocks which were previously licensed to tele.ring to competitors with smaller market shares. The case illustrates the challenges that competition authorities will sometimes have in demonstrating that competitive harm results from the removal of a maverick.

The identity of suitable purchasers was key to securing the remedies package. The commitments specified the competitors who were to receive defined frequency blocks. Although this case raised both horizontal and vertical issues, it illustrates some familiar themes that recur in vertical foreclosure cases, most notably the issue of network effects. In particular, tele.ring had started with a small customer base that it had increased through an aggressive pricing strategy.

[16] Competition Commission, *Macquarie UK Broadcast Ventures Limited/National Grid Wireless Group, Completed acquisition, Final Report*, 11 March 2008.

[17] Case COMP/M.3916 *T-Mobile Austria/ tele.ring*, Commission decision of 26 April 2006.

(v) Unconditional clearance

It is worth mentioning *News Corp/BSkyB*. The European Commission gave phase I unconditional clearance, that is, no remedies were required. It conducted a detailed assessment of the competitive nature of the various stages of the vertical chain and identified no competition problems.[18]

6.5.3 US Experience

The US agencies have reviewed mergers in the media and communications sectors in diverse areas including telecommunications, newspapers, radio and films. Pozen, in her capacity as Assistant Attorney General of the Department of Justice Antitrust Division, recently commented that such cases 'have benefited consumers, competition and the marketplace for ideas'.[19]

In order to provide an insight into how the US has approached competition issues in mergers in the media and communications sectors it is useful to consider the recent case of *Comcast/NBCU JV*.[20] The transaction was allowed to proceed, subject to detailed commitments.

On 18 January 2011 the US, together with individual states, brought a civil action against a joint venture between Comcast and NBCU. The Antitrust Division filed a proposed settlement imposing restrictions on the conduct of the joint venture which was approved by the court on 1 September 2011.

Comcast was the largest cable and television and internet provider in the US. NBCU was the owner of the NBC television network. The Antitrust Division determined that the joint venture would be likely to harm competition in the distribution of video programming by enabling the joint venture to refuse access to or raise the price of NBCU's programming to Comcast's rival distributors, among other practices. The Antitrust Division was particularly concerned that the transaction would have enabled Comcast to foreclose new entry from online video distributors (OVD).

The Antitrust Division worked with the FCC both on the substantive aspects of the case and in formulating the remedies package. The key elements of the package were:

— The joint venture must make available to OVDs the same package of broadcast and cable channels that it sells to traditional video programming distributors.

[18] Case M.5932 *News Corp/ BSkyB*, Commission decision of 21 December 2010.

[19] Pozen, S, 'Insights into Antitrust Enforcement in Media Industries' (2013) *Competition Law International*.

[20] Department of Justice press release, 'Justice Department allows Comcast-NBCU joint venture to proceed with conditions', 18 January 2011. (NBCU was formerly NBC Universal).

- The joint venture must offer an OVD broadcast, cable and film content that is similar to, or better than, the content the distributor receives from any of the joint venture's programming peers. These peers are NBC's broadcast competitors (ABC, CBS and Fox), the largest cable programmers (News Corp., Time Warner Inc., Viacom Inc. and The Walt Disney Co.), and the largest video production studios (News Corp., Sony Corporation of America, Time Warner Inc., Viacom Inc and The Walt Disney Co.).
- Comcast may not retaliate against any broadcast network (or affiliate), cable programmer, production studio or content licensee for licensing content to a competing cable, satellite or telephone company or OVD, or for raising concerns to the department or the FCC.
- Comcast must relinquish its management rights in Hulu, an OVD. Comcast must continue to make NBCU content available to Hulu that is comparable to the programming Hulu obtains from Disney and News Corporation.
- In accordance with recently established Open Internet requirements, Comcast is prohibited from unreasonably discriminating in the transmission of an OVD's lawful network traffic to a Comcast broadband customer.
- Comcast must maintain the high speed Internet service it offers to its customers by continuing to offer download speeds of at least 12 megabits per second in markets where it has upgraded its broadband network.
- Comcast is required to give other firms' content equal treatment under any of its broadband offerings that involve caps, tiers, metering for consumption or other usage based pricing.
- Comcast may not, with certain narrow exceptions, require programmers or video distributors to agree to licensing terms that seek to limit online distributors' access to content.

6.6 CONCLUSIONS AND IMPLICATIONS FOR POLICY

A number of implications for the design of policy and regulatory interventions emerge:

- Economic context: To understand the implications of vertical integration for competition and pluralism, it is important to examine the strategic rationale for the transaction or combination. One interpretation advances the view that the drivers of consolidation are underpinned by a quest for improvements in economic efficiency through merger synergies and development of economies of scale. This economic perspective provides part of the background against which vertical integration and consolidation needs to be appraised.
- Ownership and merger control: Sector-specific controls on ownership cannot be divorced from the controls that apply in the mainstream merger control regime applying to the sector. Mainstream merger control has

built within it key determinants of what amounts to ownership and what amounts to a relevant change in control. In this respect, India is no different in that it already has an established merger control system, enforced by the Competition Commission of India (CCI) under the Competition Act. Any importation of additional or different concepts of ownership or control for the purposes of regulating a particular sector must not be undertaken without careful identification of the reasons why the sector presents specific challenges which are not addressed by the standard rules. Any departure from the standard rules should be justified by a cost–benefit analysis and, in particular, the need to ensure proportionality and avoid inefficiency, duplication and inconsistency.

— Merger control 'tool box': Although competition authorities adapt their merger control jurisdiction and substantive tests to deal with the particular issues presented by vertical integration, the approach is of general sector-neutral application. Vertical integration in the media and communications sector is not a 'special case' notwithstanding the sector-specific challenges. We discern no meaningful trend towards ownership caps or outright prohibitions on extending an enterprise's vertical presence across the supply chain from one media or communications market into another or within a media segment.

— Solutions can be found: Merger control in the media and communications sectors regularly produces difficult cases where issues such as market definition and competitive effects can be complex. Competition authorities around the world have shown that they are willing and able to embrace the increasing complexities of the cases before them. There are many merger cases raising vertical issues that have been successfully resolved in similar ways and in different markets. There is no reason to doubt that India's competition regulator, the CCI, has the tools at its disposal to address concerns arising from vertical integration in appropriate cases.

— Flexible solutions can be found: The competition authorities have shown receptiveness to both structural and behavioural remedies to resolve vertical and horizontal issues in media and communications mergers. A prevailing theme is the concern to ensure access to content or infrastructure.

— Increasingly sophisticated approaches: With the phenomenon of convergence playing out, the trend internationally has been towards increasing sophistication in the evaluation of the competitive effects of mergers across multiple markets. The effects-based assessment is conducted on a case-by-case basis without any predisposition towards what is the 'right' market structure in terms of market share of concentration levels. This approach selects a remedy, if required, based on the likely harm identified. It does not rely on a priori decisions or preferences for or against a particular business model (ie vertical integration).

— Interface with sector regulation: The relationship between competition law and sector regulation is again highlighted in the merger control procedure.

Regulators should be alive to, and resist, the temptation to use the merger control procedure to attempt to correct the perceived shortcomings of the sector's regulatory regime through a merger remedy. That said, the involvement of the sector regulator may be useful in opening up the potential for a wider range of solutions, and monitoring.

— Interface with pluralism: Addressing competition concerns in mergers may also indirectly contribute to pluralism to the extent that remedies facilitate new entry. In some cases the remedy may go further than restoring the pre-merger market dynamic by creating the environment for a new player to challenge the merged entity through an assets disposal or licence. This may enable a maverick to emerge which, despite its smaller market share, may contribute to the diversity of the media landscape.
— Prohibition of mergers in the media and communications sector due to vertical issues is rare but not unprecedented. Despite the challenges presented, judging by the number of prohibitions and withdrawals, experience has shown that parties are able to get their deals through with or without conditions.

7

Cable Sector: Competition and Regulation in an International Comparative Perspective

7.1 INTRODUCTION

Globally, the broadcasting sector, and particularly cable, has developed in very different ways in different markets. In some countries the sector is regulated because it is thought that markets, when left alone, will not deliver optimal outcomes for consumers. This may arise from a belief that media, and particularly TV operations, can have a significant effect on the economy, on social and cultural life, on the political arena and ultimately on the lives of individual people.

This chapter compares the regulation of the cable TV sector internationally across three regions: Europe, Asia and the Americas. Within these regions the individual case study examples reveal further diversity in approaches to regulation. The study is by no means exhaustive but seeks to provide a description and examination of the variants. For example, and to illustrate some of the key themes which follow in this chapter and in the supporting Appendix 4:

— all the BRIC countries are represented (Brazil, Russia, India and China);
— within Europe there is no homogeneity and we discuss examples from the north (Belgium, UK) and the south (Portugal);
— within the Americas there are examples from the north (US) and south (Brazil and Mexico);
— within Asia, there are examples from countries with a more established competition regulator (South Korea), as well as from countries with newer competition regulators (China and India);
— there are examples from the longer-established antitrust and regulatory regimes (the EU and the US);
— there are examples of countries which have recently overhauled their competition law and regulatory framework and which have already made significant regulatory interventions in the sector (Mexico); and
— there are examples of countries which adopt English as their main or a principal language (India, the UK, the US) as well countries with other national languages (Brazil, Belgium, China, Mexico, Portugal, Russia, South Korea). This study has attempted to examine both cultural and economic factors. While language is only one driver of culture it can be a useful starting point in distinguishing different countries.

Table 2 lists the jurisdictions covered in this study and compares their population and gross domestic product (GDP). Population and GDP have been chosen as the most appropriate criteria for our comparative purposes.[1] When considering regulation that impacts on the cultural and economic life of a jurisdiction, the number of people (assessed in terms of population) and the size of the economy (assessed in terms of GDP) would seem to be the most relevant criteria for comparative evaluation purposes.

Table 2: Overview of jurisdictions—population and GDP

Country	Population	GDP in purchasing power parity (US$) (per capita)
Europe		
Belgium	10.4 million	US$427.2 billion (US$41,077)
Portugal	10.8 million	US$250.6 billion (US$23,204)
Russia	142.5 million	US$2,555 billion (US$17,930)
United Kingdom	63.4 million	US$2,375 billion (US$37,460)
Americas		
Brazil	201.0 million	US$2,394 billion (US$ 11,910)
Mexico	116.2 million	US$1,788 billion (US$15,387)
United States	316.7 million	US$15,940 billion (US$50,331)
Asia		
China	1,349.6 million	US$12,610 billion (US$9,344)
India	1,220.8 million	US$4,761 billion (US$3,899)
South Korea	49.0 million	US$1,640 billion (US$33,469)

Sources and notes: All data are from the most recent version for each jurisdiction contained in the CIA World Factbook and represent estimates as at July 2013.

[1] Population is ideally measured in terms of households. In the absence of comprehensive and up-to date data on households, population data may be taken as a close approximation.

Some pertinent issues emerge from Table 2. First, we have endeavoured to include countries that are both comparable to and contrasting with India. China is obviously broadly similar in terms of population size, although the GDP of India and China differ considerably with China's GDP being more than double that of India. Second, the other remaining BRIC countries (Brazil and Russia) exhibit similar GDPs to India, although their populations are smaller. Third, we have included jurisdictions which are both larger and smaller than India in terms of both population and GDP in order to provide a representative selection of comparators.

A further relevant comparator metric when examining the cable sector is land mass. The size of a country in terms of land area may not be an indicator of its economic position. However, the aggregate surface area may be a useful differentiator when considering the cable sector or other network industries. For example, the size of a country may be relevant to determining policies for efficient roll-out of infrastructure and in serving rural areas. Table 3 illustrates the countries in our study by area.

Table 3: Overview of jurisdictions—by area

Country	Total in km^2 (miles^2)	Land in km^2 (miles^2)	Comments
Europe			
Belgium	30,528 (11,787)	30,278 (11,690)	
Portugal	92,090 (35,560)	91,470 (35,320)	
Russia	17,098,242 (6,601,668)	16,377,742 (6,323,482)	Largest country in the world.
United Kingdom	242,900 (93,800)	241,930 (93,410)	Does not include the three Crown dependencies (768 km^2 or 297 miles^2) and the 14 overseas territories (1,742,857 km^2 or 672,921 miles^2).
Americas			
Brazil	8,514,877 (3,287,612)	8,459,417 (3,266,199)	The largest country in South America and in the Southern Hemisphere. Largest contiguous territory in the Americas.
Mexico	1,964,375 (758,449)	1,943,945 (750,561)	

(*Continued*)

Table 3: (*Continued*)

Country	Total in km^2 (miles^2)	Land in km^2 (miles^2)	Comments
United States	9,629,091 (3,717,813)	9,158,960 (3,536,290)	
Asia			
China	9,706,961 (3,747,879)	9,569,901 (3,694,959)	Largest country situated entirely in Asia.
India	3,166,414 (1,222,559)	2,973,193 (1,147,956)	The area given is from *Encyclopedia Britannica* and excludes disputed territories not under Indian control.
South Korea	100,210 (38,690)	99,909 (38,575)	

Source: Data are taken from the United Nations Statistics Division unless otherwise noted.[2]
Notes: (1) total area: the sum of all land and inland water bodies (lakes, reservoirs, rivers) delimited by international boundaries or coastlines; (2) land area: the aggregate of all surfaces delimited by international boundaries and/or coastlines, excluding inland water bodies (lakes, reservoirs, rivers).

Ultimately, while a study such as this is by its nature selective, the analysis reveals some interesting differences in the approach to and outcomes of regulation in these very different regions and economies. Some share a number of economic, geographic and cultural similarities with India, others less so.

The remainder of this chapter is structured as follows. First, some economic perspectives on the cable TV sector are provided. Second, the different country regulatory features are summarised and compared. Third, we draw initial conclusions for the design of policy and regulation in light of the regimes surveyed.

7.2 ECONOMIC, COMPETITION AND REGULATORY PERSPECTIVES

Governments regulate cable operators for a number of reasons. Here, we provide an overview of the rationales for cable regulation and how these have evolved over time. The aim of this section is to provide a high-level framework as background to the discussion of specific regional and national regulatory approaches in later sections.

[2] United Nations Statistics Division, 'Demographic Yearbook 2010', Table 3: Population by sex, rate of population increase, surface area and density.

7.2.1 Structure of the Broadcasting Industry

To understand the origins of and continuing rationale for regulation of the cable industry, it is helpful first to consider the structure of the industry. Figure 9 summarises the vertical structure of the broadcasting industry.

Content	Production	Packaging	Distribution	Supply	Consumer
Content rights holders (e.g. film studios, sports bodies) and advertisers	TV producers	TV broadcasters Channel owners	Terrestrial Cable Satellite Copper Fibre	Pay TV retailers (terrestrial, cable, satellite, IPTV, OTT)	TV STB PC/laptop/tablet Smartphone Home 'hub'

Figure 9: Vertical structure of the TV broadcasting industry

Source: Authors' analysis

At the content and production level, there are a variety of owners of intellectual property rights (IPR) including film studios, sports bodies and owners of rights to particular concepts, as well as production companies and companies producing advertising. The IPR are licensed to production companies or to the channel owners directly. Some of the production may be undertaken in-house by vertically integrated companies who not only produce some of their own content but also perform the downstream activities of distribution and retailing.

Content is packaged into channels or, increasingly, groups of channels. For example, free-to-air broadcasters have used the advent of digital broadcasting to expand the number of channels that each provides. While multichannel offers have been a traditional attraction of cable and satellite pay TV operators, digitalisation has enabled them to increase the number of channels they are able to offer.

A number of distribution platforms may then be used to deliver those channels to customers including analogue or digital terrestrial broadcast television, cable, satellite, and more recently, TV over copper, fibre and mobile broadband services.

The retail supply of TV services includes marketing and, for pay TV, billing, customer service and customer access arrangements such as set-top boxes. Retail pay TV services are also often bundled with other communications services including as a 'triple play' of TV, telephony and broadband or as a 'quad play' also including mobile services.

The vertical structure of the industry shows that there are a number of levels with activities at one level having implications for the performance of the industry at that level and also potentially at other levels. For example, a competition problem at one level may lead to a loss in competition upstream and/or downstream depending on the incentives and market positions of the relevant firms. Similarly, regulation applied at one level may have intended or unintended effects on outcomes at other parts of the value chain. In the next section, we explain how regulation has developed in relation to the different parts of the value chain.

7.2.2 Theories of Regulation

Two main groups of theories seek to explain the basis of regulation. Positive theories seek to explain regulation in terms of the outcome of different groups pursuing their own interests including the ability of particularly powerful or well-coordinated groups to extract rents at the expense of other groups.[3] In contrast, normative theories refer to the specific technical justification for regulation in terms of how it is purported to promote the public interest, whether this be in terms of economic or more general objectives.

Positive theories have been highly influential although they have also been subject to criticism for being incomplete and overly simplistic.[4] Positive theories may help explain regulation that has sometimes been imposed to restrict cable operators from competing with other platforms and other regulation that has restricted other platforms competing with cable. For example, in the 1960s the US cable industry was subject to a range of regulations which limited the content which could be offered by cable operators with the explicit aim of maintaining healthy ultra-high frequency television broadcast companies.[5] In many EU Member States, cable networks were prevented from being used for telecommunications services until a European Commission Directive abolished such restrictions with effect from 1 January 1996.[6]

One issue with positive theories is that the actual motivation for regulation may not be explicitly stated. Further, even regulation that is intended to promote the overall public interest may have a range of effects (some of which go against the public interest). In such cases, observers may come to differing views as to whether the regulation is really designed to promote the public interest or to advance the interests of some narrow group. Given this, a cautious approach focused on the evidence specific to the case should be followed in assessing whether particular regulation is best explained by a specific positive theory.

A large number of normative justifications have been put forward for the specific regulation of the cable industry. These justifications can be categorised as either:

- regulation aimed at improving the overall efficiency of the economy by addressing failures in specific markets ('economic regulation'); or
- regulation that is designed to achieve particular public interest objectives ('general regulation').

[3] Seminal works in relation to the positive theory of regulation include: Olson, M, *The Logic of Collective Action: Public Goods and the Theory of Groups* (Harvard University Press, 1965) and Stigler, G, 'The Theory of Economic Regulation' (1971) 2 *Bell Journal of Economics and Management Science* 3–21.

[4] See, eg, Croley, S, 'Beyond capture: towards a new theory of regulation' in Levi-Faur, D (ed), *Handbook on the Politics of Regulation*, (Edward Elgar Publishing, 2011) 50–69.

[5] Crawford, G S, 'Cable regulation in the internet era', Working Paper, Coventry: Economics Department, University of Warwick (Warwick economics research paper series, 2013) 6.

[6] Directive 95/51/EC of 18 October 1995 amending Directive 90/388/EEC with regard to the abolition of the restrictions on the use of cable television networks for the provision of already liberalized telecommunications services [1995] OJ L256.

Figure 10 provides an overview of normative rationales for regulation applied at the different levels of the broadcasting industry.

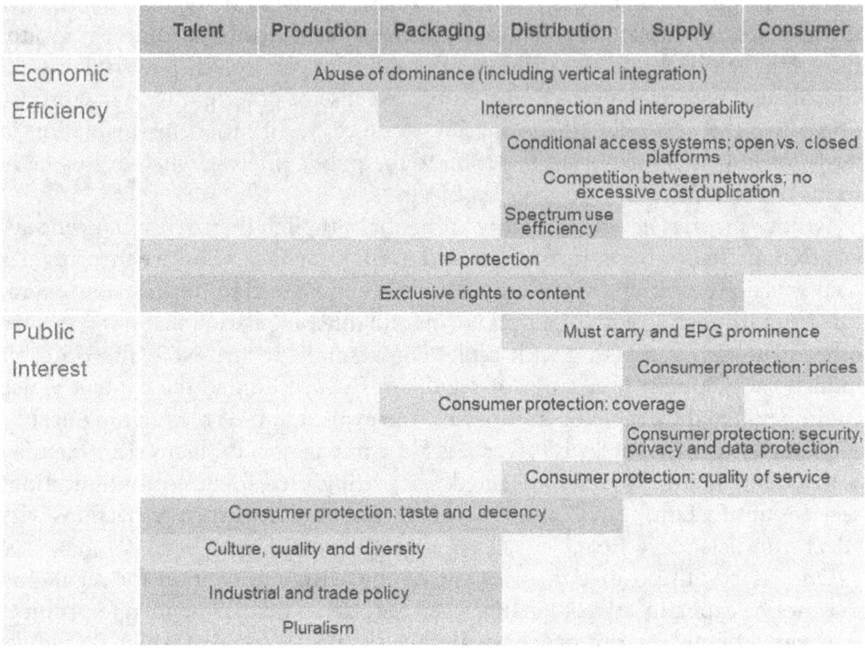

Figure 10: Normative rationales for regulation

Source: Authors' analysis and KPMG, Public Policy Issues Arising From Telecommunications and Audiovisual Convergence, a report prepared for DG XIII, London, 1996

7.2.3 Dealing with Market Power

A traditional focus of economic regulation has been to prevent the exploitation of market power in industries where there is a single dominant firm. Firms that enjoy dominant positions can harm consumers and the overall public interest by restricting their output and charging a higher price than would have been the case had the firm faced effective competition. In some markets, it may only be efficient to have one firm because of the presence of large economies of scale. In such 'natural monopolies', price or rate regulation may bring ongoing public benefit by bringing prices down towards competitive levels and thereby increasing the demand for the services. However, where there is a lack of competition in broadcasting markets, it is often due to regulations that have restricted entry, or the services that different platforms are allowed to provide. For example, many cable networks in the US were developed under municipal franchises which permitted only one cable network in the area and in return imposed regulation on rates and other service elements.[7] In these cases, while price regulation may be useful for a time, allowing for competition between platforms may ultimately bring greater benefits. In particular, a regulator may not be able to correctly estimate the competitive price (potentially harming investment if prices are set too low or harming consumers if prices are set too high) and regulation is unlikely to match the dynamic benefits of competition such as in spurring product and cost innovation.

In recognising the benefits of competitive markets, regulatory measures have been imposed to protect existing competition and help stimulate additional competition. Competition law is a key means by which authorities seek to prevent dominant companies from acting to reduce the level of competition in a market. Competition law contains prohibitions on dominant firms engaging in anti-competitive practices such as might sometimes result from bundling and tying or refusals to deal. Given the increasing importance of bundled offers by cable operators, it is important to point out that bundling can bring significant benefits including lower prices, demand-increasing price discrimination, and cost savings. Even where bundling is carried out by a dominant firm, it is likely to cause competition problems in only a narrow range of circumstances. Competition law also prohibits firms in a market from reaching agreements that reduce the level of competition, such as agreements to maintain a particular price level or to divide the market between them.

While competition law penalises conduct that has already occurred, *ex ante* regulation may also be used prospectively to protect and promote competition. Regulators may, in particular, require access to be provided to particular parts of the value chain on regulated terms and conditions. Access regulation is designed to prevent a firm that has dominance in relation to one level of the value chain from being able to leverage that dominance to weaken competition in other parts of value chain that rely on the dominant firm's services. Whether there would be an access problem in the absence of regulation would need to be assessed taking into account the specific facts of the case including whether the dominant firm would have the incentive and ability to restrict access in an anti-competitive way. A regulator would also need to consider the potential costs as well as benefits of imposing regulation, including whether access regulation may displace competition between rival networks or limit an operator's ability to efficiently coordinate the services that carry over their network.

[7] Hazlett, T, 'Cable TV franchises as barriers to video competition' (2007) 12(2) *Virginia Journal of Law and Technology*.

7.2.4 Access Issues

Access issues have arisen in relation to the sale of broadcasting rights, particularly for sports events where there has been a concern that the licensing of exclusive rights to premium content for a particular distribution company may weaken competition at the distribution level.[8]

Access has also been imposed on distribution platforms for the conveyance of particular services. For example, the Australian Competition and Consumer Commission (ACCC) decided to require access to cable networks for the carriage of analogue television broadcast signals so as to promote competition particularly through the entry of niche pay TV services.[9] Where a third party wishes to access a pay TV network to deliver its own broadcasting or interactive services, it may be necessary for it also to be able to use the network's conditional access system and related services. Conditional access systems, such as set top boxes, are used to control customers' access to services such as limiting the channels that a customer can watch to those included in the customer's tariff package. Without the ability to limit access to its content, an independent content provider may not be able to establish a viable business. On the other hand, the network owner should not have its legitimate commercial interests compromised by access regulation including its ability to receive a commercial return on its investment in conditional access.

While there has been a good deal of discussion about imposing access obligations on cable networks for the conveyance of internet services, such regulation has generally not been found to be necessary because of the presence of strong competition in the supply of internet services over telecommunications networks. One case in which open wholesale access to cable broadband has been imposed is in Denmark where large parts of the cable network are owned by the incumbent telecommunications operator.[10]

Net neutrality is a major current issue in Europe and North America which concerns whether distribution networks should be subject to various forms of non-discrimination obligation. What is actually meant by net neutrality varies widely. Some commentators see it as largely in line with existing prohibitions on dominant firms from engaging in anticompetitive practices. However, other advocates seek wider rules to be imposed on all networks which may include restrictions on charges for access and restrictions on how networks manage traffic.[11]

[8] Kienapfel, P and Stein, A, 'The Application of Articles 81 and 82 EC in the Sport Sector' (2007) 3 *Competition Policy Newsletter* 6–14.

[9] ACCC, 'Declaration of Analogue Subscription Television Broadcast Carriage Service', August 1999.

[10] European Commission press release, Telecoms: Commission endorses new Danish rules to open wholesale access to cable broadband (IP/09/394) 12 March 2009.

[11] For a discussion of net neutrality, see Hahn, R and Wallsten S, 'The Economics of Net Neutrality' (Washington, DC: AEI Brookings Joint Center for Regulatory Studies) April 2006.

7.2.5 Merger Regulation

Merger regulation represents another form of *ex ante* regulation, and prohibits mergers and acquisitions that would significantly reduce competition in a market. Many mergers between cable operators may not directly reduce horizontal competition as most cable networks are in geographically separate areas. However, there is the potential for mergers to give rise to competition concerns where there are competitive interactions with other services or, occasionally, where there are vertical effects on other parts of the value chain.

7.2.6 Public Interest

The cable industry has also been subject to more general regulation designed to achieve particular public interest objectives. 'Must carry' obligations have been imposed to require networks to carry specified television and radio channels. While a form of access regulation, 'must carry' obligations are imposed for general interest objectives such as ensuring access for disabled end-users and promoting media diversity or national content. The European Commission's Universal Service Directive provides for Member States to impose 'must carry' obligations although the use of such obligations varies widely across the EU.[12] The effect of such obligations will depend on their extent, the price (if any) that the operator receives for carrying the content, and the implications for the operation of and investment in the network. 'Must offer' obligations may also be imposed on broadcasters requiring them to make their programmes available for distribution.

Cable operators are also generally subject to at least some form of consumer protection measures. This may be general consumer protection rules such as prohibitions on misleading and deceptive conduct in relation to selling services. There may also be rules regulating the type of content that can be shown or the ways that content is shown, such as preventing content not suitable for children being shown during the day or early evening. The objective of promoting universal or at least widespread access to services may lead to obligations in relation to the geographic rollout of networks and regulation aimed at ensuring that prices (particularly of basic packages) are affordable to most customers.

Even where regulation is put forward to promote a general interest, it is important that regulators identify the full range of intended and unintended effects that are likely to result from the regulation and assess not only whether its benefits justify the

[12] Directive 2009/136 amending the Universal Services Directive (2002/22/EC), the E-Privacy Directive (2002/58/EC) and Regulation 2006/2004 on consumer protection co-operation, [2009] OJ L337/11.

costs but also whether there are alternative measures that could achieve the objective more effectively or at lower cost.

7.2.7 Convergence

Looking forward, technological convergence, and in particular the presence of competing networks offering substitute services, is likely to continue the trend towards the reduction in *ex ante* regulation of cable networks. Competition and arguments for technological neutrality can also be expected to see the gradual streamlining of public interest regulation, although the broadcasting industry as a whole can still be expected to attract greater regulation than many other sectors of the economy.

7.3 REGIME COMPARISON

The country comparative review in Table 4 at the end of this chapter, as well as the more detailed review in Appendix 4, are aimed at providing an understanding of the different regimes for regulation of the cable sector. The analysis examines the following areas:

— Market structure: What is the market structure of the pay TV sector? Which are the major players in the pay TV sector and within the cable sector in particular?
— Regulation: How is the cable sector regulated? Is there a licensing regime and specialist regulator?
— Competition law: Has competition law been applied to cable companies, whether in relation to abuse of dominance or anti-competitive agreements?
— Merger control: Does merger control apply in the cable TV sector? Have there been any cases involving prohibitions or remedies?
— Media ownership: Are there any rules restricting ownership, or cross-ownership, of a cable company and another media interest?
— Reform agenda: Are there any updates and trends in terms of proposed reforms to competition and regulation?

A summary of key findings across the above areas is provided in Table 4. Mini country 'stories' or 'case studies' are provided in Appendix 4 to illustrate the richness and diversity of the experience.

7.4 CONCLUSIONS AND IMPLICATIONS FOR POLICY

The analysis here, through an examination of the underlying economic theory, empirical evidence and policy arguments is consistent with the three basic themes of this work when viewed in the context of the pay TV/cable sector. First, the global regimes differ markedly in terms of their approach to regulation of the cable sector. Second, the regulatory regime cannot be separated from the political and cultural environment. Third, one of the most effective constraints on higher prices is competition; raising questions about whether the regulatory regime itself in prescribing the number or type of entrants might in fact constrain investment and choice.

Some markets are characterised by the presence of one or more major or even dominant cable provider, perhaps due to a legacy of state control or influence which has restricted the number of operators (eg in Russia and China). In other countries, competition has led to more than one pay TV system where cable competes with other platforms such as satellite. An initial analysis might suggest that there should be only one provider making available capacity to third parties but further examination suggests a more nuanced view. Indeed, many of the competition law investigations in the sector have arisen from complaints and concerns that a dominant owner of infrastructure or content may be foreclosing access to competition (eg Belgium, Mexico, South Korea, the UK and the US).

Accepting that the sector does have examples of abuses of market power and that these are not confined to one jurisdiction, raises the question of whether competition law alone is sufficient to address the resulting harm or whether *ex ante* intervention is needed. Indeed, this is the key question facing the Telecom Regulatory Authority of India (TRAI) as it debates whether, and if so how, to regulate the cable sector prospectively. It would seem that basic parameters need to be taken into account when deciding whether to impose further regulatory burdens on operators. These lie first in the assessment of market power and the extent to which cable faces competition. Within the sector there is the issue of duplication of infrastructure and the existence of sunk costs which might disincentivise later entrants. Even where there is no reasonable prospect that alternative infrastructure is likely to be built, a deeper inquiry is needed into the extent to which the cable operator is subject to competition from other sources of pay TV.

A further theme in the country reviews is the phenomenon whereby cases are often initiated on the back of complaints rather than being initiated by the regulator. This is a typical theme in the telecommunications and broadcasting sector not least since rivals will invariably be seeking a commercial solution such as access to content or infrastructure. The independent competition and regulatory authorities are tasked with protecting competition and not competitors which focuses on the importance of the regulator needing to take a decision independently of such pressures. However, the question remains as to whether the regulator should eliminate barriers or focus on the prevention of abuse. The promotion of competition has manifested itself in the telecommunications sector in terms of infrastructure or access. Problems in this area have largely been addressed through access conditions. However, reflecting the long-term strategy of growth it may be useful to consider whether something more should be done to foster the conditions for new entry. However, an inquiry into economies of scale might suggest that only one cable company is viable and competition should be via alternative technologies such as satellite.

Even if it is accepted that further incentives need to be provided to foster new entry, it may still be asked whether this entails more or less regulation. For example, it is quite possible that a symmetric deregulation across the board and including operators with Significant Market Power (SMP) might in fact create a more level playing field in terms of the incentives to invest. This is precisely the debate that is playing out in the UK in the ongoing regulatory review of the implications of convergence on regulation in the broadcasting sector. As yet, the outcome is not precisely defined.

Regulatory scrutiny of the TV sector has focused on economic issues which are often elided with a discussion of the 'public interest', however defined. This may be built into the framework of the authority's decision-making (ie the power of the US Federal Communications Commission (FCC) to review mergers in the cable and communications sector on the basis of public interest considerations which include, but are not limited to, competition). In others, the public interest is defined more explicitly for the media sector such as in the UK Enterprise Act 2002. One particular issue that has arisen from regulatory debates surrounding the public interest is what, exactly, do we mean by the public interest? Quite often concerns as to economic market power can be dressed up as 'public interest' concerns or the other way round. There is an important implication for the ongoing debate about control of the media in India, which manifests itself in a concern that certain political interests may be using the media for political ends. This is an issue that warrants scrutiny. If substantiated, it would seem possible to conceive of targeted remedies, such as a ban on political parties controlling segments of the media including TV channels or radio stations. However, it is important that in that inquiry a more specific concern related to the improper use of the media for political ends is not used as a justification for excessive intervention.

Against this background, it is imperative that the policy should be allowed to develop so as to answer the fundamental questions as to what type of regulation, if any, is needed to allow the market to function efficiently with respect to where it has come from (the historical background), where it is now (the status quo) and its future development.

Changing circumstances in the wider telecommunications and media markets have prompted the need to examine and re-examine the effectiveness of the prevailing regulatory environment. Almost all the regimes surveyed in this study have a reform agenda where the existing framework is being tested for its ongoing effectiveness. An exception is China which shows limited signs of moving from the legacy of state control in the near future.

This sector review of cable has been prompted by a number of factors. With convergence and competition, old styles of regulation may no longer be appropriate for resolving the challenges faced by a more complex marketplace where the distinction between regulated and unregulated spheres may be blurring. In some territories, such as Russia, the regime is looking outward to approaches in other countries (Member States of the EU) to see whether useful and relevant examples may be identified to serve as a justification for opening up the local market to competition and encouraging an environment that is more attractive to investment. Mexico has similarly relaxed its controls on foreign investment in the broadcasting sector. This appears to be predicated on a belief that times are changing and that protecting old monopolies, irrespective of how they have grown up, may not serve economic growth or customer demands. In markets which have grown largely unchecked by regulation (eg India) there has been an interest in examining whether tighter controls should be introduced either in the form of ownership caps or prohibitions on integrating across the supply chain. Interestingly, while the changes to Mexican regulation in the sector open up the possibility of such limits in the future, they have not yet been imposed.

A further theme is the role of competition law in the cable sector. Complaints have tended to involve allegations of both abuse of dominance and anti-competitive agreements with a weighting towards the former. A consistent theme has been the need to ensure access: to content, infrastructure and customers. In the EU, as in other areas where there is communications regulation, there has been a trend towards rolling back of *ex ante* interventions in cases where an operator has SMP.

Against this background, restricting entry into the cable sector through arbitrary limits that are independent of the merits of the particular case may be disproportionate, or at the very least risks resulting in ill-targeted outcomes. Mergers between cable and other services and platforms have been allowed either unconditionally or, often, subject to commitments. This approach is becoming increasingly accepted and is an inevitable consequence of convergence.

Competition is not an alternative to regulation or supervision. Where regulation has been relaxed, this has not necessarily given way to a 'free for all' market where abuse and anticompetitive activity goes unchecked. The UK and US have progressively relaxed regulatory restrictions in the communications sector but this has not displaced the role of an active communications regulator as Ofcom and the FCC have been prepared to take an interventionist role.

Finally, most of the regimes in our study remain in a state of flux. Some have recently introduced reforms (eg Belgium, UK, Mexico) while in others (eg Russia) reform is underway. In these circumstances, the ground rules are far from settled emphasising the importance of each jurisdiction adopting an approach that meets the needs of the local market. It can be guided by international best practices and there are examples where a rolling back of *ex ante* intervention—backed up by tough enforcement *ex post*—has facilitated further development and competition. At the same time, the rather mixed picture emerging means that regulators contemplating revising their regimes and testing existing ones need to adapt their approach to the new and market-specific challenges.

See specific country overviews in Appendix 4 for further detail.

Table 4: Cable sector regulation and competition—Country comparison

Country	Market structure	Regulation	Competition law	Merger control	Media ownership rules	Reform agenda
A. EUROPE						
Belgium	>80% of households receive TV services via cable.	Federal state with three regions and language Communities. Federal regulator (BIPT) works with counterparts in the three Communities.	General competition law applies and there have been decisions involving Belgian cable operators relating to abuse of dominance and anticompetitive agreements.	General merger control applies with no special rules for the cable sector. Merger cases have involved mergers between cable operators.	Virtually no cross-media ownership restrictions apart from general merger control.	New telecommunications law (October 2012). New competition law (September 2013).
Portugal	4 main pay TV players. 2 players hold 80% of the market.	Specialist media regulator licences pay TV operators.	General competition law applies to pay TV.	General merger control applies; structural and behavioural remedies have been applied in transactions involving pay TV.	None	New Competition Act 2012. Expect close monitoring of the sector by the media and competition authority.

(Continued)

Table 4: (*Continued*)

Country	Market structure	Regulation	Competition law	Merger control	Media ownership rules	Reform agenda
Russia	Largest pay TV players include Tricolor TV, Rostelecom, MTS, ER-Telekom, Akado.	No specific regulation for pay TV sector (generally governed by telecoms, media and information sector regulation).	General competition law applies with no special rules for the cable sector.	General merger control applies with no special rules for the cable sector.	Restrictions on foreign ownership of and investment in mass media (includes TV channels) and businesses having strategic importance.	Strategy Plan for Development of Competition and Anti-monopoly Regulation (2013) suggests Russian antimonopoly law will become more supportive of a competitive environment.
United Kingdom	Three providers of cable. Other pay TV offerings include satellite and IPTV.	Specific regulatory frame-work applies to the communications sector (Communication Act 2003 is the principal legislation).	General competition law applies to the cable sector. Applied concurrently by the communications and competition regulator.	General merger control law applies to the cable sector. In addition, broadcasting/ cross-media mergers may be subject to intervention on public interest grounds.	There are no specific restrictions on the ownership of cable businesses. Restrictions on media ownership in the UK have been progressively rolled back. Some restrictions remain in relation to the holding of a broadcast licence, national cross media (newspapers and Channel 3 licences).	The UK competition law framework is undergoing reform including through the creation of the Competition and Markets Authority with effect from 1 April 2014.

(*Continued*)

Table 4: (*Continued*)

Country	Market structure	Regulation	Competition law	Merger control	Media ownership rules	Reform agenda
B. AMERICAS						
Brazil	Cable and satellite are the most significant pay TV technologies. Over 150 firms currently offer pay TV services.	Cable is regulated by the telecommunications sector regulator ANATEL. Relaxation of regulatory restrictions on entry into pay TV sector since 2012.	General competition law applies to the cable sector and is enforced by CADE.	General merger control enforced by CADE applies to the cable TV sector.	Relaxation of restrictions on foreign ownership in the cable sector since 2011. Some restrictions on cross-media ownership.	2011 reforms are intended to streamline the general competition law enforcement regime. ANATEL has been strengthening its ability to deal with competition issues.
Mexico	Pay TV is offered through satellite, microwave and cable. Televisa holds over 50% of the cable segment.	Mexican Constitution was amended in 2013 to create two new regulators FTI (telecommunications and broadcasting); and FECC (competition outside the telecommunications sector).	General competition law applies to the cable and broadcasting sector. Numerous examples of cases involving abuse of dominance (relative monopolistic practices) and cartel practices.	TV sector has undergone considerable consolidation in recent years and most transactions have required pre-merger notification and approval.	No set limits but these can be imposed following the Constitutional amendment. Cross-ownership has been usual in the media sector. Competition and merger cases have raised cross-ownership.	The 2013 Constitutional amendment has brought about a major overhaul and was largely prompted by concerns in the communications sector.

(*Continued*)

Table 4: (*Continued*)

Country	Market structure	Regulation	Competition law	Merger control	Media ownership rules	Reform agenda
		Detailed legal framework applies to the broadcasting and telecommunications sector.	(absolute monopolistic practices) in the sector.		issues and remedies have been directed at such issues.	
United States	The main platforms and players in the pay TV sector are DBS, cable and internet distributors.	Cable TV is subject to regulation at the local and federal level. The FCC is the specialist federal regulator.	The FTC and DOJ regulate competition in the cable sector under general antitrust laws. The FCC also regulates competition in the cable sector under the Communications Act 1934.	General merger control applies where the thresholds under the Hart–Scott–Rodino Act apply (with notification to the DOJ/ FTC).	A single entity may own multiple broadcast networks but cannot own two or more of the top four.	Ongoing regulatory reforms relate to: retransmission consent, wholesale unbundling, exclusivity rules and public interest broadcasting.
C. ASIA						
China	The market is highly regulated and fragmented into geographic areas. The major players differ depending on the province.	Strict regulatory controls. Cable operators require a licence from SARFT and local/ provincial government approval.	General competition law under the Anti-monopoly Law applies.	General merger control under the Anti-monopoly Act applies.	Private investment in the cable sector is permitted but tightly controlled. State participation must be at least 51%.	Few indications of liberalisation of the cable sector which is viewed as an instrument of government propaganda.

(*Continued*)

Table 4: (*Continued*)

Country	Market structure	Regulation	Competition law	Merger control	Media ownership rules	Reform agenda
India	The TV sector comprises mainly cable TV, DTH, IPTV and terrestrial PV provided by the State broadcaster.	Cable operators and MSOs must register with the registering authority.	General competition law under the Competition Act 2002 applies to the cable sector.	General merger control under the Competition Act 2002 applies to the cable sector.	No current restrictions on ownership of MSOs and LCOs and no caps on the number of subscribers.	In 2013 the TRAI consulted on potential reform of cable sector regulation including introducing restrictions on ownership. The future regulatory rules are not determined as at the end of 2013.
South Korea	There are three main categories of player in the pay TV sector: satellite, cable and IPTV.	Cable is regulated under the Broadcasting Act by the MSIP. Cable operators require a licence from the MSIP.	General competition law applies to the cable sector and is enforced by the KFTC.	If the relevant thresholds are met M&A transactions in the cable are subject to pre- or post-merger notification requirements.	The Broadcasting Act imposes a variety of restrictions on ownership of cable and cable and other media businesses	Ongoing and future reforms may lead to further deregulation of the sector. Proposed amendments may at the same time limit the number of subscribers in a segment of the pay TV sector.

8

The Impact of the Internet

8.1 INTRODUCTION

We begin this chapter with some data on online developments in India. We then discuss the impact of the internet on the provision and consumption of media more generally and present a case study of the effect on news. The latter is important as it demonstrates the effect of the internet on defining markets and measuring plurality and, therefore, also for regulatory policy and intervention.

In respect of market definition, the internet obviously has implications for all media markets. While TV channels were historically delivered by terrestrial, cable and satellite distribution methods, they may now be delivered by closed internet networks (IPTV) or via the open internet ('over the top' or OTT). The internet thus adds new dimensions to market definition. In this example, the TV market would include all distribution methods.

We acknowledge that the mass audience of the media in India may lag behind many other more developed countries in respect of the availability of the internet and convergence services. However, a study by Assocham and comScore found that India is one of the three fastest-growing internet markets globally. India is the fastest-growing market among the BRIC nations,[1] adding more than 18 million internet users by July 2012, an annual growth rate of 41 per cent, yielding a total of 125 million internet users.

An Assocham spokesperson stated that: 'Interestingly, about 75 per cent of online audience [is] between the age group of 15–34 years, India is one of the youngest online demographic globally.'[2]

The five most popular categories accessed online were social networking, portals, search, entertainment and news sites. The Telecom Regulatory Authority of India (TRAI) has reported that the broadband subscriber base increased from 14.68 million by the end of July 2012 to 14.82 million by the end of August 2012—a monthly growth of 1.37 per cent.[3]

[1] Brazil, Russia, India and China.

[2] comScore, 'State of e-Commerce in India, a Research report by comScore for Assocham', September 2012, 4, available at: www.assocham.org/arb/general/Comscore_%20ASSOCHAM-report-state-of-ecommerce-in-india.pdf.

[3] Telecom Regulatory Authority of India, 'Consultation Paper on Issues relating to Media Ownership', 15 February 2013.

Figure 11 indicates the growth in BRIC internet users from July 2011 to July 2012, demonstrating that India's growth was the highest.

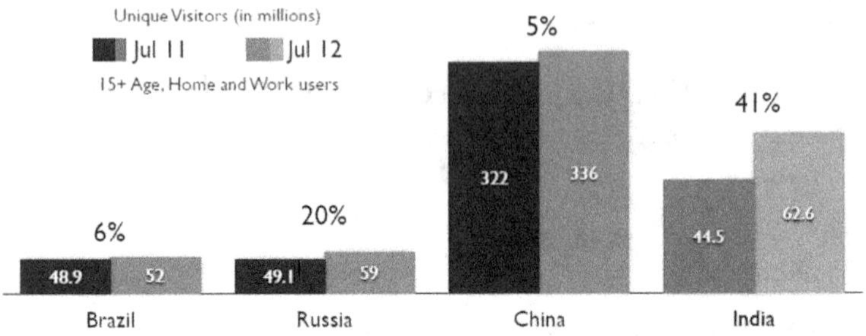

Figure 11: Growth in internet users between July 2011 and July 2012

Source: comScore, The Rise in India's Digital Consumer, August 2012, p 9

Figure 12 provides more detailed information on internet usage—fixed vs mobile access, time spent and pages viewed, all of which exhibit growth. By July 2012, internet penetration stood at 10 per cent, according to comScore. The number of unique visitors grew by more than 40 per cent between July 2011 and July 2012.

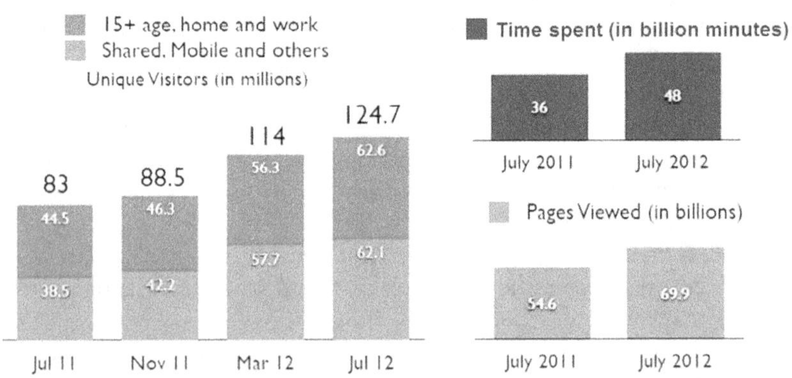

Figure 12: Growth in internet users and usage between July 2011 and July 2012

Source: comScore, The Rise in India's Digital Consumer, August 2012, p 10

Figure 13 demonstrates that as a proportion of total internet traffic in India, mobile overtook desktop around June 2012.

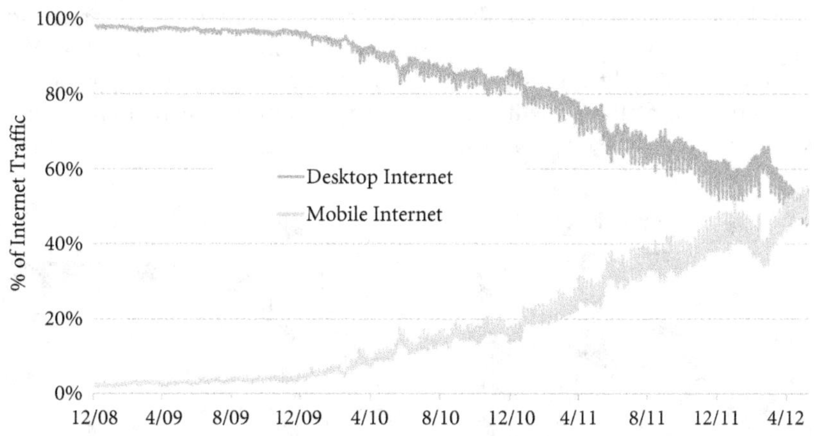

Figure 13: Trends in internet traffic between desktop and mobile internet (India)
Source: KPCB Internet Trends, 12 March 2012

In respect of the activities that India's internet users are engaging in, Figure 14 demonstrates significant growth in many activities (particularly games). comScore reports that the growth in consumption in travel, search, social networking and news exceeds the worldwide average.

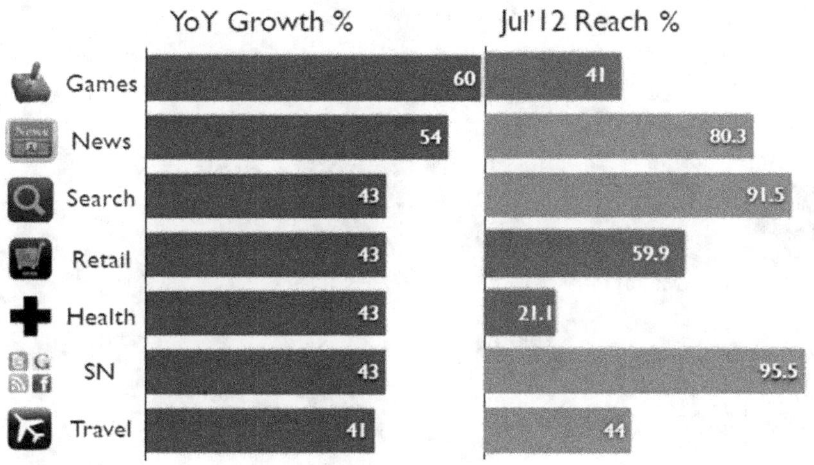

Figure 14: Growth in internet activities in India
Source: comScore, The Rise in India's Digital Consumer, August 2012, p 13

Figure 15 shows internet activity within the entertainment category. According to comScore, the category added around 15 million additional unique visitors (UVs) during the year from July 2011 to July 2012. YouTube has the greatest reach in the category and most of the growth is reported to be from Bollywood and music videos.

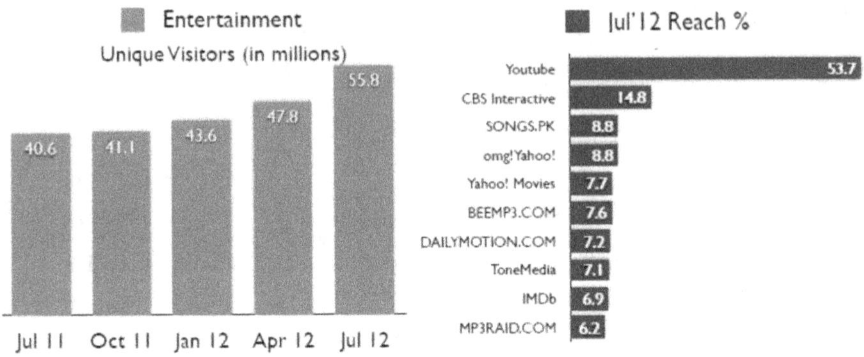

Figure 15: Growth in online entertainment in India

Source: comScore, The Rise in India's Digital Consumer, August 2012, p 13

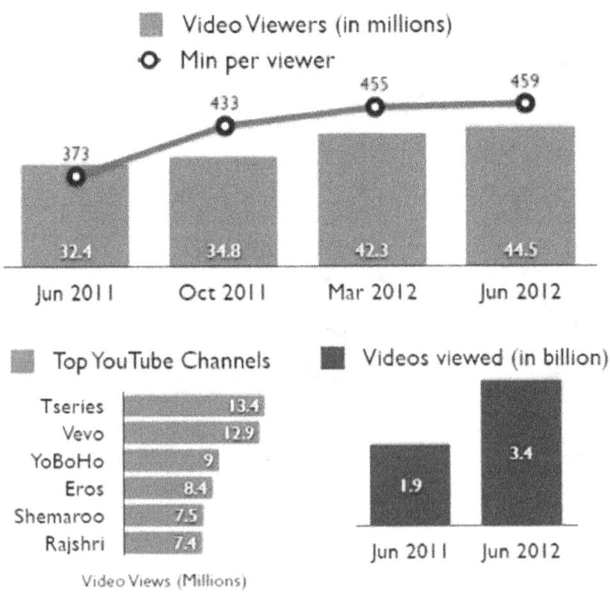

Figure 16: Online video viewing in India

Source: comScore, The Rise in India's Digital Consumer, August 2012, p 24

Data on online video viewing is reproduced in Figure 16. This demonstrates that around 3.4 billion online videos are viewed each month and that the number of video viewers has grown by more than 37 per cent. comScore reports that more than 50 per cent of the videos are in the entertainment category.

According to one industry commentator, in India mobile internet TV and OTT services are both services that have significant growth potential.[4] While TV penetration stands at 65 per cent, it is reported that online TV services may particularly appeal to households that currently have no existing terrestrial infrastructure, cable or satellite services.

According to indiantelevision.com, an independent survey of Indian consumers was conducted to find out what people want from mobile video and about their willingness to pay for the service. Of those surveyed, 54 per cent stated that they had already paid to access content and a further 88 per cent said they would consider paying for mobile video either now or in the future.

Broadband TV News announced in September 2012 that Watch India TV had launched a TV app that provides 70 channels of Indian television channels across all internet-connected devices, including TVs, smartphones, tablets and PCs.[5] While the majority of take-up may initially occur from territories outside India, the service is available domestically.

According to a report from Cisco, internet traffic in India is expected to increase nine-fold by 2015, at a compound annual growth rate of 55 per cent.[6] The principal driver of the uptake is projected to be video—internet video traffic is expected to be 63 per cent of all consumer traffic in 2015, up from 20 per cent in 2010. It reported that: 'About 99 billion minutes of video content will cross the Internet each month in 2015, up from 7 billion in 2010. Video will exceed half of India's consumer Internet traffic by year-end 2013.'[7]

Further metrics and information are provided in Appendix 5.

8.2 ONLINE'S STAGE OF DEVELOPMENT

While in India the current stage of broadband availability, penetration and device usage is lower than for many other territories, we are guided by the importance of not chilling markets today—through intrusive and excessive regulations—at the expense of digitally transformed markets tomorrow. The trends indicated above demonstrate that those who do have access to the internet in India behave in line with international trends. Presumably, policy-makers in India want the trends to date to continue and extend to the mass market.

[4] PricewaterhouseCoopers, 'Global entertainment and media outlook: 2012–2016', 8 June 2012.

[5] Available at: www.broadbandtvnews.com.

[6] The Hindu Business Line, 'Cisco says India's Net traffic will grow 9-fold by 2015', 2 June 2011, available at: www.thehindubusinessline.com/industry-and-economy/info-tech/cisco-says-indias-net-traffic-will-grow-9fold-by-2015/article2071534.ece?css=print.

[7] Ibid.

8.3 EFFECT OF THE INTERNET ON MEDIA

The internet has a number of key effects on the consumption and provision of media services, including, but not limited to the following:

— it enables a multitude of services to reach consumers via both fixed and mobile networks to a range of devices—TVs, smart TVs, smartphones, laptops, desktops and tablets;
— it provides an alternative distribution network, enabling wider availability of services to consumers;
— it facilitates the development of new services such as catch-up TV and video on demand (rental and retail);
— it allows consumers to access content 'any time and any place';
— it facilitates competition from alternative media providers—either new entrants or entry into local media markets from established overseas providers; and
— it reduces the barriers to entry with the result that established providers have to take into account the threat of potential entrants.

All of the above, discussed in chapter 2, have implications for policy and regulation.

The internet has a very specific effect on news media—reading newspapers, listening to radio news and watching television news can all be done online. Online is a truly cross-media environment and this has implications for the definition and measurement of news media markets and for media plurality. We will therefore provide a specific case study on news media.

8.4 CASE STUDY: NEWS

We cover the following key trends:

— how newspapers are becoming integrated media properties with links to online sites and social media such as Facebook and Twitter;
— how traditional media now face competition from online versions of traditional media (across all sub-sectors) and 'new' online media; and
— how the online media provides access to literally thousands of voices across the globe.

We also set out the implications of such trends for market definition and plurality.[8]

[8] The discussion is informed by FTI's previous research into media plurality including: 'Ofcom: Measuring Media Plurality (Take Two), An FTI Consulting Whitepaper', 4 February 2013 (available at: www.fticonsulting.co.uk/global2/critical-thinking/white-papers/measuring-media-plurality.aspx); 'The importance of the internet in how news is obtained in the UK today, a report submitted to the Leveson Inquiry', 24 February 2012 (available at: www.levesoninquiry.org.uk/wp-content/uploads/2012/08/Annex-B-to-Pluality-submission-from-NI.pdf); and 'Measuring Plurality in News, News Corporation/British

We note that while this case study focuses on news in order to indicate how trends in plurality may develop in future, much of the commentary applies equally to other media.

8.4.1 News Provision

In this section we outline the principal changes that have been occurring in news provision, based largely on an assessment of how the internet has changed and continues to change the landscape for news media. The wide-ranging ways in which the internet contributes to media plurality means that simple calculations of narrow, static market shares of traditional media channels no longer show the full picture of media plurality.

As reported almost six years ago by Ofcom, 'news is ubiquitous on the internet' and:

> The web offers the potential for almost limitless diversity in news, discussion and debate ... In future there will be ever more outlets for audiovisual news including through the internet with its almost limitless capacity for information, analysis and opinion ... The unprecedented availability of such a huge range of traditional and new sources of news opens up possibilities for real diversity of opinion to be heard.[9]

There has been an explosion in the number and type of news sources on the internet, including new entrants that do not originate from traditional news media. There is a vast range of available content which includes text, data, infographics, audio, audiovisual and social media, and may be delivered personally to fixed and mobile devices. Services include podcasts, rich site summary (RSS) feeds, and blogs. Owing to its ubiquity, the internet enables consumers to access news from around the world—for example, via online sites of *The New York Times*, Russia Today, France 24 and CNN.

The online news landscape contains many different types of news provider. These include:

- global, national and regional newspapers whose websites host online versions of their content;
- traditional broadcasters;
- online-only news websites, such as The Huffington Post, which have developed in the market, taking advantage of the low barriers to entry;
- news agencies such as Reuters and Associated Press, which provide news content to newspapers and other distributors;

Sky Broadcasting Group Plc, Submission to Ofcom', 14 January 2011 (available at: www.culture.gov.uk/images/publications/Annexes-NewsCorps-submission-to-SoS_14JAN2011.pdf).

[9] Ofcom, 'New News, Future News: the challenges for television news after Digital Switch-over', 26 June 2007.

- aggregators of content such as Yahoo! and Google; and
- other websites and informal sources of news such as blogs and social media.

Each of these providers distributes their content in several different ways, and typical offerings may include: a website, an email newsletter, a mobile phone app, a tablet app, a Facebook page or a Twitter feed. This allows users to consume content from different providers in different ways.

The internet has increased competition (and so reduced the influence of individual providers) through a number of routes including:

- providing competition from alternative news providers—either new entrants or entry into local news markets from established overseas providers;
- reducing the barriers to entry so established providers need to take into account the threat of potential entrants; and
- through user-generated news, as the internet provides a means for 'word of mouth' to reach a local, national and international audience.

Social media is increasingly used as a vehicle for news, particularly for breaking news. Twitter provides a complement to established newspapers and corresponding online content through discussion, and an increasing proportion of traffic to news websites is generated by Facebook.

Blogs include informal discussions by individuals and newspapers use blogs to generate interest in news stories and to attract users onto other related online news media properties. Audiences, politicians and celebrities are also involved in making the news and accessing the news in new ways. As reported by *The Economist*:

> Thanks to the rise of social media, news is no longer gathered exclusively by reporters and turned into a story but emerges from an ecosystem in which journalists, sources, readers and viewers exchange information.[10]

Thus the internet has fundamentally changed the landscape for news provision; it breaks down geographical boundaries in news provision, giving users access around the world, rather than printed newspapers in any specific market.[11]

Importantly, the development of the internet has fundamentally changed news provision for newspaper publishers who recognise the need to:

- provide an online extension of the traditional press;
- compete in a new news market that encompasses a multitude of other online providers such as broadcasters, online-only providers, and aggregators; and
- provide news through new news media—using applications, mobile sites and social media.

Through these new channels, the internet provides a means for 'word of mouth' to travel widely, reaching national and international audiences.

[10] The Economist, 'The people formerly known as the audience', 7 July 2011, available at: www.economist.com/node/18904124.

[11] Oliver & Ohlbaum, 'UK Media Enters a New Age', December 2011.

Arguably, the various structural changes have led to a change in the definition of the market—in the case of newspapers for example, they are no longer only printed copies. Essentially, the 'newspaper market' has become the 'news market'.

Such trends have led to a dynamic, vibrant news landscape. The number and variety of available voices has increased massively facilitated by the online environment. This is not only on the supply-side; the increasing trend in online news consumption, together with an increase in multi-sourcing, has led to an increase in plurality on the demand-side, which we discuss below.

8.4.2 News Consumption

While many of the trends reported below apply to a small proportion of consumers in India, as internet availability and device penetration increases and disposable incomes rise, more and more consumers will be able to access online news. As one report states:

> Consumers can also access news content produced by non-traditional and online-only providers. This ranges from commercially-produced content to not-for-profit or amateur material (or 'user uploaded content'). Blogs and the news distribution potential of social platforms such as Facebook and Twitter can also be important and influential sources of news.[12]

Access to the internet continues to change, especially access on the move. Current devices include smartphones and tablets—the latter have been found to increase both the reach and duration of reading news online. This trend is likely to continue as penetration of the devices increases. Consumers have embraced social media (such as Facebook and Twitter), generating significant reach and a large potential influence. Facebook, in particular, is a key traffic driver to newspaper sites. Newspapers provide social media links to news stories adding credibility to the available news and attracting younger audiences.

Consumers are also using more news sources, comprising both traditional and new media; multi-sourcing is becoming the norm.

Such trends are leading to a shift in cross-media news consumption patterns towards online, which is a highly plural environment. Online news consumers have a tendency to access considerably more news outlets than those who rely primarily on traditional media.

These trends are expected to continue as internet penetration and the uptake of technology increases. Therefore, as the internet becomes an increasingly important outlet for news in India it is to be expected that an increasing proportion of the population will be regularly exposed to a wide variety of 'voices'.

[12] Ofcom, 'Media Ownership Rules Review', 31 July 2009, 9.

8.5 CONCLUSIONS AND IMPLICATIONS FOR POLICY

The internet has a number of key effects on the consumption and provision of media services, including, but not limited to, the following features:

- it enables a multitude of services to reach consumers via both fixed and mobile networks to a range of devices—TVs, smart TVs, smartphones, laptops, desktops and tablets;
- it provides an alternative distribution network, enabling wider availability of services to consumers;
- it facilitates the development of new services such as catch-up TV, video on demand (rental and retail);
- it allows consumers to access content 'any time and any place';
- it facilitates competition from alternative media providers—either new entrants or entry into local media markets from established overseas providers; and
- it reduces the barriers to entry so established providers have to take into account the threat of potential entrants.

Each of the above has implications for regulation as boundaries between markets, networks and services become blurred. As we concluded in chapter 2, as a consequence regulators need to adopt a dynamic (and at the current state of knowledge and evolution) cautious approach.

The internet has a very specific effect on news media—reading newspapers, listening to radio news and watching television news can all be done online—online is a truly cross-media environment and this has implications for the definition and measurement of news media markets and for media plurality (most of what follows applies equally to other categories of media or entertainment):

- The internet has fundamentally changed the landscape for news provision: it breaks down geographical boundaries in news provision, giving users access from around the world, rather than just domestic printed newspapers or TV/radio broadcasts.
- Traditional plurality assessments are challenged: importantly, the effect that the internet has had on both the provision and consumption of news challenges the traditional approach of assessing media plurality. Indeed, we question whether such an approach remains valid. For example, in considering media plurality in respect of the press, to consider the printed copy alone would overlook two critical features on both the demand side (consumers coming to newspapers via social media and online sites) and the supply side (newspapers are now integrated with digital media—websites, videos, microblogging and social networks). Such trends are expected to continue as internet penetration and technology uptake increases. Therefore, as the internet becomes an increasingly important outlet for news, it is to be expected that an increasing proportion of the population will be regularly exposed to a wide variety of 'voices'; plurality will continue to increase.

— Online further complicates market definition: as we discussed in chapter 3, there is an inherent difficulty in measuring media plurality across traditional news media as there is no agreed upon cross-media exchange rate. Online news media further complicates matters as it becomes increasingly difficult to define markets. It is difficult to compare and contrast video material on a newspaper website or a broadcaster's online news 'broadcast'. To define the newspaper market as simply the printed copy is a simplification as newspapers are increasingly integrated with online (websites) and social media.

— Regulate explicitly and for the future: while online trends may appear somewhat distant to the mass market consumer in India, discrete parts of the population are already engaging in such online behaviour. Policy-makers need to mindful of interventions that might chill investment and innovation. This is not to say that media plurality is not important—it is—rather, that regulatory interventions should be made to address identified problems based on up-to-date empirical evidence.

— A cautious approach required: markets are dynamic and subject to much uncertainty in respect of future technological developments. Policy-makers and regulators should be cautious in applying old-style, static regulations to today's markets without empirical evidence that real problems exist today.

9

Shaping the Future Regulatory Agenda in India and Internationally

9.1 INTRODUCTION: ONGOING CONSULTATION AND DEBATE ON THE SHAPE OF MEDIA AND COMMUNICATIONS REGULATION INTERNATIONALLY

Many countries are revisiting their existing rules and procedures for regulation of media and communications markets. In some instances this has been in response to popular pressure for more—or less—interventionist approaches. In other cases, the reform agenda is prompted by developments overseas which have inspired a country to re-assess whether its own rules are fit for purpose or otherwise conform to international practices in an area where there is plenty of scope for controversy about the 'right way of doing things'. The phenomenon of convergence has also caused countries to reconsider whether traditional approaches to regulation are appropriate when the boundaries between regulated and unregulated markets are blurring.

This chapter provides a selection of case study 'vignettes' which examine ongoing reform initiatives in the international media and communications sector. We start by considering recent and ongoing reform proposals by the Telecom Regulatory Authority of India (TRAI). In order to illustrate the continuing international debate we explore recent consultations in the UK, the EU, Australia and the US. While the country comparison is necessarily focused, the examples exhibit a range of approaches, diverse geographies and varying stages of evolution in the respective regulatory frameworks. In particular, we observe the following trends.

Despite the increasing competitiveness of media and communications markets, competition and regulatory authorities have been active in launching reform initiatives. While the impetus for reform proposals shows no sign of relenting, regulators tend to be slower in implementing sea changes amid public objection; eg delays to proposed changes to the approach of the US Federal Communications Commission (FCC) to measuring media diversity.

Established jurisdictions which have a long history of regulating the media are revisiting traditional approaches and opting for more flexible tools and measures; eg Ofcom's approach in the UK to measuring plurality using a range of metrics.

Public interest considerations form a discrete topic for scrutiny, whether alone or in parallel to competition law issues; eg European Commission proposals for pan-European regulation of plurality across the Member States.

Economic and non-economic policy issues often underpin the impetus for reform. Social and cultural aspects are often pursued on the back of media and communications reforms; eg the TRAI's consultation in the cable sector contains overtones of social inclusion.

Proposals for reform are invariably hotly contested and fought out in the public arena. A compromise solution may be accepted to appease the different factions; eg the Royal Charter in the UK which fell short of the proposals by Lord Justice Leveson for regulation of the press; and the withdrawal of most of the controversial reforms to Australian media regulation in March 2013.

Further background material is provided in Appendix 6.

9.2 INDIAN EXPERIENCE AND RECENT TRAI CONSULTATIONS

9.2.1 Consultation on Media Cross-ownership

On 15 February 2013 the TRAI released a consultation paper on issues relating to ownership—particularly cross-ownership—of the media.[1] In its statement on the launch of the consultation, the TRAI observed that media markets in India are undergoing changes that it believed may have significant implications for competition and consumer choice in the sector:

> Major players of print, television and radio sectors are seeking expansion of their business interests in various segments of the print and broadcasting sectors leading to horizontal integration of media entities …
>
> Also, more and more broadcasting companies owning television channels are venturing into distribution segments ie cable TV, DTH, HITS, IPTV etc while distribution segment companies are entering into television broadcasting, leading to vertical integration in the broadcasting sector.[2]

The TRAI posed a number of detailed questions largely covering possible methods to regulate media ownership. Amongst the more controversial consultation issues were: (i) whether it would be appropriate to have a 'one out of three rule' to restrict any entity having ownership/control in an outlet of a media segment; (ii) whether it

[1] Telecom Regulatory Authority of India, 'Consultation Paper on Issues relating to Media Ownership', 15 February 2013. The authors were instructed to provide comparative commentary on international regulation, as part of a report prepared for Cable and Satellite Broadcasting Association of Asia (CASBAA). See, further, 'Issues relating to media ownership: TRAI's consultation paper, A report for CASBAA', March 2013.

[2] Reported in *The Economic Times*, 'TRAI releases consultation paper on media cross-ownership', 15 February 2013.

would be appropriate to restrict any entity having ownership/control in a media segment of more than a threshold level (say 20 per cent); and (iii) whether any entity should be allowed to have an interest in both broadcasting and distribution; ie a de facto ban on vertical integration.

In the course of this consultation, the UK is presented as a 'poster child' for the type of regulation that the TRAI is debating. In some instances, measures that the UK has now rejected in favour of a more liberal approach (eg limits on local media ownership) are cited in support of potentially replicating such a regime in India. In particular, the TRAI refers to regulation overseas in selected countries as inspiration for possible reforms in the regulation of media ownership in India.

However, the TRAI has not yet set out a discussion of identified problems in media markets in India today and/or made sufficiently explicit the policy objectives that need to be fulfilled: there is an absence of a problem statement beyond data and market analysis which predates the consultation by almost four years. Moreover, the TRAI does not appear to have considered the costs and benefits of the various interventions it is considering. These are serious omissions of the TRAI's consultation, as is the fact that while the TRAI acknowledges convergence, it does not discuss its implications for technology, networks, services or, fundamentally, regulation. Furthermore, we observe that the TRAI has not conducted a Regulatory Impact Assessment for its proposed regulation.

The objections raised here may well be rendered historical but they are raised to illustrate the cross-fertilisation between the debate on the proper scope of regulation in India and overseas. In providing this anecdotal case study we seek to emphasise our overall premise that intervention should be based on an identified set of problems and selected regulatory options and a Regulatory Impact Assessment that demonstrates that the outcome of the intervention is superior to the status quo.

9.2.2 Consultation on Monopoly and Market Dominance in Cable TV services

Within three months of the media ownership consultation, on 3 June 2013, the TRAI released a further consultation on monopoly and market dominance in cable TV.[3]

The TRAI's focus is much narrower in this consultation—it focuses on cable TV. However, the underlying approach towards evaluation of the need for reform and the appropriate type of intervention gives a sense of déjà vu. In particular, we

[3] Telecom Regulatory Authority of India, 'Consultation Paper on Monopoly/Market dominance in Cable TV services', 3 June 2013.

see the following worrying trends and thought processes that were also present in the cross-ownership consultation:

— A prima facie assumption of market dominance in cable, apparently based on market shares alone. This is not to say that further examination is not warranted but it is disappointing that such an assessment is not balanced with a consideration of historical and likely trends in penetration and investment in order to appraise the overall economic situation.
— A 'shopping list' of technical questions on how to regulate the sector but without an examination of how the TRAI's role would intersect with that of the Competition Commission of India (CCI) on competition matters.
— An attempt to superimpose sector regulation unrelated to mainstream merger control and, in one instance, a suggestion of retrospective dismantling of monopolies. The TRAI postulated that: 'Another issue that needs attention is whether the restrictions on control discussed in the preceding paras should be applicable retrospectively or prospectively.'[4]
— The use of international comparisons, on a selective basis and as (apparent) justification for automatic triggers on intervention. The TRAI cites international experience from the US, UK, Canada and South Korea. However, as with any international comparison, it is important to understand the legal and market context in which the particular rules operate. The UK is a case in point. The TRAI cites the merger assessment guidelines of the Competition Commission and the Office of Fair Trading (OFT) and mentions the various thresholds related to market concentration. However, such guidance is only that. By setting out guidance on the levels of concentration that would typically raise competition concerns, the UK authorities anchor their substantive merger assessment in established economic thinking. However, such measures are not decisive when considering whether or not a merger is challenged under UK competition law. Still less do such measures provide an automatic trigger for structural intervention based on organic growth.
— A failure to consider the full implications of trends in new platforms and distribution methods. It is a remarkable omission that the TRAI's consultation does not seek comments on the implications of market development or innovation and whether such changes could obviate or exacerbate its concerns. Of course, stakeholders are not precluded from making comments on such issues but they are not apparently at the forefront of the TRAI's inquiry.

[4] Ibid, paragraph 2.23.

9.3 EU EXPERIENCE: TOWARDS PAN-EUROPEAN REGULATION OF PLURALITY?

Two public consultations launched on 22 March 2013 suggest that the European Commission is considering a more interventionist media regulation policy.[5]

The first consultation is relatively uncontroversial—it concerns the independence of media regulators, highlighting formal, as distinct from de facto, independence.[6] The second is more controversial.[7] It advocates a much more proactive role by the European Commission in the areas of media freedom and plurality in the Member States. This would be a significant change and one that contrasts with the European Commission's approach to public service broadcasting (PSB), which essentially allows Member States significant autonomy in how they regulate PSB.

The public consultation on the independence of the audiovisual regulatory bodies considered methods of assessing the independence of the national regulatory bodies responsible for the Audiovisual Media Services Directive (AVMSD).[8] The AVMSD governs EU-wide coordination of national legislation on all audiovisual media, both traditional TV broadcasts and on-demand services. A report by INDIREG has found variation among the regulators responsible in terms of their formal and de facto independence.[9] The AVMSD provides no criteria for the independence of regulatory bodies. The consultation sought comments on a possible revision of Article 30 of the AVMSD.[10]

The second public consultation on the Independent Report of the High Level Group on Media Freedom and Pluralism sought responses on 30 recommendations in a report published by the High Level Stakeholder Group on Media Freedom and Pluralism. At a high level, this recommends that the Commission should protect media freedom and pluralism in the Member States. The recommendations on media freedom and pluralism are even more controversial since there is no consensus on the threshold question as to whether the EU is, or should be, considered competent to act to protect media freedom and pluralism at member state level. Indeed, this question is one of the issues for consultation.

[5] European Commission, 'Public consultation on the independence of the audiovisual regulatory bodies' and 'Public consultation on the Independent Report of the High Level Group on Media Freedom and Pluralism', 22 March 2013.

[6] European Commission, 'Public consultation on the independence of the audiovisual regulatory bodies', 22 March 2013.

[7] European Commission, 'Public consultation on the Independent Report of the High Level Group on Media Freedom and Pluralism', 22 March 2013.

[8] Directive 2010/13/EU of the European Parliament and of the Council of 10 March 2010 on the coordination of certain provisions laid down by law, regulation or administrative action in Member States concerning the provision of audiovisual media services [2010] OJ L95.

[9] INDIREG, 'Indicators for independence and efficient functioning of audiovisual media services regulatory bodies for the purpose of enforcing the rules in the AVMS Directive', February 2011.

[10] Article 30 provides that Member States 'shall take appropriate measures to provide each other and the Commission with the information necessary for the application of this Directive, in particular Articles 2, 3 and 4, in particular through their competent independent regulatory bodies'.

We find the European Commission's overall stance surprising as it contrasts considerably with its approach to PSB. While Member States are free to determine their PSB policies, in respect of media freedom and plurality the EU is advocating a much more hands-on role.

For stakeholders across the EU and particularly in the UK, this is a worrying state of affairs. In the UK, Ofcom spent some seven months on a public consultation on how to measure plurality, as discussed in chapter 5. The consultation involved stakeholder engagement (including written submissions), academic seminars, international benchmarking, extensive consumer research, an in-depth study of the provision of news, and a review of the academic literature. Other countries have their own specific approaches to dealing with media plurality as chapter 5 exemplifies. In our view, given the complexities, best practice knowledge sharing is to be encouraged. However, it is far from clear that there is sufficient support for harmonisation on this issue across all the Member States given the wide range of cultural, political and social contexts that suffuse the issue of plurality.

During the years 2007 to 2009, the European Commission engaged a consortium of consultants and academics to conduct a major study on media plurality across EU Member States. Its objectives were to consider appropriate metrics to measure media plurality and to monitor and indicate risks to media plurality. It developed a diagnostic tool, the 'Media Pluralism Monitor' which comprises more than 160 indicators. While a report was published in 2009,[11] there were until recently no subsequent developments. This is not surprising—it seems unlikely that 28 Member States would compile and monitor so many different metrics.

We understand, however, that the proposed risk monitor is back on the table and an announcement about its implementation may be imminent. According to the report of the High Level Group of Media Freedom and Pluralism

> a Media Pluralism Monitoring (MPM) tool has already been developed and is available online, but must be considered as a first effort which still needs considerable improvement. It has been criticised for being too cumbersome to apply and indeed has not been up and running so far. A pilot project of the European Parliament has been submitted and evaluated positively. Pending final agreement, the MPM could be put in practice in 2013.[12]

A more proactive role by the European Commission in the areas of media policy in the Member States would be a significant change since the EU has historically had a more limited role, largely in the promotion of an internal market for audiovisual media services and in consumer protection matters. The European Initiative for Media Pluralism has already urged the European Commission to prepare a new directive on press freedom and media pluralism.

[11] ICRI et al, 'Independent Study on Indicators for Media Pluralism in the Member States—Towards a Risk-Based Approach', July 2009.

[12] High Level Group on Media Freedom and Pluralism, 'A free and pluralistic media to sustain European democracy', January 2013.

The period of the consultations ran from 22 March 2013 to 14 June 2013. The future direction is unclear at the time of writing.[13]

9.4 UK EXPERIENCE: WHERE DO WE STAND AFTER *NEWSCORP/BSKYB* AND LEVESON?

9.4.1 Ofcom Review of Plurality

In June and October 2012, Ofcom provided two responses to the request from the Secretary of State (SoS) for advice on how best to measure and review media plurality. Ofcom answered the questions: 'What are the options for measuring media plurality across platforms?' and 'What do you recommend is the best approach?' as follows:

> There are three categories of metrics relevant to measuring media plurality: availability, consumption and impact. All should be included in a review of plurality, but the consumption metrics, especially reach, share and multi-sourcing, are the most important.
>
> In addition to metrics, other relevant contextual factors should be considered, for example governance and regulatory frameworks such as those which ensure impartiality. Given the dynamic nature of the news market, the metrics framework itself should be assessed during each review to ensure its continuing efficacy and relevance.[14]

Plurality is thus difficult to measure and it is important that a range of indicators are considered 'in the round'. Ofcom also stated that:

> We believe the features of a plural news market would include many or all of the following: a diverse range of independent news voices; high overall reach and consumption with consumers actively multi-sourcing; sufficiently low barriers to entry and competition to spur innovation; economic sustainability and no single organisation accounting for too large a share of the market.
>
> It may also be possible to develop a view as to what levels of the key consumption metrics provide an indication of a potential plurality concern, so that these levels are taken into consideration within a plurality review, without being regarded as absolute limits.[15]

Additionally, Ofcom concluded:

> Plurality needs to be considered both within organisations (ie internal plurality) and between organisations (ie external plurality).

[13] See, further, Sprague, A and Rab, S, 'Media Freedom and Pluralism—A Threat from the European Commission' (2013) FTI White Paper, April 2013.

[14] Ofcom, 'Measuring media plurality, Ofcom's advice to the Secretary of State for Culture, Olympics, Media and Sport', 6 June 2012.

[15] Ibid.

> In terms of scope, a review of plurality should be limited to news and current affairs but these genres should be considered across television, radio, the press and online.[16]

Ofcom ultimately recommends a sensible framework for assessment, that plurality should be considered in respect of certain market characteristics, and that the features of a plural news market include:

— the presence of a diverse range of independent news voices;
— high reach and consumption of multiple news sources;
— low barriers to entry and competition to encourage innovation; and
— economic sustainability, with no single organisation holding too large a market share.

Most encouragingly, Ofcom echoes the approach of the CC in *ITV/BSkyB*,[17] referencing a need to consider 'things in the round', and that there is a need 'to make judgements'. Crucially, Ofcom provides a clear steer away from rigid triggers.

The main conclusions of the Ofcom report are:

— measurement—Ofcom acknowledges the inherent measurement challenges and puts forward a range of measures to consider 'in the round'. It agrees that 'impact' is difficult to measure and overall appears to suggest a pragmatic framework and even suggests that the suitability of metrics be re-assessed over time;
— online news media—these are now endorsed as clear contributors to media plurality and that they: 'should be included in a plurality review as online news sources are used by a significant and growing proportion of the UK population';
— triggers—Ofcom suggests a periodic review approach (every four to five years) and dismisses the idea of reliance on discretionary interventions. It also asks whether the existing media merger regime should sit within a 'new proposed plurality regime' or exist in parallel. We await further news on how the new regime may look; and
— setting limits on news share—it is concluded that such an approach is inflexible and inadvisable and that any concerns should be addressed within the periodic review. Ofcom asks parliament to determine what constitutes sufficient plurality and whether there should be any further relaxation in cross-media ownership rules.

Ofcom has made some sensible recommendations in identifying the market characteristics that when present are indicative of sufficient plurality.

[16] Ibid.

[17] Competition Commission, *Acquisition by British Sky Broadcasting Group Plc of 17.9 per cent of the shares in ITV Plc, Report sent to Secretary of State (BERR) 14 December 2007.*

Echoing similar themes, in July 2012, the Department for Culture, Media & Sport (DCMS) submitted to the Leveson Inquiry:[18]

> any rules inevitably act as a potential constraint on that market so it is essential that they be proportionate and do not unnecessarily restrict growth and innovation … The maintenance of plurality is still vital but, as more and more services become available on different platforms, concerns over ownership have diminished to some extent and greater liberalisation has been permitted.[19]

On 29 November 2012, the report of the Leveson Inquiry into the culture, practices and ethics of the press was published. In relation to the media mergers public interest regime, Lord Leveson considered that the SoS should remain the decision-maker but he recommended certain measures to ensure the probity and rigour of decision-making.[20] At the time of writing, there is as yet no model of press regulation that has achieved industry support.

9.4.2 Ongoing Consultation—House of Lords Select Committee Call for Evidence

The topic of media plurality is once again at the forefront of the political agenda in the UK following the House of Lords' March 2013 Call for Evidence which closed on 1 May.

As the Committee reflects on the submissions made, this development is likely to be the beginning of a new period of debate as to what, if anything, should be done to improve the existing UK framework for the regulation of the media.

Over 30 separate submissions were made in response to the Call for Evidence including submissions from academics, businesses and individuals. We provide a brief summary of the authors' responses to the main issues and questions raised by the Inquiry below. The purpose of providing this excursus is to illustrate that many of the issues that the TRAI is debating are also still being discussed in the UK, despite many years of experience. The UK model—if it can be called that—is far from vindicated or decided at the time of writing. However, in the interests of synthesis and consolidation it is useful to summarise a few position points.

— Does a clearer objective for plurality policy need to be thought out and incorporated into statute than is currently the case? What should this be?

[18] Lord Justice Leveson, 'An inquiry into the culture, practices and ethics of the press' Report' No 0780 2012–13, 29 November 2012.

[19] Department for Culture, Media & Sport, 'Media Ownership: Summary', available at: www.levesoninquiry.org.uk/wp-content/uploads/2012/07/DCMS-submission_Narrative-on-media-ownership.pdf.

[20] Lord Justice Leveson, 'An inquiry into the culture, practices and ethics of the press' Report No 0780 2012–13, 29 November 2012.

Policy objectives should be clearly defined. Given the (positive) effect the internet is having on plurality, together with the fact that the last major legislative measure was made in 2003, plurality policy could be revisited and objectives reconsidered. Any incorporation into statute needs to balance certainty for stakeholders against the need for some flexibility in interpretation.

— In the absence of a definition of plurality in statute, what is the best definition, or should it be improved?

The current UK media public interest considerations are set out in section 58 of the Enterprise Act 2002. The relevant 'considerations' differ depending on whether the transaction concerns only newspapers or broadcasting/cross-media mergers. Ofcom devoted considerable attention and effort to developing its working 'definition' of media plurality. Ofcom's working definition (incorporating a range of metrics with no single measure being decisive) is an excellent first position. While there may possibly be a need for some minor enhancements/refinements, a radical revision is not advisable unless new robust evidence has come to light since the consultation.

— What should the scope of media plurality policy be? Should it encompass news and current affairs or wider cultural diversity in content provision as well?

The scope of media plurality should encompass news and current affairs only; media plurality is concerned with the plurality of viewpoints. Other genres are not directly relevant although some genres (eg soaps) may influence people's viewpoints. On the supply side, news provision is better defined and a reasonable indicator of relevant content than other genres.

— What are the appropriate triggers for a review of media plurality and with whom should discretion to trigger a review reside, or indeed should reviews be periodic?

The appropriate trigger is a relevant media merger. Ofcom reviews the status of media ownership rules on a periodic basis, and thus media plurality is implicitly assessed on a regular basis. Regulatory certainty should be paramount for all stakeholders.

— Should reviews be periodic while still retaining the possibility that a review can be triggered under certain circumstances? What should those circumstances be?

There should not be a backstop power to review that can be called upon at ministerial or regulatory discretion. This would effectively leave a 'sword of Damocles' hanging over industry and risks disincentivising organic growth.

— For the purposes of a review of media plurality, what should 'sufficient plurality' be? How should the growing role played by digital intermediaries acting as gateways to content be taken into account?

Sufficient plurality is a qualitative concept (exercising judgement based on a range of quantitative and qualitative evidence) and it must be assumed that there was sufficient plurality at the time the UK Communications Act 2003 was enacted. Essentially, there needs to be a sufficient range of viewpoints available to audiences in the UK across all media. Online news provision (and BBC services) should be included in the assessment and both the demand side (consumption, including multi-sourcing within and across media) and the supply side (news provision) should be taken into account. Companies that are successful in the plural and increasingly cross-media environment should not be penalised for their success.

— Should the BBC's output be included in a review of plurality?
The BBC cannot be excluded from the plurality landscape. If it is accepted that a commitment to impartiality, of its own, is not enough to guarantee plurality—though it contributes to it—BBC's governance structure should not prevent it being considered. It still has scope to influence the news agenda.

— How can internal plurality be sensibly measured against external plurality?
Both these mechanisms for contributing to plurality are valid. The distinction between external plurality (achieving plurality through a number of media outlets) and internal plurality (ensuring content diversity through a single supplier) has been accepted in the UK. In the context of BSkyB's proposed acquisition of a 17.9 per cent interest in ITV, the UK Competition Commission thought 'that it was appropriate to distinguish between the range of information and views that are provided across separate independent media groups (external plurality) and the range that are provided within individual media groups (internal plurality)'.[21]

— What structural and/or behavioural remedies are appropriate if insufficient plurality is found?
The choice between structural or behavioural remedies is not a binary one, ie a choice between one or the other remedy. The focus of competition authorities on structural remedies in cases raising concerns about market concentration has given way to a more sophisticated approach which selects the appropriate remedy on a case-by-case basis. In some instances, a behavioural solution may be more effective than a divestment remedy such as where access to content or prohibition from discrimination is key to ensuring the viability of independent offerings.

— How should the deployment of these structural or behavioural remedies be balanced with considerations of the wider context of news provision (eg the future of news provision and its financial viability)?
It is true that regulators face challenges when deploying remedies in fast-moving and uncertain markets. This is particularly the case in the media sector where the rise of the internet and new technologies and distribution methods presents on the one hand, the prospect of increased plurality, and

[21] Competition Commission, *Acquisition by British Sky Broadcasting Group Plc of 17.9 per cent of the shares in ITV Plc, Report sent to Secretary of State (BERR) 14 December 2007*, Executive Summary, paragraph 30.

on the other, uncertainty about how the market may develop. Accordingly, remedies should be supported by an impact assessment given the recognised ambiguous impact of technological and economic development in the media sector.

— With whom should power to deploy these remedies ultimately reside? What process for their deployment should be observed?
Historically, intervention on media public interest grounds has been the preserve of government rather than an independent regulator. However, as with any review of the substantive rules, there should also be a review of the orthodoxy that the state should be decisive on this question. The conclusion may be the same but the inquiry should focus on what safeguards can be deployed to ensure that such important decisions are in the public interest. The role of the courts to review such decisions serves as an important constitutional check on the power of regulators and should not be curtailed.
Although the first round of the consultation has closed, businesses across all media from traditional print to online will be watching developments to consider how the changing regulatory landscape will affect their interests.
As a parallel development, and indicative of the ongoing debate, on 30 July 2013, DCMS launched a consultation on media ownership and plurality.[22] This consultation sought views on the scope of the measurement framework. In particular, the DCMS invited views on the types of media that should be included (eg whether it should extend to online content); the genres it should cover; the types of organisations and services to which it should apply (whether it should be limited to publishers or extend to news aggregators and social media); whether the BBC should be included; and the audiences with which it should be concerned.

9.5 AUSTRALIAN EXPERIENCE: MEDIA REFORM TRIED, TESTED AND FAILED

9.5.1 Proposed Reforms

The month of March 2013 saw the release—and eleventh hour withdrawal—of hotly contested reforms to Australian media regulation. The proposed reforms comprised four Bills affecting media ownership and regulation of media professionals (Media Package). They attracted vociferous condemnation from the media industry's most prominent leaders, including public statements from CEOs of News Limited and Ten Networks. Serious reservations were expressed about the

22 Department for Culture, Media & Sport, Open consultation, Media ownership and plurality, 30 July 2013, available at: www.gov.uk/government/consultations/media-ownership-and-plurality.

content of the bills, and about the fact that they were 'steam-rollered' without proper consultation with industry and the Opposition.[23] In outlining the proposed reforms, we consider what they might have meant in practice, had they been implemented, in order to understand the objections raised and the reason for their rejection in the form and manner put forward.

9.5.2 Summary of the Proposed Reforms

(a) Government Oversight of the Media

The Public Interest Media Advocate Bill 2013 would establish the Public Interest Media Advocate (PIMA). The PIMA would be appointed by the Minister and have the following main functions: (i) to consider and determine applications for approval of a change of control under the new public interest test (see below); (ii) to issue remedial directions in respect of transactions which have not been approved by the PIMA; and (iii) to issue and revoke declarations of a corporate body as a 'news media self-regulation body'.

With respect to media regulatory bodies internationally, it is clear that there are a range of models in terms of the degree of independence from industry and government. The choice is often dependent on balancing the interests of accountability and also the ability to mediate between members of the industry. The reason for refraining from any legislative intervention lies in the nature of media activity and the assumption that the public interest is best served by allowing minimal interference with the right of the media to gather and impart information.

The model of private self-regulation of the press has been questioned as a result of the Leveson Inquiry in the UK which has resulted in a new proposed scheme to regulate the press under a Royal Charter. It must be recalled that this new scheme was proposed following a lengthy inquiry which found demonstrable failings in the self-regulatory system.

Although the creation of the PIMA would resemble elements of the new UK self-regulator, the Media Package differs in material respects from what was proposed by Leveson and embodied in the Royal Charter. Before any proposal to change the Royal Charter could take effect, a draft must be laid before Parliament and approved by a resolution of each House (ie, at least two-thirds of the members of the House in question who vote on the motion support it). In that respect, the outcome may be seen as a balanced compromise ensuring that the Royal Charter cannot be changed by industry without parliamentary backing while still ensuring independence from government in the manner of appointment and composition of the self-regulator.

[23] See, further, Sprague, A and Rab, S, 'The March of Media Reform: A UK Perspective on Australia' (2013) FTI White Paper, 9 April 2013.

To illustrate the divergence between the PIMA structure and the UK scheme, we contrast the Media Package against the Leveson proposals and the resulting UK model (see Appendix 6). The focus of our comparison is on the issue of the extent to which the regulatory body is legally and functionally independent from government. The results are stark: the PIMA necessarily involves government oversight of the media. This is despite the fact that the PIMA would not be subject to direction by the Minister or the government in the exercise of his or her powers. The concept of 'independence' is, of course, a relative matter. Working independence from government is unlikely to be achieved in a functional structure where the appointee is a Ministerial nominee as would be the case with the PIMA.

(b) A High Burden and Vague Public Interest Test

The Broadcasting Legislation Amendment (News Media Diversity) Bill 2013 would create a new public interest test to be applied by the PIMA. Changes of control of a 'registered news media voice' would require approval by the PIMA. The PIMA would need to be satisfied that the change of control meets the following test: (i) it will not result in a substantial lessening of diversity of control of registered news media voices (Diversity Test); or (ii) it is likely to result in a benefit to the public and that benefit outweighs the detriment to the public constituted by any lessening of diversity of control of registered news media voices (Benefit Test).

The proposed public interest test gives rise to a number of concerns. First, the Diversity Test would impose an unusually high burden by requiring the applicant to show that the control event will not result in a substantial lessening of diversity. This test is very different from the current UK public interest test which applies to media mergers. In the UK, the relevant public interest consideration for these purposes is set out in section 58(2C)(a) of the Enterprise Act 2002 being

> the need, in relation to every different audience in the United Kingdom or in a particular area or locality of the United Kingdom, for there to be a sufficient plurality of persons with control of the media enterprises serving that audience.

The meaning of 'sufficient plurality' is not developed in the Enterprise Act 2002. The Explanatory Notes to the Communications Act 2003 state in relation to section 58(2C)(a) that: 'The first limb of this subsection is concerned primarily with ensuring that ownership of media enterprises is not overly concentrated in the hands of a limited number of persons.'

The question under UK law is not whether a transaction results in a substantial lessening of plurality. Rather, it requires an assessment of whether, post transaction, there remains sufficient plurality. In these circumstances, it would be legitimate to assume that intervention on plurality grounds is warranted only when it reduces plurality to an unacceptable level. However, this does not necessarily coincide with a substantial lessening of plurality relative to the counterfactual (ie, the situation before the control event). Developments in the media market may still mean that plurality remains sufficient notwithstanding a reduction in plurality as a result of the relevant transaction.

The Diversity Test requires the applicant to prove a negative. The proposed test represents an effective reversal of the burden of proof by placing the onus on the applicant rather than the regulatory authority to show that the control event will not result in a substantial lessening of diversity of control. Although the language is deceptively similar to the 'substantial lessening of competition' (SLC) tests adopted by the Australian Competition and Consumer Commission (ACCC) and the UK competition authorities when reviewing mergers under competition law, the effect is very different. To prevent a merger on competition grounds the burden is on the ACCC or the UK Competition Commission to show that the transaction would give rise to, or would be likely to have the effect of, substantially lessening competition.

The Benefit Test places an onerous burden on the applicant. The Benefit Test similarly places the burden on the applicant to demonstrate benefits that outweigh the detriment to the public constituted by any lessening of diversity of control of registered news media voices. This is a highly unusual approach since it requires the applicant to prove the benefits of the control event. It is quite conceivable that such an event may be neutral in terms of the overall public interest assessment.

The position under the proposed Benefit Test may be contrasted with the way in which efficiency benefits are taken into account under UK merger control. When considering whether the merger may be expected to lead to an SLC, the OFT[24] may consider what efficiency gains are directly created by the merger and whether such efficiency gains would have a positive effect on competition so that no SLC would result. The OFT may take efficiencies into account where they do not avert an SLC, but will be passed on after the merger in the form of customer benefits. In this case, the exception to the duty to refer the transaction for a second stage review may apply.

If a merger is referred, the authority at the second stage may, when considering whether there is or will be an SLC, consider whether efficiency gains that are directly created by the merger would increase competition among the remaining firms in the market. In addition, should the decision-maker decide that the merger has resulted or will result in an SLC, it can consider relevant customer benefits when deciding on the question of remedies.

In the absence of guidance on how the PIMA would apply the proposed test, or at least a description of the problems or issues that it is designed to address, there are concerns about the width of discretion accorded to the PIMA. Such concerns are compounded when one considers that the Media Package was put forward without an accompanying Regulatory Impact Assessment. Given the controversial and intrusive nature of the measures, the absence of an assessment of why the proposed test is to be preferred over other approaches is even more troublesome.

[24] The OFT and Competition Commission will merge to form the Competition and Markets Authority (CMA) with effect from 1 April 2014.

(c) Position Regarding What Constitutes a Relevant News Media Voice is Neither Clear nor Consistent

The Media Package incorporates the criteria of a registrable news media voice for the purposes of the public interest test as discussed above. Providers of such services must register the services with the Australian Communications and Media Authority (ACMA). Such registrable media voices would include:[25] (i) a commercial television or radio broadcasting service that provides news or current affairs programmes or content; (ii) a subscription television service that provides news or current affairs programmes or content targeted at the public in Australia; (iii) certain subscription television platforms; (iv) print publications that include news or current affairs content, are published by a corporation engaged wholly or principally in 'media-related activities', targeted at the public in Australia and intended to be circulated by way of sale; or (v) online services that make available news or current affairs content, are provided by entities engaged wholly or principally in 'media-related activities', are targeted at the public in Australia, have paying customers and are not a news or current affairs aggregation service.

According to published criteria, a news media voice would need to be registered if the size of its audience or customer base exceeds 30 per cent of the average metropolitan commercial television evening news audience.

The above criteria appear to be a comprehensive list, presumably intended to be a 'catch-all' for news providers. We note, however, a number of possible shortcomings. The first is the 30 per cent threshold for registration. We understand that today's legislation lists all major Australian news media outlets in print, TV and AM radio.[26] The proposal aims to incorporate online. However, depending on the approach used to calculate audience share, certain voices would fall off the register. According to one observer, a quick calculation based on Senator Conroy's proposal would mean that papers such as *The Australian*, and Fairfax Media would not qualify for inclusion.[27]

That strikes us as bizarre. All voices should count in terms of contributing to plurality. Those that are successful or prominent shouldn't be penalised. Rather, everything—internal and external plurality—together with a basket of metrics should be considered in the round when assessing media plurality.

Second, the description: 'targeted to the public in Australia' could exclude online services such as the New York Times or bbc.com. Surely, these are valid voices in the mix?

Third, convergence blurs market boundaries. What constitutes a newspaper today? It has online services, social media links and twitter feeds so it cannot just be the printed copy. A further complication is that online is a truly cross-media environment—one can read the paper, watch the TV news, listen to the radio news and access thousands of online-only services.

[25] A registered news media voice is a news media voice that has been registered in the Register of News Media Voices.

[26] AM broadcasting is the process of radio broadcasting using amplitude modulation.

[27] The Conversation, 'Explainer: Conroy's proposed new media laws', 19 March 2013, available at: theconversation.com/explainer-conroys-proposed-new-media-laws-8982.

When assessing changes in media plurality during the course of a transaction, one presumably needs to assess the change before and after the transaction on both the consumption and provision side. The UK was unprepared (for many reasons beyond the point made here) because its legislation referred to media enterprises. Online—which is a massively plural environment—was not included in that definition. So the authors understand the need to get the legislation right. While the proposals attempted to be comprehensive in coverage, as discussed, the list and criteria for inclusion have many shortcomings.

(d) Unnecessary Complication to an already Complex Media Landscape

The Media Package would essentially be a 'bolt on' of additional regulation to the existing media landscape.

To illustrate the interplay between the proposals, the PIMA would be able to disclose 'authorised disclosure information' being information that is given to it in confidence in connection with the performance of his or her functions or the exercise of his or her powers and information obtained via his or her information-gathering powers. In circumstances where the PIMA is satisfied that information would assist a person or authority to perform their functions or exercise their powers, he or she would be able to disclose such information to: the ACMA; the ACCC; the Australian Prudential Regulatory Authority; the Secretary of State of the Department administering the Foreign Acquisitions and Takeovers Act 1975; or the Director of Public Prosecutions. The PIMA would also be able to authorise disclosure of information to the Minister in certain circumstances.

This strikes us as a highly complex regime. The UK is tricky enough—the SoS can order a Public Interest Test (conducted by Ofcom) alongside the competition investigation (conducted by the European Commission if certain criteria are met or in the UK by the OFT initially and then, if referred, during a second stage competition review).

The Australian regime clearly has a multiplicity of regulators concerned with transactions in the media sector. We could count at least four legislative regimes for media mergers. In the absence of a supporting Regulatory Impact Assessment, it is difficult to assess the costs and benefits of adding another one—the PIMA. The creation of this new body, superimposed on an already complex regulatory framework, adds to the burdens of compliance and may even discourage worthwhile transactions that could contribute to media diversity. Dealing with matters of plurality is a challenging and complex matter; it would be useful to at least produce a Regulatory Impact Assessment to justify a departure from the existing institutional framework.

(e) Licensing Limits and Content Quotas

The Broadcasting Legislation Amendment (Convergence Review and Other Measures) Bill 2013 would limit the number of television broadcasting licences and Australian content on such services. The proposals would impose: (i) a limit on the number of commercial television broadcasting licences that use the broadcasting services of three in a given licence area; (ii) quotas on non-core/primary commercial television broadcasting licences requiring Australian content to be 730 hours in 2013, 1,095 in 2014 and 1,460 in 2015 during targeted viewing hours; and (iii) changes to the charters of the broadcasters ABC and SBC to take account of digital media.

Dealing with the latter issue first (changes to the charters), it is reasonable to accommodate changes to the charters of the public service broadcasters to accommodate digital media. In the UK, for example, BBC online services were officially launched in 1997. At the time of writing, the BBC's first iPlayer-only series is in production.[28] The only comment to make is why digital media is only being addressed now—it is rather late in the day. This is another area where the lack of a Regulatory Impact Assessment raises unanswered questions as to the likely costs and benefits of the proposed interventions.

Quotas have a long history in many territories, not least Australia, the UK and the EU. They typically relate to two areas: the promotion of independent (ie from broadcasters) production and the broadcasting of domestic content, including specified genres. For both (ie production and broadcast), there are additionally regional quotas to ensure that the British public experiences programmes that are made in or reflect the culture of the nations and regions of the UK.

The quotas are integral to a TV ecosystem determined by spectrum availability and government policy. The BBC is, of course, a public service broadcaster (PSB) regulated by its Charter and funded by a licence fee on TV households. Channel 4 is also a public service broadcaster but a 'publisher' broadcaster with no production and funded by advertising revenue. Both the BBC and Channel 4 are public corporations. The holders of the 'Channel 3' licences (ITV, UTV and STV) are commercial TV broadcasters with public service broadcasting obligations and funded by advertising revenues. Channel 5, now owned by the newspaper/magazine publisher Northern and Shell, is similar, albeit with less stringent obligations.

Quotas are set by the EU under the obligations of the AVMSD.[29] This requires that on each channel, the majority of programmes must be European (including from the UK) and at least 10 per cent must be made by independent companies.

The level of regulatory intervention that Ofcom is required to apply depends on the category of broadcaster—public service broadcasters operate under much tighter regulations than multichannel operators—therefore some quotas apply

[28] The series, *Car Share*, produced by comedian Peter Kay, will debut on the BBC's digital catch-up service, the iPlayer, prior to being shown on the TV channel BBC 1. This is part of a trial by the BBC which includes original dramas. Previously only pilots and spin-off shows appeared as iPlayer-only shows. The BBC's regulator, the BBC Trust, approved the delivery of iPlayer-only programmes in February 2013.

[29] Prior to the AVMSD, quotas were stipulated in the Television without Frontiers Directive (Directive 89/552/EEC of 3 October 1989 on the coordination of certain provisions laid down by Law, Regulation or Administrative Action in Member States concerning the pursuit of television broadcasting activities, [1989] OJ L298).

across the board while others are specific to the PSBs. For the PSBs, the stricter quotas, as enshrined in the UK Communications Act 2003, cover:

— original productions—programmes commissioned by broadcasters from in-house production resources or independent producers;
— out-of-London productions—network programmes made in the UK outside the M25;
— independent productions—programmes made by companies that are independent of broadcasters;
— networked national and international news;
— networked current affairs;.
— national and regional programmes on Channel 3 and the BBC—to be made and shown in relevant regions.

These thus apply to PSB channels, that is, the BBC channels, ITV1, ITV Breakfast, Channel 4 (S4C in Wales) and Channel 5. They do not apply to the commercial PSBs' digital services (such as ITV2, CITV, E4, More 4, Five USA, Fiver) or to other multichannel operators (although of course, the EU restrictions do).

TV content quotas also have a long history in Australia, dating from the 1960s. The quota for Australian content on the core/ primary commercial broadcast services stands at 55 per cent and there are sub-quotas for Australian (adult) drama, documentary and children's programmes. We understand that the Broadcasting Legislation Amendment (Convergence Review and Other Measures) Bill 2013 would have had the following effects:

— broadcasting licence fees would be permanently reduced by 50 per cent (saving around AU$142 million per annum);
— the minimum 55 per cent local content quota on the free-to-air TV networks' primary channels would remain;
— restrictions on screening Australian drama, children's programmes and documentaries on the digital channels would be removed; and
— from 2013 new quotas apply to the digital channels, which will see the phasing in over three years from 1 January 2013 of an additional 1,460 hours of Australian content per network per year on the digital channels.

It could be argued that this requirement is not too onerous, all other things being equal. However, typically 'all other things being equal' applies only in textbook economics. Continued trends in technology bringing with them access to hundreds of channels inevitably means that the commercial broadcasters will be subject to increasing competition for viewers. Thus they would be losing precious advertising revenue, while facing increased production costs. Presumably the reduction in the broadcasting licence fees was set at an adequate level to take account of these changes.

In the UK both the Channel 3 and Channel 5 licensees have had some of their content obligations reduced as digitisation (and hence competition) has increased. Moreover, only their PSB channels are subject to stricter regulations than those set by the EU.

Interestingly, a number of organisations, primarily those representing all areas of screen content, argued that the digital quotas were irrelevant, stating that the digital channels already broadcast more than the base number set by the quota. Another concern expressed was that the networks would move some of the drama, children's and documentary programmes to their secondary channels, replacing them with international content. Importantly, some believe that the broadcasters would receive a cash windfall but would not have to spend it on originated Australian content. A campaign was organized by Miriam Katsambis from the Australian Writers' Guild, urging supporters to send a 'ghost of Skippy' postcard to Senator Conroy, as reproduced at Figure 17.

Figure 17: The ghost of Skippy campaign post card

Source: Available at http://mumbrella.com.au/xx-5-141490

The campaign noted that Senator Conroy's content proposals ignored Recommendation 18 of the Convergence Review final report.[30]

It would appear, at least for some stakeholders, that while some of the proposals for change (the PIMA and the public interest test) went too far, other important changes that is, those that promote Australian content, didn't go far enough.

Finally, the limit on the number of commercial broadcasting services in a given licence area is based on a recommendation of the Convergence Review:

> The new communications regulator should allocate channel capacity on the sixth planned television multiplex (known as the 'sixth channel') to new and innovative services that will increase diversity. The use of capacity on the sixth multiplex for the distribution of community television services should continue. Existing commercial free-to-air television broadcasters and the ABC and the SBS should be precluded from obtaining capacity on the sixth multiplex.[31]

Further, the Convergence Review noted that

> the sixth multiplex should not be allocated to create a full fourth commercial television network operated by a single enterprise. The Review considers that allocating individual channel capacity to a range of providers will maximise diversity. The Review considers that *this is a unique opportunity to encourage and promote innovative services on the sixth multiplex, which will give consumers new content and contribute to competition and diversity.* (emphasis added)[32]

In theory, the proposals sound sensible. The UK has six digital terrestrial multiplexes (and 26 million TV households) and boasts more than 40 free-to-air channels available. While many of the channels are PSB or PSB portfolio channels, and a multitude of others include news channels (eg Sky News, CNN, Russia Today and Al Jazeera) and digital channels from providers such as UKTV, there are also several shopping channels, and at certain times adult channels are broadcast.

A key question in the face of quotas, therefore, is what the new innovative services may be and who will provide them if not existing and established indigenous broadcasters/channel providers?

9.6 US EXPERIENCE: HOW TO MEASURE MEDIA DIVERSITY?

On 22 December 2011 the FCC proposed changes to its media ownership rules. The FCC is required by statute to review its media ownership rules every four years to determine whether they are 'necessary in the public interest as the result of competition'.

[30] Australian Government, *Convergence Review, Final Report*, March 2012.

[31] Ibid, 88.

[32] Ibid, 95.

In proposing changes to the existing regime, the FCC stated that its challenge in this proceeding is to take account of new technologies and changing marketplace conditions while ensuring that our media ownership rules continue to serve our public interest goals of competition, localism, and diversity.[33]

The existing rules prohibit, among other things, ownership of both a major newspaper and a major television station in the same media market. The proposed rules would relax the restriction on owning both types of outlets in top 20 largest media markets. In these media markets, a daily newspaper could seek to merge with a television station, provided that (i) the television station is not ranked among the top four television stations in the market, and (ii) at least eight independently owned major media outlets would remain in the market after the combination. In these circumstances, the FCC would presume that a waiver of the prohibition would be consistent with the public interest. If the conditions are not met, then a waiver would be presumed to be against the public interest.

It is notable that there are no formal guidelines governing how the FCC exercises its discretion to grant waivers from the restriction on cross-media ownership.

The final vote on the new rules was expected to take place in early 2013. However, on 26 February 2013 the FCC announced a delay while it conducts an impact study on how cross-ownership affects minority ownership.

When announcing the delay, the FCC chair, Julias Genachowski, confirmed that the Minority Media and Telecommunications Council in a filing with the agency offered to conduct and pay for the independent study; his statement recognised that this is a 'heavily-litigated area where a strong record is particularly important'.[34]

9.7 CONCLUSION

It will be clear from the above discussion that the issue of media regulation remains highly controversial. Quite apart from the debate around methodology (including measurement and procedural questions) there are a variety of institutional mechanisms, both public and private. The international experience has highlighted the core issue of the proper boundaries between private and public regulation and the interplay between them.

[33] FCC Notice of Proposed Rule Making, 22 December 2011.

[34] Julius Genachowski stated that 'the Minority Media and Telecommunications Council informed the Commission that it will conduct a focused, independent study on the effects of cross-ownership rules on minority ownership and newsgathering, in order to enhance the record in the Commission's proceeding. The study is expected to take several weeks and will be filed with the Commission, after which MMTC suggests that the agency solicit public input, to be followed by a Commission vote. In this heavily-litigated area where a strong record is particularly important, I believe this is a sensible approach to moving forward and resolving the issues raised in this proceeding.' (Statement on the status of media ownership proceeding, 26 February 2013).

The range and variety of enforcement mechanisms, which tend to co-exist, gives rise to three important conclusions.

First, a major theme is the risk of a lack of coordination between different forms of regulation both public and private, and of potential duplication. Second, there is an issue of legitimacy particularly where the bodies are not elected or are too close to industry, and of the need for some method to correct the perceived deficiencies through independent review, procedures for appointments, statutory oversight or another mechanism. Third, the prospect or occurrence of regulatory failure, whether due to political influence, weak enforcement or avoidance, pervades both the private and public mechanisms and the areas between those polar extremes.

Stepping back from the recent experiences in the selected jurisdictions, it is conceivable that the debate over the appropriate form of regulation and its independence from government will continue. Rather than considering whether the outcome is a victory for public or private regulation, the focus should be on design of regimes which emphasise coordination and transparency and above all, balance. The Leveson Inquiry lasted over a year from its appointment in July 2011 to the report in November 2012. In March 2013 there was a proposal for a new framework for regulation of the UK press under a Royal Charter and which had cross-party support. However, at the end of 2013 this was not adopted, illustrating the challenges of securing universal acceptance of such measures.. The Australian Media Package barely saw the light of day before it was pulled. We suspect it may re-emerge in another guise in the not too distant future.

The TRAI's proposals remain open for consultation. It remains to be seen whether they will be implemented and if so in what form. As the initiatives gain momentum, we hope that there will be sufficient airtime to consider whether these proposals represent good policy for India even if they contain ideas borrowed from overseas.

10

Conclusions and Implications for Policy

10.1 INTRODUCTION

The introduction and development of competition law and regulation in the information and communications sector is fraught with challenges. Government and regulators should undertake careful and forward-looking approaches.

The international experience has shown that political and industry support is vital at every stage, from identifying the need to act to developing the policy and ensuring that the regulator can implement its mandate. New or modified rules and regulatory cultures will not command the broad acceptance that is necessary for their effective implementation unless governments and business embrace their principles as legitimate and well-targeted. This means that government needs to 'buy in' to the market and constitutional principles that underpin the regime as fundamental to policy. There should be no 'special cases' to shelter vested or own interests from scrutiny. Business also need to be assured that what is put in place is important for economic development and is the minimum necessary to ensure that markets remain open for investment and growth. Balancing these goals does not dictate a 'copycat' approach by emulating what has been done elsewhere. It calls for a *nuanced* approach that takes account of the past, present and future situation in India. It must be fully anchored in the identification of problems and the justification of solutions which achieve better outcomes than the current situation.

The following are ten 'learnings' or recommendations that are suggested for building and sustaining a credible and robust competition and regulatory regime in the media and communications sector. They are based on experience from diverse international settings and are presented in light of the challenges facing India now. This chapter does not seek to replicate the insights revealed in the previous chapters, but is informed by them. Taken together, these recommendations seek to provide a pragmatic way forward in navigating complexity in a converging media and communications environment or, as we call it, the 'mediaplace'.

10.2 TEN RECOMMENDATIONS FOR COMPETITIVE AND DIVERSE MEDIA MARKETS

10.2.1 Develop a Strong Law that Respects Legal and Economic Principles

The successful operation of any law or regulation starts from an underlying policy perspective that is clearly articulated. It is important for India, as an emerging market, to lay out the policy that it considers appropriate to address the specific circumstances of the national economy and the basis for the identified problems and to explain how it is proposed to address them. A tide of opinion that 'enough is enough' or 'something needs to be done' is not sufficient to build a strong and accountable framework for real and lasting change. It may be necessary to introduce unusual provisions to address specific market failures or allow for a staged implementation that provides flexibility or gradual adoption while the market and regulators adapt to the new way of doing things.

A further question relates to whether provisions should be couched in terms of primary legislation, secondary legislation or guidance. Related to this issue is the balance between enabling flexibility and affording clarity to economic agents on their legal obligations. Either way, any change from the status quo must be supported by a Regulatory Impact Assessment, a feature that was lacking in the media ownership and cable TV consultations launched by the Telecom Regulatory Authority of India (TRAI) in early 2013.

Once consensus on the nature and extent of the issues to be addressed has been achieved, consideration needs to be given to the 'how to' (ie the mechanisms by which the policy is to be implemented). This study has attempted to identify the widely accepted principles or elements that underscore effective regulations in the media and communications sector. Recognising that this remains an area where jurisdictions around the world have forged very different ways of regulating their 'mediaplaces', we are cautious in purporting to set out a blueprint or recipe for effective adoption. That is certainly not our intention. However, drawing together the themes over where there is general consensus, the following elements emerge:

- Adherence to accepted legal principles that, as a minimum, meet the national constitutional norms and standards of natural justice (eg the right to a fair hearing and the rule against retroactive legislation);
- Regulation based on clearly defined policy objectives;
- Proportionate and 'light-handed' regulation, so that *ex ante* regulation is limited to the minimum necessary;
- Technological neutrality;
- Balance of flexibility and legal certainty;
- Balance of the need to stimulate investment and competition, including from domestic and overseas players;
- Focus on the effects of conduct rather than rigid prohibitions based on market share or the mere fact of vertical integration;

- Harmonisation of national regulatory regimes (eg between competition law and sector regulation);
- Endowment of the regulatory authority with sufficient powers and resources (including human) to undertake investigations on its own initiative;
- Calibration of interventions and sanctions according to the nature of the violation and the relevant individual circumstances, and balance of deterrence goals with financial and economic viability;
- Subjection of decisions of the authority to review by an independent appeal tribunal; and
- Periodic review.

Furthermore, where new laws are being introduced in a hostile context amid industry and other stakeholder objection, there may be good arguments for transitional implementation even after broad consensus has been reached for the underlying policy and form of reform. This should facilitate greater prospects of compliance and garner the necessary support that is needed over time, thereby minimising the risk of avoidance. In short, take small but solid and sustainable steps.

10.2.2 Stay Vigilant to Competition Issues

Even as markets become more competitive, opportunities to foreclose entry and expansion will arise in markets where there are barriers to entry. It will be important to keep sight of the effects of both newer technologies and distribution formats in reducing the market power of traditional providers and platforms. However, even in a crowded market it will be important to stay vigilant to potential competition concerns, particularly where access to content or platforms is critical to sustain market entry and expansion. While it may be tempting to presume that particular owners of content or infrastructure may occupy a gatekeeper role, that conclusion is not inevitable in changing markets.

Moreover, it is imperative to acknowledge that where there are economies of scale, new entry may not always be viable given the size of the market. Therefore, alternative regulatory tools may be required. Again, there are no fixed givens. The mere fact that a market is small does not necessarily mean that the scope for new entry and competition is remote. The authors believe that it is self-evident that consumers the world over are all similar and that any differences in the conduct and performance of law and regulation must be ascribed to the difference in context (ie the economic, demographic or other issues (if any) which make an economy different). Among the factors that are relevant to a regulatory review are: the small size of the relevant markets; the structure of government; public ownership of utilities; the scope for competition; and the prospects for cooperation with other countries in matters of competition and regulation.

Globally, particularly in the EU, there has been a reeling back of *ex ante* interventions in preference for a lighter touch approach and reliance on *ex post* competition law interventions. India appears to be exhibiting similar market trends and behaviour to those of the EU as exemplified in the expansion and adoption of new technologies and, particularly, in the take-up of the internet. This suggests that some of the insights from a carefully crafted approach to regulation elsewhere may be relevant in India. However, where internet penetration is lower and mass market delivery is imperative, it will still be important to examine the extent to which more established media and platforms enjoy a competitive advantage.

It may be tempting to minimise the relevance of competition law in a market like India which is a relatively late adopter of a more economics-based approach to competition law and regulation. However, the temptation to fall back on the blunt instrument of rigid *ex ante* controls should be resisted if all that can be said for it is that it is easier. Both competition law and sector regulation have their place but the determination of which tool is appropriate needs to be based on sound theory, evidence and experience. Interventions by a competition authority that removes a bottleneck in the provision of content or systems and allows for alternatives to incumbent business offerings, can unleash significant economic and social potential. This brings particular benefits in vertical sectors served by the media that demand an affordable, timely and unrestricted flow of accurate information (eg financial services, transportation, logistics and distribution). This is so in both newer and more established markets, quite apart from the differences in terms of technological advances and legal and institutional frameworks. Again, the theme of the need to balance incentives for investment with competition merges.

A reduced reliance on *ex ante* regulation does place greater demands on competition law enforcement (as to which, see our comments at recommendations (6) and (9) below).

10.2.3 Recognise the Role of Market Definition in all its (Product, Geographic, Temporal and Innovative) Dimensions

Defining the relevant market is a key threshold issue in any competition case. In abuse of dominance cases a necessary first step involves determining whether or not a firm is dominant in a relevant market, without which there can be no abuse. Market definition also underpins the effects-based assessment of agreements. This is particularly pertinent under Indian competition law, where section 3 of the Competition Act is predicated on there being an appreciable adverse effect (AAE) on competition in the relevant market in India. Even though certain categories of agreement are presumed to have such an effect (ie price fixing and market sharing) the presumption may be rebutted.

The competitive effects of vertical integration in the media sector have attracted a great deal of attention in the TRAI's 2013 media ownership consultations.[1] Critically for the media and communications sector, vertical agreements are treated under a 'rule of reason' type analysis under section 3(4) of the Competition Act 2002 (Competition Act) and will only infringe Indian competition law if they produce an AAE in the relevant market.

In arriving at a definition and assessment of the relevant market, it is important not to lose sight of the fact that market definition is not an end in itself. Market definition is a frame of reference against which competitive constraints operate. That is to say, market definition examines the realistic and available substitutes to which consumers may turn in the event of a small but significant increase in price which is not temporary (primarily an issue of demand-side substitution). The market definition inquiry may also examine the ability of alternative suppliers to switch their operations to provide a competing product or service (supply-side substitution).

Thus, an integrated approach that balances the production, cost-driven and often 'top down' perspective of the supplier, with the customer-focused or 'bottom up' approach can bring useful insights to competition and other regulatory authorities when seeking to define relevant frames of reference and whether and how they need to intervene.

For example, for the real-time delivery of audiovisual content, television may have few direct substitutes. There are few more direct and powerful media than television to deliver a message and provide a vehicle for political, cultural and social expression, typically directly into a person's living room. However, the parameters of television broadcasting are not so simple to define. Convergence in technologies has contributed to expanding the range of media over which audiovisual content may be delivered and consumed. This multiplicity in the range of devices over which content may be consumed, or services delivered, has made the exercise of defining relevant markets and substitutes more complex. For example, in the *Microsoft/Skype* merger[2] the European Commission had to examine the effects of the transaction across a range of platforms (including PCs, smartphones and tablets) and functionalities (including voice, video calls and instant messaging) as well as over different operating systems. Ultimately, the transaction was not found to raise any concerns.

Where media plurality is concerned, an identification of the relevant market—or audience—is a useful initial exercise. However, this must not be confused with a competition law or economist assessment. The frame of reference needs to take account of the principle expounded in this study that pluralism and competition are two separate, but related and mutually reinforcing goals.

[1] Telecom Regulatory Authority of India, 'Consultation Paper on Issues relating to Media Ownership', 15 February 2013 and Telecom Regulatory Authority of India, 'Consultation Paper on Monopoly/Market dominance in Cable TV services', 3 June 2013.

[2] Case COMP/M.6291 *Microsoft/Skype*, Commission decision of 7 October 2011.

For example, an aspect of the relevant audience that has emerged in the UK case law is the concept of a cross-media audience. The notion of an 'audience' for a particular media outlet must be based on those people who are exposed to the views and opinions of that media outlet and who could, therefore, conceivably be impacted by any alteration in its presentation of the news or current affairs. For a newspaper, the assessment must relate to the voices available to the relevant readership. For a television broadcaster the assessment must relate to the voices available to the audience which watches relevant broadcasts. For a merger between a newspaper enterprise and a TV broadcaster, the relevant audience is necessarily a cross-media audience. It is in this context that any possible effect on plurality and its adequacy needs to be assessed.

10.2.4 Question and Test Traditional Approaches in Converging Media and Communications Markets

The textbook traditional rationales for regulating media and communications markets are underpinned by the multi-faceted issue of access: to content, distribution or delivery and investment capital. Thus, interventions have taken the form of: requirements on market participants to license content or distribution platforms on fair, reasonable and non-discriminatory terms; limits in the term of exclusive arrangements; or imposition of charging structures that do not allow a party to leverage market power from one segment of the market to another. The rationale behind these interventions relies on the control and protection of distinct routes to market for service delivery.

However, in the face of convergence in some environments the traditional rationale for intervention may be questioned. While the phenomenon of convergence may not provide an answer in all cases, there may be arguments for a different approach or even a change in regulation to preserve access across different modes of distribution. Indeed, regulation can itself be a barrier to entry where it places unnecessary hindrances on market access.

The breaking down of technological divisions that used to define telecommunications, broadcasting and information technology as discrete, is also leading to the convergence of regulatory roles and responsibilities. This, in turn, may be expected to facilitate a synergised relationship between the TRAI (as sector regulator) and the Competition Commission of India (CCI) (as competition authority). Greater communication between regulators may even reduce the scope for regulatory arbitrage when parties bring their complaints in multiple fora. While it may not be obvious at the outset of a complaint or inquiry which tool—sector regulation or competition law—is appropriate, a greater communication and congruence in the methodological approaches of the two regulators (where relevant) can help obviate the worst excesses of forum shopping.

10.2.5 Ensure that the Identification of Specific Market Failures or Concerns is based on Robust Economic and Empirical Evidence rather than a Perceived 'Problem'

With regard to remedies, and in recognition of the convergence phenomenon becoming a reality, competition and regulatory authorities can and should adopt flexible and targeted approaches to remedies that take account of sector-specific features.

In the traditional telecoms sector our review of the practice of merger control authorities internationally has shown that they have not been limited to structural solutions or familiar access remedies. The authorities have shown a readiness to develop solutions that ensure the viability of new entrants or mavericks (eg *T-Mobile Austria/tele.ring*[3]). Facilitating new and innovative entry can, in certain circumstances, contribute to diversity and thereby indirectly protect pluralism.

Where plurality concerns that are unrelated to market power or competition concerns arise, there is a need to develop solutions that address the issue at hand. For example, it is quite possible that a transaction will not materially diminish concentration levels in a relevant market but could pose issues for viewpoint plurality of the merging entities previously represented the only or main sources of news representing a particular viewpoint.

If the underlying concern is a risk that editorial independence will be compromised, commitments to secure independence and impartiality, supported by internal structural safeguards such as special committees, have been used to seek to preserve the conditions for maintaining independence. The range of options needs to be explored. A number of different tools present themselves as possible mechanisms with which to protect plurality. These may differ depending on the industry segment. For example, committees and independent directors and editors have been considered in a newspaper context. Broadcasting codes and restrictions on the types of entity that may own a broadcasting licence are other examples. Such solutions are not without their challenges but should be considered on the merits with any proposed divestment remedy.

Blanket bans on cross-ownership, vertical integration or achieving a presence of a certain (arbitrary) size are blunt mechanisms to address the risks to the public interest of uncontrolled organic or inorganic corporate growth. Where such solutions are deployed in the absence of an assessment of the need for intervention in the first place, or of the particular type, it can be years before the secondary effects are observed, by which time it can be very difficult to correct the deficiencies (in terms of both under- and over-reach).

[3] Case COMP/M.3916 *T-Mobile Austria/tele.ring*, Commission decision of 26 April 2006.

There is an expanding body of practice which confirms that a particular remedy may be appropriate and feasible in one case or market, but not in another. Hence, remedies must be thoroughly tested by all relevant stakeholders, including the merging parties, competitors, suppliers and customers, and located in a coherent theory of harm.

10.2.6 Mitigate the Risk of Political Capture

Political capture—whether by politicians or industry—should not be tolerated. However laudable the objective to promote competition and diversity, this will be tainted if there is any appearance of, or actual bias in, the legal framework or its implementation.

The debate around the regulation of media and communications activities takes place in an emotionally—and politically—charged environment. This is even more apparent where interventions concerning media plurality are concerned, since this issue goes to the very heart of democracy and free expression. It is necessary, therefore, that those responsible for devising and enforcing laws in this area are mindful of the risk of making the (actual or perceived) problem worse by favouring vested interests. The following principles may assist in avoiding some of the worst features of direct and indirect political favoritism.

First, the starting point should be that the law should apply without distinction between government and private enterprise and national and foreign players. It should be neutral in its scope and application across segments of the industry. Second, any concessions (if considered necessary at all to kick-start the process) should be limited and informed by a coherent policy and objective rationale as to why special treatment is warranted. Third, the relevant authority must be ready and able to carry out its duties even where this may run counter to political interests and where the violation is as a result of government policy or the acts of specific officials. In short, there should be no political place to hide. Where the authority requires the cooperation of another agency to achieve its mandate, it should not find itself immobilised because it is dependent on the will of that agency to act.

The foregoing principles apply as much to private groups that may hijack the legal, regulatory and political process, as they do to state entities and officials. Indeed, much of the debate surrounding the need for tougher rules on plurality has revolved around concerns that private players may use their market power to distort the political process.

10.2.7 Maintain Diverse Expertise among Bodies likely to hear Relevant Cases

Regulators in emerging regimes have often been hampered in their tasks by limited human resources in terms of the range, quality, expertise and experience of their leaders and staff.

It will be apparent that a range of disciplines informs the issues under consideration including law, economics, policy, technical, public relations, and administration.

In order to promote and sustain the right balance and depth of expertise, the authority must be equipped with full-time career professionals in as many of the relevant areas as resources permit. They must be exposed to continuous professional development and on-the-ground experience. Particularly in the areas of law and economics which impact directly on the key questions of competition and plurality, there are no second-best options. Therefore, in order to recruit the right calibre of staff, such persons should have a relevant professional background rather than being secondees from an unrelated government agency. They should be paid in accordance with comparable roles in the private sector. Secondment of personnel from overseas regulators is another technique which can help build capacity and expertise and has the added benefit of wider relationship engagement between the different authorities. This can bring benefits to both regulators and facilitate ease of working on matters which may have cross-border impacts.

Although by its nature the position of leader of the authority will command prestige, it is vital that such a person has demonstrated that they have the necessary intellectual skills, experience and personality to grapple with the often difficult questions and situations that have formed the core of this study. Competence and credibility, rather than connections and cronyism, must be the criteria for appointment and advancement. This is essential in securing the authority's reputation in an area which will continue to invite criticism and debate.

Fortunately for India, there is already an institutional base in the competition law owing to the groundwork that has been undertaken by the CCI. From its inception in 2005 under the helm of the then acting chair, Mr Vinod Dhall, the CCI has steadily built capacity and made real efforts in terms of recruiting and developing staff from a wide range of professional disciplines. It also has experience of secondments from overseas, bringing wider experience and insights.

This is not to say that there is no scope for improvements in the CCI's institutional and operational set-up. However, given the interaction between competition and regulation it would be regrettable if any developments of India's regulatory regime in the media and communications sector did not benefit from the institutional experience and memory that has been gained in the CCI's first years. Unless the activities of the sector regulator are aligned with competition law insights and interventions, there is a real concern that the inevitable offset could be damaging to the effective realisation of the two complementary regimes.

Limitations in terms of expertise in competition law and economics can also affect the judiciary who are called upon to adjudicate on decisions of the competition and sector regulator. International experience in the telecoms sector, particularly in the UK, has borne out the importance of a well-educated bench well-versed in the legal and economics principles that underpin media communications competition litigation. In view of India's short history in applying economics-based competition law, there has not been sufficient time to test whether the judiciary is able to grapple effectively with the complexities of the underlying principles of competition law which, for all intents and purposes, is economics-law. There is no reason to suppose that India's judges are not keen to take up the task. However, there is a concern that without the right training they will fall back on traditional rule-based approaches to statutory construction to decide a case and will underestimate the significance of an economics-based approach.

10.2.8 Build and Strengthen Alliances with all Interest Groups affected by Competition Law and Regulation

Proposals for tougher regulation of the media and communications sector in India have already encountered diametrically opposed viewpoints. On the one hand supporters have argued for draconian measures and the break-up of alleged monopolies in the pursuit of greater competition and diversity. Such pleas have faced vigorous objection presenting their contrary case.

Of course, the issues are rarely as clear-cut as siding with one position or another and all propositions should be thoroughly tested. In these circumstances it is vital that those designing and implementing any departure from the status quo subject the arguments raised to evidence-based scrutiny. But they must go further than that, and expose the financial and relationship affinities that may work in opposition to the effective enforcement of new laws. This is especially the case when contemplating new regulation in the area of plurality which raises more complex issues beyond market or economic power. Because the issue of plurality is so intertwined with the political process, it must confront the very political links that it is designed to destroy and which have raised concerns that political actors may be using the media for political ends and counter to a healthy democratic process.

One of the ways in which an authority can seek to lay the groundwork for an effective enforcement framework which commands a broad community of respect, is to develop coalitions or buy in with those who are likely to benefit from a more predictable and accountable legal regime. This includes consumers, smaller businesses, and investors seeking to expand in markets that have traditionally been a closed shop. It also includes more established players who need to be convinced that the regulation which initially may be seen to operate against their interests will ultimately prove beneficial in creating the right conditions for them to grow on a sustainable basis within and beyond their core markets. The use of regular communications and stakeholder events can also help to bring the regulator closer to relevant interest groups, provided that this is a genuine opportunity to debate the underlying issues.

Such advocacy is no easy task. However, the sledgehammer approach which incites the hard-fought opposition of powerful players who may have a good case to make for preservation of the status quo is likely to prove counterproductive. Where a step change is needed, it is better to proceed in small but sustainable hops rather than making a quantum leap that fails because it lacks sufficient consensus among key stakeholders.

In building such alliances, moreover, the relevant architects and implementers of the new policy need to stand firm on their own autonomy. In mobilising support for any rule change, commanding respect for legitimacy depends as much on the authority's own independence of action as it does on aligning different viewpoints. This independence of action takes real courage in the face of criticism but it is essential if the authority is to make lasting change. The regulator must be feared and revered. That is to say, the authority needs to be taken seriously as ready and able to act on its mandate, while having the necessary fair-mindedness to pick its battles judiciously. This calls for transparency in those cases that the authority has decided to pursue—and those that it has not.

10.2.9 Develop Cooperation with Regulators Globally

The legal enforcement jurisdiction of the authority will generally be limited to its territorial borders yet the economic, political and social ramifications may extend much further afield. In particular, the policy approach applied to the domestic situation may not only affect competition and diversity scenarios within India itself but can impact on both inward and outbound investment.

First, the attractiveness of India as an investment destination will depend on whether it is, and is seen to be, providing a legal and regulatory regime that promotes growth and expansion without being bogged down by disproportionate red tape or protectionism. It must emphasise the need for legal certainty and continuity. This requires a commitment to delivering reforms in a timely manner—and also an assurance that the rules will not change at short notice without proper reason or engagement.

Second, a rigid approach domestically can impact indirectly on the competiveness of India's companies seeking to expand globally. If India's companies are unduly constrained in their ability to grow organically in the domestic market or are inhibited in growing through efficiency-enhancing investments at the national level, their ability to compete in global markets may be compromised.

However, it will be apparent from the issues considered in this work that the balance between national and supra-national competition is rarely simple. One route to facilitate a more informed, rounded perspective is to encourage cooperation between agencies internationally which face similar issues. India already has a track record in the competition arena where international bodies including the International Competition Network (ICN), the International Bar Association (IBA) and the American Bar Association (ABA) contributed to the development and implementation of the Competition Act. There are also indications of engagement between the CCI and other regulators including in the US and EU. This cooperation enhances knowledge share and capacity building where agencies face similar issues, albeit in different market contexts. Such engagement should not be taken as a recipe for emulation but a mechanism to share best practices so that India, its regulators and government, can decide what route it desires to pursue in light of what has worked—and not worked—elsewhere.

10.2.10 Maintain a Dynamic Approach

From the perspective of industry policy, it is understandable that the beneficiaries of a lighter approach would urge regulators to allow markets to develop without intrusive regulatory intervention. A reeling back of regulation in dynamic markets is based on the principle that businesses require the opportunity to invest in untried technologies and business formats and in new geographies where penetration has yet to develop (eg broadband in some areas). Such a check on *ex ante* regulation to allow markets to deploy new networks in the long term and against a background of uncertainty would reflect the current EU approach to regulation in the communications sector.

However, this lighter touch approach must be countered with arguments that barriers to entry may continue through technical limitations, access issues, and the conduct of individual firms. From a legal perspective, it is clear that competition law in India and internationally allows such issues to be considered where the actions of particular market participants (whether acting collectively or individually where they have market power) is likely to cause harm.

Therefore, the dynamic nature of the media and communications sector would merit consideration by policy-makers and authorities to identify both the opportunities and the threats to competition. This is especially the case given convergence between the media and communications markets, where alternative routes to the customer create diversity and choice. Such an exercise will assist in formulating a sensible market definition, in identifying the genuine risks arising from consolidation and vertical integration and in framing mandatory requirements (if any) required to keep markets open. Thus informed policy-makers, regulators and competition authorities should be in a better position to create and maintain competitive and diverse media and communications markets.

Ultimately, in the coming years, one of the main challenges for policy-makers, businesses and their advisers (including analysts) and academics, will be to unravel a commercial transaction's potential for innovation, efficiencies and consumer benefits, while being sensitive to the risk of foreclosure and harm to the public interest. It is encouraging that India's regulatory tools to seek to achieve such a balance (ie competition law) are converging with approaches that are recognised best practices internationally. Where it seeks to diverge, it is hoped that such an approach is robust in terms of policy, law and economics and also makes sense to the commercial enterprises and consumers it affects.

Appendix 1: Achieving Policy Objectives

INTRODUCTION

This Appendix provides additional material in support of the information provided in chapter 2 through case studies in the following areas:

— competition law enforcement in the EU telecoms sector; and
— sector-specific enforcement in the UK broadcasting sector.

ABUSE OF DOMINANCE

Regulatory Policy Framework: Competition Law Enforcement in the EU Telecoms Sector

The EU competition authorities have been active in enforcing competition law in the telecoms sector. Many interventions have been aimed at curtailing abuse of power by incumbents or former incumbents who have access to key infrastructure. The practices under scrutiny have ranged from charging excessive prices, margin squeezes, predatory pricing, cross-subsidisation, unfair rebate or discount schemes, tying and bundling the sale of different products, refusals to deal, refusal of access to essential infrastructure, and unjustified discrimination.

Price-Related Abuse

In July 2003, the European Commission fined France Télécom €10.6 million for predatory pricing.[1] Its retail asymmetric digital subscriber line (ADSL) access services were found to be priced below their costs of provision. The decision to impose a fine was upheld by both the General Court and the Court of Justice of the EU (CJEU), which confirmed that in order to establish an infringement it was not necessary to show that France Télécom could have subsequently recouped the losses associated with its predatory prices.

[1] Case C-202/07 P *France Télécom v Commission* [2009] ECR I-2369.

In May 2003, the European Commission fined Deutsche Telekom €12.6 million for abusing its dominant position in the German local loop market by implementing a margin squeeze under which Deutsche Telekom's regulated wholesale access prices were set at a level that did not allow new entrants to compete on the downstream voice telephony market. This was confirmed on appeal by both the General Court and the CJEU.[2]

Other Abusive Commercial Practices

On 22 June 2011, the European Commission fined TelekomunikacjaPolska (TP) €127 million for abuse of dominance in the market for wholesale access services.[3] The case differs from the previous enforcement trend in the telecoms sector where prior cases under the EU abuse of dominance prohibition under Article 102 of the Treaty on the Functioning of the EU (TFEU) have focused mainly on pricing behaviour. Here, the European Commission found some of TP's wider commercial practices, such as the manner in which it conducted contractual negotiations, to be abusive. TP has appealed the decision to the General Court, claiming that the European Commission paid inadequate regard for measures it had taken in order to remove barriers to its cooperation with alternative operators, and for a memorandum of understanding entered between TP and the Polish national regulatory authority in 2009. The appeal is pending at the end of 2013.

SECTOR-SPECIFIC REGULATION

Regulatory Policy Framework: Regulation, Competition Law and Market Investigation in the UK Broadcasting Sector

The UK has a multi-layered regulatory and competition law enforcement system comprising sector-specific regulation, mainstream competition law and the market investigations regime.

The market investigation regime in the UK is an investigation carried out by the Competition and Markets Authority (CMA)[4] *ex post*, in the sense that the CMA assesses how the market has operated in the past with a view to prescribing remedies in the future. However, it could be considered to be a rather curious example of the interface between competition law and regulation in that a market

[2] Case C-280/08 P *Deutsche Telekom AG v Commission* [2010] ECR I-000.

[3] European Commission press release, 'Antitrust: Commission fines Telekomunikacja Polska SA €127 million for abuse of dominant position' (IP/11/771) 22 June 2011.

[4] The CMA was formed in April 2014 following the merger of the OFT and the Competition Commission.

investigation may be initiated in circumstances where there is no evidence of a violation of competition law.

Currently; either the CMA or a sector regulator may refer a market/company for a second-stage market investigation. The CMA has the power to investigate markets and restrictions on competition and to impose remedies if required. The UK market investigation regime is based on the concept of an 'adverse effect on competition' (AEC). An AEC arises where 'any feature or combination of features, of each relevant market prevents, restricts or distorts competition in connection with the supply or acquisition of goods or services in the United Kingdom or a part of the United Kingdom'.[5] The test is wider in scope than Article 101/102 TFEU (and the UK national law equivalents in Chapter I and II of the Competition Act 1998). An AEC can arise from (i) the market structure; (ii) the conduct of suppliers or acquirers of goods or services; or (iii) the conduct of customers. The market investigation regime therefore complements the mainstream competition regime.

To illustrate the interface between sector regulation, market investigation and competition law it is useful to contrast two cases in the UK involving assessments conducted by the UK competition authorities into pricing and commercial practices of British Sky Broadcasting (BSkyB). References to the historic experience of the Office of Fair Trading (OFT) and the Competition Commission (prior to April 2014) are nevertheless useful in understanding the role of the CMA with effect from April 2014 as the successor to those bodies.

'Wholesale Must-Offer' (WMO)

On 31 March 2010 the UK communications regulator Ofcom made a decision requiring that BSkyB offer Sky Sports 1 and Sky Sports 2 (and the High Definition versions of the channels) on a wholesale basis to retailers on other platforms, at wholesale prices set by Ofcom.[6] This decision was not based on competition law but was an exercise of Ofcom's sector regulatory powers under section 316 of the Communications Act 2003.

On 8 August 2012, the UK Competition Appeal Tribunal (CAT) upheld appeals brought by BSkyB against the WMO.[7]

The CAT's decision contains a number of points of interest. First, the CAT found that Ofcom had misinterpreted the factual evidence when concluding that BSkyB had not engaged constructively with requests for access and had withheld the wholesale supply of its premium channels. These findings underpinned Ofcom's competition concerns which the CAT decided were unfounded. Second,

[5] Enterprise Act 2002, section 134(1).

[6] Ofcom, 'Pay TV Statement', 31 March 2010.

[7] *British Sky Broadcasting Limited, Virgin Media, Inc, The Football Association Premier League Limited and British Telecommunications plc v Office of Communications* [2012] CAT 20.

the CAT confirmed that Ofcom was not limited to imposing a remedy only in those circumstances where there was a competition law violation and, in particular, where there was found to be an abuse of a dominant position. Third, the CAT found that Ofcom did have jurisdiction to impose remedies at the wholesale level with a view to safeguarding competition at the retail level. In February 2014 the Court of Appeal found the CAT's decision was based on an incomplete set of conclusions and remitted the case back to the CAT.[8] The Supreme Court is considering an application from BSKyB to appeal the Court of Appeal's judgment. The final outcome is therefore unresolved at the time of writing.

Pay-TV Movies

In 2010 Ofcom referred to the Competition Commission concerns relating to pay TV movie content and distribution. Ofcom considered that BSkyB, being the largest provider of pay TV services in the UK had effective control over rights to premium movie content. It was concerned that BSkyB would use its market power to restrict distribution of premium movie content and charge excessive prices.

On 2 August 2012, the Competition Commission announced the outcome of its market investigation.[9] The Competition Commission concluded that there were no features relating to the supply and acquisition of subscription pay TV movie rights in the first subscription pay TV window of the major studios or the wholesale supply and acquisition of packages including core premium movies channels which gave rise to an adverse effect on competition in any market. The Competition Commission considered that there was a realistic prospect that, in the future, an independent pay TV retailer would be able to outbid BSkyB for the relevant rights of at least one major studio. However, the Competition Commission observed that, in light of BSkyB's position in the pay TV retail market and the fast-moving nature of the market, it expected that Ofcom will keep developments in this sector under review. Interestingly, this was the first market investigation where the Competition Commission concluded that there was no adverse effect on competition.

[8] *British Telecommunications, Office of Communications, British Sky Broadcasting Ltd, The Football Association Premier League, Virgin Media Inc* [2014] EW Civ 133.

[9] Competition Commission, 'Movies on pay TV market investigation, A report on the supply and acquisition of subscription pay TV movie rights and services', 2 August 2012.

Appendix 2: Media Ownership and Merger Control

INTRODUCTION

This Appendix provides additional material in support of the information provided in chapter 5 in the following areas:

- media ownership and merger control regulation applying in selected countries internationally;
- media ownership and control merger regime case studies internationally; and
- the UK media merger public interest regime.

Media Ownership and Control Merger Regimes Internationally

This chapter summarises the media ownership and merger control rules (if any) applying in the media and communications sector in the countries within our study.

The focus is on media ownership rules based on shareholding and interest and not on nationality (ie foreign ownership).

At the time of writing an overhaul of the UK framework for competition law and regulation is underway with the merger of the UK's first and second stage competition authorities (the Office of Fair Trading (OFT) and the Competition Commission respectively) to form the Competition and Markets Authority (CMA) with effect from April 2014. While references in this book to the application of competition law in the sector relate to the historic experience of the UK competition authorities (the OFT and the Competition Commission) and the UK media and communications sector regulator (Ofcom) they are informative when considering the roles of Ofcom and the CMA in the reformed UK competition law regime.

Table 5: Media ownership and merger control: Selected country summaries

Country	Media Ownership	Merger Control
Belgium	No ownership caps. The Flemish community imposes certain restrictions on broadcasters as part of their licensing conditions. These provisions only prevent cross-directorships. They do not prevent companies from having the same direct or indirect shareholders (ie being part of the same group). In the French community, the French Broadcasting Decree requires service or network providers to inform the Supreme Audio-visual Council (CSA) of their ownership structure and their shareholders' interests in other media companies. If the CSA determines that a service or network provider occupies a 'significant position' that could damage media plurality, it must ensure that media plurality is protected.	Yes. No media-specific rules.
Denmark	None	Yes. No media-specific rules.
European Union	No specific supra-national controls.	Yes. The European Commission has exclusive jurisdiction to review concentrations that satisfy certain turnover thresholds, such that the EU Merger Regulation (EUMR) provides a 'one-stop shop' for such concentrations. The test for clearance is a competition-based test. However, the EUMR also contains mechanisms for the reallocation of jurisdiction between the European Commission and the national authorities to review mergers including on grounds of 'legitimate interest'. The concept of legitimate interest covers plurality of the media.
Finland	None	Yes. No media-specific rules.

(*Continued*)

Table 5: (*Continued*)

Country	Media Ownership	Merger Control
France	Maximum holding of 49% of a company that has an authorisation to provide a national terrestrial television service, where the average audience for this service (whether digital or analogue) exceeds 8%. Any person who already holds a national terrestrial television service, where the average audience for this service exceeds 8%, may not directly or indirectly hold more than 33% of a company that has an authorisation to provide a local terrestrial television service. Detailed rules on cross-ownership including: Holder of more than 15% of a company operating a national terrestrial television channel may not hold more than 15% of another company active in the same sector. Holder of more than 5% of two companies holding an authorisation to provide a national terrestrial television channel service may not hold more than 5% of a third company active in the same sector. Similar rules apply to satellite television. 'Two-in three' rule whereby operators may not, beyond certain thresholds, operate or control more than two out of three of certain types of media. Applies at French national, regional and local level.	Yes. No media-specific rules.
Germany	Yes. Different regulations apply in most states in relation to cross-ownership of radio companies and local or regional television channels.	Yes. Transactions in the broadcasting market are reviewed by the Federal Cartel Office (FCO) and the Commission on Concentration in the Media (KEK).

(*Continued*)

Table 5: (*Continued*)

Country	Media Ownership	Merger Control
	Depending on the state, the broadcasting laws provide either for a cap on the number of radio or television channels that are operated by a broadcasting company or for restrictions of the participation in the share capital or the voting rights in broadcasting companies.	The FCO applies mainstream competition-based merger control rules. Where revenue is generated from certain media activities that are important for freedom of expression such as the publication of newspapers or the broadcasting of TV or radio programmes, the respective turnover is to be multiplied by a factor of 20. The KEK applies the Interstate Treaty on Broadcasting. Each company may operate an unlimited number of nationwide television channels unless it could exercise a controlling influence on public opinion. Such ability is presumed if its nationwide television channels achieve average viewer ratings of at least 30%. If the company holds a dominant position in a related media-relevant market or if an overall assessment concludes that its influence is equivalent to that of a company whose average viewer rating achieves 30%, the applicable threshold is 25%.
Greece	Yes. Each legal person can hold only one pay TV or radio licence, analogue or digital, per means of transmission, (terrestrial, cable and satellite). The same person can hold a licence for only one of the other two means of transmission.	Yes. Media-specific rules provide a less stringent test for prohibition. Concentration in media is prohibited if an undertaking acquires a dominant position that is defined as follows: holding more than 35% of one of the four segments of the media (being television, radio, newspapers and periodicals), each one of them taken without any further distinction as to technology, subscription or not, manner of transmission etc; or

(*Continued*)

Table 5: (*Continued*)

Country	Media Ownership	Merger Control
		if one person is active in more than one media segment: holding up to 35% in each segment; or holding cumulatively 32% in two segments; or holding cumulatively 28% in three segments; or holding cumulatively 25% in all four segments.
Italy	No content provider is permitted to hold, directly or through subsidiaries, an authorisation to broadcast more than the 20% of television programmes (or 20% of all radio programmes) nationwide by means of terrestrial technologies. No registered communication operator may earn, directly or through subsidiaries, revenues exceeding 20% of the communications integrated system (which includes all media sector activities, such as broadcasting, sponsorship, radio, cinema, advertising, publishing of newspapers and magazines, as well as e-publishing). Telecoms operators that earn 40% of their overall revenues in the telecoms sector may not accrue revenues exceeding 10% of the CIS. Television undertakings may not participate in companies that publish daily newspapers.	Yes. Sector specific rules apply to cinema exhibit in services. Certain telecoms mergers must be notified to and approved by the Italian Communications Authority.
Netherlands	None	Yes. No media-specific rules.

(*Continued*)

Table 5: (*Continued*)

Country	Media Ownership	Merger Control
Spain	Broadcasting It is prohibited to acquire a 'significant holding' in more than one national television broadcaster if the combined average audience was higher than 27% of the total audience during the 12 months preceding the acquisition. It is prohibited to acquire a significant holding or voting rights in more than one television broadcaster where: a national television broadcaster has more than two multiplexes; a regional television broadcaster has more than one multiplex; or the cross-ownership results in the existence of less than three different national television broadcasters in Spain. Radio It is prohibited to hold more than: 50% of the licences awarded for a given area; five licences for the same area; 40% of the licences awarded for an area of a particular Spanish region; and one-third of the overall total number of Spanish radio licences.	Yes. No media-specific rules.
Sweden	None	Yes. No media-specific rules.
United Kingdom	Cross-media No publisher controlling more than 20% of the national newspaper market (or company holding a 20% interest in such a national newspaper publisher) may itself hold a Channel 3 licence or more than a 20% stake in a Channel 3 company.	Yes. In addition, the mainstream UK merger regime is subject, in cases involving broadcasting or newspaper companies, to the media public interest intervention regime.

(*Continued*)

Country	Media Ownership	Merger Control
	No Channel 3 company may hold more than a 20% stake in a national newspaper publisher. NB. The Media Ownership (Radio and Cross Media) Order 2011 significantly relaxed local radio ownership restrictions. It is now possible to own a regional Channel 3 licence together with one or more local radio licences and local newspapers in the same area, regardless of audience share or circulation. Restrictions on the number of analogue and digital licences that can be owned, and on owning more than one national radio multiplex licence, were also removed.	The Secretary of State (SoS) may intervene on broadcasting/newspaper public interest grounds in a 'special merger situation', namely, where one of the merging parties has an existing 25% share of supply of the relevant broadcasting/newspaper activities in the UK or a substantial part of the UK (regardless of whether the merger enhances that share or meets the £70 million turnover test under the mainstream merger control rules). A special merger situation is subject to specific broadcasting/newspaper public interest considerations.
United States	Media ownership is subject to restrictions, including limits on: ownership of multiple broadcast television stations in a single market; ownership of broadcast television stations reaching a certain percentage of the population; ownership of broadcast radio stations within a local market; cross-ownership of broadcast television and radio stations within a local market; cross-ownership of broadcast television or radio stations and newspapers in the same geographic area; service to a certain percentage of the population by a single cable operator; ownership by a cable operator of a certain percentage of the channels it carries; ownership of two or more of the 'top four' television networks (ABC, CBS, FOX and NBC).	Yes. No media-specific rules. The Team Telecom agencies conduct national-security reviews of mergers and acquisitions in the telecoms and broadcasting sectors (and the new media sector, if there are FCC licences to be transferred or assigned in the transaction).

Source: Multiple, including 'Getting the Deal Through' (available at http://gettingthedealthrough.com) and authors' research. Current as at June 2013.

CASE STUDIES: COMPETITION AND PLURALITY REVIEW IN INTERNATIONAL MERGER CONTROL

Case 1: Competition Review—United Kingdom

Global Radio's acquisition of GCap Media is an example of a media merger which was assessed purely on the basis of competition issues. No plurality considerations arose.

The OFT cleared the London aspects of the transaction. Although each party held a 20 to 30 per cent share of radio advertising, the OFT concluded that there was no realistic prospect of harm to London advertisers or listeners because the parties were not their closest competitors in that region, and the OFT expected the transaction to generate significant efficiencies of benefit to advertisers and listeners.

Global Radio offered to divest a package of radio stations to purchasers approved up-front by the OFT to restore competition to pre-merger levels in the Midlands, where the OFT had competition concerns since the parties had overlapping interests in that region.

According to the OFT's press release, efficiencies evidence provided by the parties made a material difference to the outcome of this case. The OFT Senior Director of Mergers commented that:

> Merger efficiencies benefit customers and put pressure on rivals. In this case, they tipped the balance in favour of clearance in London. This shows that with the right facts, efficiencies can make a difference, even at first phase, and even in a horizontal merger with high market shares. The divestment remedies in the Midlands, where efficiencies were not sufficient, are about restoring competition to make sure customers will not be harmed.[1]

Case 2: Plurality—France

In 2005, the French Competition Authority raised concerns that the merger between the newspaper companies SIPA and Socpresse would result in homogenisation of the content of the affected newspapers and that this would reduce the overall quality of news for readers.[2] The parties committed, among other things, to maintain the editorial independence of the affected newspapers and ensure that each newspaper would have its own editor-in-chief. Although this review was

[1] OFT press release, 'Global/GCap radio merger: OFT seeks remedies and relies on efficiencies for the first time', 8 August 2008.

[2] E-Competitions, 'The French Minister of Economics clears a merger in the sector of daily and weekly regional press with remedies, including bundling prohibition, editorial autonomy and commitments to exclude conglomerate effects (OuestFrance/Socpresse)', 28 October 2005, no 22743.

conducted under an ostensibly competition-based assessment, it illustrates a case where a remedy was put in place which addressed issues which were grounded in pluralism (viewpoint diversity) rather than concerns as to market power.

Case 3: Competition and Plurality—Germany

In Germany, mergers in the TV and broadcasting market are reviewed by the FCO and the German KEK. The FCO applies mainstream competition law, whereas the KEK applies the Interstate Treaty on Broadcasting.

This system of double scrutiny led to a first prohibition—the proposed merger between Axel Springer AG and ProSiebenSat.1 Media AG in 2006.

The FCO prohibited the merger on the basis of competition considerations, namely that: (i) the parties would have had a 40 per cent share of the advertising market (the newspaper BILD was viewed as the only economically viable alternative to TV advertising); (ii) the merger would strengthen Springer's position in the newspaper market; and (iii) the merger would strengthen Springer's dominant position in the newspaper advertising market.

The KEK prohibited the merger on the basis of section 26 of the Interstate Treaty on Broadcasting, which empowers it to block a merger where it would result in the acquisition of a 'dominant power of opinion'. The KEK found that the merged group would hold a TV audience share of 22.06 per cent but having regard to its share of other media markets the audience share would be over 40 per cent. This exceeded the statutory threshold for prohibition. However, at the time the Treaty rules were ill suited to deal with cross-media mergers. The KEK had arrived at its audience share calculation by transposing market shares expressed as sales into audience shares. Later, the statutory provisions were modified to deal with this type of situation.

The parties appealed both the FCO and KEK decisions. In the competition case, the Federal Supreme Court confirmed the FCO's view in June 2010. In a decision of 15 February 2011, the Bavarian Higher Administrative Court overruled the 2006 decision by the KEK finding that the KEK exceeded its powers. It should not have considered Axel Springer's activities in other media markets but should only have focused on ProSiebenSat.1's television audience share which was below the statutory threshold.

Although the case revolves around the interpretation of the specific statutory provisions, it illustrates some of the complexities in devising rules to capture pluralism in the absence of competition concerns.

MEDIA PLURALITY—UK MERGER CONTROL REGIME

Merger control in the UK is voluntary in the sense that there is no requirement to inform the UK competition authorities of a merger either before or after completion. However, a completed transaction may be referred for a second stage in-depth investigation before the CMA within four months of completion. The CMA may ultimately prohibit a transaction or require remedies. Parties to a proposed merger typically seek advance clearance in order to achieve legal certainty before implementing a transaction.

The UK SoS is able to intervene in a newspaper or a broadcasting/media merger where he or she believes that a merger may raise a relevant public interest consideration and the transaction constitutes a relevant merger situation under the standard UK merger control rules. There are specific public interest considerations for newspaper cases and also broadcasting and cross-media cases.
The public interest considerations for newspaper mergers are:

- the need for accurate presentation of news in newspapers;
- the need for free expression of opinion in newspapers involved in the merger; and
- the need for, to an extent that is reasonable and practicable, a sufficient plurality of views expressed in newspapers as a whole in each market for newspapers in the UK or part of the UK.

The public interest considerations for broadcasting and cross-media mergers are:

- the need for there to be a sufficient plurality of persons with control of the media enterprises serving that audience in relation to every audience in the UK or a locality of the UK;
- the need for the availability throughout the UK of a wide range of broadcasting which (taken as a whole) is both of high quality and calculated to appeal to a wide variety of tastes and interests; and
- the need for persons carrying on media enterprises and for those with control of such enterprises to have a genuine commitment to the attainment in relation to broadcasting of objectives relating to due impartiality of news, taste and decency.

Where a transaction is identified as giving rise to public interest considerations, the SoS may intervene by issuing an Intervention Notice. If he or she intervenes, the SoS will be able to consider whether to refer the transaction, clear the merger, or direct that undertakings in lieu of reference are sought by the CMA (ie remedies). If a merger is referred, the SoS will accept the CMA's findings on jurisdiction and substantive competition issues (where relevant as not all cases will raise competition issues). However, as regards adverse public interest findings and remedies the ultimate decision rests with the SoS.

The standard public interest procedures described above focus on transactions which involve acquisitions of enterprises with relatively high UK turnover (ie more than £70 million) or have a consolidating impact (ie meet the share of supply test). However, newspaper (or broadcasting/cross-media) mergers may be scrutinised under the special public interest regime even where the standard merger control tests are not met and the acquirer does not hold an existing newspaper (or broadcasting/media) interest. Provided that one of the parties to the merger has a 25 per cent or more share of supply of newspapers of any description in the UK or in a substantial part of the UK, the SoS may intervene by issuing a Special Intervention Notice. In such a special merger situation, the review will be on the basis of public interest considerations alone—there will be no competition assessment.

If the SoS decides to intervene he or she will consider whether to: (i) refer the transaction for examination of any newspaper/media public interest considerations together with any competition issues that are identified by the CMA (in the case of mergers meeting the standard jurisdictional criteria); (ii) clear the merger; or (iii) direct that undertakings in lieu of a reference are sought (remedies).

Both the CMA and Ofcom must provide advice to the SoS within the deadline set by the SoS. In the context of a special merger situation, the CMA will assess only jurisdiction and will not carry out any competition analysis. Once a merger where a newspaper/media public interest consideration has been specified in the reference has been referred to it, the CMA will be required to conduct an investigation and publish a final report. Where the CMA investigates a special merger situation, it may have regard only to the public interest considerations specified in the reference—no competition assessment is carried out.

The SoS must take the decision on whether to make an adverse public interest finding, or make no finding at all (in which case the case will revert back to the CMA who will make the final decision), or consider the question of remedies, within 30 working days of receipt of the report. He or she must accept the CMA's conclusions on jurisdiction and competition (where applicable). Ofcom can advise the SoS following the receipt of a CMA report. The SoS has ultimate discretion to make an adverse public interest finding.

Appendix 3: Newspapers: The Story of the UK Regional Press

INTRODUCTION

In this Appendix we present a detailed case study of the drivers of consolidation in the UK regional press sector as a prelude to our examination of how the UK merger control authorities have treated such mergers.[1]

We consider the following areas:

- market trends shaping the UK regional press;
- economic features of news provision in the UK;
- case studies on innovative new business models;
- recent policy challenges;
- UK merger control and consolidation of the regional press; and
- future prospects for a healthy and sustainable regional press.

While the facts and context of our study are by their nature UK-domestic, this case vignette has significance beyond the local or regional. We invite readers to indulge us in this regional analysis in the interests of emphasising a sector-based and market-specific approach. We hope that this analysis of the UK approach in a specific media sector will yield insights beyond the UK where consolidation takes place in the quest for efficiencies or long-term viability. The case study is not held up as a stellar example of regulators 'getting it right'. Rather, we ask: what can be done to turn around distressed business models and how should regulators approach consolidation in unprecedented economic times and against understandable pleas from industry to soften their approach?

The UK regional press is in long-term decline owing to a combination of changing consumer preferences, new technology, and poor management decisions. Arguably, there have been some policy blunders and the competition regime may be hampering the future fortunes of the sector.

[1] This Appendix is based on material contained in Sprague, A and Fellas, L, 'Rags in Tatters' (2013) FTI White Paper, February 2013.

MARKET TRENDS

Patterns in Circulation and Profitability

Here we provide background on the economic environment in which UK regional press consolidation takes place. The *Press Gazette* states that between 2005 and 2011 around 70 new papers launched but around 242 local newspapers closed.[2] As a result, it identified 'news gaps' in areas including Port Talbot in South Wales, Rugeley in Lancashire, Cannock Chase in Staffordshire, Leominster in Herefordshire and Long Eaton in Derbyshire. Regional circulation trends since 2001 are shown in Figure 18.[3]

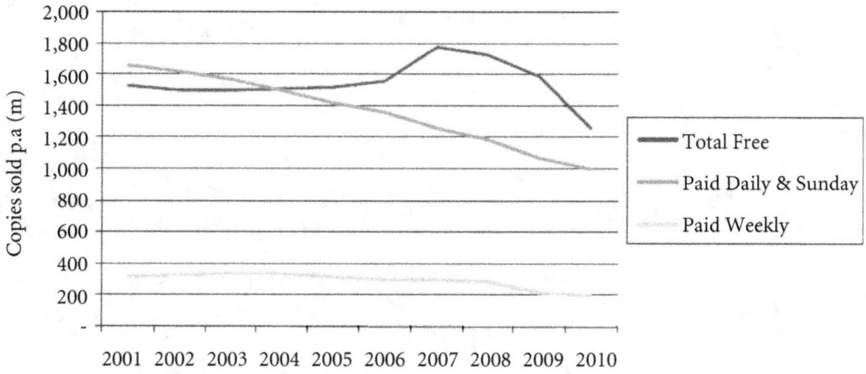

Figure 18: Regional circulation trends*

Source: Ofcom (AA/ABC/Newspaper Society)

* These are the latest data available in this format in the public domain at the time of writing.

Publicly available circulation data and numbers of titles for the regional press publishers are displayed in Figure 19. This indicates that there are around 1,100 titles provided by 87 publishers, demonstrating wide range and variety, albeit with most publishers facing continued and not insignificant circulation decline.

[2] Press Gazette, 'PG research reveals 242 local press closures in 7 years', 30 April 2012, available at: www.pressgazette.co.uk/node/49215.

[3] These are the latest data available in the public domain at the time of writing.

				January 2013		January 2012	
Rank	Group Name	Change in number of titles	Change in weekly circulation	Number of titles	Weekly circulation	Number of titles	Weekly circulation
1	Trinity Mirror Plc	-6%	-9%	132	9,197,259	140	10,087,945
2	Newsquest Media Group	-1%	-8%	186	5,741,423	187	6,247,326
3	Local World (1)	-12%	-11%	115	5,068,765	130	5,664,006
4	Johnston Press Plc	-12%	-21%	215	4,947,195	243	6,248,426
5	Associated Newspapers Ltd	0%	2%	1	3,911,980	1	3,817,120
6	Evening Standard Ltd	0%	0%	1	3,502,530	1	3,503,640
7	Archant	-2%	-7%	65	1,607,081	66	1,725,083
8	D.C. Thomson & Co Ltd	0%	-8%	6	1,453,568	6	1,588,395
9	The Midland News Association Ltd	-6%	-13%	16	1,354,629	17	1,557,750
10	Tindle Newspapers Ltd	7%	0%	78	1,124,369	73	1,122,997
	Northcliffe Media Ltd					91	4,690,109
	Iliffe News & Media					39	973,897
	Total top 20 publishers	-4%	-7%	913	41,328,086	951	44,609,342
	Total other publishers	-6%	-13%	141	1,232,642	150	1,424,931
	Total all publishers	-4%	-8%	1,054	42,560,728	1,101	46,034,273

Figure 19: Circulation of regional newspapers in the UK January 2013 and January 2012

Source: Newspaper Society Intelligence unit 01 January 2013 and 01 January 2012 ABC/VFD/ Independently audited figures. Note (1): No of titles/weekly circulation presented for Local World is the aggregate of Northcliffe Media and Iliffe News & Media

The January 2013 circulation data are summarised in Figure 20.

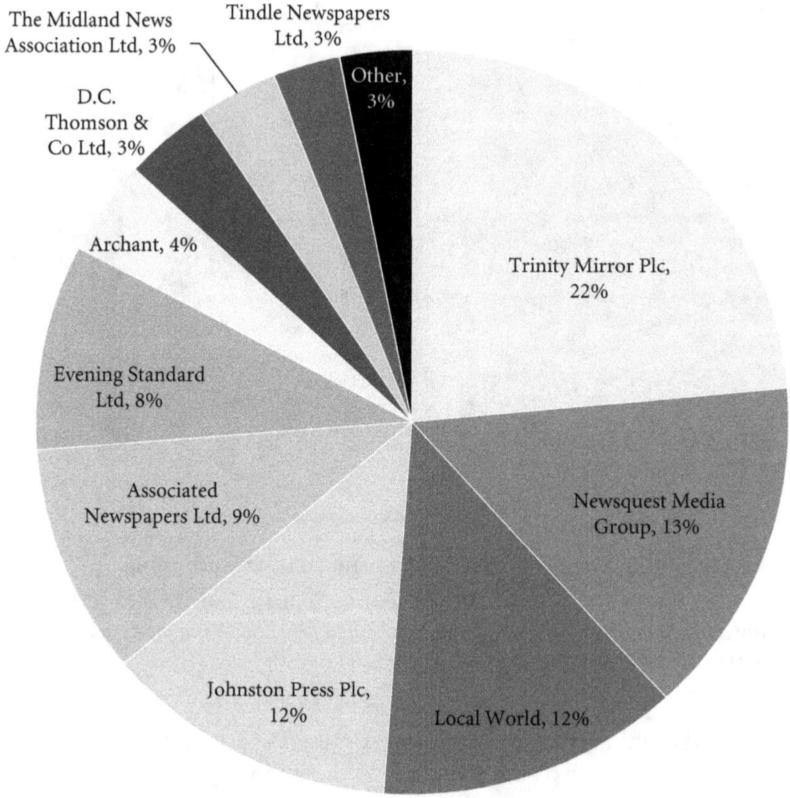

Figure 20: Share of average weekly circulation per title by regional newspaper group

Source: Newspaper Society Intelligence unit 01 January 2013 ABC/VFD/independently audited figures

Perhaps the regional press may be likened to 'indies' (ie independent TV producers) in that small and large organizations can be prosperous but rarely those in the middle, whereby the revenues generated are not sufficient to cover the companies' fixed costs. Small operations may face less loss to digital competition as the relevant titles may serve to engage particularly well with small communities.

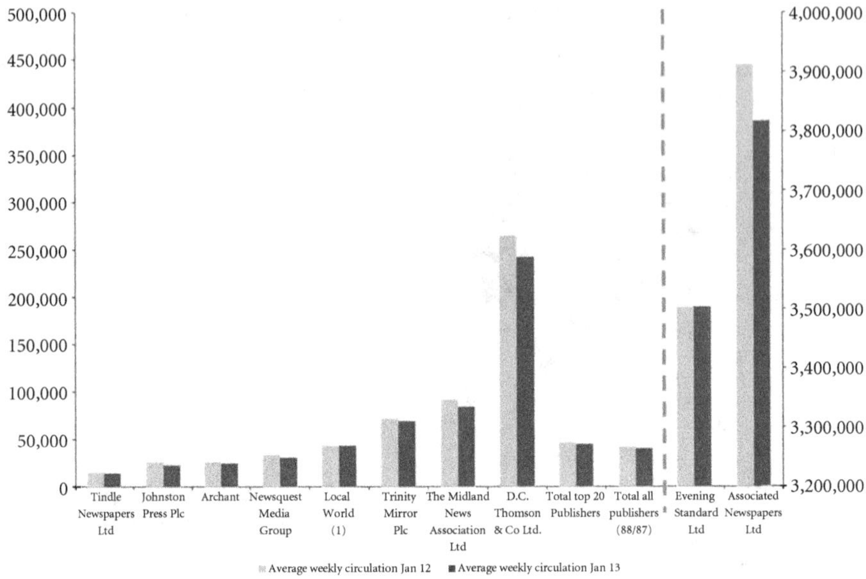

Figure 21: Average weekly circulation per title by regional newspaper group

Source: Newspaper Society Intelligence unit 1 January 2013 and 1 January 2012 ABC/VFD/ independently audited figures. Note: The weekly circulation for Local World for January 2012 is the aggregate of Northcliffe Media and Iliffe News & Media

If we consider the online trends for the local press for a number of the press groups, a much more positive trend emerges, as shown in Figure 22.

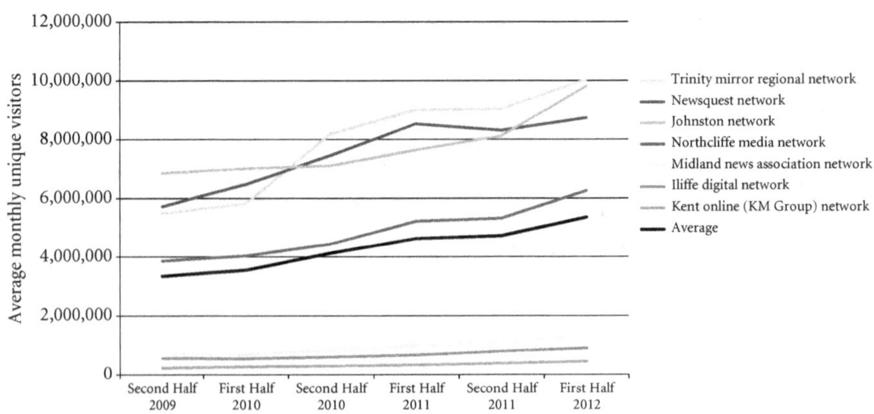

Figure 22: Regional newspaper group average monthly UV trends

Source: Press Gazette, FTI analysis

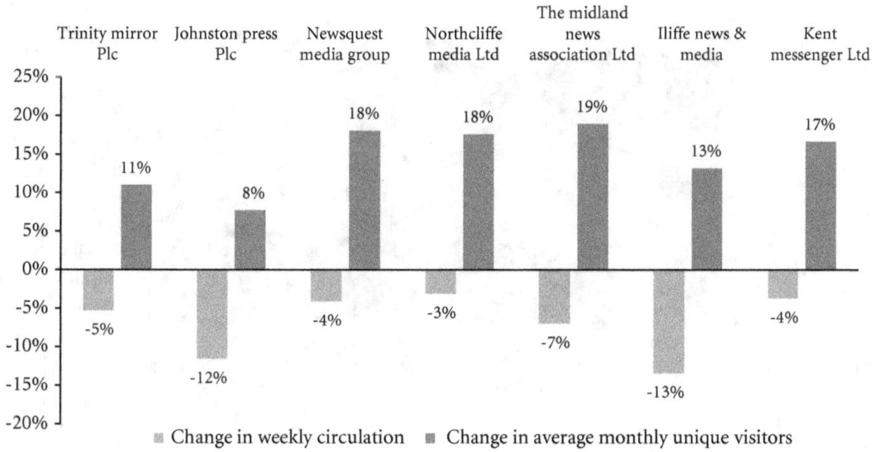

Figure 23: Regional newspaper group UV trends vs. circulation trends

Source: FTI analysis

Combining the online and circulation trends for a set of publishers, the following (neat and striking) chart emerges.

For most groups, online consumption is increasing but printed circulation continues to fall. It is accepted that the transition from offline to online tends not to be profitable. In 2008 the former CEO of NBC Universal, Jeff Zucker, told the *New York Times* in a now well-worn phrase that it is essentially trading 'analog dollars for digital dimes'.

Such metrics go straight to the bottom line, delivering a dismal downward trend in profitability, as indicated in Figure 24.

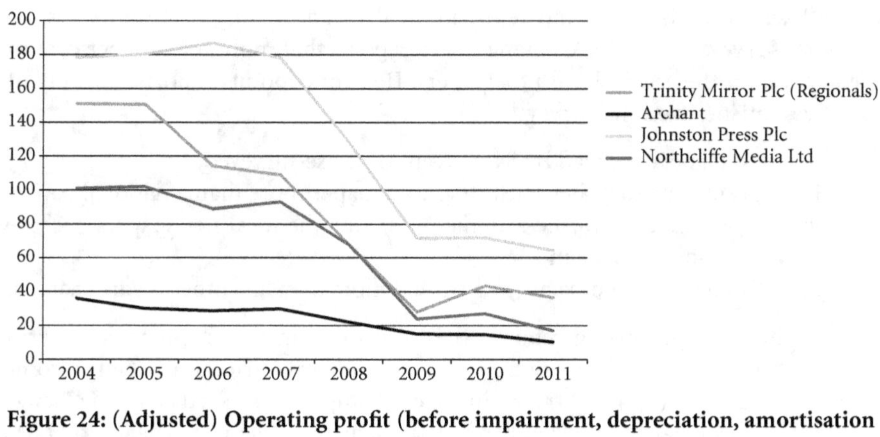

Figure 24: (Adjusted) Operating profit (before impairment, depreciation, amortisation and extraordinary items)

Source: Published annual reports and accounts; FTI analysis

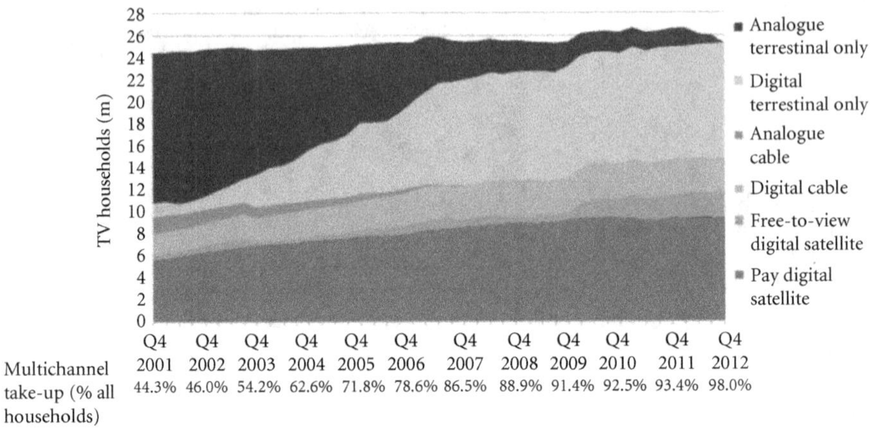

Figure 25: Multichannel take-up in UK households

Source: Ofcom Communications Market Report 2013, page 180

ECONOMIC FEATURES OF NEWS PROVISION IN THE UK

Consumer Preferences

Consumers in the UK like their local paper—according to BMRB/TGI 2012, around 31 million people read one every week (equating to 61 per cent of adults); the local press is the most widely read print medium in Britain. According to the Newspaper Society, the local press sister websites attract around 62 million unique visitors each month and advertising on local newspaper websites is 77 per cent more likely to be believed and relied upon than advertising on other websites. Another survey, CrowdDNA/Loving Local, reports that more than 60 per cent of people act on the ads in local newspapers. IPA Touchpoints reports an array of positive statistics from its survey:[4]

— free newspapers are read by 84 per cent of those surveyed;
— 72 per cent state that they trust their local paper more than a national paper;
— 99 per cent agree with the statement, 'I value the local newspapers because they cover local news'; and
— advertising in local newspapers is trusted more than any other media channel.

Yet despite such promising reports, the local press in the UK is in long-term decline. While continued and significant technological (structural) change, combined with the dire (cyclical) trends in the economy have affected all media, newspapers have been particularly badly hit by the structural changes. The internet has

[4] NS the voice of local media, 'Top Ten Facts about Local Media'.

fundamentally changed the technology for news production and consumption, broadening the market for news; newspapers face increased competition from alternative news sources—for both readers and advertising revenue. This represents a significant challenge for an industry already experiencing a long-term decline in demand for its product.

Within the newspaper sector, the local/regional press has been hardest hit. Some commentators argue that the publishers themselves are partly to blame for the extent of the damage the structural changes have had.

Chris Oakley, newspaper editor and owner of flagship regional newspapers, likens many of the regional press publishers to the Greek economy. Rather than invest for a fruitful future, Oakley argues that huge debts were racked up via reckless expenditure (on expansion). In attempting to preserve margins, cost cutting focused on letting journalists go. He says that the industry's catastrophic problems are self-inflicted and that they could largely have been avoided; newspapers 'failed to recognise the threat and opportunity of the internet and have come close to destroying an industry'.[5] According to its Annual Report, Trinity Mirror's debt stood at more than £180 million and Johnston Press's at £351.7 million.[6]

Of course, not all publishers are in the same position. Moreover, it is tricky to disentangle the data and evaluate how much of the demise is due to changing consumer preferences (long-term downward trend in circulation coupled with free online content and lower online advertising revenues) and how much it is due to management error and to what extent has public policy or the competition regime played a part.

Quality Journalism under Pressure

Notwithstanding the range and combination of possible causes of the downward trends, with such financial strain, as reported by the House of Lords, many local newspapers are unable to conduct the same amount of investigative or 'accountability journalism' stories, such as those covering events at local council and town hall level. This was highlighted in evidence by Eric Gordon, founder and Editor of the *Camden New Journal*, who, echoing Chris Oakley, stated that:

> What has happened with local newspapers is that they have been slimmed down by large groups in order to cut overheads … in my opinion, in order to maintain a good net return the large groups—which were seeking 25%, even more, in the good, buoyant years of the 1990s, whereas we would get along with 10% or so—have cut overheads by slimming down the editorial staff, which in turn means that local courts and councils are no longer covered as well as they should be. Sometimes they are not covered at all.[7]

[5] Oakley, C, 'Five Minutes to Midnight: the death and possible re-birth of the regional newspaper industry', speech to Society of Editors Manchester Conference, 2012.

[6] Trinity Mirror plc, Annual Report 2012.

[7] House of Lords Select Committee on Communications, 3rd Report of Session 2010–12, 'The Future of Investigative Journalism', 16 February 2012 (HL Paper 256) paragraph 154.

As the Select Committee on Communications points out, a vibrant local press is vital for our democracy:

> Responsible, high quality, investigative journalism matters; it is a vital constituent of the UK's system of democratic governance and accountability. At its best, it informs and educates us, enhances our democracy, and is a force for good.[8]

Some commentators contend that the well-trodden path of journalist training at a local paper, rising to correspondent in the regions and eventually to leading reporter in the nationals, is finished and that the only institution currently able to provide the groundwork is the BBC. The situation at the local level is having repercussions for training and quality across the wider news sector.

Business Strategies

The regional press continues to respond to the challenges inherent in the modern media landscape. As stated by the Newspaper Society:

> Innovation, brand extension and portfolio publishing are the name of the game for Britain's local media. While successfully building the readership of their core titles, publishers are also developing a range of targeted print, broadcast and digital channels to reach increasingly diverse audiences in their regional markets. As well as 1,200 regional and local, daily and weekly titles, the regional press now boasts 1,600 websites and hundreds of other print, digital and broadcast channels. In their individual markets, regional press brands reach more people than any other medium.[9]

Thus the press has responded, albeit, as many argue, somewhat late in the day, with investment in new platforms, special interest and ultra-local publications, converged multimedia newsrooms, video journalism, user-generated content (UGC), mobile sites, smartphone apps and other digital and print innovations. While reaching more of the population than previously, monetisation of increased reach remains tricky. We summarise below some of the headline strategy announcements made by Trinity Mirror, Johnston Press and the newly formed Local World.

Case Study: Trinity Mirror

Trinity Mirror's CEO, Simon Fox (previously at HMV), has 'merged' the regional and national businesses into one. He has opened up the executive area on the twenty-second floor of the London Canary Wharf office and hopes that digital, and in particular a focused tablet strategy aimed towards monetisation, will improve the company's fortunes.

[8] Ibid, Summary.

[9] NS the voice of local media, 'Circulation and distribution' available at: www.newspapersoc.org.uk/circulation-and-distribution.

Trinity Mirror—Key Facts

— One Trinity Mirror—a united business serving nationals and regionals
— Shared content centre
— Clear digital proposition—technology investment, improved websites, mobile and tablet applications across platforms
— Focused tablet strategy—aim towards monetisation
— Cost effective central support

'What we want is to deliver great journalism every day and to see circulation and advertising increasing … a clear, forward-looking strategy across our entire publishing operations, both print and digital, which builds on and develops our editorial strength … an efficient operation where those closest to our readers and advertisers have the autonomy to do what is best for each market.'

Simon Fox, CEO Trinity Mirror

Case Study: Johnston Press

The CEO of Johnston Press is former BBC iPlayer and Microsoft's Ashley Highfield. Highfield believes that the papers can be templated, cover prices put up and, of course, digital has to be at the heart of the company. Johnston posits that mobile will be a key growth channel and is in the process of re-launching its titles—both paper and online—following re-design and re-vamping.

Johnston Press—Key Facts

— Invest in content; platform 'neutrality' and increased UGC
— Relaunch titles: digital, combination of free to pay, daily to weekly and/ re-designs
— Drive subscription levels
— Mobile growth channel
— Digital output and inputs (mobile/digital devices for journalists)
— Partnerships with local community contributors, deeper audience engagement, journalists on the ground in every town

'I think the future for our business is to drive subscription levels … what we are trying to do is move people to a subscription where they'll get the paper, the iPad app, the website, everything in one bundles for considerably less than the cover price of the paper.'

Ashley Highfield, CEO Johnston Press

Case Study: Local World

The company is still new but Steve Auckland, Local World's CEO has embarked on a business transformation of all of its centres which is expected to take 18 months. It boasts being debt-free, will invest £10 million in digital and is focusing on 'localism'—content, sales and management. It aims to publish a high proportion of UGC.

Local World—Key Facts

- A 'one stop shop' serving content to local communities—local content, local sale, local management; high UGC
- Optimisation of local content and commerce across all platforms
- Business transformation at each centre over 18 months
- Digital-led £10 million investment
- No property, printing press and large scale distribution or legacy issues such as high levels of debt

'I'm looking forward to us building on our existing strengths, transforming our products and services, and ensuring we are the one-stop-shop for local content and commerce.'

Steve Auckland, CEO Local World

The local press is certainly not resting on its laurels. The new impetus from the combination of new CEOs and re-engineered strategies may turn its fortunes round.

INDEPENDENTLY FUNDED NEWS

In 2008 the BBC Executive set out proposals for a new local video service. Ofcom conducted a market impact assessment (MIA) of the BBC's proposed proposition and concluded that 'the launch of the proposal would have a significant negative market impact on commercial providers'.[10] The local press (and radio) supported this finding and the proposal did not obtain approval from the BBC Trust.

Independently funded news consortia (IFNC), was the brainchild of Ed Richards and was announced at a session on the local and regional media in Westminster, London. The previous government had selected the winners for the three pilot regions. Consortia comprised the regional press, TV, and experts in online and local community knowledge and, in some cases, radio. Trinity Mirror,

[10] Ofcom, 'Market Impact Assessment of the BBC's Local Video Service', 21 November 2008.

Johnston Press, DC Thomson and NWN Media were poised to receive public money and the opportunity to parade their (IFNC) brand on the ITV regional news slots. The IFNCs were immediately cancelled, as promised, by Jeremy Hunt when the coalition government was formed. To replace them, Hunt's second-favourite interest, local TV, was put on the table.[11] Local TV will, of course, be targeting local advertising revenues and may further cannibalise regional press revenues.

It seems that IFNCs may have provided a stepping stone to a more sustainable local press. Local TV, assuming it gets off the ground, could be a staunch competitor for local advertising revenues.

BACK TO THE LEGAL FRAMEWORK: UK MERGER CONTROL

Merger Control Framework

At the time of writing, an overhaul of the UK framework for competition law and regulation is underway with the merger of the UK's first and second-stage competition authorities (the Office of Fair Trading (OFT) and the Competition Commission (CC) respectively) to form the Competition and Markets Authority (CMA) with effect from April 2014. While references in this book to the application of competition law in the sector relate to the historic experience of the UK competition authorities (the OFT and the CC) and the UK media and communications sector regulator (Ofcom) they are informative when considering the roles of Ofcom and the CMA in the reformed UK competition law regime.

UK merger control provides the following alternative thresholds for mergers which qualify for investigation:

- turnover test: the UK turnover of the target exceeds £70 million;
- share of supply test—as a result of the merger a share of 25 per cent or more in the supply or purchasing of goods or services of a particular description in the UK (or a substantial part of the UK) is created or enhanced.

In the case of small-scale acquisitions it may be that the target has insufficient turnover to meet the turnover test. However, since the share of supply test is not based on an economic market definition, this gives the UK flexibility to review mergers on the basis of overlaps in narrowly defined sectors. The OFT will typically consider the share of supply on the basis of each relevant 'JICREG'[12] area and then determine whether the areas in which the share of supply exceeds 25 per cent constitute a substantial part of the UK.

[11] Hunt's favourite interest was high-speed broadband.

[12] These are areas mapped out by the Joint Industry Committee for the Regional Media Research (JICREG).

Local Media Assessment

Local Media Assessment (LMA) is a relatively new element in the UK merger review procedure. This is a formalised mechanism for Ofcom to assist the OFT in its assessment of mergers involving local media.

In media mergers involving newspaper publishing and/or commercial radio or television broadcasting, where the case raises prima facie competition concerns, the CMA asks Ofcom to provide an LMA to assist the OFT in arriving at its decision on whether to refer the merger for a second-stage investigation. The LMA will probably include Ofcom's views on:

- the relevant counterfactual to the merger (including the risk of the asset or business failing);
- the scope of the relevant product and geographic markets; and
- the competitive effects of the merger, and the exceptions to the duty of the OFT to refer the merger for a second-stage review, in particular in terms of whether the markets are of insufficient importance and whether there are 'relevant customer benefits'.

Although the decision on these matters is for the OFT, the OFT will be informed by Ofcom's views and will take them into account along with other third-party views in reaching its conclusions.

While Ofcom's expert media advice feeds into local media mergers, the OFT thus far remains unconvinced of the strength of cross-media competition. The *Kent Messenger* case discussed below provides a good illustration of the workings of the post-Digital Britain[13] competition regime. In short, local/regional press markets were defined narrowly in product and geography, competition from other media (other print, online and radio) was not considered to be effective, and the proposed merger was referred for a long, resource-intensive and costly process.

Specific challenges are posed in assessing newspaper mergers. This is because they have the characteristics of a so-called 'two-sided' product: they are effectively in two different (albeit related) markets—for readers and for advertisers. The relationship between the two markets, and hence separate groups of customers, is termed 'intermediation' by practitioners and is typically illustrated by the following example. If the cover price of a paper is increased, the paper will probably reduce in circulation and hence the number of readers will be reduced. This has a knock-on effect, reducing the demand from advertisers (or their willingness to pay a certain rate). The tension between the levels of customers and charges in the two markets are termed 'indirect network effects'. Newspapers have to cover their

[13] Department for Culture, Media & Sport and Department for Business, Innovation & Skills, 'Digital Britain, Final Report' (Cm 7650) June 2009. The Digital Britain report was a policy document which outlined the UK government's strategic vision for ensuring that the UK is at the leading edge of the global digital economy.

costs and decide on the best mix of pricing to do so—the cover price (in many cases zero) to readers and the charges to advertisers.[14]

Notably, each of the two sides of the market may have very different characteristics and dynamics which in turn affects the merger assessment, adding a layer of complexity absent from 'one-sided' product markets. In making its merger assessments the OFT takes into account the two-sided nature of the local press.[15]

The Kent Messenger *Case*

Kent Messenger Group (KMG) proposed to buy seven Kent local weekly newspaper titles from Northcliffe Media (Kent Regional News & Media, KRNM), to add to its then portfolio of seven paid for titles and seven free titles. With a long history of publishing in the county of Kent, KMG is a family-run business and the sixteenth largest news group in the UK. Compared to the larger regional press groups, it is a relatively small player.[16]

Northcliffe (now subsumed into Local World) was the fourth-largest regional publisher with a total of 115 titles across the UK, and had purchased KRNM from Trinity Mirror in 2007. These titles were run as a discrete group. Following the proposed merger, Northcliffe would have retained its remaining Kent titles within its portfolio.[17] According to KMG, there were three competitors in the Kent local newspaper sector: KMG, KRNM and *Kent on Sunday* published by Archant. Third-parties appeared to provide the OFT with compelling submissions, expressing concerns about price increases following the transaction.

Ofcom concluded in its LMA that:

> The evidence available to us suggests that the target business and the regional newspaper business of KMG will struggle to achieve profitability in their current form, which might lead them to respond by closing newspaper titles or reducing quality (or both).
>
> In light of this, a merger may provide the opportunity to rationalise costs, maintain quality and investment, and provide a sounder commercial base from which to address long-term structural change, for example by expanding the availability of online and

[14] Other media face this challenge. A prime example is Channel 4's historic switch of Film Four (and other channels) from a subscription service (with relatively fewer viewers) to a free-to-air service on the terrestrial TV platform.

[15] There is a body of empirical literature on the effects of two-sided markets on merger situations. As reported by a Federal Trade Commission Roundtable publication, several papers report on newspaper mergers. Notably, two of the papers cited, one on Canada (Chandra, A and Collard-Wexler, A, 'Mergers in Two-Sided Markets: An Application to the Canadian Newspaper Industry', Leonard N Stern School of Business Working Paper No EC-07-03 (2008), available at: ssrn.com/abstract=985581) and the other from the Benelux perspective (Van Cayseele, P J G and Vanormelingen, S, 'Prices and Network Effects in Two-Sided Markets: The Belgian Newspaper Industry' (2009) Working Paper, available at: ssrn.com/abstract=1404392) found that newspaper mergers had no or only limited impact on prices for both advertisers and readers.

[16] FTI analysis based on Newspaper Society.

[17] Ofcom, 'Local Media Assessment on the proposed acquisition by the Kent Messenger Group of seven Kent newspaper titles from Northcliffe Media', 31 October 2011.

> other digital local services. These potential benefits need to be weighed against any potential customer harm resulting from reduced competition identified in the OFT's overall assessment.[18]

The OFT, however, decided to refer the merger to the CC for a second phase review. It found that the parties (Northcliffe and KMG) were close competitors in the specific areas and that the joint share of supply in those areas amounted to 100 per cent post-merger. It concluded that the transaction would lead to a substantial lessening of competition as rivalry between the two firms would end post-merger. It was not convinced about widening the nature of the product market to include other media, stating that:

> The OFT does not consider the evidence—in relation to the constraints from print and non-print media—sufficiently compelling to justify widening the candidate market beyond the supply of advertising space in local weekly (paid-for and free) newspapers.[19]

In the context of a first-stage procedure, the OFT is more likely to fall back on accepted market definitions, making it difficult to challenge entrenched views. At the CC, there is much more open for debate but, of course, parties may abandon a deal rather than face a long and intensive CC inquiry.

Amelia Fletcher, the OFT Chief Economist in this case, said:

> Local newspapers face significant challenges, including falling readership and increased competition from other media, most notably, the internet. However, this merger would create a monopoly in local weekly newspapers in several local areas across East Kent. [Thanet, Canterbury, Swale, Dover, Ashford and Shepway] UK merger law requires the OFT to be cautious in its 'first phase' review of mergers. We require compelling evidence to dismiss concerns that the combination of such close competitors as these might result in substantially higher prices or less choice for advertisers and readers. The evidence in this case did not permit us to clear this transaction; therefore we think it is appropriate that the merger is referred to the Competition Commission for a more detailed 'second phase' review.[20]

KMG subsequently withdrew its bid for the series of Northcliffe Media titles. Throughout the process KMG had maintained that it would not be able to afford a referral to the CC, and, in such an event, would have to withdraw its bid for the titles within Northcliffe's KRNM.[21]

The chair of KMG, Geraldine Allinson, said the company had invested 'a huge amount of time' on the bid in recent months and that the costs and time necessary for a CC review (which she said would amount to £500,000) 'would be completely unreasonable for a business of our size and for a deal of this scale'.

[18] Ibid, paragraph 110.

[19] Office of Fair Trading, *Anticipated acquisition by Kent Messenger Group of several newspapers from Northcliffe Media Limited*, 18 October 2011, paragraph 47.

[20] Office of Fair Trading press release, 'OFT refers Kent newspaper merger to the Competition Commission', 18 October 2011.

[21] Kent Online, 'KM Group pulls out of bid to buy weekly newspaper group', 18 October 2011, available at: www.kentonline.co.uk/kentonline/news/2011/october/18/km_group_pulls_out_of_bid.aspx.

In response to the OFT's decision, Baron Black of Brentwood, the Telegraph Media Group's executive director, said:

> The OFT is preventing the changes in the local newspaper industry which will allow it to survive, undermining local democracy in the process ...
>
> A few years ago ... Trinity Mirror tried to sell eight free weekly newspapers in Northampton and Peterborough to Johnston Press. A ruling from the competition authorities meant the sale had to be abandoned. And ... seven of those eight titles have now closed.[22]

Black called for urgent action 'to show we understand the importance of our local press in the creative economy and in local democracy and set publishers free to renew their businesses for a new age'.[23]

The OFT decision to refer the case to the CC was also harshly criticised in the House of Lords report on investigative journalism comment that 'this case is an example of the damaging effect which the competition regime can have on the local newspaper industry, which is facing a significant economic threat'.[24]

The Topper *Case*

In 2013 industry commentators began to refer to a possible directional change by the OFT noting

> signs that the OFT's tough stance may be thawing. Last year it cleared DMGT's acquisition of free Nottingham weekly The Topper. It gave unconditional clearance despite DMGT already owning the Nottingham Post, and noting that the deal would mean the publisher would have a 'high combined share of supply of local newspapers and local paper advertising space in Nottingham'.[25]

In the *Topper* case, the acquirer, Northcliffe, stated that it did not consider that an LMA from Ofcom was required. Ofcom considered that an LMA would not materially assist the OFT's merger assessment and no LMA was requested. The OFT defined the scope of the product market to comprise both daily and weekly papers. On the advertising side, it maintained the definition of advertising in printed newspapers alone (online/other media were, however, appraised as part of the competitive assessment), taking into account advertising by category (eg display vs classified and industry segment). The geographic scope was deemed

[22] The Guardian, 'Why Black is right—block on Kent newspaper switch was a "dinosaur decision"', 4 November 2011, available at: www.guardian.co.uk/media/greenslade/2011/nov/04/guy-black-local-newspapers.

[23] Ibid.

[24] House of Lords Select Committee on Communications, 3rd Report of Session 2010–12, 'The Future of Investigative Journalism', 16 February 2012 (HL Paper 256) paragraph 158.

[25] The Guardian, 'OFT considers investigation into David Montgomery's Local World', 18 January 2013, available at: www.guardian.co.uk/media/2013/jan/18/oft-considers-investigation-local-world?INTCMP=SRCH.

to be Nottingham, the OFT stating that it believed that 'the candidate frame of reference is the supply of local newspapers in Nottingham taking into account different advertising categories where appropriate'.[26]

Interestingly, post-merger the parties would have a combined share of circulation of 90 per cent in 10 of the JICREG areas and more than 50 per cent in the remaining three JIGREG areas. However, the OFT concluded that the two papers in question, the *Post* and the *Topper,* were not close competitors and that, taken together, supply-side and demand-side constraints were *jointly* likely be sufficient to protect consumers. This is an important point—on their own, supply-side constraints (eg constraints presented by other media) were not considered sufficient. However, once demand factors were included and 'taken in the round' all potential constraints were considered sufficient to protect consumers. Notably, the two-sided nature of the product market and the so-called indirect network effects were cited as important and supported a finding that Northcliffe would not have the incentive to increase cover prices or advertising prices. While the OFT found that the merger would lead to a lessening of competition, it did not believe that the lessening would be substantial. Hence the merger was cleared.

LESSONS FROM THE US

The US is often held up as a beacon for the market, technical or regulatory development in the UK. Unfortunately, the regional press in the US is far from booming: it is, arguably, in an even worse state than its UK counterpart. According to *The Economist*, by 2011 revenues in the sector had fallen to around half of the level they were in 2000.[27]

The Pew Center, a respected US think tank on public issues and trends agrees that the printed press will continue to be a challenging market and that: 'To different degrees, executives predict newsrooms will continue to shrink, more papers will close and many surviving papers will deliver a print edition only a few days a week.'[28]

In December 2012, however, *The Economist* reported that circulation had begun to stabilise, with some papers (albeit *The New York Times* and similar) managing to stave off the fall in advertising revenues.[29] Moreover, success stories in respect of paywalls were reported. Consumer willingness to pay appears to be

[26] Office of Fair Trading, *Anticipated acquisition by Northcliffe Media Limited of Topper Newspapers Limited*, 1 June 2012.

[27] The Economist, 'News adventures: After years of bad headlines the industry finally has some good news', 8 December 2012, available at: www.economist.com/news/business/21567934-after-years-bad-headlines-industry-finally-has-some-good-news-news-adventures.

[28] Pew Center, 'How newspapers are faring trying to build digital revenue', 5 March 2012, available at: www.journalism.org/analysis_report/search_new_business_model.

[29] The Economist, 'News adventures: After years of bad headlines the industry finally has some good news', 8 December 2012.

improving, at least for content-rich papers, driven in part by tablet consumption. That said, the sector remains in a fragile state and for every success story there is probably a failure. News Corporation closed the *Daily*—a tablet-only paper. Another publisher, Advance Newspapers, moved 14 of its daily papers to three-day publications proving further evidence of the challenging nature of the sector in the US. While paywalls are becoming commonplace, revenues remain low; far too low compared to the level required to offset the decline in print revenues.

The US situation is unlikely to be a perfect indicator of prospects overseas as there are at least three important distinguishing factors. First, there is the issue of scale. In the UK, there are 26 million TV households whereas in the US, TV households total 116 million. Second, there is the issue of subscriptions. A large majority of newspaper sales in the US are by subscription whereas this is not commonplace in the UK. Third, there is the issue of revenue composition. In the US, advertising historically accounted for a relatively high proportion of newspaper revenues (more than 80 per cent), whereas in the UK, it is around 50 per cent (for paid-for copies).

The main lesson to be learned from the US is that, as in many countries, the newspaper sector is in long-term decline and that managing the digital transition is fraught with difficulty. That said, there are several success stories of turnaround—broad organisational transformation, new advertising sales management and content delivery systems combined with changes to the number and type of print days have had some promising results in staving off the inevitable downward trend. Anecdotal evidence, however, suggests that as in the UK, the quality of the journalism has also suffered.

WHAT NEXT FOR THE LOCAL PRESS?

There is a clear tension between the democratic need for investigative local journalism, current business models and the competition regime. It is not clear that the admirable new digital strategies of the regional press publishers will fully resolve the sector's problems. Trends from the US show some green shoots but this may be stalling the inevitable long-term decline. Perhaps Facebook, Twitter or the next 'big thing' will become the vital vehicle for democracy at the local level.

Public subsidies for journalism are available in Finland, France and the Netherlands. Louise Mensch, a former Member of Parliament, led a private members' debate in Westminster Hall in April 2012, calling for subsidies for the local press in the UK. This did not gain the support of fellow MPs and was swept aside in the Select Committee discussions stating that:

> [G]iven the strong independent character of the printed press in the UK and our political traditions, we do not believe that it would be appropriate for the UK Government to fund investigative journalism directly in the form of state subsidies other than with

> the continued support for zero-VAT rating for newspapers and of the BBC licence fee in broadcasting.[30]

The Select Committee did, however, propose that an investigative journalism fund could be set up, with monies coming from fines for breaches of the Editors' Code of Practice under a new system of press regulation. Such a system would require fair distribution by an accountable and independent regulatory body. While this initiative provides potentially useful support, this model is unlikely to solve the inherent problems faced by the regional press.

The internet has fundamentally changed news consumption and provision. Newspapers now have to integrate their offering with online and social media. Readers have more choice than ever and newspapers face competition from literally thousands of news sources. Such sources are often newspapers' rich content, edited news—yet available for free. While the OFT recognises the importance of the two-sided nature of newspapers, in merger cases the OFT's approach is generally to focus on the advertisers' side of the market. In some cases it has expressed concerns about a single paper serving a single JICREG area. The importance of holding MPs and allegedly rogue businesses to account is not part of the competition regulator's remit. The UK competition authorities also appear to remain unconvinced about the competition from other media (eg radio, online and social media) in exerting pressure on local press advertising rates. Competition concerns are raised and transactions tend to get referred for a second stage and resource-intensive second-phase investigation.

In any one local area, surely one paper is better than none? One option (rarely implemented by the competition authorities) would be for the competition authority to impose price regulation on press advertising rates at the local level to alleviate its monopoly concerns.[31] More seriously, there must be superior options.

In our view, as far as newspapers are concerned bigger is better or, as Sir Ray Tindle has found, small (or hyper-local) is beautiful. The middle-ground should be avoided.[32] For many publishers, therefore, further consolidation is imperative for longer-term viability, to enable cost rationalisation, test digital strategies and, most importantly, to invest in content—old-fashioned high quality journalism.

What are the stumbling blocks? The OFT's stance on market definition, its competitive assessment and its cautious approach to clearance. Two rival papers

[30] House of Lords Select Committee on Communications, 3rd Report of Session 2010–12, 'The Future of Investigative Journalism', 16 February 2012 (HL Paper 256) paragraph 216.

[31] The often quoted example of a competition authority imposing a remedy of regulated prices on a non-regulated sector dates back to the 1980s. The then Monopolies and Mergers Commission stipulated that 'price increases are limited to a weighted index of production costs minus 2%' following a merger in the white salt market. The remedy was imposed following the report by the Monopolies and Monopolies Commission, 'White Salt' (1986) Cm 9778.

[32] By this we mean that small, hyper-local papers with a loyal following appear to be able to withstand the structural decline thus far. Larger publishers are better able to build on the economies of scale and scope that medium-sized publishers find challenging to realise.

in an area coming together is unlikely to gain approval. At the local level, it appears that advertisers see newspapers as their main (and only) effective channel. However, this may change. Ten years ago advertising agencies and corporates were both struggling with online advertising and questions of whether to spend and, if so, how much, where to spend and how to measure the return on investment. Now, online and even social media are standard. If prices in the local press increased overnight, surely local advertisers would turn to other media? Over time, we would expect the constraints exerted by online to increase.

Of course, the cost of going to a second-stage merger investigation is a major barrier. In India, the Competition Commission of India (CCI) is the single arbiter of merger control at the initial (30-day) stage and in the event that a longer investigation of up to 180 days is warranted. However, the basic principle remains the same: it may be difficult to persuade the competition authority of more novel arguments in the tight time frame of a first-phase proceeding. Such arguments should get a hearing in the longer drawn out second stage—but only if the commercial rationale of the transaction can withstand the delay and cost.

Faced with a potentially drawn out regulatory proceeding, this may suggest that the legal principles at stake should be settled once and for all. In theory, therefore, a number of affected groups should come together, gather compelling evidence and bite the bullet, ultimately during a second-stage procedure if necessary. If a worthwhile transaction can be approved (accepting a few disposals in certain areas), this may set the framework for a more efficient review in future cases. Indeed, publishers could seek a set of principles from the competition authority, analogous to those for supermarkets—at least the way forward may be a little clearer. The recent CC decision on Global Radio's acquisition of GMG Radio is a good example of how the CC views the local media landscape.[33] It required divestments of overlapping stations on the grounds that local advertisers are unable to find alternative media. At root, however, there is a still a problem here—local radio and local newspapers perform valuable economic roles and aren't perfect competitors for one another. Therefore, the UK's highest competition body has implicitly said that we cannot allow two-to-one mergers either in the case of radio or (one suspects) newspapers. But this is what needs to be tested.

It has been suggested that within a regional press group, local papers that have a circulation of 30,000 may have another 30 years' life.[34] With half that circulation, it may be predicted that another 15 years remain. Yet where there is a consumer demand, as there currently appears to be, we would hope that we could expect them to stay for a lot longer than that although perhaps in a tablet or new device form rather than in the traditional printed form.

[33] Competition Commission, *Global Radio Holdings Limited and GMG Radio Holdings Limited, A report on the completed acquisition by Global Radio Holdings Limited of GMG Radio Holdings Limited*, 21 May 2013.

[34] Ashley Highfield, CEO Johnston Press.

Appendix 4: Cable Country Reviews

A. EUROPE

Belgium

Market Structure

In Belgium more than 80 per cent of households receive their TV services from cable operators.[1] Internet protocol television (IPTV) has acquired a number of customers, but alternative platforms, such as satellite, digital terrestrial and mobile TV, have not been able to gain a strong foothold in Belgium. Only Belgacom, with its IPTV offer, is a credible competitor to the cable operators. Satellite direct-to-home (DTH) reception has only achieved marginal penetration compared with cable and IPTV.

Telenet Group is the largest provider of cable broadband services in Belgium. It operates in Flanders and Brussels. Telenet's business includes the provision of both analogue and digital cable television.[2]

In Wallonia, following consolidation most cable operators now belong to Tecteo Group whose offerings are made through its VOO brand. In Brussels, the market is divided between Brutélé and Numéricable (the former Coditel). The Association Intercommunale d'Electricté du Sud du Hainaut (AIESH) cable television services have been provided by Numéricable in the Southern Hainaut (ie South Belgium) region since January 2013.

Regulation

Belgium is a federal state with three regions (Flanders, Wallonia and the Brussels region—referred to above) and three (language) Communities. The

[1] See European Commission, 'Special Eurobarometer 293, E-Communications Household Survey', June 2008 at 7: 'An analysis by country reveals that the way European households receive television differs strongly between countries: ... more than 80% of Dutch and Belgian households have cable television ....' See also 'Décision de la Conférence des Régulateurs du secteur ses Communications Electroniques of 1 July 2011' (public version) at heading 2.3.1 paragraph 67 and footnote 37.

[2] Interkabel Vlaanderen Cvba a provider of analogue and digital television services has operated as a subsidiary of Telenet NV since 1 October 2008.

three Communities are the Dutch-speaking Vlaamse Gemeenschap (Flemish Community); the French-speaking Communauté Française (French Community) and the German-speaking Deutschsprachige Gemeinschaft (German-speaking Community).

Judgments of the Constitutional Court[3] of 14 July 2004[4] and 13 July 2005[5] confirmed that the Federal State and the (language) Communities have to work together in order to manage certain areas of electronic communications, owing to the growing technological convergence between telecommunications and broadcasting. The scope of these policy areas and the terms of this cooperation are settled under a cooperation agreement of 17 November 2006 establishing the Belgian Conference of Electronic Communications Sector Regulators (CRC).

By virtue of this cooperation agreement, the Federal Regulator, the Belgian Institute for Postal Services and Telecommunications (IBPT/BIPT hereafter BIPT) works together with its regulatory counterparts in the three Communities within the CRC. Apart from the Federal Regulator, BIPT, the CRC includes:

— the Vlaamse Regulator voor de Media (Flemish Council for the Media), for the Flemish Community (the VRM);
— the Conseil supérieur de l'audiovisuel (High Council for Broadcasting), for the French Community (CSA); and
— the Medienrat (Media Council), for the German-speaking Community.

Competition Law

There have been a number a number of decisions under competition law involving Belgian cable television operators.

In the *TF1* case[6] the Brussels Court of Appeal found that collective dominance resulted from the fact that the different independent cable networks behaved like a collective interest group. However, it dismissed the case against them on the basis that such cooperation was in conformity with the requirements of the then prevailing collective bargaining requirements for the industry.

[3] The Constitutional Court was formerly known as the Court of Arbitration. Paragraph 2 of Article 107 of the 1980 version of the Constitution, which established the Court of Arbitration, provided: 'There is for the whole of Belgium one Court of Arbitration, the composition, competence and functioning of which are determined by statute.' The Court of Arbitration was officially inaugurated on 1 October 1984. It delivered its first judgment on 5 April 1985. When the Constitution was revised on 7 May 2007, the name of the Court of Arbitration was changed to 'Constitutional Court'. For information on the Belgian Constitutional Court in English see: www.const-court.be/en/common/home.html. References below are to the Constitutional Court. Copies of the judgments in the original language versions are available at the Constitutional Court's website.

[4] Constitutional Court 2004-132 judgment of 14 July 2004.

[5] Constitutional Court 2005-128 judgment of 13 July 2005.

[6] Judgment of 9 March 1999 in Case No 1998/AR/2516 *RTD and Others v SABAM*; Justel No F-19990309-1.

In the *Canal+* case[7] the Brussels Court of Appeal followed its *TFI* decision and confirmed a preliminary ruling in favour of Canal+ in its claim against a cable network operator (Coditel) for abuse of a dominant position.

When considering an application for interim measures in the *SAT 1* case (Intermosane-Interest/SABAM-AGICOA), the President of the Belgian Competition Council found an unfair and discriminatory exercise of their monopoly over the management of copyright, for musical works (by SABAM) and for audiovisual works (by AGICOA) concerning authorisations to retransmit programming of the German satellite channel SAT 1 which exceeded what was necessary to carry out the essential function of copyright-related broadcasts rights.[8] The Brussels Court of Appeal confirmed this decision.

In 2005, the LBF, a joint selling body with the exclusive right to sell TV broadcasting rights of the Jupiler League on behalf of the participating football clubs, awarded all the packages of rights to Belgacom Skynet. Telenet, Belgacom's competitor on the Belgian digital television market, as well as BeTV (formerly Canal+ in Wallonia) contested the award, given the strategic importance of access to such premium content. The Belgian National Competition Authority (NCA), however, decided on 29 July 2005 that the tendering procedure satisfied the requirements which were extracted from the European Commission's decisional practice.[9] Strengthened by the fact that Belgacom Skynet was a new entrant in the pay television market, the NCA found that the joint selling of media rights did not infringe Article 101 Treaty on the Functioning of the EU (TFEU) and should be considered to be competition enhancing. This decision was upheld on Appeal by the Brussels Court of Appeal.[10] (See also the remarks about the *Telenet/Canal+* merger below.)

Merger Control

Merger cases have included in particular the merger of cable operator Telenet and Canal+, then the only pay TV operator active in Flanders. The Competition Council cleared the concentration conditionally.

[7] Judgment of 28 January 1999 in Case No 1998/KR/334 *Canal+ Belgique SA v Wolu TV aisbl and Radio Public SA*; Justel No F-19990128-9.

[8] Belgian Conseil de la Concurrence, Second Annual Report, 1994–1995 at 44 and 45 (available at: economie.fgov.be/fr/binaries/report_competition_fr_002_tcm326-31173.pdf). Decision of 4 September 1995, 95-VMP-2, *Intermosane—Interest/Sabam—Agicoa*, confirmed by the Brussels Court of Appeal, 9th Chamber by judgment of 4 September 1996 summarised in the Juridat database at reference Justel F-19960904-7.

[9] Belgian Conseil de la Concurrence, 2005 Annual Report at §4.3.1, 37 *et seq*; (available at: economie.fgov.be/fr/binaries/report_competition_2005_fr_tcm326-36151.pdf).

[10] Judgment of 28 June 2006, in Joined Cases Nos RG 2005/MR/2 and 2005/MR/5: *Telenet v Ligue Professionnelle de football and BeTV v Ligue Professionnelle de football*—unreported. See Belgian Conseil de la Concurrence, 2006 Annual Report at §4.7.1, 56 and 57; (available at: economie.fgov.be/fr/binaries/report_competition_2006_fr_tcm326-68140.pdf).

In 2011, the Belgian Competition Council cleared the acquisition of the television channels VT4 and VIJFtv of SBS Belgium by De Vijver Media.[11]

On 31 October 2008, the Belgian Competition Council approved the concentration by which TECTEO acquired exclusive control over BeTV.[12]

As regards printed media, the acquisition of both the Flemish and Walloon business newspapers (*De Tijd* and *L'Echo*) by Mediafin (controlled by De Persgroep and Rossell) was cleared conditionally by the Competition Council.[13]

With respect to the *Telenet/Canal+* transaction, in 2003 the Competition Council imposed a number of conditions on Telenet when it approved the merger of Telenet with the pay TV channel Canal+.[14] One of the conditions required that Telenet should offer its premium film and sports channels to subscribers of alternative distribution platforms. In November 2007, Telenet asked the Competition Council to lift this condition for football broadcasting rights. The Council granted the request by a Decision of 2008[15] but its Decision was annulled by a judgment of 22 June 2009 of the Court of Appeal of Brussels[16] which referred the case back to the Competition Council. After investigation, and after hearing Belgacom and the Pro Football League, the Competition Council decided to partly review the condition originally imposed on Telenet in 2003. If Telenet acquired all live broadcasting rights for the Belgian Jupiler Pro League matches the company would have to render its pay TV channel, which will have the broadcasting rights, accessible to other platforms.

The Council found that its investigation had shown that the broadcasting markets were evolving rapidly, not only in respect of technological and competition developments between analogue and digital transmission, cable television and distribution through other platforms (eg digital subscriber line (DSL) and satellite) but also the relationships between content providers, television channels and

[11] Decision No 2011-C/C-24 of 7 September 2011 in Case CONC - C/C-11/0014; *De Vijver Media NV/ Waterman & Waterman Comm. VA, Corelio NV, Sanoma Corporation* (available at: economie.fgov.be/nl/binaries/20110927_de_vijver_beslissing_publieke_versie_tcm325-148422.pdf).

[12] Decision No 2008-C/C-57 of 31 October 2008 in CONC-C/C-08/0023 *Tecteo-BeTV/ACM*, see Belgian Official Journal (Moniteur Belge) of 6 January 2009, 240–61. Belgian Conseil de la Concurrence, 2008 Annual Report at Chapter III §§1.1 and 1.2, 42–49; (available at: economie.fgov.be/fr/binaries/2008_Rapport_annuel_FR_tcm326-219484.pdf).

[13] Decision of 20 December 2005, Belgian Official Journal (Moniteur Belge) of 30 January 2006, 1st edn at 5086. Belgian Conseil de la Concurrence, 2005 Annual Report at §§4.2.6.1–6.13, 27–36. One point that arose was whether the Members of the Competition Council should recuse themselves having regard to a previous decision that was overruled see §4.5.1 of the 2005 report at 48.

[14] Decisions No 2003-C/C-78 of 1 October 2003, Belgian Official Journal (Moniteur Belge) of 6 May 2004, 37035–40; No 2003-C/C-89 of 12 November 2003, Belgian Official Journal (Moniteur Belge) of 6 May 2004, 37071–77); No 2003-C/C-96 of 28 November 2003, Belgian Official Journal (Moniteur Belge) of 6 May 2004 (37094–97) - *NV Telenet Bidco/NV Canal+*.

[15] Decision No 2008-C/C-11 of 25 March 2008, Request by Telenet for a review of the conditions imposed by Decision No 2003-C/C-89 of 12 November 2003 in the matter of Telenet Bidco SA and Canal+ SA, (Belgian Official Gazette (Moniteur Belge) 22 April 2008, 3rd edn, 21843–21852.

[16] Judgment of 22 June 2009 in Case No 008/MR/7 *Belgacom NV v Telenet NV and VZW Liga Beroepsvoetbal, Belgian Professional Football League.*

the distribution platforms. Nevertheless, based on the strong position of the cable operator (Telenet) on the television market in Flanders and also on the substantial value of the football broadcasting rights, the Council did not believe that there were sufficient reasons to abolish the condition in its entirety.

Media Ownership

Apart from the general merger control rules contained in the Federal Act on the Protection of Economic Competition[17] there are virtually no cross-media ownership restrictions. Each legislator's scope for action is limited given the division of competencies between the Federal State and the Communities and thus enacting over-arching rules would be difficult.

A limited number of ownership rules exist for specific categories of radio and television stations, based on the number of licences (in Flanders) or capital or audience shares (in Wallonia).

In the French Community, there is a special rule for local television stations, prohibiting their control, directly or indirectly, by another radio or television broadcaster, a distributor of broadcasting services, an advertising agency or a holding company.

The VRM has responsibility for monitoring concentrations in the Flemish media sector and reporting annually.

Reform Agenda[18]

In December 2010 the four regulators of the CRC (IBPT, CSA, Medienrat and VRM) issued for consultation coordinated draft market analysis decisions on the retail markets for the provision of analogue and digital TV signals for a period of two months ending on 18 February 2011. The draft decisions imposed wholesale obligations on cable TV broadcasters found to have significant market power (SMP).[19]

[17] The Consolidated Law on the protection of economic competition (loi sur la protection de la concurrence économique coordonnée of 15 September 2006 (LPCE) entered into force on 1 October 2006. (Publication in the Belgian Official Journal (Moniteur Belge) of 29 September 2006).

[18] The 2010–2013 reform process is usefully summarised (in French) on the website of the Conseil supérieur de l'audiovisuel (High Council for Broadcasting), for the French Community available at: www.csa.be/pages/207.

[19] The draft decision covered the various business activities making up the so-called 'triple play'. Given that the retail market for the provision of analogue and digital TV signals is not identified in the European Commission recommendation of 17 December 2007 (on relevant product and service markets within the electronic communications sector susceptible to *ex ante* regulation in accordance with Directive 2002/21/EC of the European Parliament and of the Council on a common regulatory framework for electronic communications networks and services, OJ L344) the regulatory authorities devoted attention to demonstrating that the three cumulative criteria for identifying additional markets were satisfied. See, further, chapter 3, section 3.6 for a discussion of market definition under the EU Regulatory Package.

The CRC limited its ruling to cable TV and IPTV over DSL lines. It excluded all other broadcasting technologies from the market definition (terrestrial and satellite digital TV, and Web-TV). The players found to have SMP were Telenet, Brutélé/Tecteo (trading as VOO), Numericable and AIESH, with each being dominant in one of the five geographic areas into which the CRC segmented the market. The obligations imposed on the SMP players include the resale of the analogue TV offerings, access to their digital TV platforms, and broadband internet resales.

A national consultation was held which closed on 18 February 2011. The Competition Council gave its opinion on the draft decision on 21 February 2011.[20] On 20 May 2011, the CRC notified the European Commission, as required by Article 7 of the EU Framework Directive,[21] of the draft decisions. The European Commission expressed a number of concerns about the CRC's proposals. Amongst other things, it criticised the regulators' analysis of the broadcasting markets. It also asked the regulators to justify both the proportionality of the obligation on cable operators to provide an analogue resale offer and the proposed obligation to provide such access to Belgacom. Indeed, Belgacom had been quite successful in developing its IPTV offering.[22] However, the European Commission did not raise any fundamental objections involving a second-phase investigation or a veto. The four CRC members published final decisions on 18 July 2011 adopted on 1 July 2011 and applicable from 1 August 2011.[23]

In September 2011, the four cable operators (Telenet, Tecteo, Numéricâble and Brutélé) brought an action against the decisions and requested a suspension of the decision from the Brussels Court of Appeal. On 4 September 2012, the Court of Appeal dismissed the request made by Telenet.[24] On 6 November 2012, the Brussels Court of Appeal rejected the requests for suspension made on behalf of the other cable operators.[25]

A decision on the merits of the case was expected to be made in late 2013 or in 2014 but is unavailable at the time of writing. In the meantime, after analysing the reference offers from cable operators, public consultations, dialogue between regulators and notification to the European Commission, the adoption

[20] Avis 2011-A/A-02 Avis du Conseil de la concurrence du 21 février 2011 relatif au projet de décision du Conseil de l'IBPT concernant l'analyse du marché radiodiffusion télévisuelle, available at: www.bipt.be.

[21] Framework Directive 2002/21/EC as amended by Directive 2009/140/EC (Framework Directive).

[22] European Commission, 'Digital Agenda: Commission concerns on aspects of Belgian regulators' proposal to regulate broadcasting and (to a lesser extent) broadband markets' (IP/11/761), 21 June 2011.

[23] See the English language press release: 'Television broadcasting and broadband market decisions. New opportunities for consumers, new dynamics for the sector'.

[24] Brussels Court of Appeal, judgment 2011/AR/2289 of 4 September 2012 available in the Juridat database at reference Justel F-20120904-1.

[25] Unreported. See IBPT press release.

of the proposed measure has been following its normal course.[26] The European Commission has, however, expressed its concerns about the appropriateness of the proposed measures.

In the view of the European Commission, a continuation of current trends may render inappropriate at least some of the regulatory constraints imposed on the SMP cable operators, which were justified, predominantly, by the competitive advantage gained through those operators' ability to provide analogue TV. The European Commission, therefore, urged the CRC to carry out a new market analysis as soon as possible and no later than 2014, in line with Article 16 of the Framework Directive.

In a separate decision of 1 July 2011,[27] an obligation was imposed on Belgacom (identified as an operator having SMP) to provide multicast functionality in addition to the unbundling of the local loop and access to a bit rate product, so that alternative operators can offer broadband multimedia applications including digital television and internet access to their customers.

A new Telecommunications Law entered into force on 1 October 1 2012.[28] The new law provides for certain important changes, particularly as regards the consumer's rights to cancel a contract (for internet, television, fixed and mobile telephony).

The legislation of 3 April 2013 amending Belgian Competition law entered into force on 6 September 2013.[29] Although the substantive law on antitrust and merger control principles is unchanged, it contains significant institutional and procedural amendments. In particular, the 2013 measure replaces the former Competition Council and Directorate General for Competition by a single body called the Belgian Competition Authority.

[26] See Commission decision concerning Case BE/2013/1485: Retail markets for the delivery of broadcasting signals and access to broadcast networks in Belgium, Brussels 8 August 2013, C(2013) 5834 final; and Commission decision concerning Case BE/2013/1511: Retail markets for the delivery of broadcasting signals and access to broadcast networks in Belgium—Remedies, Brussels 7 November, 2013, C(2013) 7694 final. Both are comments pursuant to Article 7(3) of the Framework Directive 2002/21/EC (as amended).

[27] Décision de la Conférence des régulateurs du secteur des communications électroniques (CRC) du 1er juillet 2011 concernant l'analyse des marchés large bande. For the decision itself, see 373–74.

[28] Law of 10 July 2012 cited as the 'Telecoms Law' (loi Télécom/wet Telecom) introducing various provisions including amendments to the 2005 Belgian Act on Electronic Communications (BAEC) (loi du 13 juin 2005 relative aux communications électroniques). Amendments included, in line with EU law, a requirement for opt-in consent for cookies and a data breach notification obligation for telecommunications providers.

[29] Loi du 3 avril 2013 portant insertion du livre IV 'Protection de la concurrence' et du livre V 'La concurrence et les évolutions de prix 'dans le Code de droit économique et portant insertion des définitions propres au livre IV et au livre V et des dispositions d'application de la loi propres au livre IV et au livre V, dans le livre Ier du Code de droit économique.

Portugal

Market Structure

The Portuguese telecommunications market has evolved towards a concentrated market structure following several concentrations in recent years. At present, only four different players offer pay TV in Portugal, namely, Portugal Telecom (PT), ZON Optimus, Cabovisão and Vodafone.

To understand the Portuguese telecommunications market, it should be borne in mind that PT was a state-owned company and the incumbent operator controlling the telephone copper wire network, the cable network and the largest mobile network operator (MNO). ZON was created following the PT spin-off in 2007; it inherited PT's cable network and its market position as the largest pay TV supplier, with a market share of 65 to 75 per cent. Over the following years, PT developed the copper wire network and invested in a new optical fibre-to-the-home (FTTH) network.

Pay TV in Portugal has lost relevance as a standalone service. Demand for multiple play offers, particularly triple play, comprising pay TV, broadband internet and fixed telephony, has significantly increased in recent years. The market structure continues to be concentrated, with PT and ZON representing and sharing about 70 to 80 per cent of the triple play market. The market structure indicates that on the demand-side customers do not discriminate between copper, cable and the new FTTH networks, as both PT and ZON have about the same market share and offer triple play over different networks.

Quad play offers (triple play plus mobile services) were introduced in December 2012 and are gradually gaining market share.

Regulation

A specialist media regulator (Entidade Reguladora para a Comunicação Social (ERC)) regulates the pay TV sector. ERC grants licences for pay TV suppliers to be able to operate. ERC also monitors the market in order to defend and promote freedom and pluralism of the media, as well as the right to information and freedom of expression.

Competition Law Enforcement

The Portuguese Competition Authority (PCA) has investigated and fined several telecommunications companies for prohibited practices, but never with reference to the pay TV market. However, it should be noted that in June 2013 the PCA fined the premium sports channel Sport TV for abuse of dominance on the grounds that Sport TV applied discriminatory conditions in its commercial relationship with distributors (pay TV suppliers).[1] The case refers only indirectly to the pay TV distribution market at the downstream level, as the transactions examined by the PCA took place at the upstream (ie rights licensing) level. Sport TV has lodged an appeal with the Competition Court, which is pending.

Merger Control

Under the Portuguese Competition Act every economic activity is subject to merger control (where the thresholds that trigger the procedure are reached). In recent years the Portuguese Competition Authority has made decisions on a large number of concentrations in the pay TV market (or in the triple play market, including pay TV). Some of these cases involved structural and behavioural remedies:

PPTV—Publicidade de Portugal e Televisão, SA/PT CONTEÚDOS, S G P S, SA

The case refers to a change in control over Sport TV, which was until recently the only premium sports channel in Portugal. The PCA cleared the merger with some behavioural conditions attached.[2] The notifying parties undertook to sell the distribution rights to pay TV suppliers on a non-discriminatory basis, by applying similar conditions to equivalent transactions.

Sonaecom/PT

The case refers to a hostile takeover of Sonaecom, a telecommunications operator controlling the third-largest mobile network operator (Optimus), over Portugal Telecom, the former incumbent and the largest player in several markets, which controlled the largest MNO (TMN). The PCA adopted a non-opposition decision with several complex conditions attached, including the horizontal and vertical separation of the telephone copper wire network from the cable network followed by the divestiture of one network; returning certain frequencies to the telecommunications regulator; granting access to mobile virtual networks operators (MVNO); returning radio spectrum licences for some frequencies to the telecommunications regulator; divestiture of several businesses (eg cinema distribution and exhibition, channel production, distribution of premium sport channel, and video distribution at the upstream level).[3]

[1] Portuguese Competition Authority decision of 19 June 2013, Case No PRC 2/2010 *Sport TV Portugal, SA.*

[2] Portuguese Competition Authority decision of 8 April 2004, Case No Ccent 47/2003—*PPTV—Publicidade de Portugal e Televisão, SA/PT CONTEÚDOS, S G P S, SA.*

[3] Portuguese Competition Authority decision of 22 December 2006, Case No Ccent 08/2006—*Sonaecom/PT.*

CATVP/TVTel and CATVP/Bragatel Pluricanal Leiria* Pluricanal Santarém*

The cases relate to the acquisition by ZON (the largest pay TV supplier) of TV TEL, Bragatel and Pluricanal (minor pay TV suppliers).[4] The PCA cleared both cases with the same structural and behavioural conditions attached. ZON undertook to divest a small part of the cable network and customers in areas where an overlap between ZON and the other pay TV supplier existed; to launch a wholesale offer as regards its satellite DTH platform and to free space in the ducts network.

Kento Unitel Sonaecom/Zon Optimus

The case refers to the merger between ZON Multimedia and Optimus. Until recently, ZON was the largest pay TV and triple play provider. Optimus was a full-service telecoms provider and the third MNO in Portugal. The PCA cleared the merger with conditions.[5] The remedies included the extension of a network-sharing agreement between Optimus and Vodafone Portugal, an obligation by Optimus not to charge its FTTH customers a network disconnection charge for a period of six months, and an agreement by Optimus to provide non-discriminatory wholesale access to its FTTH network for a period of five years.

Media Ownership

There are no media ownership rules.

Reform Agenda

It should be noted that the new Competition Act (approved by Law No 19/2012) came into force on 8 May 2012. With respect to merger control it should be emphasised that the new legislation adopts the EU substantive test for merger control (ie significant impediment to effective competition) which replaced the old dominance test. The notification thresholds that trigger the merger control procedure have been adjusted to converge with the EU rules, based on the combined turnover of the undertakings involved in the concentration (although in Portugal a merger control notification can still be triggered by a combined turnover and market share threshold).

Given that the Portuguese pay TV market structure is very concentrated, with two players holding about 80 per cent of the market, it will be important in the long term to monitor different aspects such as the success and penetration of

[4] Portuguese Competition Authority decision of 24 November 2008, cases no Ccent 21/2008—*CATVP/TVTel* and Ccent 56/2007—*CATVP/ Bragatel* Pluricanal Leiria* Pluricanal Santarém.*

[5] Portuguese Competition Authority decision of 26 August 2013, Case No Ccent 5/2013 *Kento*Unitel*Sonaecom/ZON*Optimus.*

multiple play offers, the development of over the top (OTT) content and the importance of premium content to see if suppliers will agree to lower customers' switching costs.

On the other hand, it should be noted that transparency may increase in these markets and that some players are connected through structural links and operate at both upstream and downstream levels. Moreover, as operators try to soften network effects in mobile services (by offering off-net flat rates), multiple play offers tend to be less differentiated, leading customers to be more price-sensitive. These factors may favour coordination between some or all of the players and, therefore, the PCA and the telecommunications and media regulators are expected to monitor these markets closely.

Russian Federation

Market Overview

The Russian TV market is generally divided between free TV channels—mostly on-air terrestrial and, in the overwhelming majority of cases, state-controlled or affiliated—and pay channels that are distributed by cable, satellite and IPTV. Historically, in the times of the Union of Soviet Socialist Republics, TV signals were delivered via the on-air terrestrial method and were free of charge for the population. This fact has largely affected viewers' approach to pay TV services even today.

With the start of the new era after the perestroika,[1] the pay TV sector focused on cable and satellite technologies as the available markets beyond the state interest. Some of the current major players in the market started off as small local businesses exploring technologies; then new and unfamiliar for the majority of population.

According to the review of the Russian pay TV sector for the year 2012 carried out by J'son & Partners Consulting, and analysts' comments, the market is rapidly growing and will continue to grow, but the growth areas are shifting.[2] The current subscriber base of all pay TV is estimated at 31 to 32 million households with the level of penetration of up to 58 per cent, as compared to approximately 26 to 28 million households in 2012 with the penetration level at roughly 50 per cent. At the end of 2012, the largest players on the pay TV market in Russia were Tricolor TV (market share 28 per cent), Rostelecom (21 per cent), MTS (9 per cent), ER-Telecom (7 per cent) and Akado (4 per cent). However, in April 2013, another platform, Orion-Express, had surpassed Akado in its number of subscribers and thus replaced Akado as the fifth-largest player in the pay TV market.[3]

Tricolor TV and Orion Express are satellite operators; the four major cable TV operators are Rostelecom, MTS, ER-Telecom and Akado, of which ER-Telecom and Akado provide TV services exclusively via cable networks. Rostelecom and MTS count their IPTV subscribers together with the cable TV base.

The fastest growing of the technology sectors are satellite and IPTV, while the growth of cable TV has slowed considerably. The reason apparently lies in the comparative cheapness and availability of satellite services in all regions of the country and the interactivity and novelty of IPTV services. The satellite TV market growth in 2012 was mainly driven by the leading operator Tricolor TV adding 1.4 million subscribers to its base. The IPTV market is led by state-owned Rostelecom and major mobile operators MTS and Vimpelcom (operating under the brand name 'Beeline').

[1] Perestroika was a political movement for reform within the Communist Party of the Soviet Union during the 1980s associated with Soviet leader Mikhail Gorbachev and his glasnost (meaning 'openness') policy reform.

[2] J'son & Partners Consulting, '2012–2017 Pay-TV Market Current Status and Forecasts', February 2013.

[3] *Vedomosti*, 17 April 2013.

Simultaneously, the share of cable TV continues to shrink. According to J'son & Partners Consulting, cable TV companies held 57 per cent of the pay TV market at the end of 2012, which is considerably less than the 63 per cent they had occupied in 2011 and the 70 per cent they had occupied in 2010.[4] According to iKS-Consulting, the current subscriber base for cable TV services amounts to 16.8 million subscribers with approximately 13 million subscribed to four major operators and 3.8 million ordering services from small operators.[5] The central regions of Russia have the highest cable TV penetration rate (36 to 40 per cent of the cable market) while in the Far East and the North Caucasus the cable TV audience is the lowest and does not achieve 30 per cent.

The cable sector has fewer opportunities to attract new subscribers with a current growth rate of approximately 5 per cent and instead focuses on improving the quality and diversifying its services. In the last few years, the essential factor for attracting subscribers has been the number and packaging of channels. However, recently analysts have noted that consumers are no longer interested in the number of channels provided, but in the new interactive services, such as on-screen access to social networking sites, internet shops and off-air recording options. It should be noted, however, that the leading platforms for testing new services are only located in large cities, such as Moscow and St Petersburg.

While the Russian pay TV sector is still striving for growth in numbers, including expansion into new territories and provision of a large number of channels and additional services, many operators already agree that the future of the market lies in content quality development. For now, none of the pay TV channels can compete with the state-owned mass media, especially the leading on-air terrestrial Channel One. State financing allows expensive productions, exclusive transmission, and high availability to the majority of the population. In addition, Russian legislation obliges all operators to deliver free of charge to their subscribers the basic tier of all-Russian publicly available channels, consisting of 10 channels, most of which have state, governmental or close to government ownership.

These 10 channels form the so-called first multiplex, the basic tier to be delivered in digital format to 100 per cent of the country's population upon completion of the state digitisation programme aimed at the elimination of informational disparity. The programme is expected to secure the availability of two digital packages of channels (10 channels per multiplex) in DVB-T2 format to 97.6 per cent of the population by 2016. Despite the expectations of the Russian government, pay TV operators do not fear competition from the digital on air terrestrial television hoping that viewers will remain with their current subscriptions and prefer additional services and technical support provided by the pay TV sector.

[4] J'son & Partners Consulting, '2012–2017 Pay-TV Market Current Status and Forecasts', February 2013.

[5] See, further, data reported at: www.iksconsulting.ru/topics/rus_office/library/4672444.html.

Regulation

Russia has no specific regulation for the pay TV or cable sector. The statutory framework is generally formed by federal laws on mass media, telecommunications and information[6] with a number of subordinate regulations on specific requirements and procedures.

The Mass Media Law was adopted more than 20 years ago and despite being regularly amended does not provide for regulation adequate to existing market needs. Interestingly, until 2006 cable TV was not explicitly mentioned in the regulation at the federal level (although there had been some regional or municipal laws, eg the Law No 2 of the city of Moscow 'On Cable Television in the city of Moscow', dated 28 January 1998, as amended).

The Mass Media Law and the Law on Telecommunications set forth the registration and licensing requirements that are required for the distribution of information via telecommunications networks. The requirements for television include registration of a mass media (in the form of a TV channel), obtaining a broadcasting licence to release the channel and a telecommunications services licence to provide signal delivery services. In practical terms, the mass media registration and a broadcast licence are traditionally viewed as the channel's regulatory obligations, while the telecommunications services licences are held by operators providing technical services on the channel distribution to the broadcasters. Some larger media groups may have their own networks in addition to channel production, in which case they would combine all the three permits and licences required for the operation of the channel. The absolute majority of telecommunications operators tend to hold a number of licences with respect to provision of various telecommunications services, including TV signal transmission, broadband internet, data transfer and so on.

In all cases, it is the holder of the mass media registration that is viewed as the producer of the channel and that bears full responsibility for the channel's compliance with applicable regulatory requirements.

Importantly, Russian law limits foreign participation in companies holding mass media registrations for TV channels and broadcast licences. Only Russian companies in which the foreign shareholding is less than 50 per cent are eligible to hold the mass media registration in respect of a TV channel.[7] Similarly, a foreign shareholding (whether acquired at formation or subsequently) is restricted in companies carrying out broadcasting, and there the restriction is even tighter: a Russian entity with more than 50 per cent of foreign contribution to its charter capital cannot act as a founder of a Russian entity carrying out broadcasting with

[6] The Law of the Russian Federation No 2124-1 'On Mass Media', dated 27 December 1991, as amended (Mass Media Law); Federal Law No 126-FZ 'On Telecommunications', dated 7 July 2003, as amended (Law on Telecommunications); Federal Law No 149-FZ 'On Information, Informational Technologies and Protection of Information', dated 27 July 2006, as amended.

[7] The restriction was introduced in 2001 by Federal Law No 107-FZ.

consistent coverage equaling or exceeding 50 per cent of the constituent subjects of the Russian Federation or the territory in which 50 per cent or more of the population of the Russian Federation reside.[8] It is significant that there have never been any official comments or guidelines on the application of the 'consistent coverage' criteria which leaves it in the discretion of the regulator and thus may result in the restriction becoming a mere instrument of pressure.

Another substantial restriction concerns foreign investment in the business qualifying as having strategic importance for state security. The Federal Law adopted in 2008 (Law on Investing in Strategic Companies[9]) provides specific state approval procedures for any transactions resulting in direct or indirect foreign control (in the broadest sense, including in the form of negative control) over Russian companies engaged in activities of strategic importance for the Russian state. Approvals have to be obtained from a governmental commission before the transaction can be closed, and the lack of governmental approval renders the transaction void.

The list of strategic activities in the Law on Investing in Strategic Companies includes television broadcasting in the territory of residence of more than 50 per cent of the population of any constituent territory of the Russian Federation. Similar to the consistent coverage test in the Mass Media Law, the provision of the Law on Investing in Strategic Companies is ambiguous but has never been officially interpreted or clarified. Therefore, it remains unclear whether the broadcasting territory should be understood as the actual coverage (based on the network capacity) or the mere, albeit hypothetical, ability to carry out the broadcasting (a 'universal' broadcast licence, following the Mass Media Law, permits broadcasting in all territories of Russia and by all means and in all media).

Unlike in other jurisdictions, including certain CIS countries, Russian laws do not provide any exemptions for foreign channels. As a result, international channels have to set up a local presence and establish structures for their operations in Russia, involving in some cases joint ventures or agency arrangements with Russian parties holding the broadcast licences.

Although the regulatory framework still remains rather fragmentary and often lacks consistency, the substantial amendments that the regulation has undergone over the last two to three years have improved the statutory landscape by filling in certain gaps and eliminating some notorious rules. For example, until the very end of 2011 a governmental regulation restricted one entity from holding broadcasting licences for more than two channels, which resulted in major media companies establishing numerous technical subsidiaries only to hold the necessary permissions. This limitation has now been abolished.

[8] Article 19.1 of the Mass Media Law.

[9] Federal Law No 57-FZ 'On Foreign Investment in Entities Having Strategic Importance for National Defense and National Security', dated 29 April 2008 (as amended).

The regulator in the field of mass media supervising compliance with all of the above requirements, including licensing, registrations and content supervision, is the Federal Service for Supervision in the Sphere of Connection, Informational Technologies and Mass Communications (also referred to as 'Roskomnadzor'). The authority is well known for its arbitrary decisions when issuing permissions or carrying our inspections. The scope of its duties has recently been extended to include monitoring of content for illegal information which is often viewed as alarmingly close to censorship.

Competition

No specific requirements or restrictions are provided in Russian law in respect of the pay TV market. Thus only the general rules apply where the need for prior clearance or a subsequent notification to the antitrust authorities in the case of a mergers and acquisitions (M&A) transaction is determined based on the general turnover or assets value criteria which apply regardless of the sector concerned by the merger.

While discussing the state of competition in the telecommunications market in general, late in 2012, Federal Antimonopoly Service (FAS) representatives noted that some of the sectors of the telecommunications services market were dominated by a small number of companies and required further stimulation of competition. However, the authority's concerns apparently do not extend to the cable TV market, as the approval rate for acquisitions is quite high, and there are no reported cases of important approvals granted by the FAS with conditions. By way of an example, as recently as July 2013, the FAS granted unconditional approval to the acquisition of 100 per cent of one of the leading cable TV operators, Akado, by another market leader, ER-Telecom,[10] where the estimated value of the transaction was US$1 billion. In the event of successful closure of the transaction, ER-Telecom will have the second-largest market share in the Moscow pay TV market after Rostelecom. The transaction is still at the negotiation phase, and its prospects remain unclear.

Similarly, in September 2012, the FAS approved the acquisition by Rostelecom (the leading player in the communications and pay TV market) of 100 per cent of Norilsk-Telecom, an operator providing internet access, telephony and other communications services (including for cable TV) in the Norilsk region, where Norilsk-Telecom has a natural monopoly.[11]

There have been a few cases where the FAS has found what it considered to be anti-competitive agreements between cable operators in local markets in the form of price fixing for access to cable TV networks or signal delivery.[12] Fines have been

[10] Decision No АГ/28449/13 of the Federal Antimonopoly Service of 23 July 2013.

[11] See, further, fas.gov.ru/solutions/solutions_35713.html.

[12] FAS report of 19 July 2013, available at: magadan.fas.gov.ru/news/7417.

imposed on the companies infringing the competition laws in the reported cases, but the amounts have not been disclosed.

Another contentious position the FAS has addressed on numerous occasions is the intention of certain city authorities to prohibit the construction of 'air' cable networks in preference to underground cabling and impose an obligation on cable operators to move all their networks to underground trunks. The FAS has expressed a view that such restrictions are inconsistent with competition laws.

Trends in Competition Regulation

On 28 December 2012 the Government of the Russian Federation approved the Action Plan (Road Map) for the Development of Competition and Improvement of the Antimonopoly Policy (Road Map). In furtherance of the Road Map on 3 July 2013 the FAS approved the Strategy for Development of Competition and Antimonopoly Regulation in the Russian Federation for the 2013 to 2024 period (Strategy Plan). The Road Map and the Strategy Plan suggest that over the next decade Russian anti-monopoly law will become more investor-oriented and efforts will be made to enhance and protect the competitive environment in Russia. Importantly, Russia expects to join the OECD shortly, and to that end efforts will be made to bring Russian anti-monopoly law into compliance with OECD requirements and recommendations. The FAS expects to implement best practices and standards in EU competition law in order to procure an optimum business environment in Russia. The expected changes will include the following of particular relevance to the cable sector and of more general application (the list is not exhaustive):

— preparation of rules on non-discriminatory access of third parties to subsoil, broadcasting and telecommunications frequencies and other limited resources in Russia;
— extension of Russian anti-monopoly law with respect to agreements relating to the use of internet protocol rights if such agreements result in a limitation of competition;
— abolition of the FAS notification requirement applicable to certain acquisitions of minor equity interests in Russian companies;
— limitation of the period during which a company may remain listed in the register of persons owning more than 35 per cent in the relevant market to three years;
— imposition of a requirement pursuant to which fines for abuse of monopolistic powers will be calculated on the basis of the violator's turnover;
— with respect to 'vertical' arrangements, a list of per se violations based on the EU practice;
— abolition of the Law on Natural Monopolies and inclusion of new provisions in the antimonopoly law regulating natural monopolies; and
— entry into bi-lateral mutual assistance agreements with competition authorities of other countries.

As of November 2013, on the basis of the Road Map and the Strategy Plan the FAS has prepared a new set of amendments to be the Russian antimonopoly law. If adopted, such amendments will give effect to some of the changes described above and some others.[13]

[13] For example, the amendments provide that: (i) persons having less than 35% in the relevant market cannot be declared as having monopolistic power; and (ii) prohibition of abuse of monopolistic powers shall apply only if a person having monopolistic powers generally restricts competition in the relevant market (actions adversely affecting individual market players will not trigger the prohibition).

United Kingdom

Overview

Ofcom is the independent national regulator for the UK communications industries. Ofcom has regulatory powers in relation to telecommunications and broadcasting services.

An overhaul of the UK framework for competition law and regulation is underway with the merger of the UK's first and second-stage competition authorities (the OFT and the Competition Commission respectively) to form the Competition and Markets Authority (CMA) with effect from April 2014. While references to the application of competition law in the sector relate to the historic experience of Ofcom, the OFT and the Competition Commission, they are informative when considering the roles of Ofcom and the CMA in the reformed UK competition law regime.

Ofcom has concurrent powers with the CMA to apply UK and EU competition law in the communications sector. UK merger control is the responsibility of the CMA (historically the OFT (at the first stage) and the Competition Commission (at the second stage)). The CMA (and previously the Competition Commission) also has the responsibility of undertaking market investigations which enable to it to examine whether markets, including communications markets, are functioning effectively.

Market Structure

All television broadcasts in the UK are in a digital format. Digital content is delivered via terrestrial, satellite and cable as well as over closed IP networks (IPTV) and 'over the top' (OTT).

There are currently three providers of cable television, targeting different UK geographic areas. Cable TV is a subscription service, typically bundled with a phone line and broadband. Smallworld Cable is available in south-west Scotland and north-west England. WightFibre is available in the Isle of Wight. Virgin Media is available to around 55 per cent of UK households.

The UK broadcasting market is undergoing rapid change. Convergence is affecting the way in which content is delivered and consumed. An example of a hypothetical UK household will serve to illustrate the variety of ways in which consumers may access TV content. A household may have pay TV satellite services on their main television.[1] A household may have a second TV set, receiving digital TV via a Freeview box.[2] The household may also access OTT content services via a

[1] 9.6 million homes in the UK take satellite pay TV on their primary TV set. Screen Digest TV Annual Market Summary, May 2012, available at: www.screendigest.com/intelligence/tv/uk/tv_intel_uk_1/view.html?start_ser=ti.

[2] 61% of second TV sets in UK households take digital terrestrial television (DTT) services. A third of homes with at least one TV set take both DTT services, and either cable or satellite services. BARB Establishment Survey of TV Homes, annual, to March 2012. BARB is the official source of television viewing figures in the UK. See, further: www.barb.co.uk.

broadband connection. This in turn will give them access to films or TV content on demand. They may also stream audiovisual content from sites such as YouTube.

Figure 25 illustrates the extent of multi-channel take-up in UK households. While the number of digital-only terrestrial households has been relatively constant since 2008, the take-up of digital cable, free-to-view satellite and pay digital satellite has increased.[3]

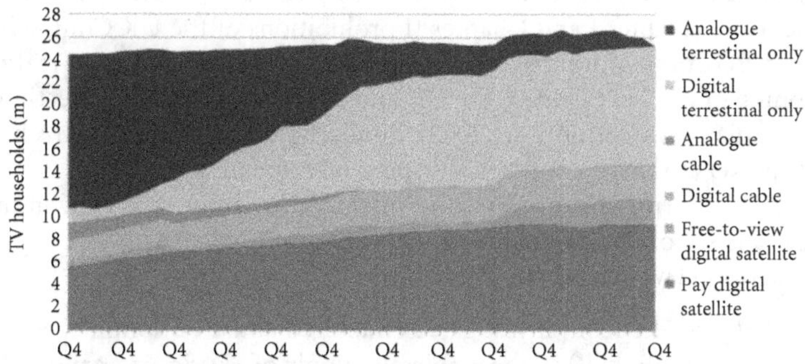

	2001	2002	2003	2004	2005	2006	2007	2008	2009	2010	2011	2012
Multichannel take-up (% all households)	44.3%	46.0%	54.2%	62.6%	71.8%	78.6%	86.5%	88.9%	91.4%	92.5%	93.4%	98.0%

Figure 25: Multichannel take-up in UK households

Source: Ofcom Communications Market Report 2013, page 180

Regulation

In addition to mainstream competition law, a specific regulatory framework applies to the communications sector.

In particular, and of most relevance to broadcasting, sections 316 to 318 of the Communications Act 2003 (Communications Act) provide for sector-specific regulation. Section 316 allows for Ofcom to include conditions for operators licensed under the Broadcasting Acts. Ofcom must include in new licences such conditions as it considers appropriate for ensuring that a provider does not engage in practices that would be prejudicial to fair and effective competition. This includes services broadcast over cable, satellite and DTT. Before proceeding under section 316, however, Ofcom must consider whether it would be more appropriate to use its competition law powers under the Competition Act 1998.

A further layer of sector-specific regulation applies at European level under the EU Regulatory Framework for the regulation of electronic communications networks and electronic communications services in the various Member States and discussed above in chapter 2 and chapter 3, section 6. This covers all forms of transmission networks, services and associated facilities including fixed and

[3] Ofcom, 'Communications Market Review 2012', 18 July 2012, figure 2.4

wireless telecommunications, broadcasting, and data transmission. It does not, however, extend to the regulation of content carried over such services.

Competition Law Enforcement

Under UK general competition law, in respect of matters in the communications sector, Ofcom and the CMA have concurrent powers to enforce UK competition law under the Chapter I and Chapter II prohibitions of the UK Competition Act 1998 and EU competition law under Articles 101 and 102 of the Treaty on the functioning of the EU (TFEU) (the UK and EU law equivalents of sections 3 and 4 of the Indian Competition Act 2002). Similarly, Ofcom and the CMA have concurrent powers to make a market investigation reference.

The UK authorities have been active in enforcing competition law in the communications sector and in the broadcasting sector in particular.

Competition law investigations include:

Sky Sports 1 and 2: Ofcom investigated an alleged abuse of dominance by British Sky Broadcasting (BSkyB) in the wholesale supply of Sky Sports 1 and 2. This followed a complaint from BT alleging that BSkyB has offered wholesale supply of the channels to BT's YouView platform conditional on BT wholesaling BT Sport channels to Sky for retail on BSkyB's satellite platform. Ofcom expected to reach a decision on whether and how to proceed in Autumn 2013 but at the time of writing the case has not been resolved.[4]

Project Canvas: Project Canvas (also called YouView) is a cooperation arrangement between the BBC, ITV, Channel 4, Channel 5, British Telecommunications (BT), Talk Talk and Arqiva offering digital terrestrial channels and internet TV via a set-top box. Following complaints by Virgin Media and IPVision, Ofcom decided not to open an investigation under the Competition Act on the basis that such an investigation would be premature in view of the stage of market development.[5] It did, however, commit to monitor YouView, particularly with regard to standards and content syndication.

IMS Media/BBC Broadcast: Following a complaint that BBC Broadcast (renamed as Red Bee Media) had engaged in predatory pricing and an abusive long-term exclusive contract with Channel 4, Ofcom decided that BBC Broadcast did not occupy a dominant position in the supply of access services to UK broadcasters.[6] It therefore concluded that there was no ground for action under the Chapter II

[4] Ofcom, British Sky Broadcasting Group plc alleging abuse of a dominant position regarding the wholesale supply of Sky Sports 1 and 2, 1 August 2013, available at: stakeholders.ofcom.org.uk/enforcement/competition-bulletins/open-cases/all-open-cases/cw_01106/?utm_source=updates&utm_medium=email&utm_campaign=cw_01106.

[5] Ofcom, *No investigation into Project Canvas*, 19 October 2010.

[6] Upheld on appeal to the Competition Appeal Tribunal in *Independent Media Support Limited v Ofcom* [2008] CAT 13, judgment of 20 May 2008.

prohibition/Article 102 TFEU. Ofcom was of the view that the contract did not appreciably restrict competition so that there was no basis to act under the Chapter I prohibition or Article 101 TFEU.

Merger Control

The UK competition authorities have considered a wide range of mergers in the TV and broadcasting sector.

Table 6 provides a summary of some recent merger control reviews.

Table 6: UK mergers in the broadcasting sector

Parties	Sector	Date (final decision/ abandonment)	Outcome
News Corporation/BSkyB[7]	Audio-visual, newspapers, advertising	25 July 2011	Referred to Competition Commission (media plurality). Reference withdrawn.
Northern & Shell/ CLT Holdings[8]	Television broadcasting, advertising and news provision	12 November 2010	Cleared unconditionally by the OFT.
BSkyB/Virgin Media Television[9]	Television channels	14 December 2010	Cleared unconditionally by the OFT.
Project Canvas: BBC/BT/Channel 4/Channel 5/ITV/ Talk Talk/Arqiva[10]	Broadcasting	14 May 2010	Found by the OFT not to qualify as a merger. Reviewed under competition law.[11]
Project Kangaroo: BBC Worldwide/ Channel 4/ITV[12]	Video-on-demand	4 February 2009	Prohibited by Competition Commission.

(*Continued*)

[7] Competition Commission, 'CC formally cancels NewsCorp/BSkyB inquiry', 25 July 2011, available at: webarchive.nationalarchives.gov.uk/+/http://www.competition-commission.org.uk/press_rel/2011/july/pdf/41_11_news_corp_bskyb_cancel.pdf.

[8] Office of Fair Trading, *Completed acquisition by Northern & Shell Network Limited of CLTUFA Holdings*, 12 November 2010.

[9] Office of Fair Trading, *Completed acquisition by British Sky Broadcasting Group plc of TV channel business of Virgin Media Television*, 14 December 2010.

[10] Office of Fair Trading, *Anticipated joint venture between The British Broadcasting Corporation, ITV Broadcasting Limited, Channel Four Television Corporation, Channel 5 Broadcasting Limited, British Telecommunications plc, Talk Talk Telecom Limited and Arqiva Limited—Project Canvas*, 14 May 2010.

[11] Ofcom, *No investigation into Project Canvas*, 19 October 2010.

[12] Competition Commission, *BBC Worldwide Limited, Channel Four Television Corporation and ITV plc, A report on the anticipated joint venture between BBC Worldwide Limited, Channel Four Television Corporation and ITV plc relating to the video on demand sector—Project Kangaroo*, 4 February 2009.

Table 6: (*Continued*)

Parties	Sector	Date (final decision/ abandonment)	Outcome
Macquarie UK Broadcast/National Grid Wireless[13]	Terrestrial broadcast transmission	11 March 2008	Cleared by the Competition Commission subject to commitments.
Arqiva/BT[14]	Satellite broadcasting services	22 February 2007	Cleared unconditionally by the OFT.
BSkyB/ITV[15]	Broadcasting	14 December 2007 (Competition Commission) 29 January 2008 (Secretary of State)	Adverse public interest finding by Competition Commission. BSkyB required to divest shareholding in ITV down to below 7.5 per cent.
NTL/Telewest[16]	Pay TV, tele-communica-tions services	30 December 2005	Cleared unconditionally by the OFT.
BSkyB Broadband Services/Easynet[17]	Telecommuni-cations, inter-net, Pay TV	30 December 2005	Cleared unconditionally by the OFT.
ITV/SDN[18]	Digital TV multiplex	15 August 2005	Cleared unconditionally by the OFT.
Carlton Communications/ Granada[19]	Television broadcasting	28 August 2003	Cleared by the Secretary of State[20] subject to commitments. This includ-ed a contract rights renewal (CRR) which provided advertisers with an option to renew the terms of their 2003 contracts.

[13] Competition Commission, *Macquarie UK Broadcast Ventures Limited/National Grid Wireless Group, Completed acquisition, Final report*, 11 March 2008.

[14] Office of Fair Trading, *Anticipated acquisition by Arqiva Limited of certain parts of the satellite broadcast services business of British Telecommunications plc*, 22 February 2007.

[15] Competition Commission, *Acquisition by British Sky Broadcasting Group Plc of 17.9 per cent of the shares in ITV Plc, Report sent to Secretary of State (BERR) 14 December 2007*. BERR, *Final decisions by the Secretary of State for Business, Enterprise & Regulatory Reform on British Sky Broadcasting Group's acquisition of a 17.9 per cent shareholding in ITV plc*, 29 January 2008.

[16] Office of Fair Trading, *Anticipated merger of NTL Incorporated and Telewest Global Inc*, 30 December 2005.

[17] Office of Fair Trading, *Anticipated acquisition by BSkyB Broadband Services Limited of Easynet group plc*, 30 December 2005.

[18] Office of Fair Trading, *Anticipated acquisition by ITV plc of SDN Limited*, 15 August 2005.

[19] Competition Commission, *Carlton Communications Plc/Granada Plc: A report on the proposed merger*, 28 August 2003.

[20] This case was a reference under a previous statutory regime where the judgment of the Secretary of State was determinative even where only competition issues arose.

Media Ownership

Restrictions on media ownership have been progressively rolled back, most notably through the Communications Act.

The current rules relate to the following areas:

- Broadcast licences: There are restrictions which prevent certain categories of persons from holding a broadcasting licence. These relate mainly to political bodies and advertising agencies.
- National cross-media ownership: A newspaper group with more than 20 per cent of national newspaper market share is prohibited from owning a Channel 3 licence or an interest in a Channel 3 licensee exceeding 20 per cent. Conversely, a Channel 3 company is prevented from owning more than a 20 per cent interest in a national newspaper.
- Previous restrictions relating to local authorities and religious bodies have been modified. Local authorities may hold broadcasting licences provided that the licensed services are used to carry out their legal functions.

There is no restriction on telecommunications providers owning cable networks. Traditionally, BT and the other public electronic communications operators were prohibited from providing broadcast entertainment services over their networks. This restriction was fully removed in January 2001. BT launched its own IPTV service (BT Vision) in December 2006. This now provides packages which include channels such as Sky Sports and ESPN which were historically provided only over satellite and cable.

Ofcom has a statutory duty to review the UK media ownership rules and make recommendations for change.

Reform Agenda

Substantial changes are likely in telecommunications and media regulation in the UK which will affect the broadcasting sector.

Proposed reforms include a new Communications Act to replace the current statute which will apply to communications media and technology. This reform package will also bring about changes in the relationship between the competition authority and sector regulators including Ofcom. In particular, there is a trend towards a preference for application of competition law by the competition authority.

The role of the media, and particularly the press, has come under scrutiny with the phone hacking scandal and which led to a judicial inquiry led by Lord Justice Leveson, with a final report in November 2012.[21] The proposals were wide ranging and included a recommendation for a new framework for measuring

[21] Lord Justice Leveson, 'An inquiry into the culture, practices and ethics of the press' Report No 0780 2012–13, 29 November 2012.

plurality. Such recommendations are likely to affect the future direction and shape of reform of the communications and media sector as a whole. The aim is to ensure high standards of professional integrity in the gathering of news across the media and to promote transparency of decision-making in respect of decisions on the public interest. A further outcome of the Leveson report was a proposed Royal Charter to underpin a new system of press reform, although the final form of regulation is unclear at the time of writing.[22]

Looking further ahead, the Department for Culture, Media & Sport has indicated it would like examine whether convergence may suggest that there is a need to overhaul the current balance of regulation between *ex ante* and *ex post* intervention in the broadcasting and telecommunications sector.[23]

[22] See, further, chapter 9, section 9.4 and Appendix 6.

[23] See, further, Department for Culture, Media & Sport, 'Making it easier for the communications and telecoms industries to grow, while protecting the interests of citizens', 30 July 2013 and available at: www.gov.uk/government/policies/making-it-easier-for-the-communications-and-telecoms-industries-to-grow-while-protecting-the-interests-of-citizens.

B. AMERICAS

Brazil

Market Structure

The Brazilian pay TV sector offers its services potentially through four different kinds of technologies: cable, satellite, microwave and ultra-high frequency (UHF) signals. However, in terms of the national market, currently only cable and satellite technologies are significant, accounting for approximately 62 per cent (10.3 million subscribers) and approximately 38 per cent (6.3 million subscribers) of the market, respectively.[1]

There are reported to be 153 firms delivering pay TV services: cable, 86 (57.3 per cent of the total of firms); microwave, 25 (16.7 per cent); UHF signal, 22 (14.7 per cent); satellite, 13 (8.7 per cent); microwave and cable, three (2 per cent); and cable and satellite, one (0.7 per cent).[2]

In 2012, the Brazilian pay TV market grew by 27 per cent[3] and currently there are nearly 17 million subscribers. Since on average there are 3.3 people per household in Brazil, pay TV is available to approximately 56 million people. Only 7 per cent of the Brazilian population has access to pay TV, so there is significant potential for growth.[4]

NET/Embratel, part of Telmex, leads the pay TV market with 53.8 per cent of subscribers (7.824 million followed by Sky/DirecTV with 30.8 per cent (4.475 million), Telefonica with 4.5 per cent (0.659 million), Oi with 3.4 per cent (0.486 million), GVT with 1.5 per cent (0.219 million), Algar with 0.7 per cent (0.104 million), ViaCabo with 0.7 per cent (0.101 million) and other groups account for 4.6 per cent (0.663 million).[5]

Regulation

The cable sector is regulated by the independent agency ANATEL (Agência Nacional de Telecomunicações), the telecommunications regulator and which is also the cable regulator.

[1] Brazilian Association of Pay TV (ABTA) at: www.abta.org.br/dados_do_setor.asp, 8 September 2013. Growth in the preceding years: 2011, 30%; 2010, 31%; 2009, 20%; 2006, 15%; 2004, 9%.

[2] ANATEL at: www.anatel.gov.br/Portal/verificaDocumentos/documento.asp?numeroPublicacao=284925&assuntoPublicacao=Dados per cent20Estat per centEDsticos per cent20dos per cent20Servi per centE7os per cent20de per cent20TV per cent20por per cent20Assinatura per cent20- per cent20-Cap. per cent2001 per cent20- per cent2049. per centAA per cent20Edi per centE7 per centE3o&caminhoRel=null&filtro=1&documentoPath=284925.pdf, 8 September 2013. Totals do not necessarily add up to 100 due to rounding.

[3] See n 1.

[4] Ministry of Communications at: www.conexaominicom.mc.gov.br/materias-especiais/1422-mais-tv-por-assinatura-no-brasil, on 8 September 2013.

[5] See n 2.

The Ministry of Communications expects that the new Law 12,485/2011,[6] which entered into force in September 2012, will lead to growth in the sector, since it opened the pay TV market to telecommunications operators and removed the obstacles to foreign investment. Based on the new law, ANATEL has enacted a new regulation, and firms interested in offering pay TV services do not have to compete for the market in public bids. ANATEL states that since the enactment of the new law, 80 new firms have been authorised to provide services in the pay TV market. Before the new rules, authorisations had been frozen since 2003. This should result in a reduction in bureaucracy, an increase in competition and enhancements in consumer welfare.[7]

Competition Law Enforcement

General competition law is applicable to cable companies and is enforced by the independent antitrust regulator CADE (Conselho Administrativo de Defesa Econômica).

With respect to abuse of dominance, there have been numerous cases bringing about a significant impact on business practices. The market growth has been opening up to new entrants which is a factor claimed in the defence of leading players.

With respect to anticompetitive agreements, the Brazilian Association of Pay TV (ABTA) has accused the Central Office of Collection and Distribution (ECAD) and six associations for jointly fixing the amounts to be paid for the public performance of musical works, literary musical works and phonograms. The complaint was made in 2010 and CADE issued an infringement decision in March 2013.[8] ECAD was also condemned for creating barriers to new entry to the market by hindering the formation and operation of new associations.[9]

Merger Control

Merger control is applied in the cable sector by CADE. Recent significant decisions have defined the product market as the offer of pay TV services, comprising cable, satellite and microwave technologies. The geographic market, in turn, has been defined as local (municipalities).[10]

[6] Available at: www.cade.gov.br/upload/LAW%20N%C2%BA%2012529%202011%20%28English%20version%20from%2018%2005%202012%29.pdf.

[7] See n 4.

[8] *Brazilian Association of Pay TV (ABTA)/Central Office of Collection and Distribution* (CADE Administrative Proceeding 08012.003745/2010-83).

[9] CADE at: www.cade.gov.br/Default.aspx?4de031f8081df33fcb79cb67fc46, on 8 September 2013.

[10] *Sky Brasil Serviços Ltda and ITSA—Intercontinental Telecomunicações Ltda* (CADE Merger Review 53500.008391/2008, vote of the Reporting Commissioner Fernando de Magalhães Furlan, 2–10, 18 August 2010); see, further, Merger Reviews 53500.002423/2003 and 53500.029160/2004, vote of the Reporting Commissioner Luiz Carlos Delorme Prado, 29, 67, paragraphs 105 and 255, 24 May 2006.

Even though it does not directly concern the cable TV sector, the merger between Sky and DirecTV in 2006 was cleared with commitments, including: a five-year prohibition on discrimination against competitors to the benefit of own group companies when acquiring audiovisual content; a five-year prohibition on the offer of exclusive audiovisual content to any pay TV company; a five-year prohibition on the exercise of exclusive broadcasting rights in respect of the five major professional soccer championships in the Brazilian territory; a five-year obligation to inform the antitrust authority 30 days before broadcasting of contracts concerning any new channel with international content; a five-year obligation to offer the same packages of channels throughout the whole Brazilian territory at the same price; among others.[11]

An interesting case in 2007 concerns the acquisition of TVA (an independent cable operator owned by a media production group) by Telefonica, the fixed mobile incumbent. Telefonica wanted to block potential competition from another cable company in the most affluent regions supplied by TVA, the cable operator. There was a great outcry, but ultimately the case was cleared. Other minor restrictions have been imposed over the years, such as bans on non-compete clauses which extend beyond the relevant geographic market and longer than five years.

Media Ownership

Foreign ownership of interests in the cable sector was restricted until 2011 but this was relaxed by the new law 12,485/2011 as noted above. Article 222 of the Brazilian Constitution rules that the ownership and management of broadcasting and news companies is exclusive to Brazilian citizens. Foreign parties may own up to 30 per cent in those companies following an amendment to the Constitution passed in 2002. Most other regulatory restrictions imposed on cross-ownership in the telecommunications sector are slowly being removed, though some still remain in force.

Reform Agenda

The Ministry of Communications, the body responsible for formulating the policies for the sector, expects the new law 12,485/2011 to enhance competition in the pay TV market.

The new competition law 2,529/2011 has set a new institutional framework in which CADE is the main (independent) antitrust regulator responsible for investigating mergers and anticompetitive practices (through an independent internal body, the General Superintendence) and also through issuing decisions on the cases challenged by the General Superintendence (through the CADE Tribunal).

[11] CADE Merger Reviews 53500.002423/2003 and 53500.029160/2004, vote of the Reporting Commissioner Luiz Carlos Delorme Prado, 80–82, issued on 24 May 2006.

The Secretariat for Economic Monitoring of the Ministry of Finance—SEAE (a subordinate of the Minister of Finance) is responsible for competition advocacy, that is, it should establish a dialogue with the sector regulatory bodies with the aim of advocating regulation based on competition, whenever possible.

The new competition law has raised a controversy about whether the role of the telecommunications regulator should be revoked. However, ANATEL has been committed to strengthening its capacity to deal with competition concerns, as indicated by the creation of its internal body 'Competition Superintendence' and the efforts to implement the General Plan of Competition Goals.[12]

[12] Resolution 600, 8 November 2012, approved by ANATEL Board of Directors.

Mexico

Market Overview

The pay TV sector in Mexico started with a cable TV service offered by Cablevisión, a division of Televisa. Subsequently, new technologies were included in the pay TV sector: Multichannel Multipoint Distribution System[1] (MMDS) and satellite services. Over recent years this sector has been subject to several procedures and analysis by the competition authority in Mexico,[2] which has identified many problems related to the concentration that characterises this market in Mexico and associated anticompetitive practices.[3] To address such issues, the telecommunications sector regime has recently been subject to regulatory amendment at a constitutional level. The impacts on the telecommunications sector of such amendment remain to be seen.

Market Structure

The pay TV sector encompasses three different technologies: satellite (or direct-to-home (DTH)), microwave and cable. According to the former telecommunications agency (the Federal Telecommunications Commission (FTC)) there were a total of 12,994,996 subscribers to the pay TV sector in Mexico in 2012.[4] As for each technology, the numbers in 2012 are as follows: 6,909,284 DTH subscribers;[5] 158,662 microwave subscribers;[6] and 5,927,020 cable subscribers.[7] Currently, according to the most recent public available information, Televisa holds approximately 56 per cent of the cable segment through Cablevisión, Cablemás, and others; and approximately 38 per cent of the DTH segment through SKY. The specific market shares for the pay TV sector are set out in Table 7.

[1] MMDS frequencies travel through the air by microwave. An MMDS signal can accommodate eight, 10 or even 12 channels of television.

[2] Until 11 September 2013 the competition authority for the telecommunication sector was the Federal Competition Commission (CFC) but as a result of a constitutional reform this power was transferred to the newly created Federal Telecommunications Institute (FTI).

[3] The CFC stated in the Opinion PRES•10•096.2006•169 that in this sector there are vertical restraints that generate significant barriers to entry and which facilitate the commission of monopolistic practices; specifically, the CFC identified the vertical restraints of Televisa and TV Azteca in the following markets: production of audiovisual contents, the sale of advertised on television, and the retransmission of TV signals (only in the case of Televisa).

[4] Preliminary figures from the Dirección de Información Estadística de Mercados, Federal Telecommunications Commission.

[5] Ibid.

[6] Ibid.

[7] Ibid.

Table 7: Mexico: Pay TV market share

Company	Market share
SKY*	39%
Megacable*[8]	17%
Dish*	15%
Cablemás*[9]	8.7%
Cablecom[10]	6.5%
Cablevisión*[11]	6%
Others[12]	7.8%
Total	100%

**Source: Competitive Intelligence Unit*[13]

The DTH segment was launched in 1995 with DirecTV of MVS, and one year later Televisa introduced its offer through SKY. Subsequently, as part of its commercial strategy and asserting its intellectual property rights, Televisa denied the retransmission of its broadcast TV channels to DirecTV, forcing it to abandon the market as Televisa's broadcast TV channels were claimed to be an important input to compete in the market.[14] Consequently, Televisa's SKY dominated the sector until Dish of MVS started offering this service at the end of 2008. Dish changed the market dynamics significantly by expanding the market (as Dish's target subscriber base is in a much lower income range) and by reducing prices by 70 per cent through a reduction in the number of channels in the bundle. As a result, SKY currently offers a cheaper service named Ve TV which includes a satellite signal with fewer channels than other SKY services. The latter service maintains an advantage on Dish since Ve TV offers its service at a low cost. This package includes Televisa's broadcast TV channels which are very popular in Mexico and are not properly received in certain zones of the republic.

[8] Megacable is the largest cable operator in Mexico, offering service in 48 major cities. In 2007, Megacable acquired a 50% stake in rival operator, Multioperadora de Sistemas, and in 2010 it acquired Omnicable. Organisation for Economic Co-operation and Development, 'OECD Review of Telecommunication Policy and Regulation in Mexico', January 2012, 24.

[9] Cablemas is the second-largest cable television operator in Mexico, and has the broadest coverage, operating in 85 cities and providing telecommunication service nationally. It is now fully owned by Televisa. It was the first cable operator in Mexico to offer a triple-play service.

[10] Cablecom offers cable pay TV, digital phone and broadband internet in several states in Mexico.

[11] Cablevision is a cable operator founded in 1966. It provides cable television, fixed telephony and broadband services, as well as leased lines. It is owned by Televisa and covers 2.2 million households in the Mexico City area, where it is the largest cable operator.

[12] Figure estimated by SAI Law & Economics.

[13] Piedras, E, 'TV de paga y servicios convergentes en el 2012' (2013) *El Economista*, 17 April 2013, available at: eleconomista.com.mx/columnas/columna-especial-empresas/2013/04/17/tv-paga-servicios-convergentes-2012. Ernesto Piedras is leader of the Competitive Intelligence Unit.

[14] Indeed, the CFC has recognised that the exit of DirecTV from the market was provoked by Televisa's denial of the right to broadcast TV channels. See Ruling in file number CNT-85-2004.

Figure 26 shows the change in the market as a consequence of the entry of Dish.

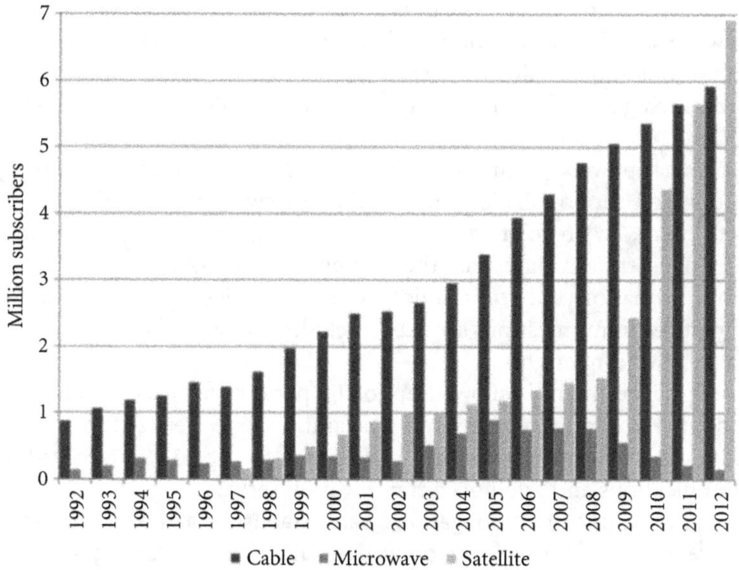

Figure 26: Mexico—Pay TV subscriptions by technology (annual 1992 to 2012)
Source: Federal Communications Commission; courtesy translation by SAI

Regulation

The Mexican Constitution provides in Article 27 that in order to operate a telecommunication network a concession granted by the state is required, since some resources necessary to exploit those services are directly owned by the state. In consequence, those activities are subject to a specific legal framework and the activities are regulated by governmental entities.

In order to address several concerns regarding the telecommunication sector, the Mexican Constitution was amended on 11 June 2013, providing for the creation of two new autonomous entities: the FTI, in charge of reviewing competition matters in the telecommunications and broadcasting sectors and all other regulatory issues in the sector; and the Federal Economic Competition Commission (FECC), the new competition authority for competition and policy for all sectors other than telecommunications.[15]

[15] Before the amendment, the FTC was the entity responsible for the regulatory review of the telecommunications sector. The CFC was the entity responsible for competition issues in the telecommunications sector, where the FTC asked it to intervene. The CFC also had the authority to authorise mergers in respect of telecommunications activities.

As a result of the constitutional amendment, the telecommunications sector was modified as follows:

— The Federal Telecommunications Commission (FTC) was substituted by the FTI, a new constitutional autonomous entity in charge of regulating the telecommunications and broadcasting sectors, even with respect to competition matters, removing such authority from the extinguished CFC, substituted by the FECC.
— The FTI also has powers within the telecommunications sector to: (i) initiate investigations on monopolistic practices; (ii) review mergers; (iii) remove barriers to entry; (iv) regulate access to essential inputs; and (v) order the divestiture of assets; attributes that the former FTC did not have.
— Access to information and communication technologies, as well as broadcasting and telecommunications services (including broadband), were established as constitutional rights.
— Direct foreign investment is allowed up to 100 per cent for telecommunications and satellite communication services, and up to 49 per cent in broadcasting. Previously, foreign investment was permitted up to 49 per cent for telecommunications and satellite communication services.
— 'Must carry' and 'must offer' obligations were established at a constitutional level. Therefore, broadcasters are obliged to allow the retransmission of their channels to all cable and satellite television providers without cost. The only exception is where the provider has been declared dominant in the telecommunications or broadcasting sector. This is one of the most important features of the constitutional amendment, since it reflects the general concerns of the CFC on competition matters regarding the telecoms sector.[16] Moreover, the FTC and several undertakings were concerned that Televisa did not provide open broadcast content to pay TV companies who were not owned by it. It was established that companies with a market share of more than 50 per cent of the national market in the telecommunications or broadcasting sectors will be considered dominant and will be subject to asymmetric regulation.[17]
— The FTI can establish limits on cross-ownership in broadcasting and telecommunications concessions that provide their services in the same market or the same geographical coverage area and hold several telecommunications media. In order to achieve such limits, the FTI can order the divestiture of assets and shares.
— The Mexican Congress may also criminalise certain monopolistic practices and punish unlawful concentrations. As of 2013, only absolute monopolistic practices (ie essentially cartels and other anticompetitive activities between competitors) are criminalised. However, as a consequence of this provision

[16] See rulings in file numbers DE-022-2007, CNT-048-2006 and CNT-018-2007.
[17] See, further, below on competition law for further discussion on this issue.

other practices could be criminalised, for example: the entry into unlawful mergers.

— The FTI may award concession rights for the installation, operation or use of telecommunications public networks, for which the interested parties should submit a request to the FTI.[18] Regarding the pay TV sector, the concessions currently awarded by the Ministry of Communications and Transportation are either regional (cable concessions) or national (DTH concessions).
— The constitutional amendment calls for a public auction for the purpose of granting concessions to establish at least two new nationwide over-the-air TV networks in Mexico.

This new configuration of the telecommunications sector regulator and other trends will shape the telecommunications policy in Mexico. It is intended that the FTI will seek to promote the efficient development of the broadcasting and telecommunications sector.

Under the current Mexican law, cable television operators are classified as public telecommunications networks, and must conduct their business in accordance with Mexican laws and regulations applicable to public telecommunications. It is expected that following the constitutional amendment various secondary laws will be modified accordingly. However, until those amendments are enacted, the existing telecommunications legislation will remain in force in so far as it does not contravene the Constitution itself. Further, any ongoing proceeding with the CFC on telecommunication matters will continue with the FTI and is unaffected by the constitutional amendment.

Competition Law

As mentioned above, a constitutional amendment was recently enacted aimed, among other objectives, to modify the structure and dynamics of telecommunications services in order to promote competition in the sector. It was precisely the problems that the former regulatory authorities identified in the telecommunications sector that spurred the need for the renewal of the legal framework regulating these matters.

The Federal Law on Economic Competition (FLEC) provides the legal framework for competition control in all sectors, including telecommunications. Nevertheless, it is expected that due to the constitutional amendment the FLEC,

[18] As provided in the Federal Telecommunications Law and a resolution issued by the Secretary of Communications and Transport and published in the Federation's Official Gazette on 29 November 2012, such request must contain, among other elements: general information of the applicant (name, address, name of the relevant stockholders for legal persons, main economic activity); description of the services to be granted; technical specifications for the project (network architecture, maps of the network, the technical standards and technologies to be used, among others); coverage, quality services and investment programmes and commitments; business plan; the legal documents to prove the legal, technical, financial and administrative capacity of the applicant; and proof of payment of the rights to apply for the concession.

and the telecommunications secondary laws and regulations, will be amended accordingly. This section discusses the main competition law interventions in the telecommunication sector prior to the constitutional amendment, and which were conducted by the CFC.

Abuse of dominance (relative monopolistic practices)

The CFC dealt with several complaints by economic agents, mostly against Televisa, for alleged relative monopolistic practices in the pay TV sector, such as tying sales of broadcast channels with pay TV channels, and anticompetitive practices related to advertising practices in the broadcast TV and pay TV sector.

In file number DE-22-2007 the CFC fined Grupo Televisa, SAB de CV and Visat SA de CV for the commission of relative monopolistic practices (tie-in sales).[19] The investigation was initiated by a complaint filed by Tele Cable Centro Occidente, SA de CV (TCCO) alleging that the three companies tied sales of their broadcast channels with their pay TV channels and also refused to offer broadcast channels to TCCO. They alleged that such practices prevented TCCO from being able to use, distribute and broadcast television signals for television broadcasting and pay television networks channels, all belonging to Televisa (such as Telehit, Ritmoson Latino, Bandamax, Unicable, De Película, Cinema Golden II, Telenovelas, Clásico, Canal 2 XEW TV, Canal 4 XHTC and others).

In the ongoing investigation in file number DE-019-2011 the CFC initiated an investigation (believed to be against Televisa) for alleged tie-in sales, refusal to supply, discounts and exclusivity agreements, cross-subsidies, and price discrimination regarding the terms of advertising services granted by broadcasters in broadcast and pay TV channels.

The ongoing investigation in file number DE-021-2011 is believed to relate to the Telmex-Dish alliance, which was previously dismissed for lack of merit.[20] In 2008, Dish reached agreement on a strategic partnership with Telmex regarding billing services and space in Telmex's retail stores for Dish to sell pay TV subscriptions. The claimants alleged that through the alliance Telmex had formed a concentration with Dish.[21] It was further alleged that through the alliance Telmex-Dish had committed relative monopolistic practices, such as tie-in sales, discounts subject to not acquiring services from third parties, and cross-subsidies. The alleged effect of these practices was to increase costs, obstruct production or reduce competitors' demand in the markets for pay TV, fixed telephony services, and broadband internet.

[19] The CFC's original ruling was challenged by Televisa through an *amparo* trial and afterwards the CFC imposed only a minimum fine on Televisa.

[20] Organisation for Economic Co-operation and Development, 'OECD Review of Telecommunication Policy and Regulation in Mexico', January 2012, 85.

[21] The claimant alleged that Dish and Televisa had merged as Dish-Echostar reviewed by the CFC in file CNT-116-2008, since Televisa and Dish had a commercial alliance regarding the lease of equipment. However, the CFC found that the Dish and Televisa commercial alliance was not tantamount to a 'concentration'.

Cartels

Collusive practices in the pay TV sector have also been investigated and penalised by the CFC.

In file number DE-001-2006-I, the CFC investigated and fined Productora y Comercializadora de Televisión por Cable SA de CV (PCTV) and its shareholders for the commission of absolute monopolistic practices. The infringing practices were identified by three companies that are cable TV concessionaires in certain cities in Mexico; ie Cable California, Jovita Rubio Martínez y Luis Miguel Oliva Cano. PCTV is an undertaking owned by 175 shareholders that, jointly, own 375 concessions to provide cable TV services. PCTV enters into contracts with programming and TV channels in order to provide them to its shareholders and other cable TV concessionaires. The CFC found that PCTV entered into exclusive agreements with TV channel suppliers regarding the acquisition and supply of TV channels, except for Cablevisión and SKY. Those agreements also allowed PCTV to determine different access conditions for channels for its shareholders and other TV operators. According to the CFC, the different conditions resulted in increases in prices or the refusal to supply channels to the TV operators who were not PCTV shareholders. The CFC fined PCTV and some of its shareholders for agreeing to allocate segments of the current and potential cable market. This activity is considered to be an absolute monopolistic practice and, therefore, it is per se illegal and punishable by the CFC.[22]

The ongoing investigation in file number DE-012-2011 deals with an alleged cartel involving the production, supply and commercialisation of fixed telephone, internet access and pay TV services to final consumers in the national territory. It has been speculated by public opinion that the investigation probably involves Cablevisión, Cablevisión Monterrey, Cablemás and Megacable, all cable companies, because of their alliance to provide double and triple play services through YOO.

Merger Control

The Mexican television market has undergone considerable consolidation in recent years. Most of the transactions required a pre-merger notification with the CFC for exceeding the monetary thresholds established in the FLEC. Indeed, Televisa has acquired within the last 10 years Cablemás and TVI, among others. Additionally, Televisa acquired control of Iusacell.[23] Regarding the cable TV segment, the following are the main mergers notified to the CFC in recent years.[24]

In file number CNT-031-2011 the CFC reviewed the merger between Televisa and Iusacell. Iusacell is a mobile company, in which interests are held by Grupo

[22] Ruling in file number DE-01-2006-I, page 2.

[23] As discussed further below, this concentration focused on other telecommunication markets. The impact in the pay TV market was highly scrutinised by the CFC.

[24] In all of the proceedings referred to here, Televisa has challenged the outcome through *amparo* claims, thus the outcome may ultimately change.

Salinas (the other major broadcast company, owner of TV Azteca and of Total Play, a triple-play services supplier). Initially, the CFC opposed the merger, among other reasons, because it determined that the transaction would give rise to coordinated effects in certain markets, including the cable sector. The merger was ultimately authorised with conditions imposed by the CFC, including must carry and must offer obligations for Televisa.[25] Regarding Total Play, the conditions imposed by the CFC required that Iusacell's shareholders sell their participation in Total Play to its controlling shareholder or to a third subsidiary within a year of the parties' acceptance of the conditions.[26]

In file number CNT-018-2007, the CFC reviewed the merger between Televisa and Cablemás, by which Televisa indirectly acquired the initial 49 per cent of Cablemás' shares (although to date Cablemás is a wholly owned Televisa entity). The CFC blocked the merger, since it would give rise to competition concerns. The CFC considered that the transaction could provide incentives to Televisa to deny access to or impose tie-in sales on its competitors in the pay TV sector regarding its broadcast channels. The CFC ultimately authorised the merger with conditions, including must carry and must offer obligations imposed on Televisa.[27]

In file number CNT-048-2006, the CFC reviewed the merger between TVI (also known as Cablevisión Monterrey) and Televisa, by which Televisa indirectly acquired 50 per cent of TVI's shares. Initially, the CFC blocked the merger because of the risks it believed would be presented to competition, for the same reasons as in the TVI merger described above. Eventually, the merger was also authorised with conditions being imposed on Televisa and TVI, including must carry and must offer obligations.[28]

Finally, on 1 August 2013, Televisa announced its intention to invest public debt in convertible shares, resulting in the acquisition of approximately 50 per cent of Cablecom.[29] With this transaction, Televisa intends to increase its participation in the cable sector. The transaction must be notified and reviewed by the FTI once the debt is converted into shares.

Media Ownership

Cross-ownership between different media companies has attracted the interest of the Mexican competition authority. In fact, cross-ownership between telecommunications undertakings has been usual in Mexico. For example, TVI is owned

[25] The CFC initiated an investigation for a probable unlawful merger. It is likely that this investigation involves Televisa and Iusacell, since evidence shows that part of the merger between Televisa and Iusacell was executed prior to its notification to the CFC since such part did not exceed the thresholds established in the FLEC for a mandatory filing.

[26] Final ruling in file number CNT-031-2011.

[27] Ruling in file number RA-026-2007.

[28] Ruling in file number RA-029-2007.

[29] Piedras, E, 'TV de paga y servicios convergentes en el 2012' (2013) *El Economista*, 17 April 2013, available at: eleconomista.com.mx/columnas/columna-especial-empresas/2013/04/17/tv-paga-servicios-convergentes-2012.

jointly by Televisa and Multimedios[30] and both are pay TV suppliers. The mergers involving Televisa described above are similar manifestations of cross-ownership in the sector. In the cases presented to it, the CFC identified that cross-ownership between pay TV suppliers and other media interests could present incentives for both absolute and relative monopolistic practices; ie cartelisation and abuse of dominance. Those concerns were identified by the CFC in the Televisa mergers and addressed by the conditions imposed.

The most significant case of cross-ownership between cable and other media interests is, perhaps, the Televisa-Iusacell merger. As mentioned, the transaction converged the only two broadcast networks (Televisa and Grupo Salinas), and Iusacell (a mobile company). The CFC noted the risks to competition arising from cross-ownership in companies operating in different telecommunications markets. In order to address its concerns regarding the negative effect on competition in the mobile phone market, the CFC imposed conditions.

In the broadcast TV market, the CFC has ruled that if in 24 months there is no public bid for a third broadcast network, then one party shall buy out the other. Televisa and TV Azteca are obliged to permit other companies in the telecommunications sector to advertise their services in the broadcast channels at an average price. Iusacell's board must not comprise employees from other Televisa or Grupo Salinas subsidiaries operating in the television sector, and likewise, Iusacell's directors shall not be appointed in any other business of those two companies.

Moreover, according to the constitutional amendment, the FTI has the power and the mandate to impose limitations on cross-ownership between telecommunications operators.

Reform Agenda

As mentioned above, the recent constitutional amendment redesigned the telecommunications sectorial regulator. The new powers of the FTI, as described above, are expected to strengthen the mechanisms to promote competition in the sector.

It is particularly interesting that the amendment granted the FTI a new power: to determine dominant/preponderant companies.[31] As for the impact it can have in the pay TV sector, the determination of dominance depends on the interpretation given to the constitutional provision. Indeed, transitory Article 8 of the constitutional amendment states that economic agents with more than 50 per cent of the national market share in telecommunications or broadcasting services will be considered as a dominant/preponderant agent and, as such, the FTI shall enact asymmetrical regulation. In this respect, it is not clear if the prescribed market share refers to any market in such sectors (telecommunications or broadcasting)

[30] Multimedios is a regional cable, DHT and broadcast supplier in Monterrey, Nuevo León.

[31] The term in Spanish is 'preponderante' rather than 'dominante'.

or the whole of such sectors. This is important since under the first interpretation companies like Televisa and Telmex could be considered as preponderant; however, under the second interpretation it would be very difficult to establish that an undertaking can be considered as preponderant in the pay TV market.

Additionally, the FTI will face an interesting challenge assuring that they must offer and must carry constitutional obligations are complied with by the main players in the pay and broadcast TV markets.[32] Further, it appears that Dish has been denied on several occasions the right to transmit Televisa's broadcast channels, a situation that will be evaluated and settled by the FTI.

The recent constitutional amendment aimed to modify at its core the structure and dynamics of telecommunications services in Mexico, granting the new regulatory agency the powers to restore, promote and strengthen competition in the telecommunications sector. It was precisely the problems that the former authorities identified in the telecommunications sector, and that are described here, that led to the need for the reform of the legal framework regulating these matters. The efficacy of this regime is still to be determined as the new structure and agency face new cases.

[32] Recently Dish began to retransmit Televisa's and TV Azteca's broadcast TV channels without paying retransmission fees. Televisa has taken legal action against Dish, arguing that the free retransmission is only possible after the secondary legislation is enacted. See, further, Sigler, E, 'Dish se 'ahorra' 61 mdd con TV abierta', *CNN Expansión*, 16 September 2013, available at: www.cnnexpansion.com/negocios/2013/09/16/dish-se-ahorra-61-mdd-con-tv-abierta.

United States

Market Structure

Pay TV in the US includes cable TV and direct broadcast satellite (DBS). Over the internet, videos can be selected directly from a distributor's website and accessed over a subscriber's internet connection, or traditional video programme distributors can use internet protocol transmission to distribute their own packages of programming.

The major players are:

— DBS: DirecTV and DISH Network;
— cable TV: Comcast, Time Warner Cable, Cox Communications, Charter Communications, Cablevision Systems (the top 5). Two national phone companies have expanded into cable TV (AT&T and Verizon) and there are also a number of local telephone companies that provide cable TV locally; and
— Over-the-top (OTT) distributors: Hulu, Google TV, Netflix, Apple TV, Amazon Prime.

Regulation

Cable TV is subject to regulation both at the local and federal level. The specialist regulator at the federal level is the Federal Communications Commission (FCC).

Local authorities can require cable operators to obtain a franchise. Each state determines which political jurisdiction (state, county, city or town) has the power to issue these franchises. Twenty-one states have enacted laws revoking the ability of local authorities to award franchises, and instead grant statewide franchises.

The local authority may (but is not legally required to) regulate the rates cable TV charges for the basic service tier, with some exceptions for cable TV operators based on the number of subscribers served and annual revenue. If a cable company is subject to 'effective competition', the local authority may not regulate the rates for the basic service tier. The rates for other video services are not subject to regulation.

Local authorities may not grant an exclusive franchise or unreasonably refuse to award a competitive franchise. Further, local franchising authorities may require cable operators to dedicate a portion of their channel capacity and provide financial support to public, educational and governmental (PEG) channels. Any PEG channels must be carried on the basic tier level of service.

At the federal level cable TV is not licensed by the FCC, but cable system operators must register with the FCC. Regulation at the federal level addresses issues such as the types of programming cable TV stations must carry, compulsory leased access to, and rates charged by, cable systems for a portion of their channel capacity, and limits on vertically integrated cable operators.

The Federal Trade Commission (FTC) and Department of Justice (DOJ) regulate competition in the cable TV sector under general antitrust laws (particularly the Sherman and Clayton Acts[1]). The FCC regulates competition in the cable TV sector under the Communications Act of 1934.[2] State attorneys-general enforce state provisions on competition law/consumer protection in the cable TV sector. Private litigants enforce federal and state competition laws by bringing private actions for damages.

Competition Law Enforcement

There have been cases relating to monopolisation and anticompetitive agreements. Recent examples include the following.

Wampler v SW Bell Tel Co[3] involved the owner of a multiple dwelling unit (MDU) who entered into an agreement with AT&T, granting AT&T the exclusive right to provide triple play services to the MDU residents, and exclusive access to the coaxial wire, copper, and other fibre optic cables, in exchange for AT&T paying a 'door fee'. Thus AT&T had exclusive control over the 'bottleneck' through which all voice, video and internet services enter the MDU. The residents of the MDU sued, claiming that the agreement was an illegal restraint of trade and also an attempt to monopolise the triple play market. The case was dismissed because the MDU was not a relevant geographic market. On appeal, the fifth circuit affirmed the district court's ruling.

In *Behrend v Comcast*[4] the court ruled that the case could go forward certified as a class. The judge found that: (i) consumers 'presented evidence from which a jury could find that Comcast had monopoly power' because of the way it bought cable firms that had previously competed with it for local service franchises, reducing competition; (ii) Comcast may have 'acted with predation' illegal under the Sherman Act when it targeted special discounts to customers of rival cable provider RCN in the hope of driving the company out of the market; and (iii) Comcast's conduct stopped RCN from expanding and offering more customers competitive service.

In *Brantley v NBC Universal, Inc*[5] a group of cable and satellite TV subscribers claimed that TV programmers' and distributors' practice of selling multi-channel cable packages is an illegal restraint of trade under the Sherman Act. They sought to compel the programmers and distributors to sell each cable channel separately. The ninth circuit ruled that the practice of 'tiering'—selling different bundles of channels together based on their level of demand—does not injure competition

[1] Sherman Antitrust Act, 15 USC §§ 1–7, Clayton Act, 15 USC §§ 12–27.

[2] Communications Act of 1934, as amended by the Telecommunications Act of 1996, 47 USC §§151 *et seq.*

[3] *Wampler v SW Bell Tel Co*, 597 F.3d 741 (5th Cir 2010).

[4] *Behrend v Comcast Corp*, 655 F.3d 182 (3rd Cir 2011).

[5] *Brantley v NBC Universal, Inc LLC*, 675 F.3d 1192 (9th Cir 2012).

under the rule of reason and dismissed the action. The Supreme Court denied a petition for *certiorari*.

Merger Control

Transactions must be notified to the DOJ and FTC if they meet the size of transaction and size of person tests. Moreover, the FCC must approve any transfer of a cable TV ownership interest, and applies the public interest standard, an assessment of which includes competition concerns; but is not limited by traditional antitrust principles. State and local authorities review transactions that involve the transfer of franchising authorisations.

Examples of recent merger cases in the broadcasting sector that were subject to remedies at the federal level follow.

The acquisition of MediaOne Group by AT&T in 2000[6] was approved by the DOJ and FCC subject to conditions. Both AT&T and MediaOne are cable multiple system operators, but in this case the DOJ was concerned that the transaction would lessen competition in the national market for the aggregation, promotion and distribution of residential broadband content based on AT&T's existing control over Excite@Home (the largest provider of broadband internet in the US) and its acquisition of 34 per cent of Road Runner, the second-largest provider of broadband internet in the US. AT&T was required to divest its interest in Road Runner. The FCC found that the merged firm would serve 41.8 per cent of the nation's multichannel video programming distributor (MVPD) subscribers, thus infringing the 30 per cent subscriber cap, subsequently overturned by the DC circuit. The FCC ordered AT&T to inform it of what it would divest within six months of closing.

The merger between AOL and Time Warner in 2000[7] was approved by the FTC and FCC subject to conditions. The FTC was concerned that the transaction would impact competition on: (i) the residential broadband internet access market; (ii) the internet transport service market; and (iii) the interactive TV market. AOL Time Warner was: (i) required to open its cable system to competitor internet services providers (ISPs); (ii) prohibited from interfering with content passed along the bandwidth contracted for by non-affiliated ISPs and from interfering with the ability of non-affiliated providers of interactive TV services to interact with interactive signals, triggers or content that AOL Time Warner has agreed to carry; (iii) prevented from discriminating on the basis of affiliation in the transmission of content, or from entering into exclusive arrangements with

[6] *United States v AT&T Corp and MediaOne Group*, Inc No: 1: 00CV01176 (RCL) (D.D.C.) (2000), available at: www.justice.gov/atr/cases/indx4468.htm. Applications for Consent to the Transfer of Control of Licenses and Section 214 Authorizations from MediaOne Group, Inc, Transferor, to AT&T Corp, Transferee FCC CS Docket No 99-251, FCC 00-202 (5 June 2000).

[7] Applications for Consent to the Transfer of Control of Licenses and Section 214 Authorizations by Time Warner Inc. and America Online Inc., Transferors, to AOL Time Warner Inc., Transferee FCC CS Docket No. 00-30 (Memorandum, Opinion and Order) (11 January 2001).

other cable companies with respect to ISP services or interactive TV services; and (iv) required to market and offer AOL's digital subscriber line services to subscribers in Time Warner cable areas where affiliated cable broadband service is available in the same manner and at the same retail pricing as they do in those areas where affiliated cable broadband ISP service is not available.

The merger between AT&T and Comcast Corp in 2002[8] was not challenged by the FTC or the DOJ. The FCC approved the transaction, which created the largest cable TV operator, subject to conditions. Before the merger, AT&T was the largest, and Comcast the third-largest cable TV operator. The FCC found there were public interest grounds for approving the transaction, because the merger would spur investment, and create synergies and efficiencies that would result in significant cost savings. It found that the transaction would accelerate the deployment of broadband services, an important policy objective of the FCC. Among other things, the merged entity was required to divest Time Warner Entertainment to avoid harm to the programming market. Consumer groups challenged the FCC's decision, but in *Consumer Federation of America v FCC*,[9] the DC circuit found in favour of the FCC.

The acquisition by Comcast Corp and Time Warner Cable of Adelphia Communications Corp in 2006[10] was investigated by the FTC and FCC. The FTC closed its investigation, but the FCC approved the transaction subject to conditions. The FCC was concerned that post-transaction, Comcast and Time Warner would be able to increase the rates for regional sports networks and therefore imposed conditions relating to (among other things) competitor access and supply of programming to MVPDs. It found that the benefits from the transaction—increased deployment of technologies, such as voice over internet protocol—outweighed the competitive concerns.

In 2011 The DOJ and FCC gave conditional approval to the joint venture (JV) between Comcast Corp and NBC Universal, Inc JV.[11] The DOJ alleged

[8] Applications for Consent to the Transfer of Control of Licenses from Comcast Corp and AT&T Corp, Transferors, to AT&T Comcast Corp, Transferee, FCC MB Docket No 02-70, FCC 02-310 (Memorandum Opinion and Order) (13 November 2002), available at: www.fcc.gov/encyclopedia/major-transaction-decisions.

[9] *Consumer Federation of America v FCC*, 348 F.3d 1009 (D.C. Cir 2003).

[10] Acquisition by Comcast Corporation and Time Warner Cable Inc of the Cable Assets of Adelphia Communications Corporation, and Related Transactions, FTC File No 051-0151, available at: www.ftc.gov/opa/2006/01/fyi0609.shtm. Applications for Consent to the Assignment and/or Transfer of Control of Licenses from Adelphia Communications Corporation, Comcast Corp, and Time Warner Inc, Transferors, to Time Warner Cable Inc, Time Warner Inc, and Comcast Corp, Transferees, FCC MB Docket No 05-192, FCC 06-105 (Memorandum Opinion & Order) (13 July 2006), available at: www.fcc.gov/encyclopedia/major-transaction-decisions.

[11] *United States, State of California, State of Florida, State of Missouri, State of Texas, and State of Washington v Comcast Corp, General Electric Co, and NBC Universal*, Inc, No 1: 11-cv-00 106 (RJL) (2011), available at www.justice.gov/atr/cases/comcast.html. Applications of Comcast Corporation, General Electric Company and NBC Universal, Inc for Consent to Assign Licenses and Transfer Control of Licenses FCC MB Docket No 10-56, FCC 11-4 (Memorandum Opinion and Order) (18 January 2011), available at: www.fcc.gov/encyclopedia/major-transaction-decisions.

that the JV would substantially lessen competition for the timely distribution of professional, full-length video programming to residential customers. It was concerned that Comcast would gain control through the JV over highly valued video content needed by Comcast's rivals to compete effectively and as a result both traditional competitors and online video distributors (OVD) would not be able to obtain sufficient programming to compete effectively against the JV. The DOJ required the JV to license its broadcast, cable and film content to OVDs in packages similar to those provided to traditional distributors, and to offer OVD cable and film content similar or better than the content received from any of its programming peers. Comcast was also required to divest its interest in Hulu, an OVD.

The merger between AOL and Time Warner in 2011[12] was permitted by the FTC subject to conditions. The FTC alleged that the merger would (among other things) restrain competition in the market for interactive TV services. The combined entity was required to make available the services of alternative, non-affiliated broadband ISPs and prevented from interfering with content passed along the bandwidth used by non-affiliated ISPs.

Media Ownership

The FCC can regulate the ownership or control of cable systems on the basis of another media interest. State or franchising authorities cannot prohibit the ownership or control of a cable system because of a person's other media interest.

Cable operators are prohibited from owning multichannel multipoint distribution services (wireless cable) licenses or offering satellite master antenna TV service within their franchise area, unless the cable operator is subject to 'effective competition'.

The FCC is further required to set limits on the number of subscribers a cable TV operator may serve nationwide and the number of channels it may dedicate to its affiliated programming networks. The FCC adopted rules doing so, but these rules were struck down by the DC circuit.[13]

A single entity can own multiple broadcast networks, but cannot own two or more of the 'top four' TV networks (ABC, CBS, FOX and NBC).

[12] In the Matter of America Online, Inc, and Time Warner Inc, File No 001 0105, Docket No C-3989.

[13] See *Time Warner Entm't Co v FCC*, 240 F.3d 1126, 1136, 1139 (D.C. Cir 2001). In 2008, the FCC once again adopted a horizontal limit preventing an individual cable operator from serving more than 30% of MVPD subscribers nationwide, using more recent empirical data to reach the result. See The Commission's Cable Horizontal and Vertical Ownership Limits, MM Docket No 92-264, Fourth Report and Order and Further Notice of Proposed Rulemaking, 23 FCC Rcd 2134, 2135, ¶ 1 (2008). Despite the inclusion of more recent data, the D.C. circuit struck down the revised horizontal ownership limit in 2009 for being arbitrary and capricious. See *Comcast Corp v FCC*, 579 F.3d 1, 10 (D.C. Cir 2009).

Reform Agenda

Retransmission consent

In relation to retransmission content cable operators are required to carry local television stations in every market they serve. Broadcasters maintain control over their signals and commercial broadcasters may request compensation from the MVPD for the carriage of their signals. In local television markets, commercial television stations must choose every three years between the right to grant retransmission consent or the right to mandatory carriage. If a station chooses 'retransmission consent', the broadcaster and an MVPD negotiate a carriage agreement, which may include compensation in return for the right to carry the broadcast signal. Without consent, the MVPD may not carry the signal. Where a station chooses 'must carry', it is entitled to the carriage of its signal but cannot receive compensation. Qualified local noncommercial educational stations have a right to mandatory carriage within the same must-carry market, but do not have retransmission consent rights. Cable operators may negotiate for retransmission consent with any other broadcast station they seek to carry regardless of the station's television market. Recently, public retransmission consent disputes have arisen out of some MVPDs' and broadcasters' negotiations, resulting in blackouts of certain channels in certain areas. The FCC is considering revisions to the retransmission consent rules. In 2011, it issued a Notice of Proposed Rulemaking.[14] Although several MVPDs support reforming the retransmission consent regime,[15] the National Association of Broadcasters, among others, is opposed to revising the rules.[16] This docket remains open and interested parties continue to make submissions to the FCC.[17]

In September 2013, Congresswoman Anna Eshoo circulated a draft bill to reform the rules on retransmission consent.[18]

Unbundling

Some small and rural MVPDs claim that in order to obtain carriage rights to the most popular networks, network owners require them to also carry less popular

[14] Amendment of the Commission's Rules Related to Retransmission Consent, MB Docket No 10 -71, Notice of Proposed Rulemaking, 26 FCC Rcd 2718, 2719, ¶ 1 (2011).

[15] See, eg, In the Matter of Amendment of the Commission's Rules Related to Retransmission Consent, Reply Comments of Verizon (3 June 2010).

[16] In the Matter of Amendment of the Commission's Rules Related to Retransmission Consent, Reply Comments of the National Association of Broadcasters (27 June 2011), available at: www.nab.org/documents/filings/RetransConsentReply062711.pdf and www.nab.org/documents/filings/RetransSupplComments052913.pdf.

[17] See, eg, In the Matter of Amendment of the Commission's Rules Related to Retransmission Consent, MB Docket No 10-71, Letter from Time Warner Cable (17 October 2013), available at: apps.fcc.gov/ecfs/document/view?id=7520947180.

[18] Video Consumers Have Options in Choosing Entertainment Act of 2013 (Video Choice Act 2013).

co-owned networks on an expanded basic tier. As a result, they have unreasonably high wholesale costs for programming in comparison to incumbent cable operators, and they are forced to pass on these costs to consumers. They also indicate that some programmers make access to traditional cable networks conditional on payment for distribution of the online version of the network. The cost of the online versions of the networks is thus bundled into basic broadband packages. The MVPDs state that the networks charge subscriber fees on the basis of the number of broadband subscribers for the online versions of the networks as well as the number of video subscribers for linear distribution. As a result, these MVPDs must either absorb the additional cost or increase end-user rates for broadband.

Senator McCain introduced a bill in May 2013 addressing bundling at both the wholesale and retail levels and allowing à la carte offering of every channel.[19] Congresswoman Eshoo's draft bill also addresses bundling as part of its reform of retransmission consent.[20]

Exclusivity rules

With respect to cable operators, the FCC's network non-duplication rules allow a local broadcast station to request that duplicated programming be blacked out when carried on another station imported by the system into the local station's zone of protection. Similarly, the FCC's syndicated exclusivity rules allow a broadcaster to assert its right to black out syndicated programming for which it holds exclusive rights when carried by a cable operator within its zone of protection. The FCC's sports blackout rule protects a sports team's or league's distribution rights to a live sporting event in a local market. This prevents a cable operator from providing the live sporting event on a distant signal to a market where the game is blacked out on the local broadcast station. The FCC has sought comment on proposed rule amendments to eliminate these exclusivity rules for cable as part of a broader reformation of the retransmission consent rules.[21]

Public interest programming

Local franchising authorities may require cable operators to dedicate a portion of their channel capacity and provide financial support to PEG channels and to carry PEG channels on their basic service tier. However, some state video franchising laws have removed or reduced the PEG requirements provided in local franchising

[19] Television Consumer Freedom Act of 2013. SCH13204, 113TH CONGRESS 1ST SESSION, available at: www.mccain.senate.gov/public/index.cfm?FuseAction=Files.View&FileStore_id=d26f11d4-7030-44ff-b980-1c0c75e8f5d1.

[20] Video Choice Act 2013.

[21] Amendment of the Commission's Rules Related to Retransmission Consent, MB Docket No 10-71, Notice of Proposed Rulemaking, 26 FCC Rcd 2718, ¶ 1 (2011).

agreements, which has led to a reduction in PEG funding and support. In 2009, the FCC received two requests to clarify the rules and responsibilities of MVPDs with respect to the carriage of PEG channels.[22] These petitions remain pending before the FCC.

Competitive Outlook

The introduction of DBS in the 1990s, and the subsequent expansion of telephone providers into the delivery of video programming in the mid 2000s, have significantly increased the level of competition in this sector. Competition continues to reduce cable's share of the US video market and cable MVPDs are expected to continue losing basic video subscribers to competing MVPDs. Cable video subscriptions have been eroded by competition from both the established DBS MVPDs and new telephone MVPDs.[23] Cable MVPDs have been losing video subscribers at an increasing rate over the last five years. At the same time, however, remaining cable customers have added subscriptions to digital video service or subscribed to cable bundles that include video, internet access and telephone services.

Although some consumers may consider online video to be a substitute for MVPD video, others may consider it to be a complement. Reports suggest that some consumers are dropping their MVPD video services ('cutting-the-cord') or eliminating subscriptions for some video services such as premium channels ('cord-shaving') in favour of video services delivered over the internet.[24] However, there are also indications that increased viewing of video programming delivered over the internet does not necessarily translate into decreased MVPD subscriptions.

[22] See Petition for Declaratory Ruling that AT&T's Method of Delivering Public, Educational and Government Access Channels over its U-verse System is Contrary to the Communications Act of 1934, as amended, and Applicable Commission Rules, MB Docket No 09-13, Petition of ACM et al (filed 30 January 2009); Petition for Declaratory Ruling on Requirements for a Basic Service Tier and for PEG Channel Capacity Under Sections 543(b)(7), 531(a) and the Commission's Ancillary Jurisdiction Under Title I, MB Docket No 09-13, Petition of the City of Lansing, MI (filed 27 January 2009). See also Entities File Petitions for Declaratory Ruling Regarding Public, Educational, and Governmental Programming, MB Docket 09-13, Public Notice, 24 FCC Rcd 1340 (MB 2009).

[23] SNL Kagan Special Report, 'US Multichannel Subscriber Update and Geographic Analysis' (2012), available at: www.snl.com/Sectors/Media/WhitepaperLibrary.aspx. See also SNL Kagan Special Report, 'US Multichannel Subscriber Update and Programming Cost Analysis' (June 2013), available at: www.snl.com/Sectors/Media/WhitepaperLibrary.aspx.

[24] Between 2011 and 2012, 7% of surveyed consumers streamed because they had cut back on MVPD services, and 10% because they had cancelled their MVPD subscription. eMarketer, 'TV Viewers Stream Content to Play Catch-up' (5 November 2012), available at: www.emarketer.com/%28S%280j0sa345o5y2wwjklat1te45%29%29/Article.aspx?R=1009461.

C. ASIA

China

Overview

The cable TV sector is highly regulated and competition is limited. Unless the Chinese government conducts a process of deregulation, it is unlikely that there will be a significant change in the situation in the foreseeable future.

Market Structure

The market is fragmented into many geographic areas. In order to provide cable services an operator needs to obtain a licence issued by the State Administration of Radio Film and Television (SARFT) and the local government. Major players differ from province to province. It is possible to identify a monopoly or near monopoly provider in selected areas: Beijing Gehua Cable TV Network Co, Ltd (Beijing); Shaanxi Guangdian Network Media Co, Ltd (Shaanxi Province); and Huangzhou Huashu Digital TV Corporation (Hangzhou City).

All of the companies who have a significant—even dominant—presence in a province or a city have state-owned capital and are strongly associated with local governments. Accordingly, in a specific province or city, there is limited competition.

Regulation

China imposes strict controls over this sector. A company is required to obtain a licence from SARFT (or its branches at provincial level) and be approved by local government (usually the provincial level government) to operate cable TV services. The local government has strong power to control the sector and could determine which company may operate in certain cities.

Competition Law Enforcement

Although frequently criticised by the Chinese public and media, cable TV operators have not yet been subject to investigations or sanctions under the Chinese Anti-Monopoly Law. As at the end of 2013, there have been no reported examples of public enforcement of competition law in the sector. However, there are a few court cases, all concerning abuse of dominance, such as *Zhen Yinglong v Huangzhou Huashu Digital TV Corporation* (2008)[1] and *Wu Xiaoqin v Shaanxi Guangdian Network Media Co, Ltd* (2013).

[1] See, www.caijing.com.cn/2008-11-28/110032663.html.

The *Wu Xiaoqin* case is the only case where the plaintiff prevailed over the defendant among more than 100 court cases in China since China's Anti-Monopoly Law took effect in 2008. Shaanxi Guangdian Network Media (Group) Co, Ltd is the only cable TV operator in the Shaanxi Province. Mr Wu Xiaoqin was one of the customers of the cable TV service. Shaanxi Guangdian Network Media (Group) Co, Ltd was alleged to be engaged in anticompetitive tie-in sales in 2012 and finally lost the case in January 2013.

Merger Control

As at the end of 2013, merger control has not yet been applied in the cable TV sector in a reported case. The key reason might be that the industry is strictly regulated by the government, each fragmented market is dominated by one company, and there is limited competition across those markets.

Media Ownership

According to the Rules on Entry of Non-Publicly Owned Capital into the Cultural Industry by the State Council of 2005, private investment in the cable TV sector may be permitted in limited circumstances. This is the first time that the Chinese government has opened the sector to private investors. However, the rules also require that state-owned capital should represent at least 51 per cent of the sector.

Reform Agenda

The Chinese government attaches great importance to the regulation of the cable TV industry since it concerns the media and may, therefore, be seen as a key instrument of policy. There are currently few indications of any easing of the government's strict control over propaganda.

The Chinese central government had tried to unify the national market by establishing one single state-owned cable enterprise. However, this effort failed due to strong resistance from local governments and dominant companies in provinces and cities.

India

Overview

The Telecom Regulatory Authority of India (TRAI) has set out its view of the broadcasting market in a 2013 consultation.[1] This provides the background to its view, espoused in the consultation that 'there is the possibility that the effects of monopoly/market dominance in cable TV distribution could also extend to other services, such as voice and broadband, which are carried on cable'.

Market Structure

The television sector in India mainly comprises cable TV, direct-to-home (DTH) services, internet protocol television (IPTV) and terrestrial TV provided by the public broadcaster, Doordarshan. The TRAI cites an industry report which states that the cable TV segment is the largest platform and it has grown from 4.1 lakh in 1992 to over 9.4 crore by March 2012.[2] The value chain for TV channel distribution in India is displayed in Figure 27.

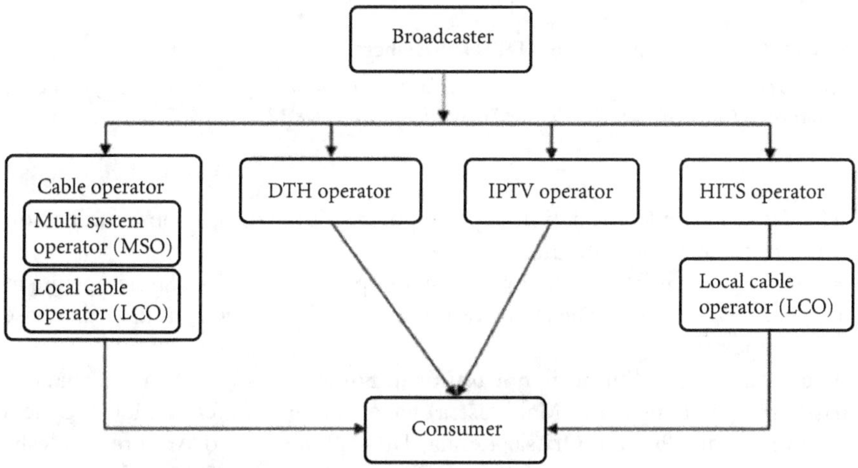

Figure 27: Broadcasting and distribution value chain in India

Source: Telecom Regulatory Authority of India, Consultation Paper on Monopoly/ Market dominance in Cable TV services, 3 June 2013, Figure 1.1, page 3
Notes: HITS = Head-end in the sky

[1] Telecom Regulatory Authority of India, 'Consultation Paper on Monopoly/Market dominance in Cable TV services', 3 June 2013 (in this appendix, Consultation Paper). Except where cited otherwise, material in this appendix pertaining to India is summarised from the Consultation Paper.

[2] Media Partners, 'Media Partners Asia report: Asia Pacific Pay TV and Broadband Market 2012', 2012.

The TRAI reports in the Consultation Paper that although DTH has emerged as an alternative to cable and its subscriber base is growing at a faster rate than cable, the percentage of cable TV homes is significantly higher than DTH homes as depicted in Figure 28.

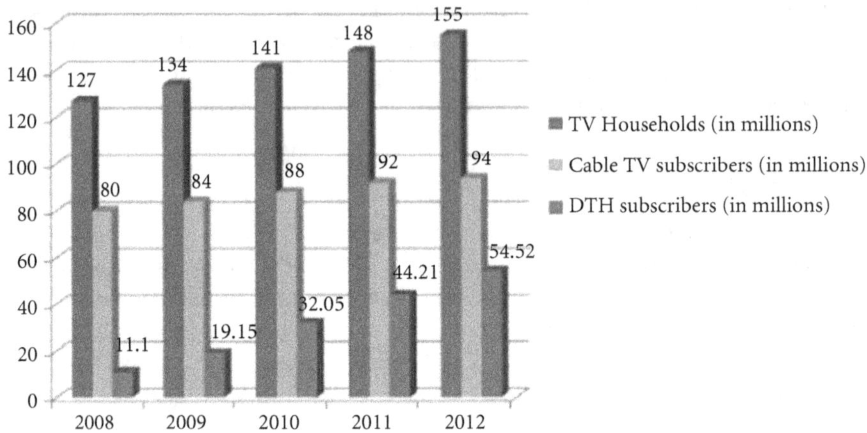

Figure 28: Growth of cable TV and DTH subscribers

Source: Telecom Regulatory Authority of India, Consultation Paper on Monopoly/ Market dominance in Cable TV services, 3 June 2013, Figure 1.2, page 12

The TRAI in the Consultation Paper reports a number of its observations on features of the market structure.

There are an estimated 6,000 multi-system operators (MSOs). Some operate at national or regional level. The majority are small local MSOs with a subscriber base of a few thousand.

The level of competition is not uniform. Some states (eg Delhi, Karnataka, Rajasthan, West Bengal and Maharastra) have a large number of MSOs. Others (eg Tamil Nadu, Punjab, Orissa, Kerala, Uttar Pradesh and Andhra Pradesh) have a single or principal MSO. The exact market shares of the MSOs are not available.

The TRAI also reports MSOs buying out local cable operators (LCOs) or smaller MSOs or entering into joint ventures with them with varying levels of ownership.

Regulation

Cable TV operators are regulated by the Cable Television Networks (Regulation) Act 1995 (Cable TV Act) and the Cable Television Network Rules 1994 (Cable TV Rules).

An operator of a cable television network is required to register as a cable operator with the relevant registering authority.[3] The Head Post Master of the Head Post Office of the local area is the notified registering authority for local cable operators.

The introduction of Digital Addressable System (DAS) led to amendments to the Cable TV Network Rules. An MSO operating in DAS notified areas is required to obtain permission from the Ministry of Information & Broadcasting (MIB) in addition to registration as a cable operator.

Competition Law Enforcement

The Indian Competition Act 2002 (Competition Act) prohibitions on anticompetitive agreements (section 3) and abuse of a dominant position (section 4) apply without distinction in the broadcasting sector.

In a relatively early Competition Act case the Competition Commission of India (CCI) imposed a penalty of INR 8 crore on three entities of cable TV operator, Fastway Group.[4] The penalty was imposed for a violation of section 4 and represented 6 per cent of its average turnover in the three previous financial years. The CCI found that Fastway Group had denied the opportunity for transmission of the complainant channel by termination of the agreement between them without any sound justification.

Merger Control

Since mandatory merger control has been effective in India since 1 June 2011 the CCI has reviewed mergers in a variety of sectors, including in the media and communications sector.

Most of the merger cases that have come before the CCI have not raised significant substantive issues. For example, the CCI cleared News Corporation's acquisition of ESPN's 50 per cent equity interest in sports broadcaster, ESS.[5] The CCI concluded that the combination would not result in an appreciable adverse effect on competition in the relevant market in India. The CCI stated, among other things, that although the proposed combination resulted in the transfer of joint control to sole control it would not result in the elimination of any competitor. The joint venture partners, News Corporation and ESPN, were not competitors for broadcasting of sports channels in India.

[3] Cable TV Act 1995.

[4] Case 36/211, *M/s Kansan News Pvt Ltd vs M/s Fastway Transmission Pvt Ltd & Ors*, 3 July 2012.

[5] Case C-2012/07/64, *Notice for acquisition by STARTV ATC Holding Limited*, 28 September 2012.

Media Ownership

As at the end of 2013 there are no ownership restrictions for MSOs and LCOs and no caps on the number of channels or subscribers in any area.

The TRAI notes that in relation to FM radio no company or Group can operate more than 40 per cent of the total FM radio channels in each city. The total number of channels that a company or Group can operate cannot exceed 15 per cent of the total number of channels allocated in India.

Reform Agenda

The TRAI received a reference dated 12 December 2012 from the MIB seeking its views on the future regulation of cable TV. This reference states that the sector is 'virtually monopolized' by a single entity in some states. MIB takes the view that it has become necessary to examine whether there is a need to introduce restrictions on MSOs and LCOs including restricting their area of operation or placing limits on the size of their subscriber base.

The following are some of the questions on which the TRAI consulted:

— Is there a need to address monopoly/dominance in cable TV distribution?
— Should the state be the relevant market for measuring market power in the cable TV sector?
— Should restrictions to curb monopoly/dominance be based on area of operation, market share or any other measure? How should the relevant market be divided amongst MSOs for providing a cable TV service?
— What should be the value of market share beyond which an MSO should not be allowed to build market share on its own? How could this be achieved in markets where the MSO already possesses a market share beyond the threshold value?
— How suitable are concentration measures such as the Herfindahl–Hirschman Index (HHI)[6] and increase in HHI for imposing restrictions on M&A?
— How should 'control' be defined for the purposes of restrictions on M&A?
— If retrospective rules are required how much time should be given to existing entities for complying with the rules by diluting their level of control?
— What information should be subject to mandatory disclosure for effective monitoring and compliance with restrictions on market dominance? What should be the frequency of such disclosures? Which of those disclosures should be made public?

[6] The Herfindahl index (also known as Herfindahl–Hirschman Index, or HHI) is a measure of the size of firms in relation to the industry and an indicator of the amount of competition between them.

Competitive Outlook

The broadcasting and, particularly, cable TV sector in India has been allowed to develop without regulation. In some cases, competition has led to more than one provider in a particular area; in others there is a single provider. While an initial analysis may suggest that there should be a preference for many rather than few operators, this conclusion is not inevitable. Now the TRAI has entered the debate of whether intervention is needed, it appears that the weighting of its questioning is focused more on the 'how to' rather than 'whether'. At the end of 2013 the outcome of the TRAI's cable TV inquiry is not yet clear. There appears to be a growing trend of policy and stricter regulation in the media and communications sector in India.

South Korea

Market Structure

In Korea, there are three broad categories of pay TV provider: (i) satellite direct-to-home (DTH) providers (launched in 2001); (ii) cable TV providers (or service operators) (since 1995); and (iii) internet protocol TV (IPTV) (since 1997).

The major player in category (i) is KT Skylife. It is the only satellite provider in Korea. In category (ii) the major players are C&M, CJ Hellovision, MB, HCN and TBroad. In category (iii) the major players are KT, SK broadband and LG Uplus (all of which are internet service providers that have moved into TV services).

Regulation

The cable TV sector falls within the scope of the Broadcasting Act most recently amended in 2013[1] (Broadcasting Act) and is regulated by the Ministry of Science, ICT and Future Planning (MSIP). A cable TV operator must obtain a systems operator (SO) licence from the MSIP. Before issuing a licence, the MSIP must obtain the consent of the Korea Communications Commission (KCC).[2] The SO licence is restricted to a specific geographical region.[3] Cable TV providers who have multiple SO licences are called multiple service operators (MSOs).

Competition Law Enforcement

Unfair trade practice

TBroad, a cable company, took advantage of its superior position vis-à-vis home shopping channels by requiring the channels to invest in a golf course.[4] Donglim Leisure Development Co, Ltd, 100 per cent owned by Taekwong Group's owner and family (which also owns TBroad), was developing a golf course. It had difficulty in raising funds and so Taekwong attempted to raise funds from its group companies. TBroad requested the three home shopping channels with which it did business (Hyundai Home Shopping, GS Home Shopping, and Woori Home Shopping) to invest money from August 2007 to November 2008. Each invested KRW 2.2 billion on the basis of its business relationship with TBroad, although each anticipated a loss since golf course membership prices were declining. A major contractual condition of the investment was that they could choose either to have the pre-invested amount returned with an annual interest of 5.22 per

[1] Broadcasting Act, Articles 2(b), 9(2).
[2] Ibid, Articles 2(b), 9(2).
[3] Ibid, Article 12.
[4] KFTC Decision No 2011—135.

cent, or to obtain golf course membership preferentially in the event that not all were sold in the public offering. Donglim Leisure Development Co, Ltd offered memberships to the public on 15 December 2009 when 30 per cent or more of the construction was completed. There was no response so it recruited members from the pre-investors. It sold memberships from 29 December 2009 to 28 April 2010. The three home shopping companies each converted their pre-invested amounts into memberships securing a total of six accounts (KRW 1.1 billion per account).

The Korean Fair Trade Commission (KFTC) found that TBroad had coerced the home shopping channels to make the purchases. In the view of the KFTC, this constituted an unfair trade practice (not an abuse of dominance) under the Monopoly Regulation and Fair Trade Act of Korea (MRFTA)[5] where a party with a superior position coerces another party to make a purchase it had no intention of making. The KFTC imposed fines of KRW 42 million, together with a corrective order.

In another case, C&M imposed a most favoured nation clause, restricting the power of contractual parties to negotiate price. The KFTC found that C&M had abused its superior bargaining position by causing disadvantage, an unfair trade practice under the MRFTA. It therefore issued a corrective order.[6]

Abuse of dominance

In the *TBroad GSD Channel* case[7] the KFTC found that TBroad had abused its dominant position. TBroad changed the channel number of a TV home shopping company (Woori Home Shopping) to a more disadvantageous channel. This change was a result of Woori Home Shopping's refusal to pay higher transmission fees. TBroad appealed, and the Supreme Court found that the KFTC had incorrectly defined the relevant market.[8] It found that TBroad was not dominant in the properly defined relevant market, which was the market for programme transmission services between a cable television company and a TV home shopping company and not the market for the transmission of programmes by a cable television company to its cable channel subscribers. The Supreme Court also noted that, even if it had agreed with the KFTC's market definition and thus found that TBroad was dominant, the KFTC failed to show any harm to competition, but merely harm to Woori Home Shopping.

The suspension of collective agreements by SOs has been the subject of abuse of dominance investigations.[9] On 25 July 2007, the KFTC issued a cease and desist order against 15 SOs, affiliates of the MSO TBroad and three SOs of CJ Group,

5 Law No 3320, 31 December 1980.
6 KFTC Decision No 2002—217.
7 KFTC Decision No 2007—153.
8 Supreme Court decision of 11 December 2008, Case No 2007Du25183.
9 KFTC Decision No 2007—458, 460, 461, 462, 463, 466, 468, 487.

and imposed fines of KRW 216 million on eight TBroad-affiliated SOs. The case was initiated in January 2005, when 15 TBroad-affiliated SOs refused to renew collective agreements to offer their services to an apartment in a broadcasting zone. Residents of the apartment complained to the KFTC. The KFTC found that the SOs were attempting to induce customers to enter into more expensive individual contracts, rather than the collective agreements. Further, in April 2005, operators unilaterally adjusted channels to incorporate popular channels of low-end packaged products into high-end products, thus adversely impacting the quality of the low-end products and triggering further complaints. The KFTC found that the SOs were dominant within the relevant broadcasting zone and that the refusal to renew the collective agreements and the unilateral repackaging of products amounted to an abuse of that dominance.

Anticompetitive agreements

Five cable operators (TBroad, CJ Hellovision, C&M, HCN and Curix) were found to have colluded to prevent programme providers from providing broadcasting programmes for IPTV. On 24 August 2011 the KFTC imposed aggregated fines of KRW 9.7 billion.[10]

Merger Control

If the thresholds for notification are met, transactions in the cable TV sector are subject to pre- or post-notification merger control requirements, as applicable. Penalties for failure to notify have been applied in the cable/pay TV sector on a number of occasions.

Examples of cases in which remedies were imposed are discussed below. At the end of 2013 there were no public details of prohibitions in this sector.

— *CJ Cable Net/Chungnam Broadcasting and Modu Broadcasting.*[11] In 2007, the KFTC imposed behavioural remedies in relation to CJ Cable Net's acquisition of stock in Chungnam Broadcasting System and Modu Broadcasting System. The acquisition merged cable-TV providers in six cities. The KFTC imposed remedies that prohibited (until the end of 2010): (i) direct or indirect price increases in service charges; (ii) reductions in the number of channels offered per subscription class; (iii) refusals to provide information on, or sell, the cheapest products; and (iv) any rejections of applications to convert subscriptions to the cheapest class of service.

— *TBroad Nakdong Broadcasting (TBroad)/Dongseo Digital (Dongseo).*[12] On 1 October 2010, TBroad entered into an agreement to acquire all the shares

[10] KFTC Decision No 2011—153.
[11] KFTC Decision No 2007—274.
[12] KFTC Decision No 2011—209.

in Dongseo, an MSO operating in the same area. The KCC requested that the KFTC review the transaction. The KFTC found that the relevant product market was the multichannel pay TV market, including cable, satellite and IPTV. The relevant geographic market comprised two areas of Busan. The KFTC found low probability of coordinated effects, but that unilateral effects were likely because: (i) the combined market share was 88 per cent, making it the largest operator, with a margin of over 25 per cent between it and the next largest competitor; (ii) in the relevant geographic market, there was significant competition pre-transaction, resulting in heavy discounts in comparison with monopolised areas; (iii) for low-price packages in these areas, the price was lower and the content quality was higher in comparison with monopolised areas; and (iv) there was no realistic prospect of entry. The KFTC approved the transaction subject to various conditions including that until 2015 there was to be: (i) no increase above inflation in the subscription for analogue services; (ii) no decrease in the number of channels in the analogue service; and (iii) no refusal to supply customers that sign up for low-priced services. This was intended to protect analogue customers in the face of digitisation, while allowing the transaction because competition between cable, satellite and IPTV is increasing.

— In 2004, the Korea cable TV provider Cheonan Broadcasting and Korea Cable TV Anyang Broadcasting acquired a 42.4 per cent share in Hanvit I&B.[13] As a result, competition in Southern Gyeonggi Province was eliminated between an affiliate of Cheonan and an affiliate of Hanvit I&B. Their combined market share was 91 per cent within this province. The KFTC allowed the transaction to proceed, citing the competitive constraints imposed by satellite, and the control of fees by the KCC, but required the company to consult with the KFTC before increasing the usage fee of any programme above the national average for the next two years.

— In 2004, three CJ Cable Net local cable companies acquired 80.6 per cent of the shares in CJ Cable Net Northern Incheon Broadcasting.[14] This led to vertical integration of CJ Home Shopping (a parent company of the acquirer), and CJ Cable Net Northern Incheon Broadcasting in the North Incheon area. As a result, the KFTC considered that other home shopping channels in the area may face a competitive disadvantage, for example, unfair channel allocation and broadcasting restraints. The KFTC approved the transaction, subject to the following conditions: (i) the CJ Home Shopping and other home shopping channels had to be within 10 listings of each other; and (ii) at least three home shopping channels had to be included within this range.

[13] KFTC Decision No 2004—254.
[14] KFTC Decision No 2004—251.

Media Ownership

Under section 8 of the Broadcasting Act, there are the following limits on holding shares in a cable TV broadcasting business and certain other media businesses:

— A corporation (and persons with which it has a special relationship) that publishes a daily newspaper or runs a news correspondence cannot hold more than 49 per cent of the shares in a cable TV operator (section 8(5)).

— A cable TV operator, a terrestrial broadcasting business and a satellite broadcaster cannot mutually and concurrently operate their business or own their stocks or equity shares in excess of the scope prescribed by the Broadcasting Act Presidential Decree in relation to market share or the number of business operators (section 8(6)). The Broadcasting Act Presidential Decree sets out detailed and complex rules, placing limits on (i) shareholdings of cable TV operators in broadcasters; (ii) shareholdings of satellite and terrestrial broadcasters in cable TV operators; and (iii) cable TV operators' market share (based on revenue) (Article 4(3)).

— A cable TV operator, a terrestrial broadcasting business and a satellite broadcaster, a programme provider, and a signal transmission network operator cannot mutually and concurrently operate their business or own their stocks or equity shares in excess of the scope prescribed by the Broadcasting Act Presidential Decree in relation to market share or the number of business operators (section 8(7)). The Broadcasting Act Presidential Decree sets out detailed and complex rules, placing restrictions on cable TV operators also operating as programme providers and vice versa based on the geographic market served (Article 4(4)).

— A cable TV operator cannot concurrently operate another cable TV broadcaster or own their stocks or equity shares in excess of the scope prescribed by the Broadcasting Act Presidential Decree in relation to market share or the number of business operators (section 8(8)). The Broadcasting Act Presidential Decree sets out detailed and complex rules, placing limits on: (i) market share based on number of subscribers; and (ii) the geographic markets served (Article 4(5)). If ownership levels exceed the prescribed limits, those shares cannot be voted, and the KCC can order that the shares are divested within a six- month period.

Reform Agenda

The deregulation of broadcast networks in 2012 may extend to cable TV operators in 2014. The KCC announced on 8 August 2013 that it would be conducting a public consultation until 18 August 2013 on proposed amendments, including easing restrictions on corporate ownership of broadcasting businesses and revising the limits on SOs' market shares.

Moreover, a proposed amendment to the Broadcasting Act and the internet Multimedia Broadcasting Service Act would limit the number of subscribers to a segment of the pay TV sector to one third of the total pay TV subscribers. Thus an IPTV, satellite or cable TV provider would be unable to increase its subscribers beyond one third of the total pay TV subscribers. KT (an IPTV provider) and KT Skylife (a satellite provider) are opposing the Bill, whereas cable TV operators are supporting it because they believe that different regulations have been applied to the different pay TV sectors, and cable TV providers have been disadvantaged by more restrictive regulations.

Competitive Outlook

Traditional cable TV broadcasting is facing a competitive threat from IPTV—the three major players in this area are likely to be significant competitors in the TV sectorin the future. They bundle their TV products together with internet and mobile at a discounted rate. Traditional cable TV providers need to find a way to compete effectively. It is envisaged that they may also move into the internet/mobile sector. For example, C&M is extending its services to include internet services, as well as bundled and discounted packages.

Appendix 5: Online Behaviour in India

INTRODUCTION

Developing the discussion in chapter 8, we provide supplementary metrics on online behaviour in India.

A granular presentation of online news consumption is provided in Figure 29.

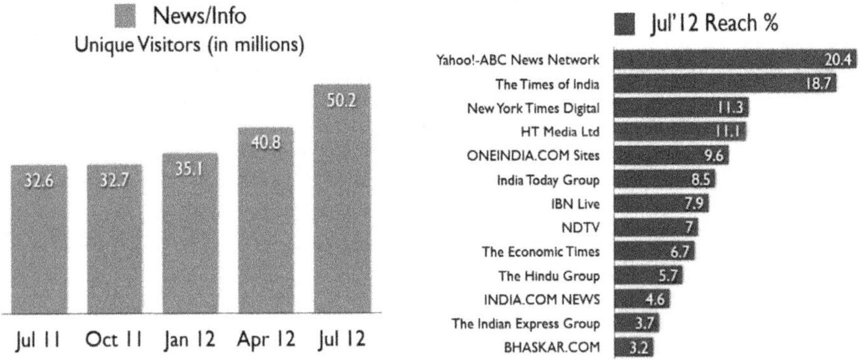

Figure 29: Online news consumption in India

Source: comScore: The Rise in India's Digital Consumer, August 2012, page 15

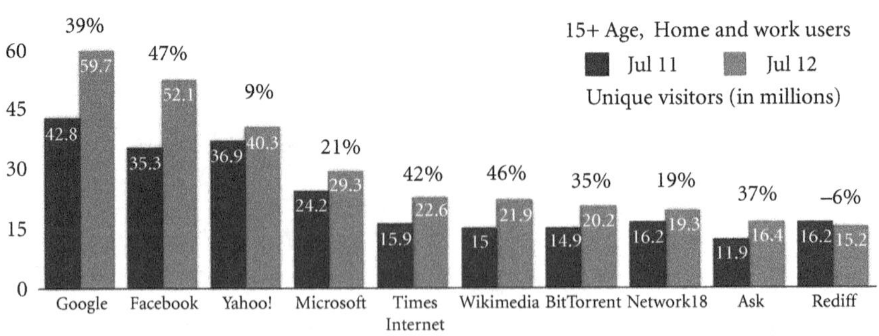

Figure 30: Year-on-year growth of the top 10 sites (India)

Note: Google is used primarily for search and news consumption

Source: comScore: The Rise in India's Digital Consumer, August 2012, page 14

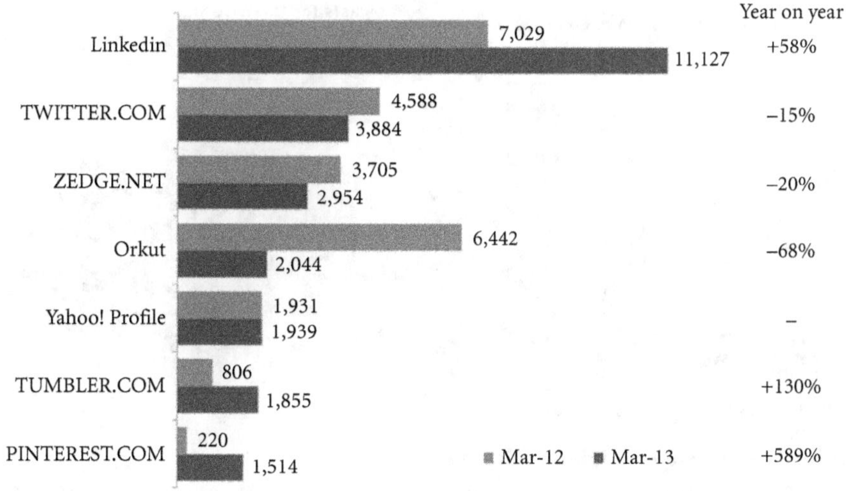

Figure 31: Visitors to social networking sites (India)

Source: comScore: India Digital Future in Focus, August 2013, page 26

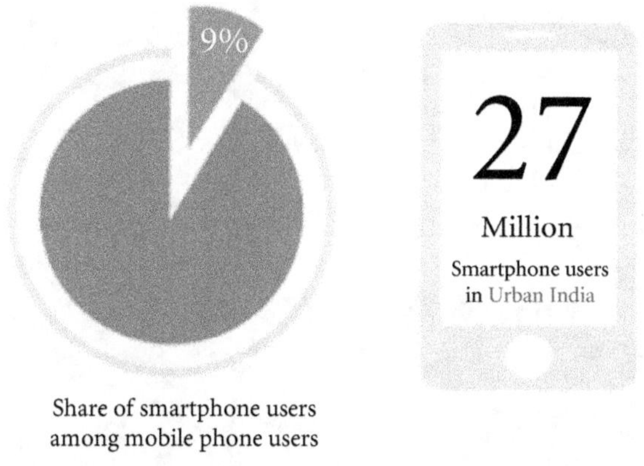

Figure 32: Uptake of smartphone users (March 2012)

Source: Nielsen Media, India: Featured Insights. Smartphones the emerging gadget of choice for the Urban Indian. Available at: http://www.nielsen.com/content/dam/corporate/india/reports/2012/Featured%20Insights_Smartphone-%20The%20Emerging%20Gadget%20of%20Choice.pdf

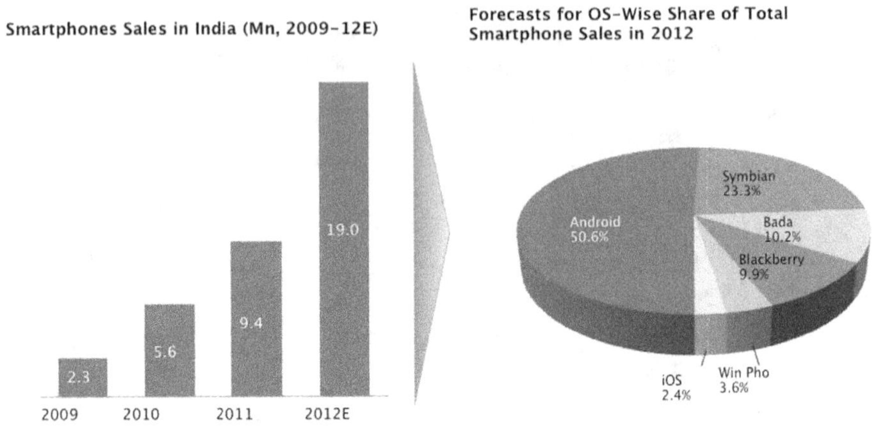

Figure 33: Growth of smartphone sales in India

Source: Convergence catalyst. Available at: http://www.convergencecatalyst.com/blog/2012/05/10/is-india-ready-for-customized-and-branded-mobile-app-stores/

Country	2013 shipment forecasts (millions)	% growth 2013/2012
Brazil	17.2	40.0
Russia	18.8	30.7
India	26.5	61.4
Indonesia	15.7	51.7
China (mainland)	239.8	29.1
Global total	827.0	22.5

Figure 34: Projected smartphone shipments 2013 (BRIIC countries)

Source: Canalys Press release, Developing markets will drive smart phone market growth in 2013, 17 January 2013

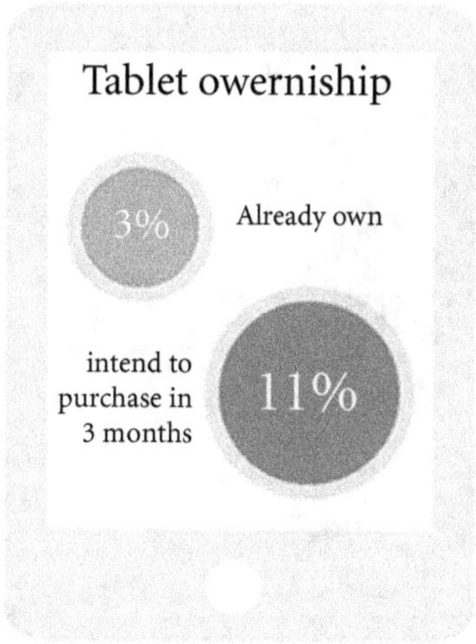

Figure 35: Tablet ownership and intention to purchase in India

Source: Nielsen. Available at: http://www.nielsen.com/us/en/newswire/2013/smartphones-keep-users-in-india-plugged-in.html

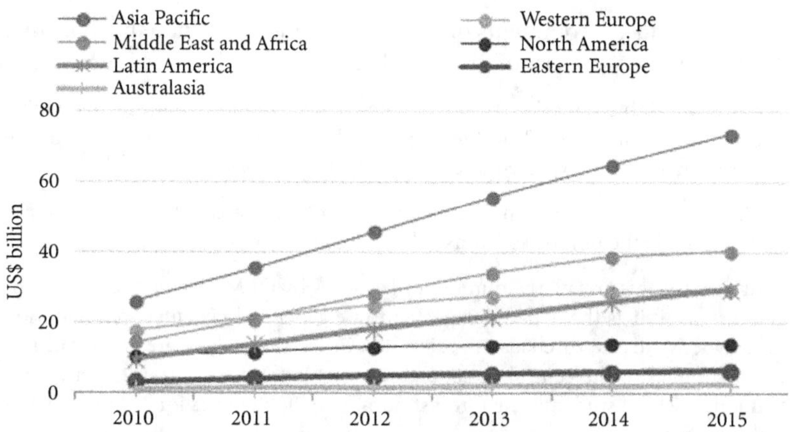

Figure 36: Projected retail sales of smartphones by region

Source: Euromonitor International. Available at: blog.euromonitor.com/2012/05/top-10-consumer-trends-for-2012-smartphone-universe.html#more

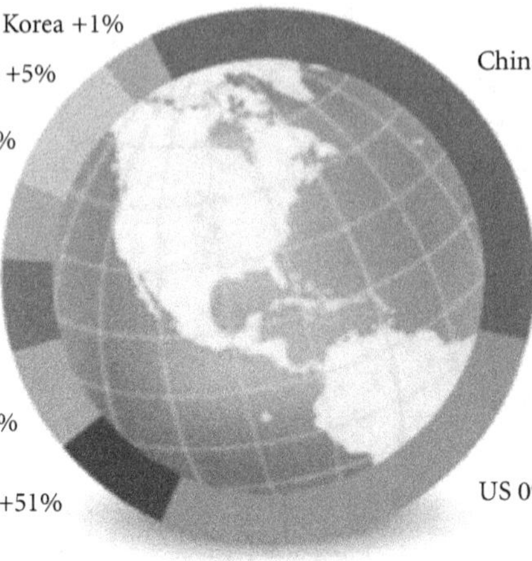

Figure 37: Year-on-year growth of the internet to 2012

Source: comScore: The State of Digital Q4 2012

RECENT PRESS COMMENTARY

Recent press and industry comments on device penetration include the following statements confirming a pattern of growth which is expected to continue:

> The overall India Tablets market recorded sales of 1.1 million units in 3Q (July–September) 2012. According to CyberMedia Research estimates, total shipments for the India Tablet PC market are expected to close at 3 million units in 2012.
>
> The research firms predicted that the market is expected to increase by at least 100 per cent in 2013 (double the number of units sold in 2012).
>
> The key drivers for this are a large number of launches by OEMs eyeing the India consumer market, as well as the demand expected to be generated via enterprise adoption of Tablets. CyberMedia Research also predicts that in case large deals are announced by vendors for supplies to the central or state governments for distribution to university, college and high school students, the forecast number of Tablet sales for 2013 could easily exceed 6 million units.
>
> The report said that in a very short span of time the India Tablets market has become one of the key drivers of data and content consumption in the country.

Source: CMR, available at: www.business-standard.com/article/technology/tablet-shipment-in-india-to-close-at-3-mn-in-2012-113010400163_1.html, and cmrindia.com/india-media-tablets-market-expected-to-touch-3-million-units-in-cy-2012-cy-2013-likely-to-see-6-million-units-or-higher-shipments-to-consumers-and-enterprises/.

> Mobile phone sales in India grew by 16 per cent to 218 million units last year on the back of rising demand for smartphones, a study by market research group IDC said.
> According to IDC's Asia Pacific quarterly mobile phone tracker, smartphone sales in the country grew by 48 per cent to 16.3 million in 2012 against 11 million in 2011.

Source: ZEEBIZ.com, Mobile phone market sales up 16% at 218 million in 2012, 6 March 2013, available at: zeenews.india.com/business/news/economy/mobile-phone-market-sales-up-16-at-218-million-in-2012_71666.html.

Appendix 6: Media and Communications Regulatory Reform Internationally Supplementary Material

This appendix provides supplementary material in relation to chapter 9. We compare two initiatives to reform media regulation in the UK and Australia through tighter controls on journalist behaviour enshrined in the UK Leveson Royal Charter and the proposed Australian Media Package.

Table 8: UK Leveson Royal Charter and Australian (proposed) media package comparison

Leveson recommendation	Area	Royal Charter (draft of 18 March 2013)	Media Package/Public Interest Media Advocate (PIMA) (proposed and withdrawn March 2013)
1	Independence of Board of self-regulator	Leveson: 'An independent self regulatory body should be governed by an independent Board. In order to ensure the independence of the body, the Chair and members of the Board must be appointed in a genuinely open, transparent and independent way, without any influence from industry or Government.' Royal Charter: The Commissioner for Public Appointments appoints the Appointments Committee and there are detailed provisions on the procedure for appointments.	The PIMA would be a single individual appointed by the Minister. There would be no Board.
2	Independence of appointment panel	Leveson: 'The appointment of the Chair of the Board should be made by an appointment panel. The selection of that panel must itself be conducted in an appropriately independent way and must, itself, be independent of the industry and of Government.' Royal Charter: In order to ensure the independence of the Appointments Committee various categories of person are ineligible including members of the House of Commons/Lords and Ministers of the Crown.	The PIMA would be a single individual appointed by the Minister. There would be no appointment panel.

(Continued)

Table 8: (*Continued*)

Leveson recommendation	Area	Royal Charter (draft of 18 March 2013)	Media Package/Public Interest Media Advocate (PIMA) (proposed and withdrawn March 2013)
3	Appointment and composition of appointments panel	Leveson: 'The appointment panel: (a) should be appointed in an independent, fair and open way; (b) should contain a substantial majority of members who are demonstrably independent of the press; (c) should include at least one person with a current understanding and experience of the press; (d) should include no more than one current editor of a publication that could be a member of the body.' Royal Charter: Largely follows Leveson.	The PIMA would be a single individual appointed by the Minister. There would be no appointment panel. Before appointing a person as the PIMA, the Minister would be required to consult the Australian Communications and Media Authority (ACMA), the Australian Competition and Consumer Commission (ACCC) and such media industry bodies as the Minister considers appropriate.
4	Appointment and composition of Board	Leveson: 'The appointment of the Board should also be an independent process, and the composition of the Board should include people with relevant expertise. The requirement for independence means that there should be no serving editors on the Board.' Royal Charter: Follows Leveson.	The PIMA would be a single individual appointed by the Minister. There would be no Board. To be eligible as the PIMA a person would require substantial experience or knowledge and significant standing in one or more of the following areas: the media industry; law; business or financial management; public administration; or economics. Since the PIMA would be a part-time appointment there would be no prohibition on

(*Continued*)

Table 8: (*Continued*)

Leveson recommendation	Area	Royal Charter (draft of 18 March 2013)	Media Package/Public Interest Media Advocate (PIMA) (proposed and withdrawn March 2013)
			outside employment provided that there is no actual or perceived conflict of interest. In principle, this would not rule out the PIMA being affiliated to a political party.
5	Chair and Members of Board	Leveson: 'The members of the Board should be appointed by the same appointment panel that appoints the Chair, together with the Chair (once appointed), and should: …(e) not include any serving member of the House of Commons or any member of the Government.' Royal Charter: Follows Leveson.	The PIMA would be a single individual appointed by the Minister. There would be no Board.

Source: Authors' own analysis. Reproduced from an article first published in FTI White Paper, 'The March of Media Reform: A UK Perspective on Australia', 9 April 2013.

Note: At the end of 2013 the Royal Charter has not been implemented.

Bibliography

GUIDANCE, CONSULTATIONS AND REGULATORY REPORTS

India

Telecom Regulatory Authority of India, 'Consultation Paper on Issues relating to Media Ownership', 15 February 2013

Telecom Regulatory Authority of India, 'Consultation Paper on Monopoly/Market dominance in Cable TV services', 3 June 2013

European Union

European Commission, 'Green Paper on the Convergence of the Telecommunications, Media and Information Technology Sectors, and the Implications for Regulation' COM (97) 623, 3 December 1997

European Commission, 'Pharmaceutical Sector Inquiry, Final Report', 8 July 2009

European Commission, 'Public consultation on the Independent Report of the High Level Group on Media Freedom and Pluralism', 22 March 2013

European Commission, 'Public consultation on the independence of the audiovisual regulatory bodies', 22 March 2013

European Commission, 'Special Eurobarometer 293, E-Communications Household Survey', June 2008

United Kingdom

Competition Commission, 'Movies on pay TV market investigation, A report on the supply and acquisition of subscription pay TV movie rights and services', 2 August 2012

Department for Culture, Media & Sport, 'Connectivity, Content and Consumers Britain's digital platform for growth', July 2013

Department for Culture, Media & Sport and Department for Business, Innovation & Skills, 'Digital Britain, Final Report' (Cm 7650), June 2009

Department of Trade and Industry, 'Guidance on the operation of the public interest merger provisions relating to newspapers and other media mergers', Guidance Document, May 2004

Hansard, Lord McIntosh of Haringey (Parliamentary Under Secretary, DCMS), 2 July 2003

House of Lords Select Committee on Communications, 3rd Report of Session 2010–12, 'The Future of Investigative Journalism', 16 February 2012 (HL Paper 256)

Lord Justice Leveson, 'An inquiry into the culture, practices and ethics of the press' Report No 0780 2012–13, 29 November 2012

Monopolies and Monopolies Commission, 'White Salt' (1986) Cm 9778

Ofcom, 'Communications Market Review 2012', 18 July 2012

Ofcom, 'Local Media Assessment on the proposed acquisition by the Kent Messenger Group of seven Kent newspaper titles from Northcliffe Media', 31 October 2011

Ofcom, 'Market Impact Assessment of the BBC's Local Video Service', 21 November 2008

Ofcom, 'Measuring media plurality, Ofcom's advice to the Secretary of State for Culture, Olympics, Media and Sport', 6 June 2012

Ofcom, 'Media Ownership Rules Review', 31 July 2009

Ofcom, 'Media plurality and news: a summary of contextual academic literature' Annex 7, 29 June 2012

Ofcom, 'New News, Future News: the challenges for television news after Digital Switch-over', 26 June 2007

Ofcom, 'Pay TV Statement', 31 March 2010

Ofcom, 'Guidance note for public interest test on the completed acquisition of GMG Radio Holdings Limited by Global Radio Limited', 3 August 2012

Other International

Australian Government, 'Convergence Review, Final Report', March 2012

Belgian Conseil de la Concurrence, Second Annual Report, 1994–1995

Belgian Conseil de la Concurrence, 2005 Annual Report

Belgian Conseil de la Concurrence, 2006 Annual Report

Belgian Conseil de la Concurrence, 2008 Annual Report

Commissariaat voor de Media, 'Media Monitor, The Dutch Media in 2010', February 2011

Organisation for Economic Co-operation and Development, 'Competition issues in television and broadcasting', Contribution from Mr Allan Fels (DAF/COMP/GF (2013)6)

Organisation for Economic Co-operation and Development, 'OECD Review of Telecommunication Policy and Regulation in Mexico', January 2012

BOOKS

Croley, S, 'Beyond capture: towards a new theory of regulation' in Levi-Faur, D (ed), *Handbook on the Politics of Regulation* (Edward Elgar Publishing, 2011) 50–69

Olson, M, *The Logic of Collective Action: Public Goods and the Theory of Groups* (Harvard University Press, 1965)

Porter, M E, *Competitive Advantage: Creating and Sustaining Superior Performance* (Simon and Schuster, 1985)

JOURNAL ARTICLES

Baudrier, A, 'The EU Regulatory Framework for Electronic Communications: Relevance and Efficiency Three Years Later' (2006) *Communications & Strategies*, No 61, 1st quarter

de Streel, A, 'A First Assessment of the New European Regulatory Framework for Electronic Communications' (2005) *Communications & Strategies*, No 58, 2nd quarter

Dobbs, I and Richards, P, 'Innovation and the New Regulatory Framework for Electronic Communications in the EU' (2004) *European Competition Law Review*, No 25

Fumagalli, C and Motta, M, 'Buyer Miscoordination, Entry and Downstream Competition' (2008) *Economic Journal* 118, 1196–222

Hazlett, T, 'Cable TV franchises as barriers to video competition' (2007) 12(2) *Virginia Journal of Law and Technology*

Hoehn, T, Rab, S and Saggers, G, 'Breaking up is hard to do—National Merger Remedies' (2009) 9 *European Competition Law Review*

Kienapfel, P and Stein, A, 'The Application of Articles 81 and 82 EC in the Sport Sector' (2007) 3 *Competition Policy Newsletter* 6–14

Piedras, E, 'TV de paga y servicios convergentes en el 2012' *El Economista*, 17 April 2013

Pozen, S, 'Insights into Antitrust Enforcement in Media Industries' (2012) *Competition Law International*

Stigler, G, 'The Theory of Economic Regulation' (1971) *2 Bell Journal of Economics and Management Science* 3–21

Tintor, V et al, 'The Legal and Economic Framework of EU Telecom Market Regulation' (2010) *Economic Annals*, Volume LV, No 185, April–June 2010, 1070–28

Waterman, D and Weiss, A, 'The Effects of Vertical Integration between Cable Television Systems and Pay Cable Networks' (1996) 72 *Journal of Econometrics* 357–95

PAPERS

Chandra, A and Collard-Wexler, A, 'Mergers in Two-Sided Markets: An Application to the Canadian Newspaper Industry', Leonard N Stern School of Business Working Paper No EC-07-03 (2008)

Crawford, G S, 'Cable regulation in the internet era', Working Paper, Coventry: Economics Department, University of Warwick (Warwick economics research paper series, 2013)

FTI Consulting, 'Strictly Media Policy', FTI Briefing

Hahn, R and Wallsten S, 'The Economics of Net Neutrality' (Washington, DC: AEI Brookings Joint Center for Regulatory Studies) April 2006

Just, N, 'Measuring media concentration and diversity instruments in Europe and the US', DOI: 10.1177/0163443708098248, (2009) 31 *Media Culture & Society* 97

Knieps, G and Zenhausern, P, 'The reform of the European regulatory framework for electronic communications: The unexploited phasing-out potentials' (2009) paper presented at the 2nd Annual Conference on Competition and Regulation in Network Industries, Centre for European Policy Studies, Brussels, 20 November 2009

Nocke, V and White, L,'Do Vertical Mergers Facilitate Upstream Collusion?' (2005) PIER Working Paper No 05-013

Sprague, A and Fellas, L, 'Rags in Tatters' (2013) FTI White Paper, February 2013

Sprague, A and Rab, S, 'Media Freedom and Pluralism—A Threat from the European Commission' (2013) FTI White Paper, April 2013

Sprague, A and Rab, S, 'The March of Media Reform: A UK Perspective on Australia' (2013) FTI White Paper, 9 April 2013

Van Cayseele, P J G and Vanormelingen, S, 'Prices and Network Effects in Two-Sided Markets: The Belgian Newspaper Industry' (2009) Working Paper

INDUSTRY REPORTS

comScore, 'The State of Digital', Q4 2012

comScore, 'The Rise in India's Digital Consumer', August 2012

High Level Group on Media Freedom and Pluralism, 'A free and pluralistic media to sustain European democracy', January 2013

ICRI et al, 'Independent Study on Indicators for Media Pluralism in the Member States—Towards a Risk-Based Approach', July 2009

INDIREG, 'Indicators for independence and efficient functioning of audiovisual media services regulatory bodies for the purpose of enforcing the rules in the AVMS Directive', February 2011

J'son & Partners Consulting, '2012–2017 Pay-TV Market Current Status and Forecasts', February 2013

KPCB, 'KPCB Internet Trends', 12 March 2012

KPMG, 'Public Policy Issues Arising From Telecommunications and Audiovisual Convergence, a report prepared for DG XIII', London, 1996

KPMG, 'FICCI—KPMG Media & Entertainment Report 2013', 12 March 2013

Mediadem, 'The regulatory quest for independent media', July 2012

Media Partners, 'Media Partners Asia report: Asia Pacific Pay TV and Broadband Market 2012', 2012

Oliver & Ohlbaum, 'UK Media Enters a New Age', December 2011

PricewaterhouseCoopers, 'Global entertainment and media outlook: 2012–2016', 8 June 2012

PricewaterhouseCoopers Economics, 'World in 2050: The BRICs and beyond: prospects, challenges and opportunities', January 2013

United Nations Statistics Division, 'Demographic Yearbook 2010'

Glossary

Unless stated otherwise references are of general application or relate to India.

References to jurisdictions outside India are denoted in brackets.

AAE	appreciable adverse effect (ie on competition in India for the purposes of the Competition Act)
ABA	American Bar Association
ABTA	Brazilian Association of Pay TV
ACCC	Australian Competition and Consumer Commission
ACMA	Australian Communications and Media Authority
ADSL	asymmetric digital subscriber line
AEC	adverse effect on competition (for the purposes of the UK market investigation regime)
AIESH	Association Intercommunale d'Electricté du Sud du Hainaut (Belgium)
ANATEL	Agência Nacional de Telecomunicações (Brazil)
API	application programme interface
AVMSD	Audiovisual Media Services Directive (EU)
BERR	Department for Business, Enterprise and Regulatory Reform
BRIC	Brazil, Russia, India and China
BRIIC	Brazil, Russia, India, Indonesia and China
Broadcasting Act	Broadcasting Act (last amended in 2013) (South Korea)
BSkyB	British Sky Broadcasting Limited
BT	British Telecommunications
Cable TV Act	Cable Television Networks (Regulation) Act 1995
Cable TV Rules	Cable Television Network Rules 1994
CADE	Conselho Administrativo de Defesa Econômica (Brazil)
CAS	conditional access system
CASBAA	Cable and Satellite Broadcasting Association of Asia
CAT	Competition Appeal Tribunal (UK)
CC	Competition Commission (UK)

CCI	Competition Commission of India
CEPS	Centre for European Policy Studies
CFC	Federal Competition Commission (Mexico)
CIS	Commonwealth of Independent States
CISAC	International Confederation of Societies of Authors and Composers
CJEU	Court of Justice of the European Union
CMA	Competition and Markets Authority (UK)
Comcast	Comcast Corporation
Compat	Competition Appellate Tribunal
Competition Act	Indian Competition Act 2002
Competition Amendment Bill	Indian Competition (Amendment) Bill 2012
CRC	Conference of Electronic Communications Sector Regulators (Belgium)
CRR	contract rights renewal (UK)
CSA	Supreme Audio-visual Council (France) Conseil supérieur de l'audiovisuel (High Council for Broadcasting), for the French Community (Belgium)
DAS	Digital addressable system
DBS	Direct broadcast satellite
DCMS	Department for Culture, Media & Sport (UK)
DOJ	Department of Justice (US)
DSL	digital subscriber line
DTH	direct-to-home
DTT	digital terrestrial television
ECAD	Central Office of Collection and Distribution (Brazil)
EEA	European Economic Area
EMPA	Eastern Motion Picture Association and Coordination of Artist and Technicians of West Bengal Film and Television Industry
ERC	Entidade Reguladora para a Comunicação Social (Portugal)
EUMR	EU Merger Regulation
FAS	Federal Antimonopoly Service (Russian Federation)
FCC	Federal Communications Commission (US)
FCO	Federal Cartel Office (Germany)
FECC	Federal Economic Competition Commission (Mexico)

FLEC	Federal Law on Economic Competition (Mexico)
FRAND	fair, reasonable and non-discriminatory
FTC	Federal Trade Commission (US) Federal Telecommunications Commission (Mexico)
FTI	Federal Telecommunications Institute, successor to the Federal Communications Commission (Mexico)
FTTH	fibre-to-the-home
GDP	gross domestic product
HHI	Herfindahl–Hirschman Index
HITS	Headend in the sky
IBA	International Bar Association
IBPT/BIPT	Belgian Institute for Postal Services and Telecommunications
ICN	International Competition Network
IFNCs	independently funded news consortia
INR	Indian Rupee
IP	internet protocol
IPR	intellectual property rights
IPTV	internet protocol television
ISP	internet service provider
JICREG	Joint Industry Committee for the Regional Media Research
JV	joint venture
KCC	Korea Communications Commission
KEK	Commission on Concentration in the Media (Germany)
KFTC	Korean Fair Trade Commission
KMG	Kent Messenger Group
KRNM	Kent Regional News & Media
KRW	South Korean Won
LCO	local cable operator
LMA	local media assessment (UK)
M&A	mergers and acquisitions
MDU	Multiple-dwelling unit
Media Package	Package of media reform proposals introduced (and largely withdrawn) in Australia in March 2013
MIA	market impact assessment (UK)
MIB	Ministry of Information & Broadcasting
MMDS	Multichannel Multipoint Distribution System

MNO	mobile network operator
MRFTA	Monopoly Regulation and Fair Trade Act (South Korea)
MSIP	Ministry of Science, ICT and Future Planning (South Korea)
MSO	multi-system operator
MVPD	multichannel video programming distributor
NCA	National Competition Authority (EU)
NBCU	NBC Universal Inc
NRA	national regulatory authority
Ofcom	The Office of Communications (UK)
OFT	Office of Fair Trading (UK)
OTT	over the top
OVD	Online video distributors
PCA	Portuguese Competition Authority
PCTV	Productora y Comercializadora de Televisión por Cable SA de CV (Mexico)
PEG	public, educational and governmental (US)
PIMA	Public Interest Media Advocate (proposed media regulator under the Media Package) (Australia)
PSB	public service broadcasting
PSTN	public switched telephone network
PT	Portugal Telecom
RSS	rich site summary
SARFT	State Administration of Radio Film and Television (China)
SEAE	Secretariat for Economic Monitoring of the Ministry of Finance (Brazil)
SIC	Integrated Communications System (sistemaintegrato dellecomunicazioni) (Italy)
SLC	substantial lessening of competition (UK and Australia)
SMP	Significant Market Power
SO	systems operator (South Korea)
SoS	Secretary of State (UK)
SSNIP	small but significant non-transitory increase in price
TCCO	Tele Cable Centro Occidente, SA de CV (Mexico)
TFEU	Treaty on the Functioning of the European Union
TP	TelekomunikacjaPolska
TRAI	Telecom Regulatory Authority of India

Treaty	Interstate Treaty on Broadcasting (Germany)
UGC	user-generated content
UHF	ultra-high frequency
UMTS	Universal Mobile Telecommunications System
UV	unique visitor
VRM	Vlaamse Regulator voor de Media (Flemish Council for the Media), for the Flemish Community
WMO	Wholesale must-offer (obligation)
YRF	Yash Raj Films Private Limited

Index